Who's Who in the Irish War of Independence
and Civil War
1916-1923

To Declan, and his courage in his own fight

Who's Who in the Irish War of Independence and Civil War
1916–1923

Padraic O'Farrell

The Lilliput Press
Dublin

Copyright © 1997 Padraic O'Farrell

All rights reserved. No part of this publication may be reproduced in any form or by any means without the prior permission of the publisher.

First published in 1997 by
THE LILLIPUT PRESS LTD
4 Rosemount Terrace, Arbour Hill,
Dublin 7, Ireland.

A CIP record for this title is available from The British Library.

ISBN 1 874675 85 6

Set in 9 on 11 Bembo
by Sheila Stephenson
Printed in Dublin
by βetaprint of Clonshaugh

CONTENTS

Preface vi
Acknowledgments ix
Abbreviations x
Chronology xiii

PART I: THE WAR OF INDEPENDENCE 1916–1921

A-Z Entries 3
The Irish Republican and Non-combatant Dead 102
The Crown Dead 121

PART II: THE CIVIL WAR 1922–1923

A-Z Entries 141
Pro-Treaty Casualties 199
Anti-Treaty Casualties 213
Executions 222

Map of Engagements and Related Events 226
Sources 228

PREFACE

A work bearing the title *Who's Who in the Irish War of Independence and Civil War 1916-1923* needs presentation under two headings, each requiring explanation and qualification.

The period of Irish history between Easter Monday 1916 and the signing of the Treaty on 6 December 1921 is surpassed only by the ensuing Civil War as a controversial topic of conversation. Its very name is often the subject of contention.

The complete period is called the *War of Independence* by most commentators. Others prefer to allude to two separate eras: *1916* and the *War of Independence*. Some quarrel with the latter, pointing out that full independence was not achieved. They prefer to talk about the *Anglo-Irish War* or the *Black and Tan War*. Then again, many like to combine the struggle with the Civil War that followed and speak of the *Troubles*.

The situation that began with the reading of the Proclamation at Dublin's General Post Office on 24 April 1916 and culminated with the signing of the Treaty justifies the taking of those years as an entity. I have done this in Part One, most of which appeared first in 1980 under the title *Who's Who in the Irish War of Independence 1916-1921*. The period between May 1916, when the leaders of the Easter Week Rebellion were executed, and the action at Soloheadbeg on 21 January 1919 was not without important incident. It must, therefore, be considered a part of the War of Independence, an event that has inspired numerous volumes from scholars and from participants in the struggle. The Civil War has its corpus too, but a less substantial one.

From both events has emerged a store of fact, fiction and anecdote. Every speaker has his or her most memorable incident: sticking a tricolour with a grenade attached in a Longford chimney so that the Black and Tans sent to impound the offending emblem would be blown up; shouting 'Hands up!' on a lonely Donegal road – to a stray donkey; Tullamore factory girls known as 'bottle-washers' tarred and feathered because they tended to the lustful needs of members of the Crown Forces. Names are whispered or called aloud according to the events with which they were connected. Lengthy arguments take place about which brother in a family of seven was wounded in some incident in 1922. Heads bend low in a bar corner as another attempt is made to determine who informed on the section ambushed in the wild Cork countryside on a late September evening. They bend lower when there is mention of Ballyseedy or Countess Bridge or Béal na mBláth.

Some names so whispered will never grace the pages of any 'who's who'. Neither will hundreds of others who contributed to this turbulent period of Irish history – simply because their efforts were not documented.

In the compilation of a work like this, the greatest problem arises after the main personalities of the wars have been noted. Then comes the difficult decision as to who of the thousands remaining – all entitled to inclusion – must be omitted. Does one major political achievement compare with the loss of life or limb in a minor incident? Does the perpetrator of a notorious deed merit inclusion before one who performed a small act of gallantry? Who *was* who, when all is said and done?

This book attempts to solve the problem by including names associated with a variety of typical incidents, facts and subjects from the two conflicts. Entries appear roughly in proportion to activity in particular regions, but it does not necessarily follow that places not represented were completely inactive; their exclusion may be the result of insufficient documentation. Some of the material came from reliable verbal sources, including names not mentioned in any previous well-known works. These are cited here to represent the vast numbers who gave service but who, intentionally or otherwise, escaped public recognition. No personal opinions are offered in the work. Widely held beliefs are cited where relevant. Emotive terms such as 'murdered', 'incarcerated', 'tortured', 'Irregulars' or 'Free Staters' are for the most part avoided.

A special word is needed about Part Two of this book. Some people still find it difficult to discuss the Civil War, and I do not wish to re-ignite old animosities, particularly at a time when peace is earnestly sought on this island. The limitations of a listing for the Civil War are enormous, for a number of reasons. Not everybody was proud of their own or their relatives' participation in this war and so involvement was often concealed or presented inaccurately. Fear existed in an environment that accommodated reports of empty coffins, unmarked graves, removal of corpses, false names and the like. Families split and friends parted. Accounts were exaggerated or softened, depending on the allegiance of the narrator. Geographically, too, there were research problems. Activity is documented adequately in some areas; elsewhere, coverage is less satisfactory. For these reasons, I dispensed

PREFACE

with home addresses in the main Civil War listing and in some of the appendices. Also, because more formal unit structures were established during the Civil War, I use military abbreviations more widely here.

Often in the course of my research, documents showed conflicting spellings of names, different dates, etc. When this occurred, I selected the form accepted by the majority of sources or by the formal, official documentation, when available. Even official documents posed problems. Files on people deeply involved might have had their contents removed. Individuals close to participants or their relatives helped me work through such difficulties. Two, three, or even four sources might contain differing accounts so I was forced to make my own judgment in many cases; I accept responsibility for any incorrect decisions in that regard.

In the book *With the IRA in the Fight for Freedom* (Tralee, n.d.), Sean MacEoin contributed a feature on 'The Constitutional Basis for the National Struggle'. He attempted to list the leaders of all the battalions that took part in the War of Independence. A large number of gaps appear where information was not to hand. If that was the case within twenty years of a war whose participants were proud of their involvement, the difficulty of compiling adequate listings three-quarters of a century after a less lauded conflict becomes apparent.

The two sides in the Civil War are designated, in the main, as anti- or pro-Treaty. When a name is followed by AT or PT, membership of either fighting force is noted by the addition of an abbreviated rank description, where known. Descriptions of ranks and appointments presented considerable problems, however. For example, the military *rank* of commandant was often mixed up with an *appointment* as Battalion Commandant. Also, compilers of records often attached a higher rank than that actually held.

The PT attack on the Four Courts on 28 June 1922 is given by most commentators as the start of the Civil War. A number of actions took place before that, however, and so Part Two recognizes the events in early 1922 that precipitated that shelling. Similarly, persons involved in engagements that took place after the cease-fire but that were directly related to the Civil War, are recorded.

Who's Who in the Irish War of Independence and Civil War attempts to embrace all classes and all creeds from all sides of the conflicts. The work is one of reference and many sources exist for elaboration. It is, by its nature, incomplete, and as I worked I was concerned lest a worthy participant or a relative with a just pride in the part played by a loved one should be offended by an exclusion. If it be so, I beg indulgence and offer the hope that some day all those names will be published.

ACKNOWLEDGMENTS

I wish to acknowledge the assistance of the staffs of the National Library; the University College Dublin Archives; Trinity College Library; Westmeath County Library, particularly Tony Cox and Carmel Geraghty; the King's Inns Library; the National Archives; Patrick Melvin, Oireachtas Library; Comdts Peter Young and Victor Laing and staff, Army Archives; the Franciscan Archives, Dún Mhuire, Killiney; Lt Col Declan O'Carroll; Sgts Hudson and Jessop; Mary Guinan-Darmody and Tipperary County Libraries; Catherine O'Rourke, Wexford County Librarian; Sean O'Sullivan, Leitrim County Library; Donegal and Roscommon County Libraries; numerous interviewees (many mentioned in the list of sources); correspondents and willing helpers, especially Jim Kemmy, Sean MacBride, Peadar O'Donnell, Kathleen Napoli McKenna, Sean Dowling, Dr C.S. Andrews, Sighle Bean Uí Dhonnchadha, Cormac O'Malley, Kathleen Trapp, Dr Breandán Mac Giolla Choille, Gerry Deignan, Niall Mac Fionngaile, Mary O'Neill, Paddy Dennehy, John Joe Joyce, Pat (Forbes) Desmond, Sean Ua Cearnaigh, Jack Sullivan, Bridie O'Sullivan, Minnie McKenna, Dónal Mac Suibhne, Louis Emerson, Mary Woods, Donal McCarthy, Liam Collins, Tom O'Neill, Joe Dowling, Mary Duffy, Mary McCarthy, Lt General M.J. Costello, T.C. O'Connor, TD, Lt General M. Brennan, Col Dan Bryan, Col D. Neligan, Lt Col N. Harrington, Col J.P. Kane, Captain Donncadha Mac Suibhne, Mai Savage, Brendan Mahony, Justin Wallace and many others who gave generously of their time in assisting my research.

I thank all who loaned rare books and documents or who passed on helpful information. Some who assisted my research for *Who's Who in the Irish War of Independence 1916–1922* (Dublin & Cork, 1980) and for my later biographies – *The Sean MacEoin Story* (Dublin & Cork, 1981), *The Ernie O'Malley Story* (Dublin & Cork, 1983) and *The Blacksmith of Ballinalee* (Mullingar, 1993) – have passed away since. Their help is reflected in the following pages. Ar dheas Dé go raibh a n-anam.

Mrs Patricia Clinton assisted with typing and indexing Part One, my daughter Aisling, with arduous indexing and word processing for Part Two. Seamus Hunt read the first draft of Part Two and offered useful comments. I thank my agent Jonathan Williams, publisher Antony Farrell and editors Brendan Barrington and Amanda Bell for friendship and efficiency, and my wife Maureen for proofreading.

Deserving of special thanks are my wife and family – for their patience and tolerance of inconveniences, leading to many minor Truces and Treaties but reasonably civil wars!

ABBREVIATIONS

2 i/c	second in command
2/Lt	Second Lieutenant
AC	armoured car
ACS	Assistant Chief of Staff
ADC	aide-de-camp
Adj	Adjutant
AG	Adjutant-General
AOH	Ancient Order of Hibernians
APM	Army Provost Marshal
A/Sgt	Adjutant-Sergeant
ASU	active service unit
AT	anti-Treaty
Att	attached to
Aux	Auxiliary (or Cadet).
BA	British Army
Bde	Brigade
Big Four	Dan Breen, Sean Hogan, Seamus Robinson and Sean Treacy, 3rd Tipperary Brigade
Bman	batman
BN	British Navy
Bn	Battalion
Brig Gen	Brigadier General
C na mB	Cumann na mBan. (*See Part One, A-Z*)
Capt	Captain
Cdt	Cadet (military rank, not to be confused with Auxiliary)
CID	Criminal Investigation Department
CIGS	Chief of Imperial General Staff
C-in-C	Commander-in-Chief
CM	court-martial
Col	Colonel
Comdr	Commander
Comdt	Commandant
Const	Constable
COS	Chief of Staff

ABBREVATIONS

Coy	Company
Cpl	Corporal
CQMS	Company Quartermaster Sergeant
C/Sgt	Company Sergeant
CW	Civil War
D/	Director of (*e.g.* D/Int – Director of Intelligence)
Det	Detective
Dist Insp	District Inspector
Div	Division/Divisional
DMP	Dublin Metropolitan Police
DOW	died of wounds
DSM	Distinguished Service Medal
DSO	Distinguished Service Order
Dvr	driver
Fianna Éireann	male youth movement
F/Lt	Flight Lieutenant
Fus	Fusiliers
GCM	general court-martial
Gen	General
Gnr	Gunner
GOC	General Officer Commanding
GPO	General Post Office
GSW	gunshot wounds
i/c	in command
IFS	Irish Free State
Insp	Inspector
Int	Intelligence
IO	Intelligence Officer
IRA	Pre-Civil-War Irish Republican Army. (*See Part One, A-Z*)
IRB	Irish Republican Brotherhood. (*See Part One, A-Z*)
ITGWU	Irish Transport and General Workers' Union
KC	King's Counsel
KIA	killed in action
L/Cpl	Lance Corporal
Lt	Lieutenant
Lt Col	Lieutenant Colonel
Lt Comdr	Lieutenant Commander
Lt Gen	Lieutenant General
Maj	Major
MP	Member of Parliament
Mun	Munitions
NA	National Army
NI	Northern Ireland
OC	Officer Commanding

ABBREVIATIONS

OIC	Officer in Charge
PG	Provisional Government
POW	prisoner of war
PP	Parish Priest
PT	pro-Treaty
Pte	Private
QM	Quartermaster
QMG	Quartermaster General
RAF	Royal Airforce
RAMC	Royal Army Medical Corps
RASC	Royal Army Service Corps
RC	Roman Catholic
RDS	Royal Dublin Society
REME	Royal Electrical and Mechanical Engineers
Rgt	Regiment
RIC	Royal Irish Constabulary
RUC	Royal Ulster Constabulary
SC	Special Constabulary
Sec Cdr	Section Commander
Sgt	Sergeant
SM	Sergeant Major
Sr	Sister, Army Nursing Service
S/Sgt	Staff Sergeant
TD	Teachta Dála (Dáil Deputy)
Vol	Volunteer (military rank, not to be confused with Irish Volunteers or National Volunteers)
WI	War of Independence. When this appears at the end of an entry it signifies that the person also appears in the War of Independence section of the book. Its omission does not suggest that the subject took no part in that war.
WIA	wounded in action ('from WIA': from wounds received in action)

CHRONOLOGY

1916-1923

1916

IRB Military Council. 19-22 Jan. Padraic Pearse, Joseph M. Plunkett and Sean MacDermott meet and co-opt James Connolly to the IRB Military Council. They decide on an early rebellion.

The Aud. *20 April.* In Tralee Bay a British naval patrol vessel, *Bluebell*, intercepts the *Aud*, bearing arms from Germany for Irish Volunteers.

Casement arrested. 21 April. Karl Spindler, the *Aud*'s German captain, scuttles the craft as it is escorted into Cobh, Co. Cork. Roger Casement lands from a German submarine at Banna Strand, Tralee Bay, Co. Kerry, to warn of a severe deficiency in the quantity of German arms expected. He is arrested. The car heading to meet him plunges over Ballykissane Pier and its occupants are drowned.

MacNeill's order. 22 April. Eoin MacNeill orders the cancellation of the rebellion.

IRB meeting. 23 April. MacNeill's order cancelling 'manoeuvres' appears in the *Sunday Independent*, causing widespread uncertainty. Plunkett leaves his nursing home to join an IRB Military Council meeting at Liberty Hall, Dublin, which decides to go ahead with the rebellion next day.

Rebellion begins. 24 April. Irish Volunteers, led by Pearse, and Irish Citizen Army, led by Connolly, seize important Dublin installations. From the portico of the GPO in Sackville Street, Pearse reads a Proclamation headed 'The Provisional Government of the Irish Republic to the People of Ireland'. The occupation succeeds without violence and the rebellion begins at midday. During the afternoon the British garrison in Dublin is reinforced from the Curragh.

The Helga. *26 April.* Heavy resistance by rebels at Boland's Mills. British sustain heavy losses. The *Helga* opens fire from the Liffey, demolishing Liberty Hall and the upper storey of the GPO.

Ashbourne attack. 28 April. Successful raid on RIC barracks in Ashbourne, north County Dublin.

Surrender. 29 April. Nurse O'Farrell bears Pearse's unconditional surrender to General Lowe.

Deportation. 1 May. Deportation of prisoners to Britain begins.

First executions. 3 May. Pearse, Thomas MacDonagh and Thomas Clarke are executed at Kilmainham, Dublin.

Further executions. 4 May. Ned Daly, Micheál Ó h-Annracháin, Willie Pearse and Plunkett are executed.

Execution. 5 May. John MacBride is executed.

Executions. 8 May. Eamon Ceannt, Cornelius Colbert, Sean Heuston and Michael Mallin are executed.

Cork execution. 9 May. Thomas Kent is executed in Cork.

Prisoner release. 15 June. The release of Easter Week prisoners is announced by Andrew Bonar Law. Releases begin in days following.

Internees released. 22 Dec. 600 internees are freed from Frongoch in Wales.

Prisoners return. 23 Dec. Bonfires and torchlight processions greet the returned prisoners.

1917

Roscommon by-election. 3 Feb. The Sinn Féin candidate, Count Plunkett, wins the Roscommon by-election by 2314 votes but refuses to take his seat in the House of Commons.

South Longford by-election. 9 May. The imprisoned Sinn Féin candidate, Joe McGuinness, wins the South Longford by-election by 32 votes.

General amnesty. 15 June. Bonar Law announces the release of Easter Week Rebellion prisoners.

Releases. 16 June. McGuinness, Eamon de Valera, MacNeill and Countess Markievicz are among the 120 remaining prisoners released from serving sentences for crimes associated with the rebellion.

East Clare by-election. 10 July. The Sinn Féin candidate, de Valera, wins the East Clare by-election by 2975 votes.

Ashe dies. 25 Sept. After being forcibly fed, Thomas Ashe dies on hunger-strike in Mountjoy Prison, Dublin.

Sinn Féin Ard Fheis. 25-26 Oct. At the tenth Sinn Féin Ard Fheis, held in the Mansion House, Dublin, de Valera is elected President. He embarks on a programme to (a) decide on a suitable form of government and (b) seek recognition of the Irish Republic abroad.

1918

Franchise. 6 Feb. The Representation of the People Act in Britain gives the franchise to men over 21 and women over 30. A concurrent Redistribution of Seats Act provides for constituencies roughly equal in size.

Conscription. 18 April. Lloyd George's Military Service Bill, introduced on 9 April, becomes law. As a protest against its being extended to include conscription in Ireland, John Dillon withdraws his Home Rule Party from Westminster. The Lord Mayor of Dublin calls members of the Irish Parliamentary Party, Sinn Féin, the Irish Labour Party and the All for Ireland League to a 'National Cabinet' meeting in the Mansion House to protest against conscription measures. A delegation from the meeting later goes to Maynooth where a Roman Catholic Synod of Bishops is also convened.

Anti-conscription pledge. 21 April. An anti-conscription pledge is signed by nationalists.

'German Plot.' April-May. Alleged treasonable communications between Ireland and Germany are used as justification for wide-scale arrests and deportations.

Organizations banned. 3 July. Sinn Féin, the IRA, and other nationalist organizations are banned.

General Election. 14 Dec. Sinn Féin takes 73 seats in a general election. Countess Markievicz becomes the first woman to be elected to the House of Commons.

1919

First Dáil. Soloheadbeg raid. 21 Jan. The returned Sinn Féin members (*above*) who are not in prison meet in the Mansion House and form the First Dáil Éireann. They issue a Declaration of Independence and an 'Address to the Free Nations of the World', and adopt a provisional constitution and a democratic programme. On the same day at Soloheadbeg, Co. Tipperary, Dan Breen, Seamus Robinson, Sean Treacy and others raid a gelignite patrol in the first action of the War of Independence proper.

De Valera elected President. 1 April. At the second session of Dáil Éireann, de Valera is elected President with Sean T. O'Kelly as Ceann Comhairle.

Knocklong rescue. 13 May. Sean Hogan is rescued from custody in a daring attack at Knocklong railway station, Co. Limerick.

The IRA. 20 Aug. Dáil Éireann approves Cathal Brugha's motion that its members and staff and the Irish Volunteers should swear allegiance to the Irish Republic and the Dáil. Thus the Irish Volunteers become the IRA – the army of the Irish Republic.

Fermoy actions. 7 Sept. The IRA, under Liam Lynch, fires on British troops at Fermoy, Co. Cork. In reprisal, troops loot shops.

Nationalist organizations suppressed. 10 Sept. A proclamation is issued suppressing Sinn Féin, the IRA, the Gaelic League and other nationalist-aligned organizations in Co. Cork.

Dáil declared illegal. 12 Sept.

Republican news-sheets and newspapers banned. 20 Sept.

Sinn Féin Ard Fheis. 15 Oct. Proclamation of 10 September is extended to cover the entire country. Nevertheless, Sinn Féin holds its Ard Fheis.

Cork sacked. 10 Nov. Crown Forces sack and loot Cork's main thoroughfares.

Irish Bulletin. 11 Nov. First issue of the *Irish Bulletin*, the Sinn Féin and Dáil Éireann news-sheet.

Commons statement. 18 Dec. In the House of Commons Winston Churchill reports that there are 43,000 troops in Ireland. Other commentators place the number of raids on private houses at 5588 during the first nine months of the year and 12,589 since 1917.

Ashtown ambush. 19 Dec. At Ashtown, Dublin, the IRA ambushes the Lord-Lieutenant, Lord French. Martin Savage is killed but the Lord-Lieutenant escapes.

1920

Black and Tans recruited. 2 Jan. Retired British Army personnel are enrolled for service in Ireland as reinforcements for the Royal Irish Constabulary. They were later given the nickname 'Black and Tans'.

PR introduced. 15 Jan. For the first time, the proportional representation system is used in urban and borough elections. Nationalist and Labour parties take control of 172 bodies out of 206. Later, on 12 June, the trend continues in elections for county council, boards of Poor Law Guardians and rural district councils, giving Sinn Féin control of 36 out of 55 district councils in Ulster.

Ballytrain capture. 14 Feb. The IRA, under Ernie O'Malley, captures its first Ulster RIC barracks at Ballytrain, Co. Monaghan.

Government of Ireland Bill. 25 Feb. The Government of Ireland Bill is introduced in the Commons, providing for separate Northern and Southern parliaments and administrations.

MacCurtain killed. 20 March. Tomás MacCurtain, Lord Mayor of Cork, is shot dead in his home.

Black and Tans arrive. 25 March.

Magistrate shot. 26 March. Michael Collins's 'Squad' shoots dead Alan Bell, the magistrate investigating Dáil Éireann and Sinn Féin funds.

Ballylanders attack. 27 April. The IRA attacks Ballylanders RIC barracks, Co. Limerick.

Limerick affray. 28 April. In retaliation for above, the Black and Tans go on the rampage in Limerick city.

Mile Bush ambush. 5 June. At Mile Bush, near Midleton, Co. Cork, the IRA carries out a successful ambush against the Cameron Highlanders. The action, led by Diarmuid Hurley, succeeds through other Volunteers distracting attention by mingling with spectators at a game of bowls, a Cork pastime played on the road. (*See Manley, Tadhg*)

Listowel mutiny. 16-19 June. RIC personnel engage in mutinous behaviour in Listowel, Co. Kerry, protesting exhortations by Col Brice-Ferguson Smyth, RIC Div Comdr in Munster, for repressive actions.

Smyth shot. 17 July. Smyth is shot in Cork by IRA in retaliation for above.

Derry disturbances. 19 July. Civil disturbances take place in Derry, resulting in 18 deaths.

Belfast riots. 21-24 July. Civil disturbances take place in Belfast. Roman Catholics are expelled from factories and shipyards. Riots follow, resulting in 13 deaths.

Auxiliaries formed. 27 July. Retired British Army officers are formed into a paramilitary division of the RIC. They became known as 'Auxiliaries' or 'Auxies'.

Swanzy assassination. 22 Aug. Dist Insp Swanzy is assassinated in Lisburn, Co. Antrim. Attacks on nationalists in the town and in Belfast follow.

Military Courts. 9 Sept. Secret Military Courts of Inquiry replace Coroners' Inquests in ten counties.

'Blackcastle Races'. 12 Sept. A flight from the 3 Tipperary Bde Conference raided by Crown Forces becomes known as the 'Blackcastle Races'.

Sack of Balbriggan. 20 Sept. The Black and Tans sack Balbriggan in north County Dublin.

Mallow capture. 28 Sept. Lynch and O'Malley lead the only capture of a military barracks during the War of Independence, at Mallow, Co. Cork. Crown Forces retaliate by sacking the town.

Fernside. 11-12 Oct. At 'Fernside', the home of Prof Carolan at Whitehall, Drumcondra, Dublin, a dramatic fight takes place before Breen and Treacy escape raiding forces.

Commons statistics. 20 Oct. The Foreign Secretary reports on IRA activity to the House of Commons. Destruction between 1 Jan 1919 and 18 Oct 1920 included 64 courthouses, 492 vacated RIC barracks, 21 occupied RIC barracks, and 148 private residences of citizens loyal to the Crown. In addition, 114 RIC barracks were damaged; there were 741 raids on the mail and 40 on coastguard stations and lighthouses; 117 policemen were killed and 185 wounded; 23 soldiers were killed and 71 wounded; 32 civilians were killed and 83 wounded.

MacSwiney dies. 25 Oct. The Lord Mayor of Cork, Terence MacSwiney, dies on the 74th day of his hunger-strike in Brixton Prison, London.

Barry executed. 1 Nov. Kevin Barry is executed for killing a soldier.

Battle of Ballinalee. 2-9 Nov. Sean MacEoin defends his native Co. Longford village in 'The Battle of Ballinalee'.

Bloody Sunday. 21 Nov. Collins's 'Squad' shoot dead 14 British Secret Service agents in their Dublin homes. Auxiliaries retaliate by killing Dick McKee, Conor Clune and Peadar Clancy while Black and Tans open fire indiscriminately at a Gaelic football match in Croke Park, killing 12.

Kilmichael ambush. 28 Nov. 3 Cork Bde wipes out a patrol of 18 Auxiliaries in an ambush at Kilmichael, Co. Cork.

Martial law. 10 Dec. Martial law declared in counties Cork, Kerry, Limerick and Tipperary. Certain relatively minor offences are included in a list of capital offences.

Cork burning. 11 Dec. RIC, Black and Tans and Auxiliaries destroy part of Cork city by fire after an IRA ambush on an RIC patrol near Victoria Barracks.

Partition of Ireland. 23 Dec. The Government of Ireland Act provides for two parliaments, one for the six north-eastern counties (Northern Ireland) and one for the remaining 26 (Southern Ireland), marking the enshrinement of partition.

Bruff shootings. 26 Dec. Five shot dead and 17 injured when the RIC opens fire in a dance-hall in Bruff, Co. Limerick.

1921

Midleton burnings. 1 Jan. The military governor in Cork, General Strickland, authorizes, with government backing, the burning of seven houses in Midleton, Co. Cork.

Crozier resignation. 19 Feb. The commander of the Auxiliaries, General Crozier, resigns, due to their excesses.

Cork shootings. 28 Feb. Six IRA prisoners are shot in Cork. In retaliation, the IRA shoots six British soldiers in the city.

Limerick shootings. 7 March. The former Lord Mayor of Limerick, George Clancy, and two other leading citizens are shot dead in the city.

Dublin executions. 14 March. Frank Flood and five others are executed in Dublin. The Labour Party calls a succesful work stoppage in the city.

Crossbarry ambush. 19 March. Successful IRA ambush at Crossbarry, Co. Cork.

Compensation awards. April. Rates in some counties increase up to 35 per cent, due to substantial awards in respect of lootings, burnings and killings.

Cost of operations. 13 April. The War Office announces that military operations in Ireland since 1919 have cost £20m per annum.

Election nominations. 13 May. 124 Sinn Féin and four Unionist Independent (Trinity College) candidates are nominated for as many seats in Southern Ireland. All are thus effectively elected.

Northern election. 24 May. In the Northern Ireland election, 40 Unionists, six Nationalists and six Sinn Féin candidates are elected in the UK's first poll using proportional representation.

Custom House burning. 25 May. The IRA sets fire to Dublin's Custom House. Local Government records are destroyed in a blaze that lasts five days and causes a number of deaths.

Truce. 11 July. A Truce, signed two days previously, comes into effect.

Second Dáil. 16 Aug. Returned Sinn Féin members meet and declare themselves the Second Dáil. They unanimously reject terms of settlement offered earlier by the British.

Plenipotentiaries chosen. 14 Sept. Dáil Éireann chooses five delegates to negotiate a settlement with the UK: Arthur Griffith, Michael Collins, Robert Barton, Eamonn Duggan and George Gavan Duffy. The British team consists of David Lloyd George, Lord Birkenhead, Winston Churchill, Sir Hamar Greenwood, Austen Chamberlain, L. Worthington Evans and Gordon Hewart.

Treaty negotiations. 11 Oct.-6 Dec. Treaty negotiations take place in London.

Treaty Signed. 6 Dec. After difficult negotiations which included a British threat of a resumption of war, the Treaty is signed at 2.10 a.m.

Opposition to Treaty. 8 Dec. De Valera denounces the Treaty.

Release of internees. 9 Dec. IRA internees released by Britain.

Treaty debates. 14 Dec.-7 Jan. 1922. Dáil Éireann debates the Treaty.

1922

Belfast boycott. January-March. Because of ill-treatment of Roman Catholics in Belfast since 1920, merchandise from that city is boycotted.

Treaty approved. 7 Jan. The Anglo-Irish Treaty is approved in the Dáil by 64 votes to 57.

De Valera resignation. 9 Jan. De Valera resigns his position as President of Dáil Éireann but stands for re-election.

Dáil adjourns. 10 Jan. De Valera defeated in vote for Dáil Presidency by

60 votes to 58. He and all AT deputies walk out. Dáil adjourned until 8 June.

Provisional Government. January. Sixty PT TDs and four Unionist MPs for Trinity College meet on 14 January and pass resolutions approving the Treaty and setting up a Provisional Government, pending the establishment of Saorstát Éireann (IFS). The Provisional Government exists from 16 January to 6 December 1922, authorized by Article 17 of the Treaty to administer 26 counties. In effect, the Provisional Government and the Dáil overlap. Its chairman is Michael Collins, but Arthur Griffith retains Presidency of Dáil Éireann. Britain recognizes the Provisional Government as the instrument for drafting a constitution and expediting the transfer of authority from Britain to Ireland. The Provisional Government receives a £1m loan from the Bank of Ireland and £500,000 from the British government. With a fighting army to support, this is totally inadequate. Richard Mulcahy is appointed Minister for Defence with powers of command over the Army, led by General Eoin O'Duffy, COS. Elected TDs who oppose the Treaty refuse to recognize the Provisional Government, regarding themselves as the lawful Second Dáil with de Valera their President.

British handover. 16 Jan. The Lord-Lieutenant, Edward Talbot Fitzallen, formally hands over power to Michael Collins at Dublin Castle. From this point British troops begin vacating barracks and posts and the Royal Irish Constabulary prepares for disbandment. PTs and ATs occupy various barracks throughout the country. The IRA of the War of Independence divides on pro-Treaty and anti-Treaty lines, each formation adopting the stance supported by the majority of its members. Isolated clashes take place, resulting in some deaths and much bitterness.

Unionist acceptance. 19 Jan. At a meeting in the Engineers' Hall, Dawson Street, Dublin, Southern Unionists unanimously agree to recognize both the Provisional Government and the IFS.

PT Army HQ established. 31 Jan. The PT army sets up its HQ in Beggarsbush Barracks, Dublin.

Limerick confrontation. February-March. British forces plan to vacate Limerick on 23 February. During February and early March, PTs from outside Limerick city move in to take over positions. Their leader is arrested by ATs. Michael Brennan assumes overall command of PT troops in the city. Ernie O'Malley's 2 Southern Div (AT), refusing to recognize the authority of Dublin GHQ or Dáil Éireann, moves in and occupies positions. Some British troops still remain. O'Malley unsuccessfully appeals to Rory O'Connor and Liam Lynch for explosives to breach PT stronghold in St John's Castle. The Mayor of Limerick and a number of prominent leaders from both sides, including Collins, de Valera, Lynch, Mulcahy, O'Duffy, Frank Aiken and Oscar Traynor, strive to prevent an outbreak of hostilities. Eventually, the ATs are persuaded to withdraw from the city.

Arms landing. 2 March. Arms from Germany are landed at Helvic Head, Co. Waterford, for ATs in Dublin.

Cumann na Poblachta. 15 March. Cumann na Poblachta, the AT League of the Republic, is formed under de Valera's leadership.

AT Executive. 26-27 March. AT Executive formed. Regarding the Treaty and the resulting Provisional Government as an abrogation of the Irish Republic declared by the First Dáil, a number of prominent officers demand an army convention. Mulcahy accedes to the demand but the Cabinet of the Provisional Government proscribes the meeting. Mulcahy issues instructions through O'Duffy that attendance would be construed as termination of membership of the army. Only AT officers attend. From 223 present in the Mansion House, Dublin, a temporary Executive of 16 is appointed under the chairmanship of Traynor. The authority of Mulcahy and O'Duffy is repudiated, and the meeting calls on the Provisional Government to cease recruiting for the National Army and the Civic Guard.

Collins-Craig agreement. 30 March. Collins and Northern PM James Craig sign an agreement promising peace, action on discrimination against Catholics in Northern Ireland and a curb on AT activities. This brings an end to the Belfast Boycott (*see Jan. 1922*).

Saorstát Éireann. 1 April. Churchill and Collins sign transfer of power from UK to Saorstát Éireann (IFS).

AT Army Convention. 9 April. An AT Army Convention, with an attendance of 217, drafts a new constitution for the IRA which places it under the authority of an Executive (elected at the convention) and its COS, Lynch. The members of the Executive are Frank Barrett, Liam Deasy, Tom Hales, Tom Maguire, Joseph McKelvey, Liam Mellows, Sean Moylan, Joseph O'Connor, Rory O'Connor, Peadar O'Donnell, Florrie O'Donoghue, Sean O'Hegarty, Ernie O'Malley, Seamus Robinson and P.J. Ruttledge.

Four Courts take-over. 13 April. ATs, under Rory O'Connor, establish their HQ in the Four Courts, Dublin.

Sligo confrontation. 16 April. Local AT leader in Sligo issues a proclamation forbidding a planned public speech by Arthur Griffith. Various positions are seized by both sides and there is high tension. Under a heavy military escort, Griffith arrives and delivers his speech.

Peace Committee. April-May. A Dáil Peace Committee meets a number of times before the final breakdown of talks on 16 May 1922. It comprises Treaty supporters Sean Hales, MacEoin, McGuinness, Seamus O'Dwyer and Padraic Ó Máille, and opponents Harry Boland, K. Clarke, Mellows, Moylan and Ruttledge.

Army Document. 1 May. Senior officers sign a document aimed at army unification. It proposes acceptance of the fact that a majority of Irish people support the Treaty and an election to form a government that would have the confidence of all citizens. It calls for army unity pending the expedition of these proposals. Signatories are Sean Boylan, Breen, Collins, Tom Hales, Mulcahy, Humphrey Murphy, O'Donoghue, O'Duffy, O'Hegarty and Gearoid O'Sullivan.

Election agreed. 20 May. In January the Dáil had agreed that, in order to give the electorate an opportunity to hear debates on the Treaty, an election should be held in June. On 20 May Collins and de Valera agree the drawing up of a panel of Sinn Féin candidates for a general election on 16 June, organized by the Provisional Government. The existing PT and AT Dáil representation would provide the basis for its ratio. Britain disputes the arrangement and calls Collins and Griffith to Whitehall. (Collins eventually repudiated the pact on 14 June 1922, two days before polling day.)

'Pact Election'. 16 June. General election held in 26 counties. Result: PT Sinn Féin, 58; AT Sinn Féin, 36; Labour, 17; Farmers, 7; Independents, 6; Trinity College (University of Dublin), 4. After the election the Dáil sits to formalize transfer of authority. There is another adjournment. The Dáil is prorogued on 4 August.

Kildare raid. 17 June. ATs raid the Civic Guard barracks in Kildare, removing arms and ammunition.

AT dissent. 18 June. At an AT Extraordinary Convention in the Mansion House, Tom Barry proposes a resumption of hostilities against British forces remaining in the country. Although 12 of the 16 Executive members support the motion – only Lynch, Deasy, Moylan and Barrett are against it – the convention defeats it by a small margin. The minority refuse to accept the decision, leave the meeting and lock themselves into the Four Courts, appointing McKelvey as their COS.

Wilson assassination. 22 June. The military adviser to the government of Northern Ireland, Gen. Sir Henry Wilson, is assassinated in London. This incident leads to the British authorities demanding action from the Provisional Government. (*See Dunne, Reginald and O'Sullivan, Joseph*)

Henderson arrest. 26 June. PTs arrest prominent AT activist Leo Henderson.

O'Connell arrest. 27 June. In reprisal for above, ATs kidnap Gen J.J. O'Connell, A/COS of the Provisional Government's army, and hold him in the Four Courts.

Lynch COS. 27 June. Liam Lynch is again agreed as COS of AT troops but he is still not in the Four Courts.

Firing on Four Courts. 28 June. At 0400 hours, PT troops direct artillery fire against the Four Courts; 375 rounds are fired during the operation. Lynch sends a message of encouragement to the besieged garrison. Fighting also breaks out in O'Connell Street, Dublin. The CW is fully under way.

PT Proclamation. 28 June. In a Proclamation and National Call to Arms, the Minister for Defence, Richard Mulcahy, exhorts further resistance to ATs. (*See 7 July*)

AT Proclamation. 29 June. In the *Poblacht na hÉireann War News* No 2, dated 29 June 1922, the AT Executive issues a proclamation declaring that 'our rightful cause is being treacherously assailed by recreant Irishmen' and exhorting former comrades to 'return to that allegiance and thus guard the Nation's honour from the infamous stigma that her sons aided her foes in retaining a hateful domination over her'. In the same publication de Valera places the blame for the CW on Britain's threat of war and on those who, he claims, yielded to it.

CHRONOLOGY   30 JUNE–10 OCTOBER 1922

Surrender of Four Courts. 30 June. Four Courts garrison surrenders, having set fire to the Public Record Office. Two hundred ATs are taken prisoner.

Early actions. June-August. A number of actions are fought in Leinster and Munster, mainly in counties Cork, Kerry, Limerick, Louth, Tipperary, Waterford, Wexford and Wicklow.

Baldonnel Plan. July. ATs make plans to capture Baldonnel Aerodrome with a view to bombing Leinster House or Beggarsbush Barracks. They also make plans to isolate Dublin city by cratering roads, blowing up bridges, etc.

Dublin fighting. 1-5 July. PTs attack and clear a number of AT city strongholds, leaving Dublin in Provisional Government hands. Spasmodic actions continue into August.

Blessington fighting. 2-7 July. Fighting in Blessington, Co. Wicklow, one of the main early actions.

Call to Arms. 7 July. National Call to Arms issued by the Provisional Government. The title 'National Army' is formalized.

War Council. 12 July. The Provisional Government appoints a War Council, with Collins as Commander-in-Chief.

Cities captured. 20 July. PTs capture Waterford and Limerick.

Sea-borne landings. July-August. AT troops deploy a defensive screen to secure Munster but the National Army makes a number of landings behind these. A trial landing is made at Westport on 24 July 1922. On 2 August 450 Dublin Guards land at Fenit, Co. Kerry. Their armaments included one armoured car (*The Ex-Mutineer*), Lewis guns, rifles, grenades and a considerable quantity of ammunition. The Western Div lands at Tarbert next day. On 8 August a further contingent of Dublin troops land at Passage West, Youghal and Union Hall, Co. Cork.

Cork and Fermoy captured. 10-11 Aug. PTs capture Cork and Fermoy, the last urban areas occupied by ATs.

Griffith's death. 12 Aug. Arthur Griffith, President of the Provisional Government, dies from a cerebral haemorrhage.

Collins shot dead. 22 Aug. Michael Collins, Commander-in-Chief of the National Army, is shot dead in an ambush at Béal na mBláth, Co. Cork. Mulcahy succeeds him.

Chairman appointed. 25 Aug. William Cosgrave is appointed Chairman of the Provisional Government, in place of Collins.

Third Dáil meets. 9 Sept. Members of the Third Dáil, elected in June, finally assemble. Cosgrave is elected President. AT deputies do not attend the sitting.

Constitution Bill introduced. 18 Sept. Cosgrave introduces a bill to enact a constitution for Saorstát Éireann (the IFS), as envisaged by the Treaty.

Emergency Powers. 28 Sept. The Dáil approves the Army Emergency Powers resolution. (*See 15 October*)

Amnesty offer. 10 Oct. The government offers an amnesty to ATs willing to hand in arms and discontinue fighting. On the same day, the Irish Hierarchy meets in Maynooth and issues a joint Pastoral Letter in support of the move. It condemns strongly any further resistance to the Provisional Government, describing attacks on the National Army as murder and assassination.

Emergency Powers Bill effective. 15 Oct. Following a request from Mulcahy, the government agrees to extend the army's powers significantly by making the Army Emergency Powers Bill effective. This gives authority to military courts to impose death penalties for certain offences. The bill allows for any measures deemed fit to crush the ATs.

AT decision to fight on. 16-17 Oct. The AT Executive meets in Nugent's, Ballybacon, Glen of Aherlow, Co. Tipperary, and decides to continue the fight. They appoint an army council whose functions are similar to those of the Executive when the latter was not in session. The meeting passes a resolution calling on de Valera to form a government and council of state that would 'preserve the continuity of the Republic'. The Executive would formalize this on 25 October, the same date upon which the Dáil enacted the Constitution of the IFS.

Constitution enacted. 25 Oct. The Dáil enacts the Constitution of Saorstát Éireann (the IFS). (See 5 and 6 Dec.)

First executions. 17 Nov. The first executions under the Army Emergency Powers Act take place. In Kilmainham Jail, Dublin, four ATs are executed for possession of revolvers.

Childers executed. 24 Nov. Erskine Childers is executed for unlawful possession of a revolver.

Saorstát Éireann approved. 5 Dec. The Dáil approves the Saorstát Éireann Act, which ratifies the Constitution of the IFS. T.M. Healy becomes Governor-General designate.

Saorstát Éireann established. 6 Dec. Saorstát Éireann comes into being with Cosgrave its President. AT TDs declare themselves an alternative Dáil and de Valera the President of the 'Irish Republic'.

Hales shooting. 7 Dec. ATs assassinate Sean Hales, TD, and wound the Leas Ceann Comhairle, Padraic O'Maille.

Four ATs executed. 8 Dec. In reprisal for above, Rory O'Connor, Liam Mellows, Joe McKelvey and Richard Barrett are executed.

1923

Property burning. January.-March. A number of Senators' houses are burned or blown up by ATs.

Deasy document. 18 Jan. After Liam Deasy's capture, court-martial and sentence, he signs a document pledging to assist the immediate unconditional surrender of arms by ATs and appeals for similar action from the recipients of copies of the document: Aiken, Barrett, Tom Barry, Frank Carty, M.P. Colivet, de Valera, Tom Derrig, Lynch, Sean MacSwiney, Con Moloney, Humphrey Murphy, Donal O'Callaghan, Seamus O'Donovan, Robinson, Ruttledge and Austin Stack.

Another amnesty offer. 8 Feb.

Lynch repudiation. 9 Feb. Liam Lynch issues a repudiation of both Deasy's and the government's calls (*above*).

Knocknagashel incident. 6 March. Six PT troops are killed when inspecting an arms dump in Bairanarig Wood, Knocknagashel, Castleisland, Co. Kerry. As a result, GOC Kerry Command orders that AT prisoners are to be used in similar operations in the future.

Ballyseedy incident. 7 March. While in captivity, eight ATs are blown up in a mine explosion at Ballyseedy, Co. Kerry. Official reports later state they were removing a stone road-block and that a PT captain, a lieutenant and a sergeant were injured, two seriously. Evidence of an AT escapee suggested that they were tied to a mined log forming a road-block before it was detonated. At Countess Bridge, Killarney, and at Caherciveen, similar incidents followed, in which four and five AT prisoners, respectively, were killed.

Nire Valley meeting. March-April. Most, but not all, of the AT leaders believe a summer campaign would be ill-advised. Despite the danger involved, a meeting is arranged to discuss this in a remote part of the Nire Valley, near Ballynacarbry, Co. Waterford. The meeting begins in Cullinane's, Bliantas, after some discussion about admitting de Valera, who had arrived there. Intelligence reports on PT search-and-sweep operations in the area lead to a move to Wall's of Glenanore on 25 March. The debate continues until 26 March but agreement to discontinue resistance is not reached. The meeting is adjourned until 10 April with de Valera continuing to negotiate acceptable terms for a cease-fire through intermediaries.

Lynch shot dead. 10 April. Intense search-and-sweep operations in the South Tipperary-Waterford area result in the shooting of Liam Lynch, who was making his way to attend the adjourned meeting (*above*). Aiken succeeds him as AT COS.

Offensive operations suspended. 30 April. Aiken orders ATs to suspend all offensive operations.

Cease-fire ordered. 24 May. Aiken announces a cease-fire and orders the dumping of arms.

De Valera backs cease-fire. 27 May. De Valera reiterates Aiken's cease-fire order.

General election. 27 Aug. Cumann na nGaedheal wins 63 seats, Sinn Féin (abstentionists) 44, Independents 16, Farmers 15, Labour 14, Independent Labour 1.

Hunger-strike. 13 Oct. A hunger-strike among AT prisoners begins in Mountjoy Prison and spreads to other locations. It lasts until 23 November.

PART I

The War of Independence
1916–1921

A–Z

Order of details, when given: name, home address, rank, affiliation, details of involvement. Bracketed cross-references are given only for persons, organizations or events not otherwise named in the entry.

AHEARN, Philip: Tullamore, Co. Offaly. RIC Sgt. Wounded when he raided Sinn Féin rooms in William Street, Tullamore, 20 March 1916. He was fired upon and his assailants were censured by their superiors for anticipating the Rebellion.

AHERNE, James: Cobh, Co. Cork. Killed in 20 February 1921.

AHERNE, John: Ballyrickard, Co. Cork. Killed in action at Ballymoe Cross 16 February 1920.

AHERNE, Liam, Jeremiah and Josie: Midleton, Co. Cork. Brothers. Liam and Jeremiah shot in ambush at Clonmult, Co. Cork, 20 February 1921.

AIKEN, Frank: Camlough, Co. Donegal. Capt Camlough Coy IRA 1918. Comdt Camlough Bn 1919. Vice-Comdt Newry Bde 1920. Comdt 4th Northern Div (South Down, West Armagh, North Louth) 1921. Secretary South Armagh Sinn Féin.

AIMES, Peter Ashmunt: Morristown, New Jersey, USA. Ex-Grenadier Guards BA. Member of 'Cairo Gang' leadership. Taken from his bed at 38 Mount St, Dublin, and shot dead by Collins's execution squad Bloody Sunday morning 21 November 1920. (*See* Bennett)

ALBERT, ALOYSIUS & AUGUSTINE: Priests of Church St Capuchin community, Dublin. Attended to spiritual needs of Irish Volunteers in Easter Week Rebellion and to Ceannt, Mallin, Colbert, Heuston, W. Pearse, Ó h-Annrachain and Plunkett before executions. Fr Albert arrested in winter raids of 1921.

ALDRIDGE, John W.: Sgt 10th Royal Dublin Fusiliers. NCO in charge of Portobello Barracks guard 26 April 1916 when Sheehy Skeffington, McIntyre and Dickson were shot.

ALLAT, H.T.N.: Col Royal Irish Rifles BA. Retired but taken on as a draft-conducting officer. Present at raid on house of Hanna Sheehy Skeffington two days after her husband's killing, although not empowered to hold command. Killed in action at South Dublin Union. Posthumously mentioned in despatches for distinguished service.

ALLEN, Sean: Bank Pl., Tipperary. Officer of 3rd Tipperary Bde. Arrested for possession of arms and documents February 1921. After an unsuccessful application for *habeas corpus* by T.M. Healy he was shot at Victoria Barracks, Cork, 28 February 1921.

ALLMAN, Daniel: Headford Junction, Ballymacelligot, Co. Kerry. IRA

Comdt Operations Officer Kerry No 2 Bde. He co-ordinated the Headford Junction attack on a British provisions train 21 March 1921. He was killed in action there. (*See McEllistrim, Tom*)

ALTON, E.H.: Capt BA. Commanded the Dublin University Officers' Training Corps. At outbreak of hostilities 24 April 1916 he arranged a hasty defence of Trinity College. Awarded the Military Cross for his actions during Easter Week.

AMIGO (Dr): Bishop of Southwark. Allowed his cathedral to be used for Terence MacSwiney's funeral despite protests from the establishment.

ANDREWS: Col BA. Replaced Kirkwood i/c of British troops in Kilkenny area 1920. Later transferred to Clare.

ANDREWS, C.S. ('Todd'): Summerhill and Terenure, Dublin. Rathfarnham Coy 4th Dublin Bn. Detained at Arbour Hill and interned at Rath Camp, Curragh. Escaped after Truce. Adj Cork No 2 Bde. Active in takeover of installations from British.

ANDRUS: Col Comdt. Superintendent of Internee Camps and Prisons in Ireland. Visited Cork Detention Barracks, Spike Island, Bere Island and other camps October 1921.

ANGLISS: Lt BA. Alias for McMahon. Recalled from Russia to British Secret Service and formed their Dublin Intelligence Section. After involvement in the John Lynch shooting, he was constantly trailed by Collins's 'Squad'. This and a drinking problem led to his becoming a type of double agent. He passed on valuable information on the names of other British agents to the Squad. He was killed by the IRA at 22 Mount St, Dublin, on Bloody Sunday morning 21 November 1920.

ARCHER, Liam: Dublin. Civil servant retained in GPO during Easter Week occupation. After the execution of the leaders, he became active with 1st Dublin Bn and commanded 3rd Bn in 1919.

ARMSTRONG-HOLMES, Philip: Maj Gen BA. Div Commander of Police for Cork and Kerry. He and his escort ambushed by Newmarket Flying Column and some East Kerry Volunteers under Sean Moylan at Tureengarriffe, Co. Kerry, 28 January 1921. He was wounded and died the following day.

ASHE, Thomas: Kinnard, Lispole, Co. Kerry. National Teacher at Lusk, Co. Dublin, and Comdt 5th Bn Dublin Bde. Led successful attack on Ashbourne Barracks Friday 28 April 1916 (Easter Week). Arrested, court-martialled and sentenced to death after surrender. Sentence commuted to penal servitude for life. Released by general amnesty 16 June 1917. Re-arrested in August for a seditious speech made at Ballinalee, Co. Longford. Sentenced to further imprisonment. Began hunger-strike 20 September. Died from pneumonia (after forced feeding) 25 September 1917.

ASQUITH, Herbert Henry (First Earl of Oxford and Asquith): Liberal Prime Minister of Britain 1908-16. Approved of Easter Week leaders' executions but later admitted British failure in halting insurrection. Failed to establish Irish Home Rule. Resigned Premiership and was succeeded by Lloyd George 6 December 1916. Became First Lord of the Admiralty. Urged Dominion

Home Rule 1920. Condemned killing of Michael O'Callaghan March 1921 and other atrocities in Ireland.

AUGUSTINE (Fr): *See Holohan, Patrick.*

AUXILIARIES ('Auxies', 'Cadets'): Paramilitary division of RIC, recruited 1920. Mostly ex-British Army officers. Elected own commanders. Wore Glengarry caps and were paid double the Black and Tan salary.

BAGALLY: 19 Eccles St, Dublin. Capt BA. Court-Martial Officer. Allegedly caused John Lynch's assassination by mistaking him for Liam Lynch and reporting his whereabouts. Killed during Bloody Sunday operation 21 November 1920. (*See Lynch, John*)

BAILEY or BEVERLEY, Daniel Julien: Member of Casement's Irish Bde in Germany, accompanied Casement and landed with him in Ireland 1916. Charged with Casement but released when the Crown entered a *nolle prosequi*, having pleaded joining the Irish Bde in order to get back from Germany, where he was a prisoner of war, to rejoin his rgt. (*See Brittain, F.A.*)

BAILEY, James: *See McEllistrim, Tom.*

BALCH, C.A.: Maj BA. Medical Officer in Portobello during Easter Week Rebellion. Examined bodies of Sheehy Skeffington, Dickson and McIntyre. Was immediately transferred to Sierra Leone. Simon Commission refused to produce him when so requested by Denis S. Healy K.C.

BARNETT: Galway. Youth arrested with Thomas Whelan for alleged part in Bloody Sunday morning operations.

BARRETT, Benjamin: *See 'Twelve Apostles'.*

BARRETT, Dick: Hollyhill, Co. Cork. Bde Staff Officer, sometimes acting Bde Comdt West Cork Bde. Continued teaching to avoid suspicion and organized fund-raising activities for comrades on the run. QM 1920. Arrested after Crossbarry ambush March 1921 and imprisoned at Cork and Spike Island.

BARRETT, Frank: Daragh, Co. Clare. Comdt Mid-Clare Bde 1918-21. (*See Brennan, Michael*)

BARRETT, Joe: Daragh, Co. Clare. QM Mid-Clare Bde and OC Mid-Clare Flying Column. Led successful attack on British patrol in Ennis on eve of Spancil Hill Horse-fair 23 June 1920. Adj 1st Western Div 1921.

BARRINGTON (Miss): Glenstal Castle, Co. Limerick. Shot dead in ambush 14 May 1921 when accompanying British officer to a social function. (*See Biggs*)

BARRY, Denis: Cullen, Riverstick. Member of AOH, Gaelic League and Irish Volunteers. Arrested 3 May 1916 in Kilkenny. Imprisoned there and Frongoch. OC Republican Police 1st Cork Bde, April 1921. With Michael Burke, planned rescue of prisoners from Spike Island 29 April 1921.

BARRY, Kevin: Toombeag, Co. Carlow; 8 Fleet St, Dublin. University student and Irish Volunteer. Captured after the ambush of a military vehicle in King St area, Dublin, 15 August 1920. Tortured during interrogation on whereabouts of his fellow Volunteers. Details of torture set down in a sworn statement made before a Justice of the Peace. Court-martialled, sentenced to death and hanged at Mountjoy Jail 1 November 1920. (*See Keogh, Myles*)

BARRY, Leslie (Bean Thomais de Barra): Rosscarbery, Co. Cork. Director of C na mB 1916-23. Served in the GPO during Easter Week.

BARRY, Tom: Rosscarbery, Co. Cork. Was serving with BA in Mesopotamia in 1916; returned to Cork February 1919. Became IRA IO, Training Officer West Cork Bde May 1920. Became OC Bde Flying Column. Led column at Tooreen causing four British casualties and four wounded 24 October 1920. Led column at Kilmichael 28 November 1920; sixteen killed outright, one wounded who died later, one escaped. Hospitalized December 1920. With C. Hurley feigned attack on Innishannon Barracks 16 January 1921. Led Bandon attack 24 January 1921. Occupied Burgatia House 2 February 1921. Ordered shooting of Essex Rgt troops on sight. Attacked Bandon 23 February; an RIC Const and four British killed and two BN Warrant Officers taken prisoner. Fought Auxiliaries at Castletown-Kenneigh in March. Led outstanding action at Crossbarry 19 March 1921 against a large contingent of Crown Forces which sustained heavy losses. Led the column against Rosscarbery Barracks 30 March 1921. Active in Union Hall arms landing April 1921. Led third attack on Bandon 14 May 1921. Deputy Comdt and Training Officer 1st Southern Div. Resigned September 1921, requesting a transfer back to 3rd Bde. (*See Higginson*)

BARTON, John: Dublin. Det DMP. Arrested looters and arms-carriers during Easter Week, including 27 on first night. Awarded the King's Medal for conspicuous gallantry and promoted as a result. Alleged to have ill-treated prisoners taken after the surrender. Killed by Collins's 'Squad' as part of a campaign against policemen prominent in harassing Volunteers.

BARTON, Robert: Wicklow. Served with BA during 1916 Rebellion. Resigned and joined Volunteers, reaching the rank of Comdt. Elected for West Wicklow 1918. Represented Wicklow/Kildare and read the English version of the 'Message To Free Nations' at the First Dáil sitting 21 January 1919. Arrested for making seditious speeches February 1919. Escaped from Mountjoy 16 March. Minister for Agriculture 1 April 1919. Instigated Land Bank Schemes. Re-arrested January 1920. Sentenced to three years' penal servitude. Released after six months on declaration of Truce. Minister for Economic Affairs. Member of Truce Observation Committee. Treaty negotiator and signatory. Cousin of Erskine Childers.

BEALEN, Patrick: Loan, Castlecomer, Co. Kilkenny. His body was found in the cellar of the public house where he worked at 177 North King St, Dublin, after Easter Week. A Coroner's Jury's verdict that he had died of wounds inflicted by soldiers was considered by commentators to be unsatisfactory. (*See Healy, James*)

BÉASLAÍ, Piaras: Liverpool and Dublin. Journalist. Vice Comdt to Ned Daly at North Dublin Union, Easter Week 1916. Arrested and sentenced to penal servitude. Imprisoned Mountjoy, Belfast and Manchester. Escaped twice. Elected for East Kerry 1918.

Liaison Officer between government Department of Publicity and IRA HQ 1919. Editor of *An t-Oglach*. Helped draft the constitution for the First Dáil. IRA Director of Propaganda. (See O'Connor, Rory)

BEGLEY, Flor: Bandon, Co. Cork. Bn QM 1st (Bandon) Bn West Cork Bde January 1919. Bn Adj from August 1919. Formed Bandon Volunteer Pipe Band. Played lament at Charlie Hurley's funeral. Arrested 1 January 1921. Imprisoned in Wormwood Scrubs. Released in April after hunger-strike. Bde Acting Adj April 1921. Played war tunes on his pipes at Crossbarry ambush 19 March 1921.

BELL, Alan: Banagher, Co. Offaly; Dublin. Magistrate. Served in Athenry, Ballinrobe, Lurgan and Belfast prior to appointment in Dublin Castle in 1920 where he assisted British Intelligence. Investigated Dáil Funds and National Loan 1920. In March 1920 signed order forcing banks to disclose details of clients' accounts. Taken from a tram at Merrion stop, Dublin, and shot dead, March 1920.

BELLEW, Henry Grattan (Sir): Magistrate and Deputy Lt for HM in Galway in August 1920 when he and 148 Irish magistrates resigned because military law was being substituted for civil law in Ireland.

BENNETT: Temporary Capt, Royal Artillery. Informer and co-leader of 'Cairo Gang' with Aimes. Shot dead at 38 Mount St on Bloody Sunday morning 21 November 1920. (See Aimes, Peter)

BERGIN, John: Nenagh, Co. Tipperary. Wounded in an action near Loughglynn Wood, Co. Roscommon, 18-19 April 1921. He was later shot dead with another participant, Stephen McDermott. Joe Satchwell and Toby Scally were badly beaten and the former imprisoned.

BEVERLEY: *See Bailey, Daniel Julien.*

BIGGS: Maj. Dist Insp RIC Limerick. On 14 May 1921, while motoring with the only daughter of Sir C. Barrington of Glenstal Castle, he was ambushed near Newport, Co. Tipperary. Miss Barrington was shot dead.

BIRKENHEAD, F. E. 'Galloper' Smith (Lord): Lord Chancellor. Counsel for the Prosecution (Attorney General) at Casement trial. Befriended Collins during Treaty negotiations.

BIRRELL, Augustine (Rt Hon.): Chief Secretary for Ireland 1907-16. His ineptitude gave rise to the word 'Birrellism'. The Royal Commission of Inquiry into the Easter Week Rebellion held him responsible for the outbreak of hostilities. Admitting his underestimation of Sinn Féin, he resigned.

'BLACK AND TANS': Former BA personnel recruited for service in Ireland as reinforcements for RIC March 1920. Haphazardly dressed in khaki tunics and black trousers (or vice versa).

BLAKE (Dist Insp and Mrs): *See Cornwallis.*

BLAKE, Henry (Sir): Youghal, Co. Cork. His submission to the Royal Commission of Inquiry into the Easter Week Rebellion summed up conditions prevailing in Ireland and was included as an appendix to the report.

BLYTHE, Ernest: Magheragall, Lisburn, Co. Antrim. Deported with Liam Mellows prior to Easter Week. Assisted in organization of Volunteers in Bantry-Beara area. Imprisoned with Sean Treacy at Dundalk. Elected for North Monaghan in 1918. Member of Sinn Féin Executive October 1919. Director of Trade and Commerce in First Dáil. Appointed Minister for Trade and Commerce 1921.

BOLAND, Gerry: Manchester and Dublin. Member of Jacob's garrison Easter Week. Arrested and imprisoned after surrender. In 1920 his family accepted custody of portion of the Russian Crown jewels which had been given as security for a loan of £20,000 made to win recognition for the Irish Republic. Brother of Harry Boland.

BOLAND, Harry: Clontarf, Dublin. Imprisoned at Dartmoor with Stack and Ashe and in Dundalk with Treacy. Member of Sinn Féin Executive October 1917. Accompanied Collins in organization of de Valera's escape from Lincoln prison February 1919. TD for South Roscommon 1919. Sent to USA in an attempt to heal the rift among Irish bodies there 1919-20. Brother of Gerry Boland.

BOLSTER, Frank: See 'Twelve Apostles'.

BOURNE (Cardinal): England. Conveyed RC bishops' desire for withdrawal of Auxiliaries from Ireland to Lloyd George April 1921.

BOWEN-COLTHURST, J.C.: Capt Royal Irish Rifles, Portobello Barracks, Dublin. Shot Sheehy Skeffington, McIntyre and Dickson at Portobello 26 April 1916. Also shot a young witness. Court-martialled and found guilty of three murders. Plea of being of unsound mind being accepted 26 June, he was committed to Broadmoor Criminal Lunatic Asylum. (*See Coade, J.*)

BOYD: Gen BA Bde Commander Dublin District September 1920.

BOYLAN, Sean: Dunboyne, Co. Meath. Family participated in Easter Week Rebellion. Sean, Joseph, Peter and Edward imprisoned at Kilmainham, Wandsworth and Frongoch. Commandant Meath Bde 1919-20. Active at Trim Barracks attack 30 September 1920. Chairman of Meath Sinn Féin and Director of Elections there. OC 1st Eastern Div 1921.

BOYLE, Jeannie: Young bride-to-be trampled to death at Croke Park when Black and Tans raided a Gaelic football match during the afternoon of Bloody Sunday 21 November 1920.

BRACKEN, Peadar: Tullamore, Co. Offaly. Fought in Dublin in Easter Week Rebellion. Member of Volunteer Executive and active in the leadership of Athlone Area and Offaly Bde. Moved to GHQ Staff 1920. Organizer in Kildare, North Tipperary and Offaly. Interned at Rath Camp, Curragh, from which he escaped October 1921. Republican Court organizer Longford/Westmeath.

BRADY, Christopher: Dublin. Member of party that seized Dublin Castle guard room during Easter Week. Fought in Castle St area until his capture on the Wednesday. Imprisoned Wandsworth and Frongoch. Released in bad health November 1916. Died 28 January 1917.

BRADY, James: Co. Cavan. Arigna Volunteer Coy. Miner interned at Rath Camp, Curragh, who gave his name to the 'Brady Tunnel' through which 70 prisoners escaped in September 1921. Scottie Regan of Keadue, Co. Roscommon, was his chief accomplice.

BRADY, P.S.: Magistrate. When his motorcar broke down at Ballineer Road, Dunmanway, Co. Cork, on 15 December 1920, Canon Magnier and a youth, Tim Crowley, went to his assistance. Both were shot dead by Auxiliaries who threatened Brady also. Production of identification saved him.

BREEN, Dan: Soloheadbeg, Co. Tipperary. Capt Lisheen Grove Coy, Tipperary. Bn Comdt April 1916 to August 1917. QM 3rd Tipperary Bde October 1918. One of the 'Big Four'. Co-planner of Soloheadbeg ambush, staged on the first day of Dáil 21 January 1919. It was the most significant encounter with British forces since Easter Week and represented the start of the War of Independence proper. Two policemen were killed and a reward of £10,000 was afterwards offered for his capture. Seriously injured in Knocklong rescue of Sean Hogan. Active in Dublin 1919. Wounded in Ashtown ambush of Lord French 19 December 1919. Returned to Tipperary 1920. Wounded in Rear Cross attack 11 July 1920. Active in Dublin 1920. Received five bullet wounds in 'Fernside' fight, Drumcondra, when he and Treacy escaped capture. Admitted to Mater Hospital Nursing Home two days before Treacy's death October 1920. (*See Robinson, Seamus*)

BREEN, Lar: Brother of Dan (*above*). Member of 3rd Tipperary Bde. Worked in Soloheadbeg quarry and observed movements for the Bde.

BRENNAN Brothers: Carrickteel, Co. Roscommon. Prominent Volunteer organizers. Both arrested after Easter Week Rebellion; Michael imprisoned in Glasgow, Jack in Lewes. Campaigned extensively for Harry Boland's election in Roscommon.

BRENNAN Brothers: Meelick, Co. Clare. Prominent Volunteer organizers. Michael: Chairman County Council. North Munster member of Supreme Council of IRB. Arrested Easter Week having attempted to move to Galway to contact Mellows. Imprisoned Limerick, Richmond Barracks, Wakefield, Frongoch, Reading. Released December 1916. Rearrested February 1917 and detained at Arbour Hill and in open detention at Wetherby from where he escaped. Courtmartialled in Cork 12 July 1917, he was one of the first to adopt the tactic of refusing to recognize the court. Imprisoned Cork. Went on hungerstrike which was called off on Collins's orders. Moved to Mountjoy and again to Dundalk. Released November 1917. With Paddy (*below*) assisted in South Armagh election of 1918. While undergoing a further sentence in Dundalk, he witnessed Diarmuid Lynch's wedding. Released January 1919 and became Comdt East Clare Bde. Was active in the struggle, participating in the Kilmallock attack among other actions. Took custody of Gen Lucas for a period. Severely wounded in action at O'Brien's Bridge and continued operating with the use of one arm. Participated in Glenwood action where a Dist Insp and five Consts were killed. OC 1st Western Div 1921. Initially Frank Barrett's Mid-Clare Bde was excluded but later came under his command, Barrett becoming 2 i/c of the Div (see *Hogan, James*). Austin: Appointed Comdt East Clare Bde and remained its Comdt when 1st Western Div was formed 1921. In action at Glenwood 20 January 1921 and many of encounters mentioned above. Paddy: Collected boats and arranged passage through Ennis to Galway for expected arms from Germany prior to Easter Week. Arrested in Carrigaholt during the week. Imprisoned Limerick and Frongoch. Comdt of the original Clare Bde, he resigned when GHQ initiated the new organization splitting the Bde. (See *Casement, Roger*)

BRENNAN, J.: See *'Twelve Apostles'*.

BRENNAN, J.J.: Dublin. Fought at Mendicity Institute Easter Week. Court-martialled at Richmond Barracks and sentenced to death, commuted to life imprisonment. Imprisoned Mountjoy, Portland, Lewes and Pentonville until the June 1917 amnesty.

BRENNAN, Maurice: Participated in Easter Week Rebellion and in Mountjoy hunger-strike April 1920. Helped evacuate Dan Breen to Mater Hospital.

BRENNAN, Richard: Knockanure, Co. Kilkenny. Vice Comdt 9th Kilkenny Bn IRA. Led Sinnots Cross ambush near Mooncoin, Co. Kilkenny, June 1921.

BRENNAN, Robert: Wexford. Comdt. Led Wexford Volunteers and occupied Enniscorthy during Easter Week. Held out until he received a surrender order from Pearse in Dublin. Court-martialled and sentenced to death, commuted to life imprisonment. Imprisoned Dartmoor. On release, became Director of Elections for Sinn Féin December 1918. Headed Government Department of Publicity 1919.

BRENNAN-WHITMORE, W.J.: Ferns, Co. Wexford. Senior Staff Officer in Easter Week Rebellion; helped prepare a handbook on guerilla tactics. Sinn Féin delegate for Wexford. Arrested and deported for alleged part in supposed 'German Plot' May 1918.

BRENT, George: See *Nolan, George*.

BRERETON, J.P.: Ladywell, Athlone, Co. Westmeath. Col BA. Captured and held at Four Courts by IRA during Easter Week. Testified as to good character of his captors, stating that they were incapable of acts of brutality. (See *Daly, John Edward*)

BRESLIN, Ned: See *'Twelve Apostles'*.

BRETT: RIC Const shot dead in Cork 1920. Growing hostility to RIC caused undertakers' refusal to attend to his remains.

BRIND, J.: Col. BA representative at the final drafting of Truce terms.

BRISCOE, Robert: Dublin. Returned from USA after Easter Week. Member of Fianna Éireann. Became an IRA agent for arms purchase in Germany 1920.

BRITTAIN, F.A.: Tralee, Co. Kerry. Dist Insp RIC. Extracted story of the *Aud* and Casement from Bailey at Abbeydorney Barracks, Co. Kerry, while Casement was held in Tralee after his arrest. (See *Bailey, Daniel Julien*)

BROSNAN: SM Royal Irish Fusiliers. BA. Musketry instructor at Armagh and Buncrana. Holidaying with wife and children in Dublin Castle when Castle was attacked 24 April 1916. Offered services, disarmed one Volunteer attacker before being shot dead by a soldier who mistook him (being a stranger and in mufti) for an attacker.

BROSNAN, Tadhg: *See O'Connor, Tom.*

BROWNE, John: Ballymacelligot, Co. Kerry. KIA during the first attack on an RIC barracks in Kerry at Gortalea 18 April 1918. The RIC members who attended an inquiry into the affair 14 June 1918 were fired upon in Tralee. (*See Laide, Richard*)

BROY, Eamonn: Rathangan, Co. Kildare. One of Collins's 'Castle Spies'. Allowed Collins access to HQ of Dublin Det Force in Brunswick St (now Pearse St) April 1919. Arrested March 1921. His superior Superintendent, although unaware of his activities, burned Broy's papers, thus leaving no evidence to convict him. Broy pleaded another was responsible for his own activites, naming a man who lived in England. Collins had this man transported to make him appear guilty. Broy was held in custody until after the Truce. Secretary to Collins during the Treaty negotiations. (*See Neligan, David; Redmond, William*)

BRUCE: Maj BA. Discharged by Crozier 1920. Returned as RIC officer to raid Kilkenny creameries. Arrested and imprisoned for one year.

BRUGHA, Cathal (Charles Burgess): Richmond Ave, Dublin. 2 i/c, under Eamon Ceannt, at South Dublin Union during Easter Week. Severely wounded there. Held at Dublin Castle hospital after the Rebellion. Released as 'incurable' and was lame for life. Member of Sinn Féin Executive. COS Irish Volunteer Organization November 1917 to April 1919. Helped build Volunteer Force. Elected for Waterford in 1918 election. Presided at First Dáil meeting 21 January 1919 and was appointed Acting President (de Valera and Griffith in jail). Proposed the swearing of allegiance to the Irish Republic and the Dáil August 1919. Minister for Defence April 1919 and August 1921 cabinets. Rejected an execution list prepared as a reprisal for Bloody Sunday. Disapproved of independent action by Volunteers without Dáil approval. Supported de Valera's exclusion from Treaty negotiations and declined to participate himself. (*See Mulcahy, Richard*)

BRUNSWICK, Sean: Dublin Bde Volunteers. Active in attempts to protect Breen and Treacy after 'Fernside' fight, warning Peadar Clancy of Crown Forces' activities. Witnessed shooting of Treacy and removed documents from his possession.

BRYAN, Dan: Dunbell, Co. Kilkenny. While a medical student joined C Coy 4th Dublin Bn in 1917. As a result of participation in raids, armed patrols and observation work, he was appointed Assistant Bn IO in January 1921 when Joe Kinsella became involved in grenade manufacturing. With Bn Comdt Sean Dowling, Coy Capt Sean McCurtain of G Coy, Coy Capt F.X. Coughlan of E Coy and the Bn Int Section, his activities included the correlation of intelligence from Tommy Daly at Kildare St Club.

BRYAN, Thomas: Dublin. Arrested after abortive 'Drumcondra ambush' when a proposed attack on an RIC tender was thwarted due to the activities of an informer. Sentenced to death and hanged 14 March 1921. (*See Flood, Frank*)

BUCKLEY, Jeremiah: *See O'Brien, Patrick*.

BUCKLEY, Sean: Bandon, Co. Cork. IRA organizer. West Cork Bde IO 1919-21. Organized Civil Administration in the Bandon area. Escaped recognition by Hampshire Rgt troops at Ballinphellic when Charlie Hurley was killed.

BURKE Brothers: Det Insp and Sgt RIC. Killed and wounded respectively at Balbriggan, Co. Dublin, by IRA who intervened in a fracas when RIC declined. Action led to the 'Sack of Balbriggan' 20 September 1920.

BURKE, Frank: 2 Lt Rathfarnham Coy Dublin 4th Bn. Former pupil of Pearse, fought beside him during Easter Week. Arrested and interned at Frongoch. Maintained close relationship with Pearse family after Padraic's and Willie's executions.

BURKE, Michael: *See footnote to Murphy, Joe*.

BUTTERFIELD, T.C.: Lord Mayor of Cork 1916. Together with Assistant Bishop of Cork, negotiated with MacSwiney and MacCurtain to prevent Easter Week uprising there. Negotiated for the handing in of Volunteer arms. These were later impounded by Crown Forces.

BYRNE, Ben: *See 'Twelve Apostles'*.

BYRNE, Charlie: *See Intelligence Section*.

BYRNE, Eddie: *See 'Twelve Apostles'*.

BYRNE, J.A. (Sir): Brig Gen, Derry. Deputy AG on Sir John Maxwell's staff. Succeeded Sir Neville Chamberlain as Insp-Gen of the RIC. Appointed Commander of the Order of the Bath in recognition of distinguished service during Easter Week Rebellion. Given leave with pay, supposedly because of disagreement with British policy, January 1920.

BYRNE, Vincent: Dublin. Member of Collins's 'Squad'. Participated in Ashtown ambush. (*See 'Twelve Apostles'*)

BYRNE, William Patrick (Sir): Succeeded Sir Robert Chalmers as Under-Secretary to the Lord-Lt of Ireland 27 October 1916.

BYRNES, Robert: Limerick. Adj 2nd Limerick City Bn. Imprisoned in Limerick Jail for alleged possession of arms. Went on hunger-strike. Moved to Limerick Union Hospital. Escaped but was wounded and died that evening 16 April 1919.

CADETS: *See Auxiliaries*.

CAFFREY, Sean: *See 'Twelve Apostles'*.

CAHILL, Paddy: Tralee, Co. Kerry. Comdt Kerry No 1 Bde 1919. In March 1921 refused Gen Strickland's proffered guarantee of safety for desisting from IRA activities. Led the Lispole ambush March 1921. His replacement by Andy Cooney after the formation of the 1st Southern Div led to some confusion at the Castlemaine ambush 1 June 1921.

'CAIRO GANG': A group of British Intelligence Officers, so called because they met in Cairo at the behest of Sir Henry Wilson, CIGS. Carried out raids and searches in Ireland in 1920, attempting to break Collins's system. Their action led to the Bloody Sunday executions 21 November 1920.

CALDWELL, Paddy: *See Intelligence Section*.

CALLANAN, Eugene ('Nudge'): Student at University College Cork and member of the College IRA Coy. Abandoned his studies to become Assistant Bde Medical Officer with the West Cork Bde 1921. Fought also at Clashinimud 2 December 1920. Assisted in treating the wounded after Crossbarry 19 March 1921.

CAMPBELL, James Henry Mussen (Lord Glenavy): Unionist MP for Dublin University. Attorney General for Ireland 1916. Not notified of any possibility of trouble before Easter Week Rebellion and so testified before Royal Commission of Inquiry. Lord Chief Justice 1916-18 when he became Lord Chancellor. Made Baron 1921.

CARBERY, Christopher: Dublin. First appointee to the Volunteer GHQ intelligence staff after its inauguration by Eamonn Duggan May 1918. Captured 1921.

CAREW, Thomas: Golden Garden, Cashel, Co. Tipperary. Recovered and concealed on his farm the gelignite dumped after Soloheadbeg ambush. Served three months in Cork jail for refusal to comply with deportation order. Received further deportation order on release, forcing him to go 'on the run'.

CARNEY, Frank: OC 1st Northern Div until May 1921. Volunteer who was active with Joe Sweeney in Donegal area. Involved in blowing up of Port Nua coastguard station. Arrested in a raid in Burtonport.

CARNEY, Winifred: Belfast and Dublin. Sometimes referred to as 'Carew'. Irish Citizen Army and James Connolly's secretary. One of the last three women to leave the GPO after its evacuation towards end of Easter Week Rebellion. Attended to Plunkett and MacDonagh after the surrender when they were detained in the open at the Rotunda Hospital.

CAROLAN (Professor): Owner of 'Fernside', Drumcondra, Dublin, where Treacy and Breen fought their way to avoid capture 12 October 1920. DOW received in raid by Crown Forces.

CARRAGHER, Lily: New York C na mB. Enthusiastic fund-raiser in USA.

CARROLL, Patrick: Dublin. Fifteen-year-old messenger killed during the shooting of Sean Treacy in Talbot St 14 October 1920.

CARSON, Edward Henry: Harcourt St, Dublin. Member of British Cabinet. First Lord of the Admiralty 1916-17. Strongly opposed Home Rule. Advocate of a six-county instead of a nine-county Northern Ireland 1920. Refused to vote for Partition Bill 1920. Lord of Appeal 1921.

CARTY, Frank: Clooncunny, Ballymote, Co. Sligo. Comdt South Sligo Bde and Commander of Flying Column. Imprisoned for arms raid at Templehouse. Rescued from Sligo Jail 26 June 1920. Effected a daring escape from Derry Jail 15 February 1921 by sawing through the bars of his cell; despite cordons thrown about the city, escaped on a boat to Glasgow. There, under instructions from GHQ, he spent some months training Glasgow Volunteers. Arrested, charged and sentenced, he again figured in a spectacular escape attempt: Volunteers attacking the van conveying him from court to prison attempted to shoot the lock off the van but jammed it instead. Police Insp Robert Johnson was shot in the unsuccessful escapade. (*See Kilcoyne, Tom; Perceval*)

CASEMENT, Roger David (Sir): Ballycastle, Co. Antrim; Lawson Tce, Sandycove, Co. Dublin. Commander of the Order of St Michael and St George. Clan na Gael envoy in Germany prior to Easter Week. Arranged shipment of arms for the Rebellion aboard the *Aud*, himself landing from a German submarine at Banna Strand. Arrested there 21 April 1916. After a three-day wait off the Kerry coast the *Aud* was arrested and escorted to Cobh, Co. Cork, where it was blown up by its crew. Casement imprisoned in Tower of London and Brixton. Convicted of High Treason. Converted to Roman Catholicism before death. Hanged 3 August 1916 at Pentonville prison, London. (*See Bailey, Daniel Julien; Spindler, Karl*)

CASEMENT, Thomas: Brother of Roger (*above*). Solicited support of Gen Smuts and other South African statesmen for Imperial Conference of 1921. Smuts was then Premier of the Union and was working for co-operation within the Commonwealth.

CASEY, Patrick: *See Maher, Jerry.*

CASSIDY, Frank: Corlough, Co. Cavan. With his comrade Tom Darcy, he marched to Co. Fermanagh for arms and equipment to form a Flying Column from the Volunteer Coy at Corlough, Co. Cavan.

CASSIDY, Martin: Vice-Comdt Kilkenny Bde 1921. Attempted to bomb the home of County Insp White of the RIC March 1921.

'CASTLE ORDER' (also 'Castle Document'): A document, alleged to have been copied from Dublin Castle files, that included plans for the arrest of members of national organizations. It was produced by Rory O'Connor and circulated prior to the Easter Week Rebellion in order to sway dissenters. Castle authorities denied that such a document ever existed.

CEANNT, Eamon: Ballymoe, Glenamaddy, Co. Galway. Member of IRB, Comdt 4th Dublin Bn. Member of the National Council and the Military Council of the Volunteers which planned the Easter Week Rebellion. A signatory of the Proclamation. Commanded his Bn at the South Dublin Union during Easter Week. Court-martialled and sentenced to death. Executed at Kilmainham 8 May 1916.

CHALLONER (Col and Mrs): *See Lambert.*

CHALMERS, A.D.: 2 Lt 14th Royal Fusiliers. On sick leave and in vicinity of GPO at outbreak of Easter Week Rebellion. Held prisoner there throughout the week.

CHALMERS, Mackenzie Daizell (Sir): Member of Royal Commission of Inquiry into the Easter Week Rebellion.

CHALMERS, Robert (Sir): Succeeded Sir Matthew Nathan as Under-Secretary for Ireland May 1916. Was in turn succeeded by Sir William Patrick Byrne October 1916.

CHAMBERLAIN, Austen Joseph (Rt Hon): His father, Joseph Chamberlain, resigned from Gladstone's cabinet due to Irish Home Rule policy. Austen joined Churchill in pressing for strong measures in Ireland in 1921. Leader of House of Commons and British delegate in Truce negotiations. Participated in final Treaty talks.

CHAMBERLAIN, Neville Francis Fitzgerald (Sir): Col Insp Gen of RIC 1916. Gave evidence before Royal Commission of Inquiry into Easter Week Rebellion, stating that he had repeatedly warned of impending dangers. Resigned July 1916.

CHANDLER, Richard: Balbradagh, Trim, Co. Meath. His premises were raided by a large convoy of Auxiliaries 9 February 1921. He was abused, his shop and public house looted and his invalid sister manhandled. Members of the convoy reported the incident to Gen Crozier, resulting in the suspension of some of the raiders.

CHARTRES, John: Chief of Intelligence Section of War Office Armaments Output Committee. Collins allegedly had him returned to London from Germany. War Department business in Dublin during 1916 interested him further in the Irish struggle. He became a leader writer and contributor to *Nationality* and assisted in the procurement of arms. Active in collecting, collating and disseminating intelligence for the IRA. One of three assistant secretaries with Erskine Childers for Treaty negotiations 1921. He pointed out the difficulty surrounding the symbolism of the Crown in Ireland. (*See Lynch, Fionan; O'Hegarty, Diarmuid*)

CHEYLESMORE (Lord): *See Lucas, A.L.*

CHILDERS, Erskine: London and Glendalough House, Co. Wicklow. Former Clerk of House of Commons Committees and BA officer. Often mistrusted because of background. Secretary of Lloyd George's Irish Convention of 1917, which sought agreement on a Home Rule Bill. Irish prisoners in England were released to provide favourable climate for the convention, which nevertheless failed. Elected to Dáil for Wicklow 1921. Dáil's Director of Propaganda March 1921. With three assistants, acted as secretary to the Irish delegation at the Treaty negotiations. Irish secretary of subcommittee dealing with observation of the Truce. (*See Chartres, John; Lynch, Fionan; O'Hegarty, Diarmuid*)

CHRISTIAN, Francis: Sgt. Member of British Intelligence party observing Sean Treacy's movements after 'Fernside' fight. Closed in on Treacy in Talbot St, Dublin, 14 October 1920. Mortally wounded in exchange of fire in which Treacy was shot dead.

CHURCHILL, Winston Leonard Spencer (Rt Hon Sir): Secretary of State for War, House of Commons, January 1919. Member of British delegation in Truce negotiations 1921. Participant in final Treaty talks.

CITIZEN ARMY: Originated in the 1913 labour lock-out. Jim Larkin and James Connolly fashioned the force, which aimed at protecting the workers. Participated in Easter Week Rebellion.

CLANCY Brothers: Ballylanders, Co. Tipperary. David: Lt in Ballylanders Coy IRA. Housed Treacy and Breen during night following Knocklong rescue 13 May 1919. Patrick: Vice-Comdt of 3rd Tipperary Bde Flying Column, was active in the struggle and was shot dead in Kanturk, Co. Cork, 17 August 1920.

CLANCY, George: Former Lord Mayor of Limerick shot dead in his home 7 March 1921. 'Cairo Gang' presumed responsible; they had been foiled in a plot to kill the Bishop of Killaloe. His wife was shot through the hand during the struggle. (*See Crozier, F.*)

CLANCY, J.J.: *See Pilkington, William.*

CLANCY, Pat: Comdt Kanturk Bn Cork No 2 Bde. Assisted Liam Lynch at capture of Gen Lucas.

CLANCY, Patrick: Allensbridge, Newmarket, Co. Cork. IRA Comdt prominent in the establishment of the East Limerick Bde Flying Column. Killed with Jack O'Connell of Derrygallon, at the latter's home 17 August 1920.

CLANCY, Peadar: Cranny, Co. Clare. Vice-Comdt Dublin Bde IRA. Involved in many of Collins's Dublin operations including jail-rescue bids. Guiding force behind the Mountjoy hunger-strike of April 1920 when he refused all proffered concessions, including political status and negotiated release of all hunger-strikers. Proprietor of the Republican Outfitters, where activities preceding Treacy's death took place. Active in attempts to save Treacy and Breen. Captured with Dick McKee, Bde Comdt, in the Gloucester Diamond on 20 November 1920, the eve of Bloody Sunday. Both alleged to have been tortured, and killed when they refused to give information. Official communiqué stated they were shot while trying to escape from Dublin Castle. (*See Hardy; Munro; O'Malley, Christopher*)

CLARKE, Basil: Operated British Propaganda Department, Dublin Castle. Issued highly inaccurate and exaggerated reports on ambushes, etc.

CLARKE, Joseph: Rush, Co. Dublin. Fought at St Stephen's Hall during Easter Week and took part in the Mount St Bridge encounter. Believed strongly that his garrison was let down by not receiving reinforcements from nearby Boland's Mills.

CLARKE, Kathleen: Wife of Thomas J. (*below*). After husband's execution, worked for Irish National Aid Association and Irish Volunteers' Dependants' Fund. Member of Sinn Féin executive 1917. Arrested 17 May 1918. Deported and imprisoned without trial. Appointed a justice of the Republican Courts established in 1920. (*See McGuinness, Joe*)

CLARKE, Thomas J.: South Africa; Isle of Wight; Dungannon, Co. Tyrone; USA; Fairview, Dublin. Sometimes referred to as the 'Father of the Revolution', having been a Fenian. Closely involved in planning of Easter Week Rebellion. Strongly deplored MacNeill's interference in the plans. Presided at Easter Sunday morning meeting which decided to go ahead with the Rebellion. Had the distinction of being the first to sign the Proclamation. Fought in the GPO. Court-martialled and sentenced to death. Executed in Kilmainham 3 May 1916. Left £3100 to his wife for relief of the distressed.

CLAYTON, E.M.: County Insp RIC in Galway East Riding. Gave evidence before the Royal Commission of Inquiry into the Easter Week Rebellion. Later Div Insp of RIC. One of six prominent persons named by the Coroner's Jury that brought in a verdict of murder in the Tomás MacCurtain case.

CLEAR, Frank: Coolcullen, Co. Kilkenny. Active organizer of Coolbawn ambush of 1921 when intending IRA ambushers were themselves set upon by Crown Forces.

CLERY, Arthur: Prof of Law, University College Dublin. Appointed member of Supreme Court, Republican Courts, 1920.

CLIFFORD, Patrick: Mitchelstown, Co. Cork. One of two sentenced Volunteers to have had a Writ of Prohibition applied for by Michael Comyn, KC. Appeal heard by House of Lords 16 June 1921 when Military Courts were deemed to be illegal. (See *O'Sullivan, Michael*)

CLUNE (Most Rev Dr): Archbishop of Perth, Australia. Met Lloyd George and Griffith to discuss possibilities of a Truce in December 1920. An uncle of Conor Clune (*below*).

CLUNE, Conor: Raheen, Quin, Co. Clare. Arrived by chance in Dublin on the eve of Bloody Sunday. Was in Vaughan's Hotel when it was raided by Auxiliaries. Shot dead with Dick McKee and Peadar Clancy Bloody Sunday 21 November 1920. Officially reported as having been shot while attempting to escape. There exists a conflict of views as to whether he was a member of the IRA and whether he was tortured before death. (*See McLysaght, Edward; Pearson, William*)

COADE, J.: Upr Mount Pleasant Ave, Dublin. A youth who witnessed the meeting of Bowen-Colthurst with Sheehy Skeffington and was consequently shot dead at Rathmines Rd on night of 25 April 1916. Simon Commission of Inquiry pronounced the shooting as being completely unjustified. (*See O'Loughlin, F.; Simon, John*)

COCKERILL: Brig Gen MP. Made an unheeded call for unconditional truce discussions as early as October 1920.

COGAN, James: Stonefield, Oldcastle, Co. Meath. Member of Republican Police. Shot dead by Auxiliaries while accompanying a cattle thief to his trial 21 July 1920.

COHALAN, Daniel: New York. Justice of the Supreme Court of New York State. Irish-American leader of the Friends of Irish Freedom. Sought self-determination for Ireland rather than recognition of the Irish Republic. Clashed with de Valera on the Dáil Loan issue. President Wilson refused to meet a delegation from the Irish Race Convention of 1919 until Cohalan withdrew. A close associate of John Devoy.

COHALAN, D.F. (Most Rev Dr): Assistant Bishop of Cork 1916. With Lord Mayor T.C. Butterfield, he prevailed on MacCurtain and MacSwiney to abandon the rising in the city during Easter Week. In December 1920 he issued a decree stating that those taking part in IRA ambushes were guilty of murder and were liable to incur excommunication from the RC Church if they persisted.

COLBERT, Cornelius: Monelena, Athea, Co. Limerick. One of Clarke's IRB members on the Committee of the Volunteers. Member of 4th Dublin Bn under Eamon Ceannt during Easter Week. Commanded the garrison at Watkin's Brewery, Ardee St, and Jameson's Distillery, Bow St. Also fought at Marrowbone Lane. Executed at Kilmainham 8 May 1916.

COLEMAN, Dick: St Peter's Rd, Phibsborough, Dublin. Volunteer Capt Fingal Bde, Swords, Co. Dublin. Fought in successful attack on Ashbourne Barracks during Easter Week. Also led reinforcements from Swords to relieve garrison at Mendicity Institute on the Tuesday of Easter Week. Underwent three prison terms including one with Thomas Ashe in 1917. Died of pneumonia in Usk prison, Monmouth, Wales, 7 December 1918.

COLGAN, Patrick: Co. Kildare. Maynooth Coy. Very prominent in the movement of Maynooth troops to Dublin for Easter Week Rebellion. On the reorganization of the Volunteers in 1917 he was appointed Comdt North Kildare Bn. (*See ua Buachalla, Domhnall*)

COLIVET, Michael: Limerick. Comdt Limerick Volunteers. Personally went to Pearse to ensure receipt of plans for Easter Week Rebellion. Totally confused then by MacNeill's countermand. Led his unit to Killonan on Easter Sunday. Remained mobilized until a vote taken on Tuesday suspended further action.

COLLINS, Con: Monegay, Newcastlewest, Co. Limerick. IRB and Volunteer leader. Sent from Dublin to assist Austin Stack at the projected *Aud* arms reception. Arrested in Tralee, Co. Kerry. Imprisoned until 1917 amnesty. Signatory of address to the President and Congress of the USA 18 June 1917. Elected Sinn Féin TD for West Limerick 1919. Assisted in preparations for first Dáil sitting January 1919.

COLLINS, Johnny: Woodfield, Clonakilty, Co. Cork. Brother of Michael. Provided safe house. Arrested Shannonvale Railway Station 7 April 1921. Interned on Spike Island. Home burned by Essex Rgt.

COLLINS, Mrs Maurice: Parnell St, Dublin. Her home was used to imprison Bulmer Hobson, who was opposed to the Rebellion, during Easter Week. Her husband acted as guard over him. Handled vital messages during the Breen/Treacy manhunt 12-14 October 1920.

COLLINS, Michael: Woodfield, Clonakilty, Co. Cork. Private secretary to Count Plunkett. Staff Capt and ADC to James Connolly in the GPO during Easter Week. With The O'Rahilly led the first party out of the GPO immediately before its surrender. Arrested and imprisoned. Released December 1916. Director of Organization, Irish Volunteers, November 1917. Chairman of Supreme Council of IRB, he formed an elite corps for its strengthening. Organized massive demonstrations at Thomas Ashe funeral. Elected for Cork South December

1918. Helped organize de Valera's escape from Lincoln Jail February 1919. Minister for Home Affairs and later Finance in April 1919 Government. Organized highly successful National Loan. In 1920 was simultaneously AG of the Volunteers, D/Organization, D/Int and Minister for Finance. Developing his crack Intelligence Section, he ruthlessly struck out at RIC informers. Despite £10,000 offered for his death or capture, he went about openly, bluffing his way through interrogations. Only member of Volunteer HQ who approved of attacks on RIC barracks in independent operations throughout the country. Built up an execution squad nicknamed the 'Twelve Apostles', a.k.a. 'the Squad'. Practically eliminated the British Secret Service in Bloody Sunday morning operations 21 November 1920. Acting President of the Republic November 1920. Elected for South Armagh May 1921. Minister for Finance 26 August 1921 Dáil. Took part in negotiations leading to Truce. Reluctantly accepted co-leadership (with Griffith) of Treaty delegation. Appointment sanctioned at Dáil meeting 14 September 1921. First met Lloyd George 11 October. Signed Treaty, with Griffith and Barton, at 1430 hours, December 1921.

COLLISON, John: Toomevara, Co. Tipperary. Comdt North Tipperary ASU. Participated in various operations including the ambush at Modreeney.

COMERFORD, James: Coolraheen, Coon, Co. Kilkenny. Took part in the Coolbawn ambush near Castlecomer 18 June 1921. Held hostage during Uskerty Wood ambush May 1921.

COMERFORD, Máire: Rathdrum, Co. Wicklow. Reported to St Stephen's Green garrison during Easter Week in order to join Countess Markievicz but was turned away because of her youth. Became an active C na mB member after 1916.

COMPTON-SMYTH: Maj Royal Welsh Fusiliers. Captured by 6 Bn Cork No 1 Bde and held hostage for release of prisoners taken at Mourneabbey and Clonmult. Gen Strickland was warned that Compton-Smyth would be shot if the prisoners – Thomas Mulcahy, Patrick Roynane, Maurice Moore and Patrick O'Sullivan – were executed, which they were in February and April 1921. Pleas were made by Kerry IRA to Collins to intervene, alleging that Compton-Smyth was of good character. Collins acted on his behalf but was too late.

COMYN, Michael: Senior Counsel for IRA. Acquired a Writ of Prohibition halting the holding of Military Courts 16 June 1921. (*See Clifford, Patrick; O'Sullivan, Michael*)

CONBOY, Martin: Solicitor. Assisted in re-organization of Volunteers after Easter Week. Assisted in legalizing bonds for raising of Dáil Loan June 1919.

CONDON, Larry: Fermoy, Co. Cork. Vice-Comdt Fermoy Bn who led the main attack there 7 September 1919. Arrested. Later became Comdt Fermoy Bn and member of Cork No 2 Bde Flying Column 1920.

CONLON, Bobby: Dublin. Messenger for Collins's Finance Department. Held for lengthy questioning on Collins's movements early in 1921 but refused to co-operate with authorities.

CONNOLLY, Cornelius: Comdt Skibbereen Bn West Cork Bde. Escaped from Strangeways Jail, Manchester. Joined Tom Barry's Flying Column after Crossbarry ambush 19 March 1921. Fought at Rosscarbery 30 March 1921. Commanded unit which shot Const McLean dead and wounded Const Cooper near Skibbereen before Union Hall action of May 1921. Also known as Nelius Connolly.

CONNOLLY, James: Edinburgh; Monaghan. Socialist. Ex-BA. Organized, trained and became Comdt Gen of the Citizen Army and of Dublin District during Easter Week Rebellion. Alongside Pearse, with whom he had argued vehemently, he led a party from Liberty Hall at noon on Easter Monday 24 April 1916 to occupy the GPO. Signed the Proclamation. Commanded the GPO garrison during hostilities as well as being in charge of operations in Dublin. Wounded after leading a party to occupy Independent House, Middle Abbey St. He continued directing operations from a couch. Captured, court-martialled and sentenced to death. Executed at Kilmainham while still severely wounded 12 May 1916. Some sources say he sat for his execution, others that he stood.

CONNOLLY, James: See 'Twelve Apostles'.

CONNOLLY, John: Bandon, Co. Cork. IRA Capt. Arrested unarmed September 1920. On 1 October members of the Essex Rgt shot him dead in Castle Bernard Park, Bandon, having held him for a week.

CONNOLLY, John & Michael: Whitegate, Co. Clare. Brothers. Victims of the 'Killaloe Bridge Murders' when RIC Consts shot persons held in their custody 17 November 1920.

CONNOLLY, Nora: Daughter of James (*above*). Actively supported the struggle for independence. Assisted in bringing Liam Mellows back from England, where he had been under open arrest, to attempt an uprising in Galway Easter Week. Carried instructions from Pearse to offset MacNeill's countermand.

CONNOLLY, Sean: Philipsburg Ave, Dublin. Actor and Capt Citizen Army. Commanded the City Hall garrison at outbreak of Easter Week hostilities. His brothers George, Eamonn and Matthew and sister Kathleen (Barrett) also in garrison. Another brother, Joseph, fought in St Stephen's Green. Deployed parties to occupy various buildings, including Dublin Castle guard room where George was among those who overpowered the guard. They retired from the guard room, not realizing that the Castle itself was practically undefended. Shot dead Easter Monday. (*See O'Reilly, Sean; Shields, Arthur*)

CONNOLLY, Sean: Ballinalee, Co. Longford. 2 i/c of Longford Bde 1919. Assisted in training of Roscommon Bdes. Shot dead by Crown Forces at Selton, Co. Leitrim, 11 March 1921; member of a party ambushed allegedly as a result of information given by an informer. (*See Reilly, John & Joseph*)

CONNOLLY, T.: *See McGrath, John.*

CONNORS, Timothy: Greenane, Co. Tipperary. Eleven-year-old son of a worker on Sean Treacy's farm. Arrested and detained in Dublin for a month's questioning after Solohedbeg ambush. RIC found guilty of illegal detention in resulting legal action.

CONROY, James: See 'Twelve Apostles'.

CONWAY, Christopher (Kit): Burncourt, Cahir, Co. Tipperary. Fought with D Coy 3rd Bn 3 Tipperary Bde and with Denis Lacey's column.

CONWAY, Jim: See 'Twelve Apostles'.

COONEY: RIC. Const on Collins's list for execution because of harassment of Volunteers. Shot dead in an exchange of fire with Frank Davis at Breaghy, near Granard, Co. Longford, 2 November 1920.

COONEY, Andrew: Dublin. Volunteer 3rd Bn Dublin Bde. Took part in the action against British agents at 2 Pembroke St, Dublin, on Bloody Sunday morning 21 November 1920.

COONEY, Andrew: GHQ Staff Officer appointed Comdt Kerry No 1 Bde in 1921, allegedly because of an internal command problem there. (See Cahill, Paddy)

COONEY, Kathleen: Official in Longford Post Office. Passed vital information to the Intelligence Section Longford Bde.

COOPER, Becky: Waterford St, Dublin. A 'Monto' madam in whose premises British agents were alleged to have passed on their information regarding Volunteer activities.

COPE, Alfred W.: Assistant Under-Secretary for Ireland. Extended peace feelers to the IRA in 1921. Informed London that agreement or all-out war were the only alternatives. Secured de Valera's release from prison within days of his arrest on 22 June 1921 in order not to jeopardize the chances of a truce. Party to the Truce 11 July 1921. Member of the subcommittee dealing with its observance.

CORISH, R.: Wexford. Alderman. Supported by Sinn Féin, became the only Labour Mayor appointed to office in Ireland. Arrested and deported for nationalist activities prior to his election 15 January 1920.

CORKERY, Dan: Comdt 7th Macroom Bn Cork No 1 Bde. The Bn was active at Kilmurray 3 January 1919, at Carrigadrohid 9 June 1919, and at Lissarda and Coolavokig.

CORKERY, Jack: Cloghane, Co. Cork. Ballindee Coy 1st Bn West Cork Bde. Active throughout the struggle. Member of the party that carried out a mine attack on Drimoleague 11 February 1921. In action at Inishannon before Union Hall, Crossbarry, etc.

CORNWALLIS: Capt BA. Ambushed near Gort, Co. Galway, with Dist Insp and Mrs Blake, Mrs Robert Gregory of Coole Park and Lt McCreery, 17th Lancers, 15 May 1921. The incident took place as the party was leaving Ballyturin House, having been entertained by J.G. Baggott, JP. Mrs Blake returned fire and was killed in the action. The ambushers took possession of the car and personal documents before executing Cornwallis and McCreery in retaliation for the Fr Griffin killing. A Const Kearney, arriving at the scene, was also mortally wounded.

CORRIGAN, Charles: North Frederick St, Dublin. Glasgow-born Gaelic League enthusiast. Fought in GPO Easter Week. Killed in action with The O'Rahilly 28 April 1916 during the first attempt to evacuate the GPO.

CORRINGHAM, Joseph: Civilian bystander killed by three bullets at scene of Treacy's shooting in Talbot St, Dublin, 14 October 1920.

COSGRAVE, W.T.: James's St and Templeogue, Dublin. Vice-Comdt South Dublin Union garrison Easter Week. Sentenced to death, commuted to life imprisonment. Imprisoned Frongoch until amnesty 1917. Joint Treasurer, with L. Ginnell, of Sinn Féin 1917. Won Kilkenny by-election 1917. Re-elected 1918. Minister for Local Government in April 1919 Government. Tackled the task of setting up an independent administration adopting a policy of non-co-operation with the British authorities. First President of the Executive Council of the IFS.

COSTELLO, Michael J.: Cloughjordan, Co. Tipperary. In charge of Fianna Éireann in Cloughjordan up to 1920. IO 2 Bn North Tipperary Bde from 1920 until the Truce. Accounts and Records Officer Div Staff 3rd Southern Div.

COSTELLO, Sean: Athlone, Co. Westmeath. 2 Lt Irish Volunteers. Wounded in fighting at Grand Canal St during Easter Week. Among large number of wounded brought to Sir Patrick Dun's Hospital by its doctors and nurses. Died there 26 April 1916.

COTTER, Sean: Skibbereen, Co. Cork. Adj 5th (Bantry) Bn West Cork Bde. Participated in attack on Durrus RIC Barracks 31 March 1920. Arrested the following day. Taken as hostage on a number of Black and Tan raids before transfer to Belfast and Wormwood Scrubs after intervention by Col Hudson. Released in May after 23 days of hunger-strike. Participated in raid on naval vessel at Bantry. Recaptured November 1920.

COUGHLAN, F.X.: *See Bryan, Dan.*

CRAIG, James: Belfast Parliamentary Secretary to British Cabinet. Approved Ulster Volunteers in their attacks on Catholics and in their establishment as Ulster SC. Leader of Northern Unionists February 1921. Met de Valera in secret 5 May 1921 in Dublin, each under the illusion that the other desired the meeting. Nothing transpired. Refused further meeting with de Valera July 1921 and subsequently gave little ground in negotiations. First Prime Minister of Northern Ireland 31 May 1921.

CRAKE, F.W.: Capt, ex-Bedfordshires. Commander of Auxiliaries in Macroom, Co. Cork, 1920. Led contingent active in the Ballyhalwick-Dunmanway area when Canon Magnier/Timothy Crowley incident took place. Shot dead in Kilmichael ambush 28 November 1920.

CRAVEN: Lt Comdr. In charge of Crown Forces at Clonfin ambush, Longford, 2 February 1921. Surrendered to Sean MacEoin while dying there. Said to have warned MacEoin of arrival of reinforcements.

CRONIN, Felix: Active in North Tipperary. Captured and imprisoned in Wormwood Scrubs. Endured hunger-strike there. (*See McCormick, Michael*)

CRONIN, Patrick: Henry St, Tullamore, Co. Offaly. RIC Sgt shot in reprisal for Kevin Barry's execution. Died 1 November 1920.

CROWE, Edmund: *See Crowe, Maurice, below.*

CROWE, Maurice: Glanbane, Co. Tipperary. Volunteer organizer in South Tipperary. With Sean Duffy and Denis Lacey, carried on Treacy's work after his early arrest April 1918. Accompanied Dan Breen to Dundalk for proposed rescue of Treacy. Adj South Tipperary Bde June 1918. Active in planning Soloheadbeg ambush and in harbouring personnel involved, and arms and ammunition captured. His brother, Edmund, assisted. Captured and imprisoned Mountjoy. Participated in hunger-strike of April 1920.

CROWE, Tadhg: Solohead, Co. Tipperary. Participated in planning Soloheadbeg ambush. Assisted at dumping of captured arms at Glenbane. (*See Dwyer, Paddy*)

CROWLEY, Daniel: Clogheen, Co. Tipperary. RIC Const. On 21 May 1920, accompanying Black and Tans to the home of Maurice Walsh, quarrelled with them about their authority to shoot civilians. Black and Tans responded by firing on him and other members of the RIC. This and other such incidents led to his resigning from the force 1 June 1920. He gave evidence before the American Commission on Conditions in Ireland, outlining the treatment of Sinn Féin members ordered by Gen Lucas after the murder of the Lord Mayor of Cork, Tomás MacCurtain, March 1920.

CROWLEY, Diarmuid: Member of Republican Supreme Court 1920. Arrested at Ballina, Co. Mayo, and sentenced to imprisonment 1921. Helped draft Constitution and Rules of Republican Court.

CROWLEY, Jack, Peter & Tadhg: Ballylanders, Co. Limerick. Brothers. Their father's premises were blown up by Black and Tans 25 July 1920. Jack and Peter: Participated in a 94-day hunger-strike in Cork. Tadhg: Member of East Limerick Bde Flying Column.

CROWLEY, John: *See footnote to Murphy, Joe.*

CROWLEY, Mick: Kilbrittain, Co. Cork. Engineer Officer West Cork Bde. Sec Comdr No 3 Section of Flying Column 1921. Active in a number of operations including Kilbrittain and Drimoleague. With Tom Barry and two volunteers, took on Auxiliaries at Castletown-Kenneigh March 1921. Commanded his section at Crossbarry and Rosscarbery March 1921. Active in Bandon operations of February and May 1921.

CROWLEY, Paddy: Kilbrittain, Co. Cork. Organized training camp for West Cork Bde April 1918. Associated with actions at Tooreen, Rathclarin, Howes Strand Coastguard Station and Newcestown. Due for promotion to Bn Comdt when killed by Crown Forces in large-scale search-and sweep-operation at Maryboro-Timoleague 4 February 1921.

CROWLEY, Peter: *See footnote to Murphy, Joe.*

CROWLEY, Timothy: Dunmanway, Co. Cork. Youth shot dead by Auxiliaries as he assisted a motorist, Magistrate P.S. Brady, at Ballineen Rd, Dunmanway, Co. Cork, 15 December 1920. Canon Magnier witnessed shooting, protested and was in turn shot. (*See Harte*)

CROZIER, F.: Brig Gen BA. Arrived in Ireland to command Aux Div of RIC July 1920. Intervened as two Aux were about to shoot Frank Teeling on Bloody Sunday morning 21 November 1920. Discovered murder plot against Catholic Bishop of Killaloe. His instructions to pass a warning to the Bishop were disobeyed but Dr Fogarty was in any event absent. Dismissed many undisciplined Aux but was constantly thwarted. He was silenced on the Fr Griffin case but after the Chandler (Trim) affair and the Drumcondra shootings he dismissed 21 Aux. When they were reinstated, he resigned February 1921.

CULLEN, Tom: Wicklow. Capt Wicklow Volunteers. With Liam Tobin and Frank Thornton, led Collins's Intelligence Section. Assistant QM in charge of Supplies and Mun IRA HQ 1918. Led a successful arms raid on the Provost Marshal's house in Haddington Rd, Dublin, 1918. Prominent in Breen/Treacy cover operations after 'Fernside' fight October 1920. Survived interrogation by 'Cairo Gang' at Vaughan's Hotel prior to Bloody Sunday. (*See Mulloy*)

CUMANN na mBAN: Women's League. Auxiliary force of Irish Volunteers.

CUMMING, H.R.: DSO Col Comdt East Lancashires. OC Kerry Forces. Adopted practice of conveying civilian hostages in military vehicles. Shot dead in action against an IRA ambush at Clonbanin, Co. Cork, 5 March 1921.

CUNNINGHAM, Joseph: Co. Westmeath Republican Justice. Beaten unconscious by RIC 22 August 1920.

CURTIS, Lionel: Secretary of British delegation in Treaty negotiations 1921. Presented a memorandum on Dominion status. Co-secretary with Thomas Jones on British Truce Observation subcommittee 1921.

CURZON, George (Lord): British Home Secretary throughout Truce and Treaty negotiations.

DALTON: *See Deed, Con.*

DALTON, Charles: One of Collins's Intelligence Section. Took part in robbery of mail from Dublin Castle, including documents for the Lord-Lt, Chief Secretary, *etc.*, 1919. Participant in Bloody Sunday morning operations 21 November 1920 and in the attempt to rescue Sean MacEoin from prison.

DALTON, Emmet: USA and Drumcondra, Dublin. Former BA officer. D/Mun GHQ staff of IRA. Acting Director of Training 1921. Dressed in his old BA uniform, gained access to Mountjoy jail in a commandeered armoured car with a rescue party in a bid to release Sean MacEoin. With Joe Leonard got as far as overpowering the governor and his personal staff when gunfire was opened by other members of the raiding party, causing abandonment of the attempt. Director of Training 1921.

DALY, Agnes: Limerick. Sister of Ned Daly (*below*). Despite being ill, set upon by unidentified assailants who shaved her head and inflicted a deep wound in her hand January 1921.

DALY, Charlie: Comdt Kerry No 2 Bde, later Vice OC 1 & 2 Northern Divs.

DALY, James: Tyrrellspass, Co. Westmeath. While serving with 1st Bn of the Connaught Rangers in Jullunder, India. he heard of Black and Tan atrocities at home and led a mutiny on 28 June 1920 which resulted in his being executed 2 July 1920. (*See Hawes, Joseph*)

DALY, John Edward (Ned): Frederick St, Limerick; Fairview, Dublin. Brother of Tom Clarke's wife. Commanded 1st Bn Dublin Bde on Easter Monday 1916 and was Comdt in charge of Four Courts garrison. Held Col J.P. Brereton, Athlone, captive there. Brereton later commended the behaviour of the garrison. Court-martialled, sentenced to death and executed at Kilmainham 4 May 1916.

DALY, Nora: Limerick. Despatch-carrier for Pearse. Carried instructions to Cork leaders at Sheares St on Wednesday of Easter Week. Brought back their intent to remain at their HQ and retaliate only if attacked. Her sister Laura carried despatches to Michael Colivet in Limerick. (*See Dore, Eamonn; Perolz, Marie*)

DALY, Paddy (Also O'Daly): 69 Parnell St, Dublin. 2 i/c of Collins's 'Twelve Apostles' on its formation July 1919. Often in full command. In charge of Ashtown ambush 19 December 1919. Studied RIC Assistant-Commissioner Redmond's movements as part of preparations for his execution near Standard Hotel, Harcourt St, Dublin, 21 January 1920. Present 17 October 1920 at execution of Sgt Roche, RIC, at Parliament St.

Roche had come from Tipperary, possibly to hunt down Sean Treacy. He was accompanied by a detective who pointed him out to Daly and William Stapleton.

DALY, Tommy: Member of Intelligence Section 4th Dublin Bn. Operated in the billiard room of Kildare St Club where top British officials discussed their affairs. His accurate reporting on events preceding the intensification of British military activities brought about his being appointed to work directly with GHQ Intelligence. (*See Bryan, Dan*)

DARCY, Finbar: Ex-Alexian Brother shot dead in the Imperial Hotel, Cork, on Wednesday 5 January 1921 during a raid by Crown Forces. A military inquiry alleged his having struggled with two soldiers and having been shot while trying to escape.

DARCY, Louis: Headford, Co. Galway. Comdt Headford Bn. Informed upon and arrested off the Dublin-Galway train at Oranmore 24 March 1921. Wounded trying to escape. Discovered dead in Galway later, allegedly after being dragged behind a military vehicle from Oranmore.

DAVIS, Frank: St Patrick's Tce, Longford. QM Longford Bde. IRB member. Selected by Cathal Brugha for proposed bombing of Whitehall, London, which never materialized. Participated in raids on RIC barracks at Drumlish, Longford and Ballinamuck. A police constable was shot dead in an exchange of fire with him at Breaghy, Clonbroney, near Granard, 2 November 1920. (*See Cooney*)

DAVITT, Cahir: Ballybrack, Co. Dublin. Circuit judge, Republican Courts, 1920-21.

DEASY, Liam: Kilmacsimon Quay, Bandon, Co. Cork. Brother of Patrick (*below*). Joined Volunteers 1917. Organizer and Capt of Innishannon Coy. Adj West Cork Bde August 1919-April 1921. Bde Comdt 1921, succeeding Charlie Hurley. Member of Flying Column. Participated in Tooreen ambush and attacks on Black and Tan barracks at Bandon 24 January 1921 and Crossbarry 19 March 1921. Adj of 1st Southern Div under Liam Lynch 1921.

DEASY, Mick: Timoleague Coy 1st (Ballindee) Bn West Cork Bde. Young member of Barry's Flying Column who took part in most of its actions. Highly rated as a soldier by Barry.

DEASY, Patrick: Kilmacsimon Quay, Bandon, Co. Cork. Brother of Liam, (*above*). Lt. Signal Officer Bandon Bn at sixteen years of age. Because of his age forbidden to march to Kilmichael but followed the Flying Column and was KIA 28 November 1920.

DE COURCY-WHEELER: Maj BA. Accepted the surrender of Comdt Mallin and Countess Markievicz on behalf of the College of Surgeons garrison at York St, Saturday 29 April 1916.

DEED, Con: Only member of quartet to escape death in the Valley of Knockanure-Gortnaglanna, Co. Kerry. The three killed in the encounter were Dalton, Lyons and Walsh.

DELANEY, William: Roscrea, Co. Tipperary. Volunteer 3rd Tipperary Bde. Taken from custody in Cashel Jail and shot dead at Kilfeakle 18 December 1920. (*See Looby, J.J. & Lawrence*)

DE LOUGHREY, Peter: Parliament St, Kilkenny. Town Commissioner. Deported for alleged participation in supposed 'German Plot' May 1918. Inmate of Lincoln Jail with de Valera. Said to have fashioned one of the keys used in his escape. Elected Mayor of Kilkenny 1919. Imprisoned 1920. Comdt Kilkenny Bde IRA. His family's foundry was used to manufacture grenades.

DE MONTMORENCY, Hervey: Maj. Aux IO for Westmeath. Authorized house-burnings in Moate and Coosan areas which preceded the IRA burning of Lord Castlemaine's house and shooting of RIC in Kilbeggan. Castlemaine was County Lt. Noted for organizing large-scale arrests.

DENNEHY Family: Midleton, Co. Cork. Dan: Killed at Clonmult 20 February 1921. Denis: Arrested and imprisoned, Kilmainham. Nell and Nora: C na mB. Family home housed and fed members of 4 Bn Cork No 1 Bde.

DERHAM, John: Member of Balbriggan Town Council, Co. Dublin. Physically assaulted and house ransacked by Black and Tans from Gormanstown garrison after the shooting of one of their men 20 September 1920. This and other events of the same night became known as the 'Sack of Balbriggan'.

DERRIG, Tomás: Westport, Co. Mayo. Student leader in University College, Galway, in 1916. Organized a College Corps of Volunteers. Arrested, deported and interned with Prof Steinberger. Comdt West Mayo Bde 1919. Interned in Curragh. Elected Sinn Féin MP for Mayo.

DE VALERA, Eamon: Manhattan, New York; Bruree, Co. Limerick; 'Croiglaith', Greystones, Co. Wicklow. Comdt 3rd Dublin Bn and Boland's Mill garrison during Easter Week. Last Comdt to surrender. Sentenced to death at court-martial 10 May 1916. Sentence commuted to life imprisonment. Served sentence at Dartmoor, Lewes and Maidstone. Released 16 June 1917 under general amnesty. Elected Sinn Féin candidate for East Clare July 1917. President of Sinn Féin October 1917. President Irish Volunteers November 1917. Arrested May 1918 and imprisoned in Lincoln Jail for leading anti-conscription outcry. Lost to Joe Devlin in West Belfast, elected in East Mayo and returned unopposed for East Clare December 1918 election, while in prison. Escaped from Lincoln Jail 3 February 1919. Priomh Aire (President) of Dáil Éireann 1 April 1919. Formally installed as President of Sinn Féin 8 April 1919. Delegate to Paris Peace Conference 1919. Went to USA June 1919 promoting Dáil Loan and recognition of the Irish Republic. Clashed with Irish-American groups, notably John Devoy, Daniel Cohalan and Friends of Irish Freedom. Pleaded with President Woodrow Wilson for recognition of the Republic of Ireland as a sovereign independent state October 1920. Returned from USA December 1920 having raised a $6 million loan. Elected for Down May 1921. Arrested 22 June 1921 but speedily released to expedite the pending Truce negotiations. Re-elected President of the Irish Republic 26 August 1921. Declined leadership of Treaty delegation September 1921, having negotiated with Lloyd George (July 1921) and having rejected his terms (August 1921). Disapproved the Treaty terms and issued a proclamation recommending their rejection 8 December 1921. Appealed for their rejection in the Dáil 15 December 1921. (See *Cope, Alfred W.*)

DEVLIN, Joe ('Wee Joe'): Hamill St, Belfast. Nationalist MP for West Belfast. On his querying the action of British Forces in Croke Park on Bloody Sunday afternoon 21 November 1920, shouted down in House of Parliament. With John Dillon, represented the Parliamentary Party on the 'National Cabinet' of April 1918. Defeated de Valera in West Belfast December 1918 election. On first meeting of Northern Parliament at City Hall Belfast 7 June 1921 refused to take his seat but did so later. (See *Greenwood, Hamar*)

DEVOY, John: Kill, Co. Kildare. Clan na Gael leader in USA. Assisted in fund-raising efforts for Volunteers and many other Irish organizations. Negotiated for arms from Germany for 1916 Rebellion. Clashed with de Valera during latter's visit to USA in 1919, being desirous of Irish-Americans' retaining control of affairs there.

DEVOY, Seamus: Dublin. Member of GPO garrison Easter Week. Commissioned by Connolly there. One of Connolly's stretcher-bearers during his evacuation. Arrested and deported.

DICKSON, Thomas: 12 Harrington St, Dublin. Civilian editor of *Eye*

Opener, a gossip publication on affairs of British officers. Shot dead by Crown troops at Portobello 26 April 1916, one of the 'Portobello Murders'. The Simon Commission found that he was in no way connected with the Rebellion. (*See Bowen-Colthurst, J.C.; McIntyre, Patrick; Sheehy Skeffington, Francis; Simon, John*)

DILLON, John: Blackrock, 2 North Great George's St and Ballybrack, Dublin. Nationalist MP for East Mayo until defeated by de Valera in December 1918. In March of that year had taken over leadership of waning Irish Party from Redmond. Spoke out against 1916 executions and led a protest against the Conscription Bill in the House of Commons. Joined Joe Devlin in representing the Parliamentary Party at the 'National Cabinet' of 1918. Vigorously campaigned against Arthur Griffith in the East Cavan by-election of 21 June 1918 but his candidate, O'Hanlon, lost. Although still averse to Sinn Féin, did not oppose their candidates in the May 1921 election.

DINEEN, Michael: Kilcorney, Co. Cork. Volunteer Kilcorney Coy Cork No 2 Bde. Shot dead at Toureenbawn in reprisal for Rathcoole ambush of 24 June 1921.

DOBBIN, William: 2/Lt 3rd Royal Irish Fusiliers. Commanded the main guard at Portobello on night of Sheehy Skeffington's and McIntyre's shooting. He was transferred after the incident but the Simon Commission of Inquiry was postponed to await his return from France to give evidence of witnessing the shooting.

DOBBYN: Kerry. Assistant County Commissioner RIC. One of the party faced by mutinous RIC members at Listowel 19 June 1920. (*See Smyth, Brice-Ferguson*)

DOCKERY, Michael: Comdt North Roscommon Bde. Offered £50 for purchase of arms to the first battalion in his area to produce a workable plan for striking at Crown Forces, then playing havoc in the area. Led the Keadue ambush 19-20 March 1921 where he disarmed a constable about to fire on him. Shot in foot attempting to escape capture at Cootehall later. Captured but rescued from Boyle Military Barracks.

DOCKRELL, Maurice (Sir): South Great George's St, Dublin. Chairman, City and County of Dublin Recruiting Committee. Gave evidence before the Royal Commission of Inquiry into Easter Week Rebellion. Presided at ceremony at Trinity College after Easter Week when members of the Officers Training Corps were presented with silver cups in recognition of their services in the College defence and in other areas of the city during the fighting. Met de Valera in the Mansion House 4 July 1921 to discuss minority views.

DOHERTY, Joe: *See footnote to Sweeney, Joseph A.*

DOLAN, J.N.: Won a seat for Sinn Féin in Leitrim at the 1918 election. It is of interest to note that a namesake, Charles J. Dolan, MP for North Leitrim, resigned his seat ten years previously, calling for political independence for Ireland.

DOLAN, Joe: Dublin. Member of Collins's Intelligence Section.

Involved in the Redmond shooting at the Standard Hotel January 1920. (*See Redmond, William C. Forbes*)

DOMINICK, Rev Fr (O'Connor): Chaplain to Lord Mayor of Cork. Attended Terence MacSwiney during his hunger-strike. Arrested at Church St, Dublin, December 1920. Court-martialled and imprisoned for possessing an incriminating document.

DONEGAN, Maurice: *See Hudson.*

DONNELLY, Michael: 113 St Stephen's Green, Dublin. Lt in Citizen Army. Allowed the occupation of his home during Easter Week. Arrested and imprisoned Knutsford and Frongoch. Secretary to the Citizen Army Council 1919. Pressed for more involvement by Citizen Army in War of Independence. (*See Kelly, Michael; Robbins, Frank*)

DONNELLY, Simon: See *O'Malley, Ernie.*

DONOVAN, Thomas: *See footnote to Murphy, Joe.*

DONOVAN, Tom: Glengoole, Co. Tipperary. Comdt 7th (Drangan) Bn South Tipperary Bde 1918-20. Assisted Treacy in leading attack on Drangan RIC barracks 3 June 1920. Killed in an action at Glengoole, Killenaule, 31 October 1920.

DOOLEY: Fermoy, Co. Cork. Draper. Taken from his bed by Auxiliaries, who feared he had information on the Prendergast drowning. His house was fired; he was thrown into the River Blackwater and shot at. Saved from drowning when raised by a millwheel.

DORAN: Porter at Wicklow Hotel, Dublin. Alleged British spy. Executed by Collins's squad.

DORAN, John: Loughinisland, Co. Down. Volunteer. Was refused political status in Belfast Jail December 1918. Sympathizing Sinn Féin prisoners seized him from ordinary criminals' wing and held him until the authorities met their demands on his behalf. (*See Stack, Austin*)

DORE, Eamonn: Glin, Co. Limerick. Courier for the Military Council of the Irish Volunteers. On receipt of a coded message from Sean MacDermott, took a train to Dublin to become his bodyguard during the Easter Week Rebellion. Escorted the Daly sisters to Kingsbridge Station through a number of British checks and interrogations, thus enabling them to bring despatches to Cork and Limerick Volunteers. (*See Daly, Nora*)

DOWLING, Joseph: Former member of Casement's Irish Bde who landed from a German submarine 12 April 1918. Arrested, court-martialled and sentenced to life imprisonment, of which he served six years. The 'German Plot' fabrication was conceived by this incident.

DOWLING, Sean D.: Comdt 4 Bn Dublin Bde. Energetic organiser whose Bde was involved in a number of major actions in Dublin. (*See Bryan, Dan*)

DOWNES, Barney: Wexford. Bosun based in Liverpool. Involved in various undercover transportations including de Valera's return after escape and his passage to USA in 1919.

DOYLE, Joseph: Dublin. Sgt Citizen Army. Commanded section at Davy's public house (later Searson's), Portobello Bridge, which put up a stubborn resistance, repulsing Crown Forces on a number of occasions.

DOYLE, Patrick: St Mary's Place, Dublin. One of six men hanged at Kilmainham 14 March 1921 during a rash of violent operations by Crown Forces. (See Ellis, John)

DOYLE, Patrick: Milltown, Dublin. KIA at Clanwilliam House during battle of Mount St Bridge 27 April 1916. His body was burned in the building.

DOYLE, Seamus: Gorey, Co. Wexford. Wexford Volunteer Capt active in Enniscorthy during Easter Week. With Capt Etchingham, went to Dublin on Saturday 29 April to receive surrender order from Pearse before standing down Volunteers. Deported. Elected to Second Dáil. Interned in Ballykinlar. (See Brennan, Robert)

DOYLE, Sean: See 'Twelve Apostles'.

DROHAN, Frank: Clonmel, Co. Tipperary. Tipperary delegate IRB. Arrested and deported for alleged part in supposed 'German Plot' May 1918. Comdt 4th (Clonmel) Bn South Tipperary Bde 1919. (See Morrissey, Sean)

DRURY, Pat: See 'Twelve Apostles'.

DUFFY, George Gavan: Monaghan. Solicitor. Instructed Sgt Sullivan in Casement's defence 1916. Called to Irish Bar 1917. Elected for South Dublin 1918-21. With Sean T. O'Kelly and Piaras Béaslaí arranged First Dáil sitting and helped draft its constitution. Participant in Paris Peace Conference 1919 from which he was threatened with expulsion for anti-British propaganda. Member of the Treaty delegation and a reluctant signatory 1921.

DUFFY, Sean: Adj 1st Longford Bn Longford Bde which attacked Drumlish, Edgeworthstown, Ballinamuck Barracks and fought the Lancers in Longford town's 'Top Barracks'. Participated in Clonfin ambush 2 February 1921.

DUFFY, Sean: Monaghan. Member of IRB and Comdt 1st (Tipperary Town) Bn South Tipperary Bde. Organized and drilled Volunteers with Denis Lacey and Maurice Crowe after Treacy's arrest February 1918. Arrested 1918. Shot dead by Auxiliaries at Monard, Limerick Junction, 1 May 1921.

DUGGAN, Eamonn: Longwood, Co. Meath. Comdt 1st Bn Dublin Bde Volunteers Easter Week. Arrested and imprisoned until general amnesty June 1917. As prisoners' solicitor, assisted 1919 jail escapes. IRA D/Int for a short period. Unrecognized, talked Rt Hon James MacMahon, Under-Secretary, into annulling his own (Duggan's) deportation order. Re-arrested late 1920. Released July 1921. Solicitor for Thomas Ashe's next of kin. Elected for South Meath 1918 and 1921. Read English version of Declaration of Independence at First Dáil session January 1919. Acting Joint Treasurer, with Pearse, of Sinn Féin, 8 April 1919. Army representative at Truce agreement 9 July 1921. Chief Liaison Officer after the Truce. Member of Treaty delegation and signatory.

DUKE, Henry (Rt Hon.): MP. Chief Secretary for Ireland 31 July 1916 to 1918. Prominent during lead-up to release of 1916 prisoners from Frongoch and Reading December 1916, and during Thomas Ashe's hunger-strike. Removed from office May 1918.

DUNNE, Barney: Dunboyne, Co. Meath. Prominent figure in Meath Bde. Comdt 1st (Dunboyne) Bn 1919. The Bn was later led by Comdt Kit Lynam, who led the capture of RIC personnel coming from church during the Trim Barracks attack of 30 September 1920. Married de Valera's secretary, Kathleen Keegan, who was in charge of Meath C na mB. (*See Moore, Patrick*)

DUNNE, Eugene: Adrigole, Co. Cork. IO Adrigole Coy 6th (Beara) Bn West Cork Bde. Employee of Bantry Bay Steamship Coy. Initiated Bere Island explosives raid 5 June 1918.

DUNNE, J.J.: Callan, Co. Kilkenny. Comdt 7th Bn Kilkenny Bde. Drove Treacy and Sean Hogan to Dublin before former's death, using various ruses to outwit the Auxiliaries.

DUNNE, John: *See 'Twelve Apostles'*.

DUNNE, Peadar: 1st Comdt Mid-Limerick Bde. Active with Peadar McMahon in organizing and recruiting Volunteers during the re-organization of 1917. After his arrest he was succeeded by Tomás Malone ('Sean Forde').

DUNSANY (Lord): Wounded when his car was fired upon after his driver had refused to stop for Volunteers in Church St area Easter Tuesday 1916. He and his fellow-passenger Capt Lindsay were held captive in Four Courts. Father of Sir Horace Plunkett.

DUNVILLE, Robert: *See McGee*.

DWYER Brothers: Ballydavid, Co. Tipperary. Edward and Frank shot dead before their parents and sister 18 October 1920. Another brother, Jerry, was also a Volunteer.

DWYER, Paddy: Hollyford, Co. Tipperary. Member of IRB and South Tipperary Bde. Observed movement of gelignite escort to Soloheadbeg and participated in ambush. With Tadhg Crowe, dumped captured arms. Ignored Treacy's advice to go 'on the run'. Daringly watched as RIC members purchased newspapers to read of ambush. Saved Treacy, Ernie O'Malley and Gowan by shooting an RIC Sgt during attack on Rear Cross Barracks 11 July 1920.

DWYER, Seamus: IO 'G' Coy 4th Dublin Bn. Obtained the views of senior British civil servants in Dublin Castle from a former college companion who occupied a very influential position there. Worked with Collins on policy but not on local military activities. Member of Second Dáil which sat on 16 August 1921.

DWYER, Tadhg: Commanded Grovestown Coy 3rd Tipperary Bde. Mobilized during Easter Week. Comdt 3rd Bn in whose area Hollyford Barracks attack took place 10-11 May 1920. Present at and escaped from the raided Bde Conference 12 September 1920 – the 'Blackcastle Races'.

EASTWOOD, F.R.: Maj BA. Bde Maj 17th Infantry Bde Cork 1920. Ordered and enforced closing of shops in Cork during the funeral of the British victims of Kilmichael December 1920.

EDGEWORTH-JOHNSTONE, Walter: Lt Col. Chief Commissioner DMP 1916. Gave evidence before the Royal Commission of Inquiry into the Easter Week Rebellion. Testified that he had urged the British government to take drastic action before the Rebellion. Was praised for his own and his forces' zeal and loyalty.

EDMONDS, Michael: Tipperary. Pulled from his bed where he was sleeping with his wife 16 December 1920. Body found in hills with bullet wound in head. Auxiliaries held responsible.

EGAN, Barry: See Ó Cuill, Micheál.

EGAN, Michael: Scarriff, Co. Clare. Member of East Clare Flying Column 1920. Killed while a prisoner of RIC 17 November 1920 in what became known as the Killaloe Murders.

ÉIRE: See Nationality.

ELLIS, John: English hangman. Travelled to Dublin and was conveyed by armoured car to Mountjoy Jail to carry out execution of Frank Flood, Thomas Whelan, Moran, Patrick Doyle, etc. 14 March 1921.

EMMET, Thomas Addis (Dr): President of Irish Relief Fund in USA 1916.

ENNIS, Peter: Tinahely, Co. Wicklow. Caretaker, Liberty Hall, Dublin. Reported developments in that area each day of Easter Week Rebellion to Connolly in GPO. Announced the arrival of the gunboat *Helga*.

ENNIS, Thomas: Comdt 2nd Bn Dublin Bde 1920. Carried out reconnaissance of Custom House in preparation for its burning May 1921. Wounded in the action itself.

ENRIGHT: Thurles, Co. Tipperary. Const RIC. One of Sean Hogan's escorts on train which was boarded by the IRA at Knocklong to rescue Hogan. Mortally wounded in that action 13 May 1919.

ERVINE, St John Greer: Ballymacarret, Belfast. Playwright. Manager of the Abbey Theatre during Easter Week, his anti-nationalist views influenced a decision by the actors not to perform on 29 May. They offered patrons notices saying they would not appear under Ervine's management and were dismissed.

ETCHINGHAM, Sean: Courtown Harbour, Co. Wexford. IRA Capt. Went to Dublin with Seamus Doyle to ensure that Pearse had, in fact, surrendered after Easter Week Rebellion. Arrested for alleged part in supposed 'German Plot' May 1918. Deported.

EYRE-MAUNSELL: Castlecomer, Co. Kilkenny. Dist Insp RIC. I/c of Crown Forces at Uskerty Wood ambush 2 May 1921.

FAHY, Frank: Galway. Arrested for alleged part in supposed 'German Plot' May 1918. Elected for Sinn Féin in Galway December 1918.

FAHY, Sam: 3rd Tipperary Bde. Received deportation order after Soloheadbeg ambush. Ignored it on Collins's advice. Arrested, court-martialled and sentenced to imprisonment.

FALVEY, Batt: Ballymurphy, Upton, Co. Cork. Participant in many West Cork Bde actions. Shot dead at Upton ambush 16 February 1921.

FARRELL, Katherine: Domestic servant at 38 Mount St. Answered door to IRA raiders on Bloody Sunday morning 21 November 1920 and was forced by them to point out the rooms of British agents there.

FARRELL, Patrick: Parnell St, Dublin. Had severed connections with Volunteer movement but joined in the Easter Week Rebellion and was killed in the Church St area 25 April 1916.

FARREN, Thomas: Chairman of the National Executive of Trade Unions. Co-signatory of call for general strike in support of hunger-strikers 12 April 1920. Arrested December 1920. (*See Johnson, Thomas*)

FAY, Michael: Rathvilly, Co. Carlow. One of few Carlow fatalities in war. Killed in action at Ballymurphy, near Borris, 18 April 1921.

FEELEY, James: Boyle, Co. Roscommon. Comdt Boyle Bn North Roscommon Bde. Member of First Sinn Féin County Council in Roscommon 1919. Prominent in many actions including the raid on Rockingham House. Interned at the Curragh Camp 1921. (*See McCabe, Alec*)

FEENEY, Henry (Rev Fr): Clarinbridge, Co. Galway. Acted as Chaplain to Galway Volunteers and handled despatches for them during Easter Week.

FFRENCH-MULLEN, Adeleine: Leader of Women's Section Citizen Army Easter Week. Commanded the medical detachment at the College of Surgeons. Imprisoned at Richmond Barracks.

FIGGIS, Darrell: Rathmines, Dublin. Writer. Deported from Achill and imprisoned May-December 1916. Joint Secretary with Austin Stack of Sinn Féin 25 October 1917. Arrested for alleged part in supposed 'German Plot' May 1918. Deported. Editor of *The Republic* 1919. Secretary of the Inquiry into Industrial Resources September 1919 to 1921. His wife nursed the Volunteer daringly rescued from Mercer's Hospital after a leg amputation. (*See MacBride, Sean*)

FINLAY (Dean): Brackley House, Bawnboy, Co. Cavan. An octogenarian whose death 11 June 1921 was investigated by a military court in Swanlinbar. Members of the household, testified that they heard no shooting during the raid by a large party. Medical evidence suggested that the wound in his head could have been caused by a sharp instrument, possibly in a fall.

FINN, Seamus: Co-Vice-Comdt Meath Bde with Sean Hayes 1919. Participant in Trim Barracks attack 30 September 1920. Vice-OC 1st Eastern Div 1921.

FINN, Sean: Rathkeale, Co. Limerick. Bde Comdt West Limerick Bde 1919. Organized safe movement through his area for Hogan and Breen after Solotheadbeg ambush and for 'Big Four' after Knocklong rescue. Killed in action at Ballyhahill 30 March 1921.

FITZALAN, Edward Talbot (Lord): Last Lord-Lt of Ireland. Appointed 1 April 1921. First RC to hold the appointment.

FITZGERALD: Capt BA. Son of a Tipperary doctor. Barrack Defence Officer for Co. Clare 1920. Taken by IRA who attempted to shoot him with his own revolver. After one misfire and one miss he feigned death and escaped. While recuperating after hospitalization for an arm injury he was shot dead at 28 Earlsfort Tce on Bloody Sunday morning 21 November 1920.

FITZGERALD, Desmond: London; Bray, Co. Wicklow. Member of GPO garrison during Easter Week. Arrested and sentenced to life imprisonment, commuted to twenty years. Served in Maidstone and Dartmoor until his release in 1917. Arrested for alleged part in supposed 'German Plot' May 1918. Elected for Sinn Féin in Pembroke (Dublin) constituency 1918. Liaison Officer (with Piaras Béaslaí) between Government Publicity Department and GHQ Staff of the Volunteers from April 1919 until his arrest and internment March 1921. Produced *The Irish Bulletin*. Released after Truce. Minister of Propaganda outside the Cabinet August 1921. Conveyed the text of the Treaty to the Mansion House 6 December 1921 when de Valera refused to take it.

FITZGERALD, Jack: Kilbrittain, Co. Cork. Coy Capt Kilbrittain Coy. Participated in Rathclarin ambush 16 June 1919. Commanded raiding party which captured arms at Howes Strand Coastguard Station 22 June and 2 July 1920. Active in many other engagements including Newcestown 9 October. Captured 18 October.

FITZGERALD, Mabel: Bray, Co. Wicklow. Wife of Desmond (*above*). Assisted him in his publicity campaigns. Played a major role in the Sinn Féin election successes of December 1918. Contacted the United Press of America and the *Manchester Guardian* when her husband was arrested; journalists then contacted Dublin Castle publicity section to intercede for improvements in his treatment.

FITZGERALD, Martin: Proprietor of the *Freeman's Journal*. Arrested, court-martialled and sentenced to twelve months' imprisonment; newspaper fined £3000 for publication of a report concerning ill-treatment of a prisoner by Black and Tans. Arson attack on office November 1920.

FITZGERALD, Michael: Fermoy, Co. Cork. Fermoy Coy 1st Bn Cork No 2 Bde. Member of the Bde Flying Column formed September 1920 after earlier action at Araglen Barracks and arms capture at Fermoy, 7 September 1919. Untried and unsentenced, went on hunger-strike at Cork Jail and died 17 October 1920, eight days before MacSwiney.

FITZGIBBON, Sean: Vice-Comdt 3rd Dublin Bn prior to outbreak of Easter Week hostilities when sent to convey details of the *Aud* landing to the Kerry leaders and instructions from Pearse concerning the distribution of the expected arms. Helped convince MacNeill that the 'Castle Order' (*q.v.*) was a forgery.

FITZPATRICK, Matt: Officer North Monaghan Bde. Injured in action and hospitalized in Monaghan County Hospital. Successfully rescued from there 30 March 1921. (*See Hogan, Dan*)

FITZSIMONS, Anna (later Kelly): 'Miss Fitz'. Prominent in political and propaganda fields. Often held custody of secret documents of the Volunteer movement during raids.

FLAHERTY, Const: *See Harris, Thomas*.

FLANAGAN, Paddy: Capt later Comdt Dublin Bde. Oldest of Collins's 'Twelve Apostles'. Took part in four shootings at 28 Pembroke St on Bloody Sunday morning 21 November 1920. Leader of the ASU Dublin Bde 1921.

FLEMING, D. & K.: Drumcondra, Dublin. Daughters of James and sisters of Michael (*below*). Scouts and observers for Breen and Treacy before 'Fernside' fight 12 October 1920. Warned them of their movements being observed. Interrogated during the raid. Told of the conduct of the raiders by Prof Carolan before his death.

FLEMING, James: Drumcondra, Dublin. Father of D. & K., above, and Michael (*below*). Owner of house where Breen and Treacy stayed before moving to 'Fernside' for expected safety. Arranged with Prof Carolan for the move. Fleming house raided as expected. Defied raiders and thwarted attempts to plant incriminating documents in the house. Taken to Mountjoy for questioning. Released.

FLEMING, Michael: Drumcondra, Dublin. Son of James and brother of D. & K. (*above*). Member of Jacob's garrison during Easter Week. Took part in successful attack on Ashbourne Barracks. Acted as decoy to allow Breen and Treacy leave Fleming home for 'Fernside'. Arrested and interrogated, refusing £10,000 for information. Court-martialled and imprisoned. (*See Ashe, Thomas; Mulcahy, Richard*)

FLEMING, Patrick: Laois. Endured various punishments in Portlaoise ('Maryboro') Jail during 1918. Carried on an incessant campaign of obstreperous behaviour in seeking special status. Demands were eventually satisfied by a reduction of his sentence and transfer to Mountjoy. Escaped 29 March 1919. (*See O'Connor, Rory*)

FLOOD, Frank: 30 Summerhill Parade, Dublin. Brother of Thomas (*below*). 1st Lt ASU Dublin Bde. Leader and victim of the abortive 'Drumcondra Ambush' when a proposed attack on a DMP tender was thwarted due to the actions of an informer. Captured at Clonturk Park when attempting to escape from the scene of the ambush. Court-martialled and found guilty of High Treason. Hanged at Mountjoy 14 March 1921, the only student besides Kevin Barry to have been executed. His hanging gave rise to demonstrations and protests. (*See Doyle, Patrick; Ellis, John; Moran, Patrick; Ryan, Bernard; Whelan, Thomas*)

FLOOD, Matthew: Fermoy, Co. Cork. Ex-BA, joined Volunteers in September 1917. In action at Fermoy 7 September 1919, Mallow 28 September and Ballydrochane ambush. Arrested after Mick Fitzpatrick's funeral October. Imprisoned at Cork, Kilworth, Spike Island and Bere Island from where he escaped hours before the Truce in 1921.

FLOOD, Robert: QM Sgt 5th Royal Dublin Fusiliers. Tried for the murder of William Rice, a clerk in Guinness's Brewery, and Lt A.L. Lucas, King Edward's Horse, 28 April 1916. Acquitted.

FLOOD, Thomas: Brother of Frank (*above*). Participated in Custom House burning 25 May 1921. Captured and charged with treason. Acute appendicitis on the eve of his trial caused its postponement. The Truce was declared on the eve of the date selected for his retrial.

FLYNN, Patrick: Solohead, Co. Tipperary. Carter of the gelignite patrol ambushed at Soloheadbeg 21 January 1919.

FOGARTY, Michael (Most Rev Dr): Bishop of Killaloe. Was, with de Valera and James O'Mara, a trustee for the Dáil Loan June 1919. Escaped being drowned in the Shannon 3 December 1920 by visiting Dublin. A warning of the attempt on his life was sent by Gen Crozier but was not delivered. Participated in peace efforts during 1921.

FOLEY, Edward: Galbally, Co. Tipperary. Took part in Knocklong rescue of Sean Hogan. Sentenced to death for shooting an RIC Sgt there. Hanged with Patrick Maher 7 June 1921.

FOLEY, Michael: Dublin. First communicator between Eamonn Broy and Collins.

FORBES Family: Ballinaboy, Ballinhassig, Co. Cork. Dan, Dick, Jack: all 5 Bn 3 Cork Bde. Peg: active in C na mB. Jack: escaped to USA. Others interned.

FORDE, Sean: *See Malone, Tomás.*

FOX: Thurles, Co. Tipperary. RIC Det. Persistently questioned by a Miss Meagher regarding arrangements for Sean Hogan's train transfer to Dublin, to be passed to the IRA planners of Hogan's rescue. He did not report the obvious interest. As a result, Treacy forbade his execution at a later date.

FRENCH, John Denton Pinkstone (Lord): Commander-in-Chief British Home Forces. Despatched the 59th Rgt to Dublin when Easter Week Rebellion commenced. Lord-Lt of Ireland 1918-21. A number of ambushes set for him including the well-known Ashtown ambush of 19 December 1919. Proclaimed martial law in Ireland 10 December 1920, mainly in Cork, Kerry, Tipperary and Limerick. One of a number of prominent persons named by Coroner's Jury as being guilty of the murder of Tomás MacCurtain. (*See Breen, Dan; Hogan, Sean; Macpherson, Ian; Robinson, Seamus; Savage, Martin; Treacy, Sean*)

FRIEND, Lovick Bransby: Maj Gen in charge of Administration and General OC BA in Ireland up to 28 April 1916 but on leave in England during the outbreak of hostilities. Maxwell took command then, leaving Friend in charge of administration only. Gave evidence before Royal Commission of Inquiry into the Rebellion. Military Governor of Dublin 1918. Issued deportation orders.

FURLONG, Matthew: Summerhill, Co. Wexford. Volunteer injured while testing munitions in Dunboyne, Co. Meath, causing his hospitalization. His pursuers raided the Mater Hospital, Dublin, just as Dan Breen was being conveyed there. Died Mater Hospital 15 October 1920.

GAFFNEY, T. St John: USA Consul-Gen in Munich. A Clan na Gael leader in USA. Founder member of Friends of Irish Freedom Movement 1916.

GALLAGHER, Andy: *See McCormick, Michael.*

GALLAGHER, Frank: Cork and Dublin. Member of Dáil Éireann Publicity Department 1919-1921. Assisted in the production of the underground publication, the *Irish Bulletin.* (*See Childers, Erskine; Fitzgerald, Desmond; McKenna, Kathleen*)

GALLAGHER, H.T.: Crown State Solicitor for Donegal dismissed because of Sinn Féin loyalties. Moved to Dublin where his wife, Eileen, made sweets, fudges and jams in her own kitchen in Tallaght, the beginnings of a major chocolate firm.

GALLAGHER, Patrick & Bridget: Curraghboy, Co. Roscommon. Husband and wife, IRA and C na mB. Patrick interned Pentonville and witnessed Tom Hales' torture marks. Bridget active in Boland election campaign.

GALVIN, Daniel: RIC Const stationed in Galway and Tipperary. Gave evidence before the American Commission on Conditions in Ireland regarding the prohibition of fairs, markets, etc., in Tipperary after its being declared a prohibited district.

GANTLEY, Mick: *See McCormick, Michael.*

GAY, Thomas: Librarian, Capel Street Library, Dublin. IRB. Brought list of proposed arrests to Harry Boland, having been given it by Joe Kavanagh. No action taken and the May 1918 arrests followed. Ensured safe meetings in the library and in his home between Castle agents and IRA Staff Officers.

GAYNOR, Sean: Nenagh, Co. Tipperary. Leader of the Modreeney ambush. Comdt Tipperary No 1 Bde. Appointed OC 2nd Southern Div in 1921 although some sources claim otherwise.

GIBBONS, John: Balbriggan, Co. Dublin. Hauled from his bed at 0100 hours, interrogated, beaten and shot at dawn 21 September 1920 with James Lawless during the 'Sack of Balbriggan'. His body was discovered almost disembowelled. (*See Derham, John*)

GIBSON: Tullamore, Co. Offaly. RIC Const. An attempt was made on his life in reprisal for the hanging of Kevin Barry November 1920. He resigned from the RIC as a result.

GIFFORD, Grace: Dublin. Sister of Nellie (*below*). Fiancée of Joseph Mary Plunkett for four months. Married him in his cell at Kilmainham Jail a few hours before his execution 4 May 1916.

GIFFORD, Nellie (Mrs Donnelly): Dublin. Sister of Grace (*above*). Brought rations to College of Surgeons and cooked for the garrison there during Easter Week.

GINNELL, Laurence: London; Delvin, Co. Westmeath. MP for North Roscommon. After the 1916 executions accused the British government of murder in the House of Commons. Resigned his seat and campaigned vigorously for Count Plunkett in the subsequent by-election. Became active in the struggle. Joint Treasurer, with W.T. Cosgrave, of Sinn Féin, October 1917. Imprisoned in Mountjoy and deported on completion of his sentence 1918. Minister for Propaganda in First Dáil 1919.

GLAVEY, Michael: *See O'Rourke, Dan.*

GLEESON: Tipperary, Waterford and Longford. Head Const, Lanesborough, Co. Longford, 1919. Champion RIC marksman. Ordered Auxiliaries out of Lanesborough; they shot the chimneys off the barracks in anger. He saved civilians from execution and eventually resigned from the force.

GLEESON, Frank (alias Aidan Redmond): Fairview, Dublin. In action in Easter Week Rebellion. Died after an operation for appendicitis having been on hunger-strike in Mountjoy during May 1920.

GLEESON, Michael: Meelick, Co. Clare. Full-time member of the East Clare Flying Column 1920-1 while not yet 20 years of age. In helping the wounded Comdt G. McCarthy to safety at Meelick on 10 June 1921 was himself overcome, having wounded several British soldiers. DOW 15 June 1921.

GLEESON, Mollie: Manageress, Hughes' Hotel, Dublin. Handled despatches for the 'Big Four' during their Dublin operations. Said to have identified the body of Sean Treacy at King George V Hospital (now St Bricin's) October 1920.

GLYNN, Patrick: *See O'Rourke, Dan.*

GOFF, John W.: USA judge. A Clan na Gael leader in USA. Chairman of the committee that formed the Friends of Irish Freedom Movement.

GOGAN, Dick: Member of the GPO garrison during Easter Week. One of Connolly's stretcher-bearers during his evacuation.

GOGGIN Brothers: Youghal, Co. Cork. Ned and John: active in Youghal area. Dan: participated in Dripsey ambush.

GOLDEN, Peter: National Secretary of American Association for the Recognition of the Irish Republic (AARIR). Raised money for relief in Ireland 1916. General Secretary of the Irish Professional League in USA 1917. Assisted in the promotion of Bond Certificates.

GONNE, Maud (Madame Gonne MacBride): Roebuck House, Clonskeagh, Dublin; France; 73 St Stephen's Green. Resident in Paris until 1917. Her husband John MacBride executed after Easter Week Rebellion. Member of Sinn Féin and prominent leader of women's organizations. Her Inghinidhe na hÉireann (Daughters of Ireland) movement was active within the ranks of C na mB. Arrested for alleged part in supposed 'German Plot' May 1918. Deported and imprisoned in Holloway. Justice of Sinn Féin parish courts 1920. After the 'Sack of Balbriggan' and other atrocities, she formed an organization for the relief of victims which ultimately became the Irish wing of the White Cross Fund.

GORE-BOOTH, Constance: *See Markievicz, Constance.*

GORMAN, James: Hollyford, Co. Tipperary. Lt 3rd Tipperary Bde and member of Flying Column. Irish-Australian First World War marksman. In action at Hollyford Barracks attack 10-11 May 1920. Wounded in attack at Rear Cross Barracks 11 July 1920. Prominent in Thomastown ambush 28 October 1920.

GOULDING, W. Joshua (Bart): Prominent businessman appointed by British government as chairman of the commission to deal with the victims of the Easter Week fire in Dublin.

GOWAN: *See Dwyer, Paddy.*

GREALY, John: Shanwalla, Aghamore, Co. Mayo. QM Ballyhaunis Bn East Mayo Bde. Participated in a number of actions before being imprisoned. Nicknamed 'Morrissey', he was often mistaken for another prisoner named John Morrissey.

GREENE, John P.: Kitchener Scholar, University College, Galway, with no Sinn Féin connections. Taken from Reilly's public house by Black and Tans 14 May 1921 and made to keep walking out to sea as shots were fired about him. Then taken and made to stand by sea wall, having been shot in back and neck, while preparation for his final execution was feigned. Batoned harshly and freed.

GREENWOOD, Hamar (Sir): Under-Secretary of State. Chief Secretary for Ireland 1920-1. In August 1920 he assured the House of Commons that the Army, Black and Tans and Auxiliaries would wipe out all Irish resistance. In November he answered questions on the disappearance of Fr Michael Griffin. His decrying of the Bloody Sunday morning killings without alluding to the afternoon massacre in Croke Park prompted Joe Devlin's outburst in Parliament. He supported Lloyd George's suppressive measures in 1921. Instigated the *Weekly Bulletin*, aimed at goading Crown Forces into more violent action, 1921. Also responsible for the *Weekly Summary*, a somewhat similar publication. Member of British delegation in Truce negotiations 1921 and a member of the Truce Observation subcommittee.

GREER: Drafted proposals to apply Home Rule Act of 1914 to twenty-six counties in 1916. Lloyd George sent the draft proposals to Carson with a covering note suggesting a permanent partition of the six north-eastern counties.

GREGORY, Isabella Augusta (Lady): Roxborough and Coole Park, Co. Galway. Co-director of Abbey Theatre. Wrote in support of Easter Week Rebellion and War of Independence.

GREGORY, Mrs Robert: *See Cornwallis.*

GRENNAN, Sheila: Sir John Rogerson's Quay, Dublin. C na mB. Conveyed instructions concerning Easter Week Rebellion to the country. With Elizabeth O'Farrell, carried message from Pearse to the leaders of the British forces complaining that wounded Volunteers were being fired upon while being evacuated from the GPO.

GRETTON, John: Spokesman for the Conservative Unionists in the House of Commons. Denounced the Government for negotiating with Sinn Féin in 1921.

GREY, Mick: *See McCormick, Michael.*

GRIFFIN, Michael (Rev Fr): Gurteen, Co. Galway. Ally of Irish language and Volunteer causes. Taken from his residence at 2 Mountpelier Tce, Galway, during night of 14-15 November 1920, to HQ of Crown Forces in Taylor's Hill. On Saturday 20 November his body was found buried in a boggy field at Cloghscoltia, near Barna. A military inquiry held at Eglinton Police Station found that he died as a result of a gunshot wound in the head, fired feloniously, wilfully and with malice by some person or persons unknown. (*See Greenwood, Hamar*)

GRIFFIN, Paddy: See 'Twelve Apostles'.

GRIFFITH, Arthur: 4 Dominick St and 122 St Lawrence's Rd, Clontarf, Dublin. Pursued a policy of passive resistance. Did not take active part in Easter Week Rebellion, yet had the respect of Volunteers. Arrested because of his outspoken writings May 1916 and imprisoned in Reading Jail. Was a member of the committee to organize a National Council in May 1917. Devised the Sinn Féin policy initially disapproved of by Republicans, was its president and founder and yet stood down in favour of de Valera at October 1917 National Convention. Accepted joint vice-presidency with Fr O'Flanagan. Member of the National Cabinet of April 1918. Arrested for alleged part in supposed 'German Plot' May 1918. Deported and imprisoned without trial. Won East Cavan by-election while in prison. Elected for North-west Tyrone and East Cavan in general election, again while in prison, December 1918. Minister for Home Affairs April 1919. Released from prison to become delegate to Paris Peace Conference of 1919. Arrested 26 November 1920 while Acting-President of the Republic, de Valera being in the USA. Involved in the Archbishop Clune peace moves while held in Mountjoy. Elected for Tyrone and Fermanagh May 1921. Released from Mountjoy July 1921. Minister for Foreign Affairs 1921 Cabinet. Chairman of Treaty Delegation 1921. (*See Clune, Most Rev Dr*)

GUCKIAN, Pat: *See Sweeney, Bernard.*

GUILFOYLE, Joe: *See Intelligence Section.*

GWYNN, Stephen: Capt BA. Member of Recruiting Council refused a hearing by Waterford Corporation 1918.

HACKETT, Rose: Dublin. Employed at ITGWU co-operative shop. Warned Liberty Hall of all suspicious movements. Her first-aid post for the College of Surgeons wounded during Easter Week was said to have been fired upon despite displaying a red cross.

HACKETT-PAIN, G.W.: Brig Gen BA. Commanded Ulster troops during Easter Week. Mentioned in despatches for distinguished service.

HALDANE (Lord): Carried out unsuccessful secret mission here in 1919, promising the release of prisoners held in British jails in return for the cessation of fighting, violence and excessive claims.

HALES, Sean: Ballinadee, Co. Cork. Brother of Tom (*below*). Bn Comdt 1st (Bandon) Bn Cork No 3 (West Cork) Bde 1919. Led attack on Timoleague 12 February 1920. Led ambush of Essex patrol at Brinny 28 August 1920. Led attack on two truckloads of Crown Troops at Newcestown Cross in which a British officer was shot dead and a number of troops wounded. Section Commander in Flying Column 1921. Commanded the left section of the attack at Crossbarry 19 March 1921.

HALES, Tom: Ballinadee, Co. Cork. Brother of Sean (*above*). Comdt 1st (Bandon) Bn 1917-19. Bde Comdt Cork No 3 (West Cork) Bde 6 January 1919-July 1920. Led attack on Allihies RIC Barracks 12 February 1920. Arrested 27 July 1920. Torture before sentence to Pentonville prison included the pulling of his flesh and toenails with pliers, planting of cartridges on himself and Pat Harte, and the feigning of his execution preparations. I/c of prisoners in Pentonville. (*See Gallagher, Patrick*)

HALLEY: Det Sgt RIC. Lord French's bodyguard. Wounded in the Ashtown ambush. His was one of the first houses raided in Collins's campaign against over-officious members of the RIC.

HAMMOND: Col BA. Ordered the mounted Lancers to advance on the GPO from Parnell Square to occasion the first shootings of the Easter Week Rebellion 1916. Four Lancers were shot by the GPO garrison.

HANLON, Jack: *See 'Twelve Apostles'*.

HANLY, Anne: Limerick. Elderly woman visiting in Lahinch, Co. Clare, forced to leap from an upstairs room of a house set on fire by Crown Forces September 1920.

HANNIGAN, D.: *See Ó hAnnagáin, Donncadha*.

HANNIGAN, Donal: Vice-Comdt Louth Volunteers 1916. Escaped imprisonment after the Easter Week Rebellion and went to the USA where he assisted Liam Mellows. Returned March 1918.

HANNON Brothers: Milltown Malbay, Co. Clare. Canon, PP: spoke out against April 1920 reprisals. Austin, Jim and Tim: active with East Clare Bde, Jim becoming QM 1st Western Div with special responsibility for munitions and chemicals. Family home burned because of allegiances.

HARBISON, Thomas: Parliamentary Party. Beat Sinn Féin's Sean Milroy in East Tyrone by-election April 1918.

HARDINGE (Rt Hon Lord, Baron of Penhurst): Chairman of the Royal Commission of Inquiry into the causes of the Easter Week Rebellion of 1916. The commission first sat on Thursday 18 May 1916.

HARDY: Capt BA. Interrogator at Dublin Castle. Carried out in-depth interrogation of McKee and Peadar Clancy 20 November 1921, eve of Bloody Sunday.

'HARDY', F. Digby: Other aliases: Harling, Saville, Gooding. A criminal who offered his services as a spy to Lord French. Accepted, he was assigned the task of collecting information leading to the capture of Collins. Collins detected his ploy, led him on and invited him to a meeting chaired by Arthur Griffith. 'Hardy' presented a plan for a supposed IRA operation which would, in fact, have led to the capture of Collins. Griffith replied by reading the Intelligence Section's file on 'Hardy'. He was instructed to leave the country immediately, which he did.

HARLING: *See 'Hardy'*.

HAROLD, Owen: *See Sullivan*.

HARRELL, David (Rt Hon Sir): Gave evidence before the Royal Commission of Inquiry into the Easter Week Rebellion stating that a turbulent minority had led astray a peaceful majority.

HARRINGTON, Dan: Knocksaharing, Co. Cork. Accompanied the O'Sullivan brothers to Millstreet, 23 April 1916. Arrested at Ballyvourney, Co. Cork, 27 April, and imprisoned in British jails, including Frongoch. Released December 1916.

HARRINGTON, Niall C.: Boyle, Co. Roscommon. Son of Timothy C. Harrington, MP, Lord Mayor of Dublin. Member of A Coy 1st Bn North Roscommon Bde. Participated in successful arms raids at Boyle, Cootehall, Grange, Ballinameen and Kingsland, and in burning of Grevisk RIC Barracks and Cootehall Tax and Revenue Office Easter 1920. Received a notice threatening his death from a local 'Anti-Sinn Féin Society' because of his activities in connection with the boycotting of the RIC in August 1920. When notice was ignored he was taken by Black and Tans and disguised RIC personnel, badly beaten and released. GHQ of the IRA then transferred him to C Coy 2nd Dublin Bn where he served until the Truce.

HARRIS, G.A.: Maj. OC 1st Dublin Bn Irish Association of Volunteer Training Corps. With some members of Officers' Training Corps, held Trinity College until arrival of regular troops Easter Week.

HARRIS, Thomas: Participated in Easter Week Rebellion. Capt of Prosperous Coy 1917. Vice-Comdt North Kildare Bn. On division of the area in Naas 1920 became Comdt No 2 Kildare Bn. Led the Kill Coy at an attack on RIC there 21 August 1920. Arms were captured, Sgt O'Reilly and Const Flaherty killed. Arrested November 1920.

HARRISON: *See McCartney.*

HART, Christopher: Porter at Vaughan's Hotel who kept Collins and his staff informed of any danger. Arrested and held for five days on one occasion. Refused £5000 and a free passage to a destination of his choice abroad if he informed.

HARTE: Aux. Found guilty of Canon Magnier's murder on 14 December 1920 but pronounced insane at time of the shooting. (*See Crowley, Timothy*)

HARTE, Pat: Clonakilty, Co. Cork. Bde QM Cork No 3 (West Cork) Bde August 1919 till his capture on 27 July 1920. Tortured until insane by Essex Rgt. Tortures included strapping of guncotton to his back and feigning its explosion, strapping to Tom Hales and both bayoneted, *etc*. Committed to a mental hospital where he died a few years later.

HARTNETT, Patrick: *See Huckerberry.*

HAWES, Joseph: Kilrush, Co. Clare. Pte Connaught Rangers. One of the ringleaders of the Connaught Rangers mutiny at Jullunder, India, 28 June 1920. (*See Daly, James*)

HAYES (Rev Fr): Newcastlewest, Co. Limerick (native of Bruree). Named in despatches between Gen Maxwell and Dr O'Dwyer, Bishop of Limerick, in 1916. Maxwell's disapproval unheeded by Dr O'Dwyer.

HAYES, James: Killucan, Co. Westmeath, Portarlington, Co. Laois. Vice-OC, later OC Offaly No 1 Bde.

HAYES, Pat: See McLysaght, Edward.

HAYES, Sean: See Finn, Seamus; Mooney, Patrick.

HEAD, D.: Seville Place, Dublin. Volunteer who tossed a grenade from the Loop Line Bridge into a truckload of Black and Tans during the Custom House burning operation 25 May 1921. KIA at the same operation.

HEALY, James: Little Green St, Dublin. His body was found with that of Patrick Bealen in a North King St cellar after Easter Week Rebellion. The Coroner's Jury verdict that he had DOW inflicted by soldiers was considered by commentators as unsatisfactory.

HEALY, Jeremiah: See Huckerberry.

HEALY, Sean: Phibsborough, Dublin. Fianna Éireann. Allegedly the youngest victim of Easter Week Rebellion. Assisted his father with arms movement and reported to Jacob's garrison in defiance of orders forbidding the use of youths in the Rebellion. Sent with despatches to the Phibsborough garrison. Called to his home for a meal en route. Shot dead when he emerged from his home 24 April 1916.

HEALY, T.M.: Bantry, Co. Cork; Chapelizod, Co. Dublin. Independent member of the National Cabinet April 1918. Not permitted to attend the inquiry into the burning of Cork city December 1920. Unsuccessfully applied for habeas corpus on behalf of Sean Allen June 1921. Appointed Governor-General of the IFS after the Treaty.

HEARD: Comdt of the RIC Depot, Phoenix Park, Dublin. Administered the Oath of Allegiance to prevent and detect crime in the King's name to Gen Crozier July 1920.

HEARN, Thomas: Ardfert, Co. Kerry. Sgt RIC. Arrested Roger Casement at McKenna's Fort and took him to Tralee.

HEGARTY, Daniel: Mallow, Co. Cork. Vice-Comdt Cork No 2 Bde 1919. Assisted in transfer of arms captured at Fermoy 7 September 1919. One of the men that Head Const Sullivan refused to arrest.

HENDERSON, Arthur: MP. Demanded and was refused an inquiry into the 'Sack of Balbriggan', October 1920. Subsequently chaired the Labour Party's own inquiry into the affair. Presented his findings to Lloyd George, without result.

HENDRICK, John Joseph: Citizen Army. Came from London to participate in Easter Week Rebellion. Fought with the College of Surgeons garrison.

HENNESSY: See McGuinness, C.J.

HENNESSY, Sean: See footnote to Murphy, Joe.

HENRY, Denis: KC, MP. Senior Crown Counsel for Co. Westmeath 1916. Member of the Royal Commission of Inquiry into the deaths of Sheehy Skeffington, Dickson and Coade.

HEPPELL-MARR, Constance: Assistant Director, City of Dublin Branch of the British Red Cross Society and Joint Red Cross. Organized a field hospital and attended to the wounded in the streets during the Easter Week Rebellion.

HERLIHY, Michael: Brade, Union Hall, Co. Cork. Enlisted in Myross Coy 1919. Became Capt of Bandon Coy and participated in Kilmichael ambush.

HERON, Archie: Portadown, Co. Armagh. Full-time IRB organizer. Worked with James Connolly towards organizing ITGWU. Married Connolly's daughter Ina.

HEUSTON, Sean: Dublin and Limerick. Active Fianna Éireann organizer in Limerick and Dublin. Capt D Coy 1st Bn Dublin Bde. Comdt in charge of occupation of Mendicity Institute, South Quays, at outbreak of Easter Week hostilities. Defended it with a tiny garrison until Wednesday, although orders only demanded its occupation for a few hours. Court-martialled, sentenced to death and executed at Kilmainham 8 May 1916.

HEWART, Gordon (Sir): Attorney General 1921. Adviser to Truce delegation 1921.

HEWETT, H: Lance-Cpl 2nd King Edward's Horse. Shot dead during a charge on the Volunteers' North King St barricade on Thursday of Easter Week. Until then he had harassed Volunteers in South Quays, Thomas St, Cork Hill, South George's St and Dame St areas and was one of the most active of the British troops.

HIGGINSON: Brig Gen BA. Military Governor of the Martial Law Area of Munster. With Gen Strickland he conducted a search and sweep operation involving 1000 troops in an unsuccessful attempt to wipe out Tom Barry's West Cork Bde Flying Column.

HILL, H.O.H.: County Insp Kerry RIC. Gave evidence before the Royal Commission of Inquiry into the Easter Week Rebellion.

HILLERY, Michael (Dr): Milltown Malbay, Co. Clare. Attended to wounded after Monreal ambush 18 December 1920 and other engagements. Director of Medical Services 1st Western Div 1921.

HITZEN, E.H.: Capt BA. Received de Valera's surrender at Boland's Mills Easter Week 1916.

HOBSON, Bulmer: Holywood, Co. Down. Northern leader of the IRB, founder-member of the Irish Volunteers and their Secretary in 1916. Was opposed to the use of force except in the event of being attacked or in resisting conscription. Was denied information concerning the Easter Week Rebellion until Holy Thursday when, on his own suspicions, he accompanied Eoin MacNeill to a meeting with Pearse. He was given authority over all Dublin Volunteers by MacNeill but was placed under arrest by the Military Council of the Volunteers on the following evening, Good Friday. Withdrew from revolutionary activities after the Rebellion. (*See* Collins, Mrs Maurice)

HOEY, Daniel: Det RIC. Particularly active in apprehending Volunteer leaders, notably Sean McDermott, for execution after Easter Week Rebellion. Shot dead in Brunswick St, Dublin, 12 September 1919, as part of Collins's campaign against members of the RIC who harassed Volunteers.

HOEY, Patricia: 5 Mespil Rd, Dublin. Home used for GHQ Intelligence work by Volunteers. Raided 1 June 1921. Gave misleading information on Collins during interrogation and had to feign her mother's illness. Passed a message to Collins through her mother's doctor to prevent his arriving into a trap.

HOGAN, Dan: Monaghan. Participated in Ballytrain attack, Monaghan, 14 February 1920. Led the party that rescued Matt Fitzpatrick from Monaghan Hospital 30 March 1921. Succeeded Eoin O'Duffy as Bde Comdt 1921 and led attack on Carrickmacross Barracks. OC 5th Northern Div 1921. (See O'Malley, Ernie)

HOGAN, David: Active in Volunteers 1917-21. Sentenced for a seditious speech at Myshall, Co. Carlow, 1919. Figured in a number of jail escapes.

HOGAN, David: Dublin. Lt IRA. Member of Erskine Childers' Publicity staff 1921. Arrested and interrogated at Royal Barracks May 1921. A member of the raiding party on the Provost Marshal's house, Haddington Rd, Dublin, 1918. (See Cullen, Tom)

HOGAN, James: Brother of Michael (below). Prominent in many actions with Michael Brennan in Clare and Galway, including Broadford. With Brennan, was hunted by the Black and Tans, escaping on several occasions. IO 1st Western Div 1921. Established liaison with Limerick and Galway Bdes and a type of 'Secret Service' among non-Volunteers in the area.

HOGAN, Matthew: Tipperary. Fifteen-year-old brother of Sean Hogan detained and interrogated for weeks after Soloheadbeg ambush.

HOGAN, Michael: Brother of James, (above). Active with East Clare Bde. After the Truce he was sent to London with Ned Lynch to procure arms for 1st Western Div. They availed of a chance to acquire arms from an Irish Guards depot. The plan misfired and newspapers sensationalized the incident as a serious breach of the Truce.

HOGAN, Michael: Grangemockler, Co. Tipperary. Member of the Tipperary Gaelic football team shot dead in Croke Park during the raid by Black and Tans on Bloody Sunday afternoon 21 November 1920. (See Ryan, Thomas)

HOGAN, Sean: Tipperary. One of the 'Big Four'. Took part in the Soloheadbeg ambush of a gelignite patrol 21 January 1919. Arrested 12 May 1919 at Meagher's of Annefield. Rescued by his comrades at Knocklong 13 May. Operated in Dublin as well as Tipperary. Took part in Ashtown ambush of Lord French 19 December 1919. Back in Tipperary 1920, took part in Drangan Barracks attack 3 June. Commanded the Flying Column of the 3rd Tipperary Bde.

HOLMES: Botanic Ave, Drumcondra, Dublin. Unionist and Loyalist who nonetheless gave Dan Breen refuge and dressed his wounds after the 'Fernside' fight.

HOLMES, Philip Armstrong: Cork. Maj Gen. Div Commissioner of the RIC in Munster. Replaced Col Brice-Ferguson Smyth July 1920. Injured at Tureengarriffe ambush 28 January 1921. He and other injured RIC personnel transported to the County Infirmary by their attackers. He died from his injuries next evening.

HOLOHAN, Patrick: Dublin. Comdt. Senior Officer of Fianna Éireann 1916. With his brother Garry participated in the attempt to blow up the Magazine Fort in the Phoenix Park on the morning of Easter Monday 1916. Followed on to fight in the North Quays area. Received the surrender order from Pearse in North Brunswick St. His party was cut off and he had refused to surrender until Fr Augustine arranged a truce. Pearse's order followed on Sunday morning. Led an arms raid on Collinstown 19 March 1919.

HOOLAN, Liam: Dunkerrin, Co. Offaly. Comdt North Tipperary (No 1) Bde. Prominent in many actions including the attack on Borrisokane Barracks. (See McCormick, Michael)

HOTBLACK: Capt BA. A ruthless officer who served under Percival in the Bandon area, Co. Cork. Shot dead while leading a pincer movement against the IRA at Crossbarry 19 March 1921.

HOULIHAN, Brian: Kenmare. Active in 1916. Lost his right arm after two years' hospitalization.

HOURIHAN, Jack (officially Jeremiah): 'Jack the Tailor', Tooreen, Skibbereen, later Drimoleague, Co. Cork. In action Ballinhassig, Newcestown and Kilmichael ambushes, all Co. Cork.

HOWE, T.A.: Chief Insp of the RIC in Cork. His statement to the Royal Commission of Inquiry into the Easter Week Rebellion was included as an appendix to the report.

HUCKERBERRY: Notorious Black and Tan operating in the Abbeyfeale area of Co. Limerick. Patrick Hartnett, a young postman, and Jeremiah Healy, an eighteen-year-old blacksmith, were shot dead by him as they passed by the RIC barracks.

HUDSON: Col King's Liverpool Rgt. Stationed at Skibbereen, Co. Cork. Was praised by Tom Barry for his soldierly behaviour. He saved Donegan, Keyes, O'Sullivan and Cotter of Barry's Column from the Black and Tans and had them interned instead November 1920.

HUGHES, Hector: Barrister and member of the committee that drafted the Constitution and Rules of Court June 1920.

HUNT, Jim: Gurteen, Co. Sligo. Resigned from the RIC after the execution of the Easter Week Rebellion leaders. Joined the Volunteers and became Comdt Gurteen Bn Sligo Bde in 1918, succeeding Owen Tansey who died in the influenza epidemic of that year. Active in many engagements including attack on RIC barracks at Collooney and Ratra ambush 1920. Served sentences in Sligo and Mountjoy. (See MacDonagh, Tomás)

HUNT, Michael: Thurles, Co. Tipperary. Dist Insp RIC. Shot dead in Thurles 23 June 1919. The incident was considered a major factor in the decision by the British Government to have Sinn Féin proclaimed throughout Co. Tipperary.

HUNTER, Thomas: Volunteer Capt. Succeeded Tomás MacDonagh as Bn Comdt 2nd Dublin Bn, having served with him at Jacob's factory during

Easter Week Rebellion. Was Adj to de Valera at Lewes Prison 1917.

HURLEY, Charlie: Kilbrittain, Co. Cork. Volunteer organizer. Arrested April 1918 and sentenced to five years imprisonment for possessing plans of Bere Island. Served in Cork and Portlaoise before his release after hunger-strike. Commanded detachment that ambushed an RIC patrol at Ahawadda, killing three, wounding one and capturing all arms and ammunition April 1920. Vice-Comdt 1st (Bandon) Bn January 1920. Became Comdt West Cork Bde after Tom Hale's arrest. Commanded the Bde from August 1920 until his death. In action at Tooreen ambush. Walked fifteen miles to meet the Flying Column after Kilmichael and guarded them as they rested. Commanded the Column during Barry's illness December 1920. Ambushed the Black and Tans at Gaggin but the plans went awry, leading to death of IRA Lt McLean. In action at Innishannon 16 January 1921 and Bandon 24 January 1921. Wounded at Upton ambush 15 February. Shot dead while attempting to escape from a raid on Forde's of Ballymurphy where he was recuperating as Crossbarry ambush was about to begin 19 March 1921.

HURLEY, Diarmuid: Bandon, Co. Cork. OC 4 Bn Cork No 1 Bde. Led Mile Bush ambush, Midleton, 5 June 1920, and disarmed Cameron Highlanders. Killed in action at Carrigona, Midleton, 28 May 1921.

HURLEY, Frank: Laragh, Bandon, Co. Cork. Member of Barry's Flying Column West Cork Bde. Guided Barry from Crossmahon to deliver his attack on Brandon curfew patrol 24 January 1921. Shot dead by Essex Rgt 9 May 1921.

HURLEY, Jim: Clonakilty, Co. Cork. Bn Comdt 2nd (Clonakilty) Bn West Cork Bde from January 1921. Participant in an engagement in which RIC Const Brick of Rosscarbery was shot dead. Injured while destroying a bridge near Clonakilty March 1921. In action at Rosscarbery and Dunmanway.

HURLEY, Sean: Drinagh, Co. Cork. Secretary of the English Council of the IRB. In action during Easter Week Rebellion. Killed as he attempted to re-capture a lost barricade in the Church St area 28 April 1916.

HYDE, Sean: Dublin. Volunteer officer involved in intelligence work 1920. While in bed in his lodgings at Mount St following Bloody Sunday, the agent 'Peel' actually burst into his room asking where Hyde (himself) slept. Hyde replied that he had not returned the previous night and 'Peel' left.

HYLAND Brothers: Batty, a garage owner of Denzille Lane, Dublin, was Collins's regular driver. His brother Joe also drove him on occasions. They always had a car ready when needed.

HYLAND, Mary (later Mrs Michael Kelly): Actress active with Countess Markievicz in searching for arms to equip the College of Surgeons garrison during the Easter Week Rebellion.

HYNES, Frank: Galway. Active with Liam Mellows during Easter Week in Galway.

HYNES, Mick: Trim, Co. Meath. Assisted Patrick Mooney in attack on Trim RIC Barracks 30 September 1920.

'IGOE GANG': Members of the RIC from the provinces operating in Dublin for the purpose of identifying IRA personnel reporting to GHQ.

INTELLIGENCE SECTION: Prominent in Michael Collins's Intelligence Section were: Liam Tobin and Tom Cullen in charge; Charlie Byrne; Paddy Caldwell; Charles Dalton; Joe Dolan; Joe Guilfoyle; Ned Kelleher; Patrick Kennedy; Dan McDonnell; Peter Magee; Frank Saurin and Frank Thornton. (*See 'Twelve Apostles'*)

IRISH VOLUNTEERS: Irish nationalist military organization formed in response to the formation of the Ulster Volunteers in 1913. Participated in Easter Week Rebellion. Came to be known as the Irish Republican Army during the War of Independence.

IRISH REPUBLICAN ARMY: Initially an unofficial title for Óglaigh na hÉireann, the Irish Volunteers. Came into popular use after institution of First Dáil, 21 January 1919.

IRISH REPUBLICAN BROTHERHOOD. Founded 1858, and generally referred to in the 19th century as the 'Fenians'. Secret society with aspirations to Irish independence, to be achieved by force if necessary. The Easter Week Rebellion was planned by the IRB's Military Council, which included a faction of its Supreme Council. Developed strong ties with the Irish Volunteers, who came to be known as the Irish Republican Army during the WI.

ISAACS, Rufus: Lord Chief Justice presiding at the trial of Roger Casement at the Old Bailey 26 June 1916.

'JAMESON': Limerick-born British Secret Service agent formerly named Burns. Claimed to be a representative of the Russian Government anxious to stir up mutinies in BA to avenge Churchill's interventionist policy. Claimed to have access to arms from Birmingham Small Arms factory. Made contact with Collins through Art O'Brien in London. Exposed by being given the supposed location of a document he had requested. The address given was promptly raided by Crown Forces. 'Jameson' left Ireland but soon returned and persisted with his activities until executed in Dublin, February 1920. (*See MacNamara, James*)

JOHNSON, Robert: *See Carty, Frank.*

JOHNSON, Thomas (Dr): Belfast. English-born Secretary of the Irish Labour Party and Irish Congress of Trade Unions. Campaigned against conscription 1918. Labour representative on the National Cabinet of 1918. Disapproved of force. With William O'Brien, prepared a draft on social and democratic issues for the First Dáil 1919. With Cathal O'Shannon represented Ireland at the International Labour Conference at Berne 3 February 1919. Presided over the Investigation into Food Resources 1919. Co-signatory of the call for a general strike in support of hunger-striking prisoners 12 April 1920. Arrested in December 1920 raids. (*See Farren, Thomas*)

JOHNSTONE, Walter Edgeworth: Chief Commissioner DMP throughout war. Denied appropriation of Dáil notepaper upon which threats were widely issued during 1920.

JONES: Pte. (*See Sullivan, Head Const*)

JONES, Thomas: Lloyd George's private secretary. Member of British delegation in Truce negotiations. Advocated a Boundary Commission for Northern Ireland November 1921. (*See Curtis, Lionel*)

JOYCE, James: Dublin. Citizen Army. Porter at Davy's public house. Took part in its occupation and stubborn defence during Easter Week.

KAIN, Thomas: Dublin. Lt Citizen Army. Mobilization Officer. Occupied Upper Castle Yard guardroom on Easter Monday 1916. Later moved to Lahiff's, Castle St. Hid out in cellar when British occupied the area.

KAVANAGH, Ernest: Oxford Rd, Ranelagh, Dublin. ITGWU clerk and cartoonist for *The Irish Worker*. Killed in Liberty Hall area, Easter Week 25 April 1916.

KAVANAGH, Joe: Dublin Castle Det. Offered favours to 1916 prisoners which were mostly refused out of suspicion. Later, with Broy, Neligan and James McNamara helped pass on vital information to Collins's Intelligence Section. Gave warning of many raids including those of May 1918 in connection with the supposed 'German Plot'. Died 1920. (*See Gay, Thomas*)

KAVANAGH, Matt: *See O'Brien, Seamus*.

KAVANAGH, Ned: Sailor employed by a coal importing company. Throughout the war was involved in the smuggling of arms and in two-way movement of personnel, including escapees from English prisons.

KAVANAGH, Seamus: Lt Irish Volunteers. Led reinforcements sent from Tomás MacDonagh at Jacob's factory to Michael Mallin at St Stephen's Green and occupied the Turkish Baths there during the Easter Week Rebellion.

KAVANAGH, Sean: *See Maher, Jerry*.

KEANE: Editor, *Kilkenny People*. Paper suppressed after he had proposed W.T. Cosgrave for Kilkenny City by-election August 1917.

KEANE, Michael: *See O'Rourke, Dan*.

KEANE, Thomas: Limerick. Executed at Military Detention Barracks Limerick 4 June 1921. Mourners praying outside were attacked, beaten and abused by police and Black and Tans.

KEARNEY, John: Burncourt, Cahir, Co. Tipperary. Coy Capt D Coy 6 Bn 3 Tipperary Bde. Close associate of Sean Treacy.

KEARNEY, Peadar: 68 Lr Dorset St, Dublin. Returned from a tour of England with the Abbey Theatre in time to participate in Easter Week Rebellion. Fought at Jacob's factory. Assisted in re-organization of Volunteers after Easter Week. Wrote poems in favour of Sean Treacy and other heroes of the war. Arrested and interned for a year in 1920.

KEARNS, Linda: Sligo. Nurse. Arrested by Auxiliaries April 1921 for driving Volunteers and supplies. Interrogated and abused. Tried in Belfast and claimed responsibility for car and its contents in order to protect Volunteers. Sentenced to ten years' imprisonment.

KEATING, Con: Cahirciveen, Co. Kerry. Wireless expert with Volunteers; drowned off Ballykissane Pier, Killorglin, Co. Kerry, while attempting to meet up with Casement. The car in which he was travelling plunged into the sea 21 April 1916. (*See McInerney, Thomas; Monaghan, Charles; Sheehan, Donal*)

KEATING, Pat & Thomas: Comeragh, Kilmacthomas, Co. Waterford. Brothers. Both active in war. Pat was 1st Comdt Comeragh Bn and was killed in an ambush at Burgery, Dungarvan, 19 March 1921.

KEEGAN, Kathleen: De Valera's secretary. In charge of Meath C na mB. Married Comdt Barney Dunne.

KEENLYSIDE, H.B.: Capt 1st Bn Lancashire Fusiliers. Shot dead on Bloody Sunday morning 21 November 1920 at 28 Upr Pembroke St.

KELLEHER: Dist Insp, Granard, Co. Longford. On Collins's list for execution. Killed by Longford Bde members at Greville Arms Hotel, Granard, 31 October 1920.

KELLEHER, Michael: Youghal, Co. Cork. Active with 4th Bn there. Imprisoned on Spike Island and in Frongoch. Endured a 21-day hungerstrike.

KELLEHER, Ned: *See Intelligence Section*.

KELLEHER, Thomas: Clonbroney, Co. Longford. Orderly to Longford Bde Comdt. In May 1921 while accompanying a machine-gun instructor to Roscommon Bde, came upon Auxiliaries at Drumlish and shot one dead. Fire was returned and Kelleher was killed.

KELLEHER, Thomas: Upton, Co. Cork. Section Commander Flying Column West Cork Bde, greatly praised in various documents. In action at Upton ambush, at Crossbarry (where his section met the heavy British reinforcements arriving from Ballincollig), at Rosscarbery, and at Bandon. His older brother Pat was also active.

KELLY, Brian: *See Sullivan, Head Const.*

KELLY, Frank: Assisted in a number of escape bids from English prisons including that of de Valera from Lincoln Jail.

KELLY, Joseph: *See footnote to Murphy, Joe.*

KELLY, Michael: Dublin. Citizen Army Lt. In action Harcourt St and Portobello area Easter Monday 1916 and College of Surgeons Easter Tuesday. Imprisoned Knutsford. With Frank Robbins and Michael Donnelly, negotiated for closer co-operation with Volunteers 1918. Wounded four DMP constables during incident at Connolly Commemoration 5 June 1919.

KELLY, R.C.: Capt BA. Mun Dept, Dublin. Gave evidence before the Royal Commission of Inquiry into the Easter Week Rebellion 1916.

KELLY, Thomas: 7 Belgrave Rd, Dublin. Alderman Dublin Corporation, to which he read a decoded order proposing action against national organizations on the Wednesday prior to Easter Week. Member of a committee that organized the Sinn Féin National Council April 1917. Acting Joint Secretary, with Hanna Sheehy Skeffington, of Sinn Féin during the absence of executive members in April 1919. Arrested and deported December 1919. Elected Lord Mayor of

Dublin while in prison after local elections of January 1920. Read the Democratic Programme, in English, at the First Dáil sitting.

KELLY'S: 'The Halfway House'. Public house from where the Ashtown ambush of 19 December 1919 was launched.

KEMPSON, Lily: Dublin. Assisted Countess Markievicz in searching out arms and supplies and conveying them to St Stephen's Green garrison Easter Week 1916. Active there and in College of Surgeons.

KENNEDY, Joe: Castlepollard, Co. Westmeath. Sinn Féin organizer prominent in events leading up to 1918 election. Was arrested and jailed for two days before election.

KENNEDY, Mick: See 'Twelve Apostles'.

KENNEDY, Patrick: Dublin. Youth arrested on suspicion at Talbot St, Dublin, with James Murphy 9 February 1921. His dead body was found in a field at Clonturk Park, Drumcondra, next day. Black and Tans court-martialled in connection with the incident were acquitted. (See King, 'Tiny'; Murphy, James)

KENNEDY, Patrick: See Intelligence Section.

KENNEDY, T.J.: Cookstown, Co. Tyrone. Lt Royal Inniskilling Fusiliers, former editor of *Northern Standard*. Commanded troops in Pro-Cathedral area during Easter Week Rebellion. Was complimented by its clergy on his conduct and was mentioned in War Office despatches.

KENNY, James: Terenure, Dublin. Volunteer 4th Bn Dublin Bde. Was present at the occupation of the GPO on Easter Monday 1916. Accidentally wounded by a Dutch sailor on the premises, thus becoming the first casualty of the Rebellion. Lt Rathfarnham Coy throughout the war.

KENNY, Joseph: See footnote to Murphy, Joe.

KENT Brothers: Bawnard House, Castlelyons, Coole, Co. Cork. Defended themselves and their home against an armed raid by RIC 1 May 1916. William: Imprisoned in Cork Jail after the action. Acquitted. David: Wounded in the action. Captured and sentenced to death. Execution postponed owing to his condition. Sentence later commuted to imprisonment. Released by the amnesty June 1917. Richard: Wounded in the action. Died Fermoy Hospital 4 May 1916. Thomas: While resisting arrest the following day shot an RIC officer. Imprisoned and executed in Cork Military Detention Barracks 9 May 1916. Requested that he not be shot by an Irishman. (See Rowe, William)

KENWORTHY: Lt Comdr BN. Later Lord Strabolgi. Repeatedly called for justice in Ireland. Questioned the Chief Secretary on the Dermot O'Sullivan case. Called a traitor by his colleagues because of his stand.

KEOGH: Lt Hampshire Rgt. Participant in Hales and Harte interrogation Bandon July 1920. (See Hales, Tom; Harte, Pat)

KEOGH, Margaret: Leighlinbridge, Co. Carlow. Nurse. Shot dead at No 2 Hospital, South Dublin Union, Easter Monday 1916. Upon hearing gunfire, rushed to call in patients walking in the grounds. Some sources say she was shot in error by Volunteers, others that she was shot by British troops.

KEOGH, Myles (Dr): Dublin. Visiting Justice at Mountjoy during the May 1920 hunger-strike. Signed Kevin Barry's sworn statement of 28 October 1920 in which details of interrogation and torture were given.

KEOGH, Tom: Dublin. Assisted in the manufacture of munitions for Volunteers. A distinguished marksman, he participated in the Ashtown ambush 19 December 1919. Took over and drove the horse-drawn mail car in the Castle Mail raid of 1919. Active in attempt to prevent Treacy's capture after 'Fernside' fight October 1920. One of the 'Twelve Apostles'. Shot two Auxiliaries while escaping from 22 Mount St, Bloody Sunday morning 21 November 1920. A member of the party that captured an armoured car at the City Abattoir, Blackhorse Ave, for use in the MacEoin rescue bid. Captured after his involvement in the burning of the Custom House May 1921. (*See Dalton, Emmet*)

KERR, Neil: Dublin and Liverpool. Purser on a shipping line. Agent for Collins in England. Brought messages from Sam Maguire of Whitehall civil service. Assisted in the acquisition and importation of arms after Easter Week Rebellion. Assisted in cross-channel movement of key personnel. Arranged Harry Boland's passage to USA in April 1919. Left hospital to attend to arrangements for de Valera's passage to the USA. Arrested and imprisoned 1920.

KETTLE, Tom: Dublin. Former MP, Prof of National Economics and believer in Home Rule. Joined the Dublin Fusiliers while still a Volunteer. Easter Week Rebellion and the subsequent executions disillusioned him to the extent that he requested a transfer to the front line in First World War. He was killed in the Battle of the Somme September 1916.

KEYES, Ralph: Coy Capt Bantry Bn 1917. Participated in numerous actions with West Cork Bde, including the raid on a naval sloop at Bantry Bay 17 November 1919 when a valuable collection of arms was captured. In action at Durrus and Clonee and led a small party at the shooting of a notorious member of the RIC in Bantry 30 November 1920. Arrested and interned. (*See Hudson*)

KIERNAN, John: With Fred Lawlor, took over the switchboard of Tara St Fire Station when the station was occupied by 3rd Dublin Bn IRA during the burning of the Custom House 25 May 1921.

KIERNAN, Sean: Director of Mun Irish Volunteers. Involved in attempts to protect Sean Treacy after 'Fernside' fight.

KILCOYNE, Tom: Achonry, Tubbercurry, Co. Sligo. Marched to Tubbercurry to receive expected arms from Germany during Easter Week preparations. Was a close associate of Frank Carty and was himself involved in an unsuccessful tunnelling escape attempt from Castlebar Jail.

KILDEA, Martin: Woodlawn, Co. Galway. Full-time member of East Clare Flying Column. Arrested and killed while in confinement with others in what became known as the Killaloe Murders.

KILLALEA, Martin: Doon, Co. Roscommon. QM North Roscommon Bde and extremely active in all its activities including the Rockingham raid. Was on the run until arrested and interned at the Rath Camp, Curragh. Some sources say he escaped through the 'Brady Tunnel' in September 1921, others that he was released about that time.

KILLALOE MURDERS: East Clare Volunteers shot dead on Killaloe Bridge and vicinity 17 November 1920: Michael Mc Mahon, Alphonsus Rodgers, Michael Egan and Martin Kildea.

KILROY, Michael: Comdt 1st (Castlebar) Bn West Mayo Bde and leader of Flying Column. Came to the rescue of South Mayo Bde after Tourmakeady action 3 May 1921. OC 4th Western Div 1921. (*See Maguire, Tom*)

KING: 2nd Lt Royal Irish Fusiliers. One of a number of prisoners held by the Volunteers at the GPO during Easter Week Rebellion 1916.

KING: Capt BA. Interrogator at Dublin Castle. Involved in McKee-Clancy interrogation.

KING Brothers: Three brothers of GPO garrison Easter Week. Patrick: A member of the Liverpool Coy of the Irish Volunteers that came here to join the Kimmage Coy. Arrested after the Rebellion and interned at Frongoch. Re-arrested 1921 and interned at Rath Camp, Curragh.

KING, 'Tiny': Maj Coy Commander 'F' Coy (Dublin Castle) Auxiliaries. With two Aux Cdts, was seen taking Patrick Kennedy and James Murphy from Castle prior to their being discovered dead 9 February 1921.

KINSELLA, Joe: *See Bryan, Dan.*

KIRKWOOD: Col BA. Commander of Kilkenny Coy October 1920. When dining with the McCalmont family at Mount Juliet the residence was raided by IRA seeking weapons. Other tensions, including disloyalty from subordinates, caused his deteriorating health and he was returned to England by Gen Crozier.

LACEY, Denis: Annacarty, Co. Tipperary. Gaelic League and Volunteer organizer 1916. Supervised Shrough and Knockharding munition manufacturing locations. Participated in raid on Kilmallock RIC barracks 28 May 1920. Comdt 3rd Tipperary Bde Flying Column August 1921. Active in Thomastown ambush 28 October 1920 where three British soldiers were killed and five wounded, and at Lisnagaul where two RIC members were shot dead while two others died later from wounds received. (*See Crowe, Maurice; Duffy, Sean*)

LAIDE, Richard: Ballymacelligott, Co. Kerry. Killed in action at the first attack on an RIC barracks in Kerry 18 April 1918. The RIC members involved were fired upon in Tralee, having attended the inquiry into the affair on 14 June 1918. (*See Browne, John*)

LAMBERT: Col Comdt BA. Commander of 13th Bde, Athlone. Returning home after a tennis game with Col and Mrs Challoner and Mrs

Lambert 9 June 1921, the party was called upon to halt at Moydrum, Athlone. Their chauffeur increased his speed, the car was fired upon and Lambert was killed. Mrs Challoner received facial injuries.

LANIGAN, Stephen: Customs Official in Liverpool. Assisted Neil Kerr in his activities. Arrested December 1921 and interned.

LARDNER, Larry: See Murphy, Seamus.

LATYMER: Col. Commanded K Coy RIC in Cork. He was suggested by Lt Commander Kenworthy as having been implicated in the Cork burnings of December 1920. In the House of Commons 28 February 1921, the Chief Secretary admitted to his being suspended from duty but did not concede implication.

LAW, Andrew Bonar (Rt Hon.): British Chancellor of the Exchequer and Leader of the House of Commons December 1916. On 15 June 1917 he announced the release of the Easter Week prisoners in a general amnesty aimed at creating a favourable atmosphere for the Home Rule Convention. Lord Privy Seal and again Leader of the House January 1919. Objected to any form of Truce until the IRA surrendered their arms 1920. Spoke in favour of the Treaty 1921.

LAWLESS, Frank: Swords, Co. Dublin. Associate and close adviser to Thomas Ashe. Played a major part in preparations for Ashbourne attack in which his son Joe (*below*) also participated. As QM 5th Dublin Bn he collected arms, *etc*, in a horse and cart in preparation for Easter Week Rebellion. Arrested for alleged part in supposed 'German Plot' May 1918. Deported.

LAWLESS, James: Balbriggan, Co. Dublin. One of those raided in the 'Sack of Balbriggan'. Taken from his home and shot dead 20 September 1920. (*See Derham, John; Gibbons, John*)

LAWLESS, Joe: Swords, Co. Dublin. Son of Frank (*above*) who also fought at Ashbourne. Two brothers, Colm and Frank, also participated in Easter Week Rebellion. Deported and interned in Knutsford and Frongoch until the amnesty. Manufactured bombs in his Parnell St engineering works until its discovery late in 1920. Supplied transport to Collins, McKee and Boylan. Interned at Arbour Hill and Curragh Camp 1921.

LAWLESS, Tom: *See McCormick, Michael.*

LAWLOR, Fred: Dublin. With John Kiernan, took over the switchboard of Tara St Fire Station when members of 3rd Dublin Bn IRA occupied the building during the burning of the Custom House 25 May 1921.

LEAHY, Denis: *See McGee.*

LEAHY, Michael: Vice-Comdt Cork No 1 Bde. Selected for trip to Italy to procure arms for IRA 1921.

LEATHAM: Resident Magistrate. One of the group who faced a mutiny of RIC personnel at Listowel, Co. Kerry, 19 June 1920.

LEAVY, Sean: Ashbrook, Co. Roscommon. Comdt 3rd Bn North Roscommon Bde in action at Scramogue ambush 23 March 1921. (*See Madden, Pat*)

LEHANE, Dan: Lahinch, Co. Clare. Shot dead in front of his wife 22 September 1920 in reprisal for the loss of six RIC consts at Milltown Malbay two days earlier. Body burned. (*See Salmon, Joseph*)

LEMASS Brothers: Ballybrack, Co. Dublin. Sean: left school at 15 to join de Valera's Volunteer Coy. Fought in GPO during Easter Week having been separated from his own unit. Arrested December 1920 and interned in Ballykinlar until after the Treaty. Noel: also fought in GPO.

LENNON, George: *See Whelan, Pax*.

LEONARD, Joe: Dublin. One of 'Twelve Apostles'. Involved with William Stapleton at the execution of Capt Newbury BA at 92 Lr Baggot St on Bloody Sunday morning 21 November 1920. Participated in Ashtown ambush of Lord French 19 December 1919. Involved in attempts to protect Treacy and Breen after 'Fernside' fight. Partnered Emmet Dalton in the attempted rescue of Sean MacEoin from Mountjoy.

LIDDY, Sean: Comdt West Clare Bde 1919-21.

LINDSAY: Capt. *See Dunsany, Lord*.

LINDSAY (Mrs): Coachford, Co. Cork. Seen entering Ballincollig Barracks before the arrest of six Volunteers. When five were sentenced to death she was apprehended by Cork No 1 Bde. The British authorities were warned that any execution of Volunteers would be followed by hers. The warning went unheeded and the Volunteers were executed. Mrs Lindsay and her chauffeur were executed around 5 March 1921 without the sanction of IRA HQ.

LITTLE, P.J.: Editor of *New Ireland* 1916-19. The publication used the contributions of established writers sympathetic to Sinn Féin.

'LITTLE TOMMY': British spy disguised as a tramp and active in the Kilkenny area. Captured at Ballymurphy September 1920. Tried by the IRA and executed at Knockmore, Co. Carlow, 30 September 1920.

LLOYD GEORGE, David (First Earl Lloyd George of Dwyfor): Prime Minister of British Coalition government 6 December 1916 to 1922. Set up Convention on Irish question June 1917. Passed Conscription Bill for Ireland April 1918. With Lord French, Rt Hon Ian Macpherson and high-ranking officers of the RIC, was found guilty by Coroner's Jury of the murder of Tomás MacCurtain 1920. Took part in Treaty negotiations.

LOGUE, Michael (Cardinal): Carrigart, Co. Donegal. Supporter of Gaelic League but opposed to force. Strongly opposed to partition although he accepted the Treaty.

LONG, Walter: Chairman of the British Cabinet Committee given a mandate to draw up a settlement to the 'Irish Problem' after the Dáil was declared illegal September 1919.

LONSDALE, John (Sir): Ulster Unionist representative on Lloyd George's Convention of 1917.

LOOBY, J.J. & Laurence: Dualla, Co. Tipperary. Shot dead at Kilfeakle 20 December and at Ballysheehan 19 December 1920 respectively, while in custody of Crown Forces. (*See Delaney, William*)

LORDAN, Denis: Kilbrittain, Co. Cork. Vice-Comdt Bandon Bn 1919, having been most active organizing Bandon Volunteers after 1916. In action at Upton. Led a section at Crossbarry and was in action at Gloundaw.

LORDAN, Jim: Brother of John (*below*). Interrogated by Capt Crake before Kilmichael ambush but his explanation was accepted and he was freed. Fought in his brother's section at Crossbarry. (*See Crake, F.W.*)

LORDAN, John: Newcestown, Co. Cork. Vice-Comdt Bandon Bn 1921. Followed Flying Column to Kilmichael and asked to take part. Commanded the Newcestown Section. In action at Bandon 23 February, Crossbarry 19 March and Bandon 14 May.

LOUGHNANE, Henry & Patrick: Shanaglish, Gort, Co. Galway. Brothers. Arrested by RIC 26 November 1920 while threshing corn. Handed over to Auxiliaries who informed their mother three days later that her sons had escaped from custody at Drimharsna Castle, Ardrahan. Their bodies were found in a pond at Dombriste 6 December.

LOWE, W.H.M.: Brigadier i/c of Curragh forces 1916. OC Crown Forces in Dublin during Easter Week Rebellion 1916. Accepted the surrender from Pearse at Parnell St on the afternoon of Saturday 29 April at approximately 1430 hours. Mentioned in despatches for his conduct during the hostilities and promoted to Honorary Maj Gen.

LUCAS: Brig Gen Shropshire Rgt. OC 18 Bde. Captured by a party under Liam Lynch while fishing the Blackwater 27 July 1920. Held hostage in East Limerick. Escaped when he happened to be a passenger in a mail truck ambushed by a party under Sean Treacy near Oola, Co. Limerick. Wounded in the action. (*See Brennan Brothers (Michael); Clancy, Pat*)

LUCAS, A.L.: 2nd Lt King Edward's Horse. Shot by British troops while on duty at Guinness's Brewery 28 April 1916. A Lt Worswick and a civilian, William Rice, also shot. Impressions given that both officers were involved with Sinn Féin were vehemently denied by Lord Cheylesmore, who presided at the trial of Coy QM Robert Flood for the murder of Lucas and Rice.

LUCEY, Con: Student at University College, Cork. Abandoned studies to act as Medical Officer for the West Cork Bde from April 1921. Also took part in combat. Set up a field dressing station and attended to the wounded at Crossbarry.

LUMLEY, Richard: Rear Cross, Co. Tipperary. Shot dead 4 July 1920 at Ballingeary, one of a number sniped at by Black and Tans from the backs of their trucks as they drove through the countryside.

LYNAM, Kit: *See Dunne, Barney*.

LYNCH, Diarmuid: Dublin. Member of Supreme Council of IRB. Worked closely with Tom Clarke on plan for Easter Week Rebellion 1916. Staff Capt in GPO. One of the prominent IRB members elected to the Sinn Féin Executive October 1917. As Controller of Food for Sinn Féin in 1918, ordered the seizure of pigs due for export. Sentenced to two months' imprisonment. Managed to become married during a visit from his fiancée, Miss Quinn, to the annoyance of the

Dundalk Jail authorities. Deported in reprisal. Became Secretary of the Friends of Irish Freedom in USA May 1918. Resigned from the Dáil in 1920 as a protest against frictions between Irish interests in the USA.

LYNCH, Fionan: Officer of Dublin Bde imprisoned after action in GPO during Easter Week Rebellion. With Stack and Ashe, led the Mountjoy hunger-strike of May 1917. Released by amnesty. Re-imprisoned August 1917 for inflammatory speech. Released in November after another hunger-strike. Re-imprisoned on the same charge May 1918. Released August 1919. Helped plan escape of other prisoners. Was one of Erskine Childers' Assistant Secretaries on the Treaty Delegation. (*See Charters, John; O'Hegarty, Diarmuid*)

LYNCH, John A.: Kilmallock, Co. Limerick. Member of Limerick County Council. Director of Elections for Sinn Féin. Republican Court Justice. Collector of monies for the National Loan. While reporting to Dublin with a collection, stayed at the Exchange Hotel, Parliament St, where he was shot dead by a raiding party of Crown Forces 22 September 1920. Speculation suggested the possibility that Liam Lynch was the target. (*See Angliss; Bagally; 'Peel'*)

LYNCH, Liam: Anglesborough, Co. Limerick. Member of Supreme Council of IRB for Munster. Volunteer organizer in Cork 1917. Vigorous opponent of conscription 1918. Comdt No 2 (North Cork) Bde and led its first attack. Participated in the capture of Araglin Barracks. Active in harassing bank-robbers and recovering stolen monies. Captured Brig Gen Lucas. Led party that ambushed the King's Shropshire Light Infantry in Fermoy 7 September 1919. This drew retaliation in the burning and looting of establishments in the town. Led a successful raid on Mallow Military Barracks 28 September 1920. This was the one military installation captured by the IRA. Appointed Div Comdt 1st Southern Div 26 April 1921. Led a deputation to GHQ explaining that the fight could not be continued without extra munitions May 1921.

LYNCH, Ned: *See Hogan, Michael.*

LYNCH, Patrick: KC. Redmonite candidate defeated by de Valera in East Clare by-election 10 July 1917. Applied for *habeas corpus* in Con Murphy case.

LYNN, Kathleen (Dr): Medical Director Citizen Army Easter Week Rebellion. Member of St Stephen's Green garrison. Gave medical attention in City Hall area also and attended to Sean Connolly. Member of Sinn Féin Executive October 1917. Led Cumann na dTeachtairí, the League of Women Delegates.

LYONS: Const RIC Kerry. An inquest verdict pronounced him guilty of the murder of Daniel Scanlon, Ballybunion, Co. Kerry, but no action was taken against him.

LYONS: *See Deed, Con.*

(Names with prefixes Mc and Mac are both alphabetized as Mac.)

Mac ALLASTAIR, Sean (An tAthair): Chaplain to the internees at Ballykinlar Camp 1921.

McAULIFFE, Garret: Fought in GPO during Easter Week Rebellion. Later 2 i/c West Limerick Bde. Particularly active in Rathkeale area.

MacBRIDE, John: Westport, Co. Mayo. Father of Sean, below. Ex-BA Maj. Husband of Maud Gonne. Did not join Volunteers but fought at Jacob's factory during Easter Week Rebellion. He was 2 i/c to Tomás MacDonagh. Court-martialled, sentenced to death and executed at Kilmainham 5 May 1916.

MacBRIDE, Sean: Dublin. Son of John (*above*). Led a party that ambushed Auxiliaries at Pearse St, Dublin, in March 1921. He rescued a Volunteer injured in the ambush from Mercer's Hospital where his leg had been amputated. (*See Figgis, Darrell*)

McCABE, Alec: Keash, Co. Sligo. Member of Supreme Council of IRB for Connaught. Comdt Sligo Bde. Officer in charge of the Rockingham raid of February 1918, having been driven from Ballymote by Michael McGuire so that the car would not be known in Boyle. The house was the seat of Sir Thomas Stafford, Bart. Boldly knocking on the door of the mansion, the party overcame the butler and house staff before seizing arms from the gun-room. Elected for Sinn Féin in Sligo 1918. Imprisoned February 1918 and September 1919. Edited the *Irish Yearbook*.

McCALMONT Family: *See Kirkwood*.

Mac CAMHTHAOIL, Tomás: *See Ruttledge, P.J.*

McCAN, Pierce: Ballyowen House, Dualla, Co. Tipperary. President East Tipperary Sinn Féin Executive and County Comdt IRB in 1916. Despite lack of orders from Dublin he decided that the Rebellion should go ahead in Tipperary if Cork and Kerry rose too. Elected for Sinn Féin in 1918. Arrested and interned without charge in Gloucester Prison where he died of influenza 6 March 1919. The release of political prisoners was announced on the night of his death.

McCARTAN, Patrick (Dr): Carrickmore, Co. Tyrone. Member of IRB. Assisted in re-organization of Volunteers after Easter Week. Went to New York July 1917 bearing a petition for Irish freedom signed by 26 officers of the Easter Week Rebellion. Addressed Congress and the President of the United States. With Mellows, negotiated for arms from Germany for the Irish struggle. Was defeated in the South Armagh by-election 1 February 1918. Returned unopposed for Offaly April 1918 by-election. Was the only Irishman elected to Parliament by Sinn Féin who was out of prison, through being in the USA, in 1918. Appointed Irish envoy in Washington 1919. Returned from the USA in 1920 to encourage home support for de Valera in his difficulties with USA organizations. Sent a formal protest against British atrocities to USA State Department in October 1920.

McCARTHY: Ex-REME Capt and explosives expert. Assisted the West Cork Flying Column after Crossbarry. Prepared the mine used at Rosscarbery 30 March 1921.

McCARTHY, C.: *See McGrath, John*.

McCARTHY, G.: *See Gleeson, Michael*.

McCARTHY, Jack ('Jack James Andy'): Lissane, Drimoleague, Co. Cork. In action at Rosscarbery, Gloundaw and Kilmichael.

McCARTHY, James: Thurles, Co. Tipperary. In order to incriminate Sinn Féin he was sent a death threat purporting to come from them before being killed by RIC 30 March 1920.

McCARTHY, J.M.: East Limerick Volunteer organizer and Comdt Galtee Bn. Vice-Comdt and Adj East Limerick Bde. Officer of the Bde ASU and participated in most of its actions. Appointed Deputy Div Commander and Div Adj 4th Southern Div 1921.

McCARTHY, Michael: Dunmanway, Co. Cork. Vice-Comdt Dunmanway Bn West Cork Bde 1917 until his death, except for a brief period in 1919. Carried out the reconnaissance of the Kilmichael positions with Tom Barry. Commanded No 2 Section there and was KIA 28 November 1920.

McCARTHY, Tim: Cork. Executed in Cork 28 February 1921.

McCARTHY, William: Lixnaw, Co. Kerry. Despatch messenger for Tralee IRA. Arrested and killed, allegedly after severe interrogation and torture 26 March 1921.

McCARTNEY: Musgrave St, Belfast. RIC Sgt, allegedly the chief organizer of the notorious Cromwell Clubs. Aided by Nixon and Harrison, he engaged in harassment of Catholics in Belfast in an auxiliary capacity to the Unionist Clubs. Clubs first appeared around August 1921.

McCLEAN, D.L.: Chief IO in Dublin Castle 1920. Interrogated Michael Fleming.

McCORLEY, Felix & Roger: Belfast. Brothers. Prominent in the struggle. Roger: Comdt Belfast Bn, later commanded the Belfast Bde and was Vice-Officer commanding 3rd Northern Div. Felix: Adj and Training Officer Antrim Bde as well as being active in Liverpool.

McCORMICK, Michael: Dublin. OC 3rd Southern Div 1921. His staff included: Tom Lawless, Bluebell, Vice-Comdt; Austin McCurtin, Adj; Felix Cronin, QM; Mick Gantley, Engineer Officer; Paddy Mulcahy, Signals Officer. His Bde Commanders were: Liam Hoolan, Tipperary No 1; Andy Gallagher, Offaly No 2; Mick Grey, Laois No 1; Michael Walsh, Laois No 2. Some sources say that Austin McCurtin took command before the Treaty.

McCORMICK, Richard: Dublin. Capt Citizen Army. Occupied Harcourt St Station Easter Monday 1916. Was injured by a civilian while moving to the College of Surgeons the following day. Arrested after the surrender and imprisoned at Knutsford.

McCREA, Patrick: Dublin. Member of Collins's ASU. Assisted at Dan Breen's evacuation to the Mater Hospital after the 'Fernside' fight. Drove the armoured car captured at the City Abattoir for the MacEoin rescue attempt. (*See Dalton, Emmet; 'Twelve Apostles'*)

McCREERY: *See Cornwallis.*

McCULLOUGH, Denis: Divis St, Belfast. Sinn Féin delegate. Ex-President of Supreme Council of IRB and Member for Ulster. Organizer of Irish Volunteers in Ulster. Mobilized his Volunteers for Easter Week but lack of communication from Dublin proved detrimental to further action.

Arrested and deported for alleged part in supposed 'German Plot' May 1918.

McCURTAIN, Sean: *See Bryan, Dan.*

MacCURTAIN, Tomás: Ballyknockane and Blackpool, Cork. Cork Volunteer leader. With MacSwiney occupied a HQ at Sheare's St Easter Monday 1916. He parleyed with the assistant Bishop of Cork and Lord Mayor of Cork concerning proposed action in the city. Arrested after the Rebellion and imprisoned at Frongoch, Wakefield and Reading. Took part in an unsuccessful attempt to ambush Lord French in Dame St, Dublin. Elected Sinn Féin Councillor for Cork North-west, and was elected Lord Mayor of Cork 30 January 1920. He set out to eliminate corruption in local administration and received numerous death threats which he ignored. Was shot dead in his home in front of his wife 20 March 1920. A verdict of murder was brought against Lloyd George, Lord French, Rt Hon Ian Macpherson and high ranking RIC officers by a coroner's jury. (*See Butterfield, T.C.; Cohalan, D.F.; Crowley, Daniel; Smith, Thomas*)

McCURTIN, Austin: *See McCormick, Michael.*

McDERMOTT, Kate & Rose: Sisters. Leaders of New York C na mB and active in support of Irish causes.

MacDERMOTT, Sean: Kiltyclogher, Co. Leitrim; Jones's Rd, Dublin. Member of the Military Council of the IRB and of Sinn Féin. Member of the PG and signatory of the Proclamation. Although ill, helped plan and raise funds for the Easter Week Rebellion 1916. Volunteer organizer. Fought in the GPO. Court-martialled and sentenced to death. Executed at Kilmainham 12 May 1916. (*See Hoey, Daniel*)

McDERMOTT, Stephen: *See Bergin, John.*

Mac DIARMADA, Sean: *See MacDermott, Sean.*

McDONAGH, Joseph: Imprisoned with Sean Treacy in Mountjoy 1917. Member of Sinn Féin Executive October 1917. Organized a hunger-strike in Wormwood Scrubs prison 1920. Directed the 'Belfast Boycott' of January 1921 as Minister for Labour. Dublin stores stocking Belfast manufactured goods were ransacked in reprisal for the July 1920 Orange pogroms (*see Chronology*) and all local authorities were asked to follow suit. Suggested in the Dáil that the Treaty delegation should be subjected to some form of restriction. (*See MacSwiney, Mary*)

McDONAGH, Tom: Cloonloe, Co. Sligo. Capt South Sligo Bde. With Comdts Hunt and Marren in charge, attempted to capture arms from RIC proceeding to Ballaghadareen court. The ambush took place at Ratra, Teevnacreeva, 1 September 1920. He and two constables were killed.

MacDONAGH, Tomás: Cloughjordan, Co. Tipperary. Teacher at St Enda's and lecturer at National University of Ireland. Member of Gaelic League and co-opted to the Military Council of the IRB. One of the chief organizers of the Easter Week Rebellion. Did his utmost to undo the effects of MacNeill's countermand. D/Training Irish Volunteers and Comdt Dublin Bde. Signatory of the

Proclamation. Commanded 2nd Bn Dublin Bde at Jacob's factory, Bishop St, during Easter Week. Executed 3 May 1916 at Kilmainham.

McDONNELL: Const RIC for thirty years in Tipperary. killed with Const O'Connell at Soloheadbeg ambush, the first RIC victims since 1916 and first casualties of the war proper.

McDONNELL, Dan: *See Intelligence Section.*

McDONNELL, Mick: Participated in Ashtown ambush of Lord French. First Commander of Collins's 'Twelve Apostles'.

McDONNELL, P.: Comdt West Connemara Bde and West Connemara Flying Column. Led the ambush at Mounterown 23 April 1921, one of few actions in an area not properly activated until early in 1921. Credited by some sources as being i/c of 3rd Western Div in 1921. (*See Pilkington, William*)

McDONNELL BODKIN, M.: Co. Clare. County Court Judge. Reported on misdemeanours of Crown Forces to Sir Hamar Greenwood. Liberal in awarding compensation for destruction of property by Crown Forces. Stressed that restoration of law and order was impossible as long as what he termed 'competition in crime' continued.

* McELLIGOTT, James: Tralee, Co. Kerry. Fought in GPO during Easter Week Rebellion. Arrested, deported and imprisoned. Served part of his sentence with Collins in Stafford Jail. Released in 1917.

McELLIGOTT, Michael: Capt. Charles St, Listowel, Co. Kerry. With Comdt Michael Robert caused confusion among Crown Forces since they operated in each other's areas. The latter, better known as 'Bob', was killed in action at Derrymore 19 February 1921.

McELLISTRIM, Tom: Led the attack on Scartaglin Barracks April 1920, having earlier participated in attack on Gortatlea. With Johnny O'Connor, led Kerry No 2 Bde at Headford Junction 21 March 1921. A hand-to-hand fight took place on board a British provision train. Twenty-four British casualties reported. Dan Allman and James Bailey killed in the action.

McENTEE, John: *See McGee.*

McENTEE, Sean: Belfast. Member of National Executive of Irish Volunteers 1917-21 and active with them from 1916. Elected Sinn Féin MP 1918. Arrested for alleged part in supposed 'German Plot' May 1918. Deported.

Mac EOIN, Sean: Bunlahy, Co. Longford. 'The Blacksmith of Ballinalee'. Comdt 1st (Ballinalee) Bn Longford Bde 1919. Vice-Comdt of the Bde 1921. His Flying Column carried out an ambush in Granard November 1920. Auxiliaries and Black and Tans descended upon the town in reprisal. Returning from this, they were ambushed at Ballinalee by MacEoin and his Column 5 November. Reports say 20 Volunteers took on a hundred Crown Forces, killing up to 20. On 7 January 1921 MacEoin was raided in Miss Martin's house, Ballinalee, by a party under RIC Dist Insp McGrath. He escaped, killing McGrath. Led successful Clonfin ambush 2 February 1921 when Crown Forces surrendered and their leader Lt Comdr Craven was shot dead. Arrested 21 March 1921 at Mullingar railway station. Was severely wounded in an escape bid before being held at the military barracks prior to transfer to King George V (now St Bricin's) Hospital, Dublin. Was returned for Longford-Westmeath in May 1921 election. Charged 14 June with murder of Dist Insp McGrath. Convicted and sentenced to death. Plan to rescue him from prison failed. Before the Truce negotiations, British authorities agreed to release all imprisoned TDs except MacEoin. Urged by Collins, de Valera insisted on his release which was eventually granted. MacEoin proposed de Valera as President of the Irish Republic 26 August 1921. Comdt Midland Div 1921. He seconded Arthur Griffith's proposal that the Dáil should approve the Treaty 19 December 1921. (*See Dalton, Emmet*)

McEVER, Thomas: Co. Cork. Chemist shot dead at Dunmore, Tuam, Co. Galway, 2 May 1921, and labelled 'Convict Spy – Executed by IRA'. Alleged to have been shot by Crown Forces and to have had no connection with the IRA in the Tuam area.

McGARRITY, Joe: Co. Tyrone. Clan na Gael leader in Philadelphia, USA. With J.J. Ryan and John Devoy, compiled a Clan na Gael Revolutionary Directory. Supported the direct payment of funds raised in USA to the Dáil 1919. Established the New York HQ of the Dáil Loan.

McGARRY, Sean: Dublin. President of the Supreme Council of the IRB November 1917. Imprisoned Lewes Jail after Easter Week Rebellion. General Secretary of the Irish Volunteer Organization November 1917. Arrested for alleged part in supposed 'German Plot' May 1918. His house, thus already raided, provided a safe place for Collins to hide out during the remainder of the searches. Was deported and imprisoned. Escaped from Lincoln Jail with de Valera February 1919. (*See Milroy, Sean*)

McGEE: Castlebellingham, Co. Louth. RIC Const. Killed during an attack on Castlebellingham RIC Barracks 24 April 1916 when attempts were also made on the life of Lt Robert Dunville, Grenadier Guards. Three men, John McEntee of Belfast, Frank Martin of Dublin and Denis Leahy of Dundalk were court-martialled and sentenced to death, later commuted to life imprisonment, for the killing.

McGINLEY, J.P. (Dr): Breenagh, Letterkenny, Co. Donegal. Arrested December 1919 for advocating Sinn Féin loan. Held in Derry and Burnfoot. After a turbulent trial he was imprisoned in Mountjoy.

McGOWAN, Seamus: Dublin. Commanded the rear party at Liberty Hall after the Volunteers had marched out to the GPO to begin the Easter Week Rebellion 1916.

McGRANE, Eileen: 21 Dawson St, Dublin. Provided a refuge for Ernie O'Malley and part-time office for Collins. Court-martialled and imprisoned 31 December 1920 to 1 January 1921 when incriminating documents were found in her home.

McGRATH: Dist Insp of the RIC killed by Sean MacEoin 7 January 1921. When MacEoin was sentenced McGrath's father, mother and brothers appealed to the British Viceroy in Ireland for MacEoin's reprieve.

McGRATH, John: Rathclarin, Co. Cork. Volunteer shot dead by the Essex Rgt while digging a road trench at Crois-na-Leanbh, near Kilbrittain, 16 February 1921. Three others were also killed, J. O'Neill, T. Connolly and C. McCarthy.

McGRATH, Joseph: Dublin. In action at Marrowbone Lane Easter Week 1916. Arrested and imprisoned Wormwood Scrubs and Brixton. Elected for Sinn Féin in 1918 and 1921 elections. Arrested for alleged part in supposed 'German Plot' May 1918. Deported. Escaped from Usk prison January 1919. Re-arrested January 1920. Imprisoned. Transferred to Ballykinlar where he was Comdt No 1 Camp. After his release, he was active in arranging communications during the Treaty negotiations.

McGRATH, Sean: Secretary of the non-militant Irish Self-Determination League in England. Interned April 1921.

McGRATH, William: KC. Counsel for Dublin Corporation. Shot dead at 129 Altona Tce, North Circular Rd, 14 January 1921.

McGREEVY, John: *See Sweeney, Bernard.*

McGUINNESS, C.J. (alias Hennessy): Derry. Participated in the Derry riots of 1920. Led a Flying Column in the North-west. Assisted the escape of Frank Carty from Derry Jail and smuggled him on board collier *Carricklee* commanded by his father. Carried out actions in Glenties and Ardara after which he was captured. Sent a message to his Adj Hughie Martin that he had been informed upon. The culprit was 'executed' but his 'corpse' disappeared. He had, in fact, been wearing a bullet-proof vest and had escaped to England. McGuinness transferred to Ebrington Barracks from where he escaped. Brought two shiploads of arms from Germany to Cheek Point, Waterford, and to Wexford.

McGUINNESS, Joe: 41 Upr Gardiner St, Dublin; Longford. MP court-martialled and imprisoned after Easter Week Rebellion. Was imprisoned in Lewes Jail when nominated by Sinn Féin for the Parliamentary stronghold of Longford South. Reluctant to accept. By-election held 9 May 1917. Prominent people including Mrs Pearse, Mrs Clarke and Countess Plunkett campaigned vigorously, using the slogan 'Put him in to get him out.' They suffered severe harassment. McGuinness announced as the loser by twelve votes but after two recounts he won by thirty-nine votes. He followed Griffith's abstentionist policy and did not take his seat at Westminster. Member of Sinn Féin Executive October 1917. Arrested May 1918 for alleged part in supposed 'German Plot'. Deported. Member of First Dáil and was in prison when it met.

McGUIRE: Limerick. Purchased Vaughan's Hotel 1920. Said to have refused large sums to inform on Michael Collins and his staff.

McGUIRE, Michael: *See McCabe, Alec.*

McINERNEY, Thomas: Limerick. Driver of the car involved in an accident at Ballykissane Pier, Co. Kerry, when it went into the sea while conveying a party to meet Roger Casement 21 April 1916. He escaped but the passengers were drowned. Drove Hogan and Breen to Limerick after Solohedbeg action. (*See Keating, Con; Monaghan, Charles; Sheehan, Donal*)

McINTYRE, Patrick: Non-combatant journalist of a gossip publication on affairs of British officers called *The Eye-Opener* and other periodicals. Editor of *The Toiler*, *The Searchlight* and *Spark*. With two others, was shot dead by the BA at Portobello, Dublin, 2 April 1916. The subsequent Simon Commission of Inquiry found that he had no connection whatsoever with the Rebellion. (*See Bowen-Colthurst, J.C.; Dickson, Thomas; Sheehy Skeffington, Francis; Simon, John*)

McKEE, Dick: Finglas, Co. Dublin. Comdt Dublin Bde 1918-20. A member of GHQ Staff of the Irish Volunteers. Political prisoner at Dundalk 1918. Took part in the first unsuccessful ambush of Lord French at Dame St. With Rory O'Connor, arranged the Mountjoy escape of Béaslaí, Fleming and Walshe. Printed *An tOglach* from an Aungier St base 1920. Took part in the evacuation of Dan Breen to the Mater Hospital and in his protection there October 1920. Active in attempts to protect Treacy at same time. In charge of the Bloody Sunday morning operation until his arrest on its eve with Peadar Clancy 20 November 1920. Arrested at the Gloucester Diamond after an earlier escape from Vaughan's. Was killed, allegedly while trying to escape from Dublin Castle guardroom where he is also said to have been tortured for information concerning the operation. Despite the risk, Collins went to the Pro-Cathedral and laid out McKee's body in uniform. (*See Hardy*)

McKELVEY, Joseph: Stewartstown, Co. Tyrone; Cyprus St, Belfast. Fianna Éireann organizer. Defended the Nationalist minority during the Belfast programs of 1920 (*see Chronology, July 1920*). OC 3rd Northern Div 1921. (*See Woods, Seamus*)

McKENNA, Kathleen: Secretary to Desmond Fitzgerald and Erskine Childers in the Department of Publicity during their terms of office. Closely connected with the publication of *The Irish Bulletin*. Her brother Tadhg was interned at Ballykinlar and the Curragh.

McKENNA, Tadhg: See *McKenna, Kathleen*.

McKEON, Sean: See *MacEoin, Sean*.

McKINNON: Maj BA. Threw a journalist into the River Liffey for his condemnatory writings. While Commander of H Coy Aux Div he was shot dead by the IRA when golfing at Tralee, Co. Kerry, 17 April 1921. This followed his relentless campaign against them.

McLEAN, Michael: Lowertown, Schull, Co. Cork. Lt West Cork Bde. Killed by Black and Tans after an abortive ambush on them at Gaggin 8 December 1920. (*See Hurley, Charlie*)

McLYSAGHT, Edward: Raheen, Co. Clare. Self-described 'back room boy' for East Clare IRA Bde. Member of Irish Convention 1917-18. Member of Dáil Industrial Resources Commission. His premises were raided 25 times by Crown Forces. He assisted Michael Brennan (*see Brennan Brothers*) with transport, etc. By chance, he brought Conor Clune to Dublin instead of Pat Hayes, Adj East Clare Bde. Clune was shot and McLysaght identified the body at King George V (now St Bricin's) Hospital. He vouched for (a) Clune's body not being disfigured and (b) Clune's not being a member of the IRA. (*See Pearson, William*)

McMAHON: Lt. (*See Angliss*)

MacMAHON, James (Rt Hon.): *See Duggan, Eamonn.*

McMAHON, Michael: *See Killaloe Murders.*

McMAHON, Peadar: *See Dunne, Peadar.*

McMAHON, Sean: Dublin. QMG IRA 1920 and 1921. In that capacity, was involved in planning for provision of arms and ammunition, often in very low supply. Participated in the Custom House burning operation 25 May 1921.

McMONAGLE, James. Sinn Féin Secretary, Glenswilly, Co. Donegal. Active in Donegal area.

MacNAMARA, James: Det. An agent for Collins at Dublin Castle. Confirmed that 'Jameson', was a spy, having been a member of a raiding party called out as a result of information received from 'Jameson'. Was dismissed from the service in 1921. (*See Redmond, W.C.F.*)

MacNAMARA, Martin: East Clare Bde. Distinguished himself in an action at Mountshannon. Deported February 1920 and endured hungerstrike at Wormwood Scrubs. Released after three weeks.

MacNEILL, Eoin: Glenarm, Co. Antrim; Ballyboden and Hatch St, Dublin. COS of the Irish Volunteers before Easter Week Rebellion. Was opposed to the policy of armed insurrection. Was not informed of Rebellion plans. Became suspicious when he read of widescale manoeuvres in newspapers on Holy Thursday. Went to Pearse and on being informed of the plans, reluctantly agreed on the assurance of arms being landed at Fenit before the Rebellion. On Saturday morning, learning that no arms had been landed, he felt deceived. He inserted a notice in Sunday's newspapers cancelling the manoeuvres and sent despatches to leaders throughout the country saying that the Rebellion was cancelled. No rising took place in the country therefore; a further order from Pearse urging one caused utter confusion. Arrested after Easter Week, MacNeill accepted some responsibility for the Rebellion at his trial on 22 May. He was sentenced to life imprisonment but released under the 1917 amnesty. Member of Sinn Féin Executive October 1917. Was involved in a controversial agreement with the Irish Parliamentary Party on election tactics for Northern seats 1918. Minister for Industry and Commerce in the April 1919 Government. Professor of Early Irish History at University College Dublin from 1909. (*See Hobson, Bulmer*)

Mac NEILUS, Donncadha (Denis McNELLIS): Volunteer Cork No 1 Bde. Resisting arrest in November 1918, fired on his apprehenders, wounding a constable, thus becoming one of the first to open fire on a constable since 1916. Many disapproved but Collins supported his action. Was rescued from Cork Jail 11 November 1918.

MACPHERSON, Ian (Rt Hon.): British Chief Secretary for Ireland 1918-20. Thwarted American Peace Conference attempt to have the Irish case heard at the Paris Peace Conference of 1919. With Lloyd George, Lord French and high-ranking officers of the RIC, was found guilty by coroner's jury of the murder of Tomás MacCurtain, 1920.

MACREADY, Nevil (Sir): Chief of London Police. Appointed Commander-in-Chief of British Forces in Ireland 1918-20. Issued the December 1920 Proclamation warning of the death penalty for possession of arms, explosives, *etc*. Party to the Truce agreement 1921. Assisted the Truce Observation subcommittee.

McSWINEY, Eugene (Rev Fr): Fairview, Dublin. Gave spiritual assistance to Sean Treacy after his shooting at Talbot St, 14 October 1920.

MacSWINEY, Mary: Cork. Sister of Terence (*below*). Testified in Washington before commission on conditions in Ireland 1919. With Joe MacDonagh, sought imposition of restrictions on Treaty delegates in Dáil.

MacSWINEY, Terence: Cork. Brother of Mary (*above*). 2 i/c to Tomás MacCurtain in Cork during Easter Week 1916. With a BA permit, travelled to Kerry with MacNeill's countermanding order concerning the Rebellion. Arrested February 1917 but released under amnesty June. Elected to the First Dáil for West Cork. Seconded Cathal Brugha's motion on the swearing of allegiance to the Irish Republic and the Dáil by all deputies and Volunteers 20 August 1919. Helped establish the Arbitration Courts. Elected Deputy Lord Mayor of Cork in the January election of 1920 and Lord Mayor in March after Tomás MacCurtain's death. Comdt Cork No 1 Bde. Arrested 12 August 1920 and sentenced to two years' imprisonment for possessing an incriminating document. With ten others, went on hunger-strike. All but he were released after three days. Deported 22 August. Attempts were made to force-feed him on 21 October. Died after a 74-day hunger-strike 25 October 1920. (*See Butterfield, T.C.; Cohalan, D.F.*)

MADDEN, Pat: Comdt 3rd Roscommon Bn. Led South Roscommon contingent at Scramogue ambush 23 March 1921. (*See Leavy, Sean; Peek, Alfred*)

MAGEE, Peter: *See Intelligence Section.*

MAGNIER (Very Rev Canon): PP. Dunmanway, Co. Cork. Refused to have his bell tolled on Armistice Day. Killed by Auxiliaries 15 December 1920, having rebuked them for shooting Timothy Crowley. (*See Harte*)

MAGUIRE, Conor: Cong, Co. Mayo. Sinn Féin supporter. Helped draft Constitution and Rules of Court for the Sinn Féin Courts. Republican Court Judge. Land Settlement Commissioner. High and Supreme Court Judge 1920. (*See Ruttledge, P.J.*)

MAGUIRE, J.: Bde Commander 1st Eastern Div 1921.

MAGUIRE, Sam: Mallabracka, Dunmanway, Co. Cork. Prominent member of GAA, Gaelic League and IRB in London. Post Office civil servant.

Recruited Collins into IRB and became his Chief IO in London. Controlled all major operations in England and assisted in the communication of information through the Post Office. Was at one stage one of the most wanted men in England, without the authorities knowing he was in their employment.

MAGUIRE, Tom: Cross, Cong, Co. Mayo. Comdt South Mayo Bde. Commanded the Bde Flying Column, mainly of Ballinrobe personnel. With 30 men, held Tourmakeady against a large contingent of Crown Forces. Finally forced to withdraw, his escape route was blocked by British reinforcements. He established a hasty defence at Tournawoade and was wounded there. The action (3 May 1921) caused the withdrawal of RIC garrisons from Cuilmore, Kinnury and Derrypark. OC 2nd Eastern Div 1921. (See Kilroy, Michael; O'Brien, M.J.)

MAHER, Jerry: Sgt RIC. Confidential clerk to County Insp Supple at Naas. Passed on details of a new cipher to Collins through a confidante, Sean Kavanagh. Continued to co-operate with the passing of information and refused promotion in order to do this work. Realizing that suspicion of his activities was being aroused, resigned at the end of 1920 but was replaced by another willing member of the force, Patrick Casey, who continued assisting the Volunteers' Intelligence Section, again through Kavanagh, until Kavanagh's arrest and imprisonment in Kilmainham.

MAHER, Patrick: Galbally, Co. Tipperary. Hanged 7 June 1921 for alleged involvement in the Knocklong rescue of Sean Hogan. (*See Foley, Edward*)

MAHON, Bryan T. (Sir): Gen. C-in-C of the British Forces in Ireland 1916-18. Prohibited the unauthorized carrying or possession of arms in certain areas February 1918.

MAHON, Michael: *See Sweeney, Bernard.*

MALLIN, Michael: Emmet Hall, Inchicore, Co. Dublin. Comdt Citizen Army. Appointed its COS by James Connolly prior to Easter Week Rebellion. Suggested the GPO as HQ for the Rebellion. Commanded the St Stephen's Green garrison on Easter Monday and successfully supervised its evacuation to the College of Surgeons on Tuesday. Before the surrender he lowered the flag and flew a white flag, then joined Countess Markievicz in leading out the troops. Court-martialled and sentenced to death. Executed at Kilmainham 8 May 1916.

MALONE, Eamonn: Athy, Co. Kildare. Comdt Carlow Bde which extended into parts of Kildare, Wicklow and Laois.

MALONE, Michael: South Circular Rd, Dublin. Lt, later Capt. Killed at 25 Northumberland Rd, having played a major part in the battle of Mount St Bridge 27 April 1916, when British reinforcements moving from Kingstown (Dun Laoghaire) to the city were met, causing heavy casualties.

MALONE, Tomás: Tyrrellspass, Co. Westmeath. Using the name Sean Forde, represented IRA GHQ in Limerick, ostensibly organizing the Dáil Loan but in effect rallying the Galtee

Bn, mainstay of the East Limerick Bde. Took charge of the assault on Ballylanders Barracks, wounding three and capturing munitions. Also led the attack on Kilmallock Barracks where one sgt and one constable were killed and the barracks burned 27-28 May 1920. An outstandingly successful leader in East Limerick area, he became its Bde Comdt.

MANLEY, Tadhg: Ballinaglough, Carrignavar, Co. Cork. Member of Cork No 1 Bde. Mingled with spectators at a bowl game to assist an ambush of Cameron Highlanders. Carried out attack on Carrigtwohill Barracks 3 January 1920. Arrested Midleton. Imprisoned Cork, Maidstone and Brixton. Severely punished in prison for refusing to wear prison garb. Released after hunger-strike.

MANNIX, Daniel (Most Rev Dr): Charleville, Co. Cork. Archbishop of Melbourne 1917. Opponent of conscription and champion of Irish independence. Returning from a tour of USA in 1920, where he had met de Valera, British authorities forbade a proposed visit to Ireland. His ship was boarded off Cork and he was arrested 8 August. He was taken to Penzance and barred from speaking in predominantly Irish-populated areas in England.

MANSFIELD Brothers: *See Wyse, Joe.*

MARKEY (Rev Fr): PP, Clonbroney, Co. Longford. Escaped from RIC and Black and Tans, having been sentenced to death for not giving information on Const Cooney's death 2 November 1920.

MARKIEVICZ, Constance (Countess): Buckingham Gate, London; Lissadel, Co. Sligo; Dublin. Citizen Army. Vice-Comdt to Michael Mallin at St Stephen's Green during Easter Week Rebellion when she fought in full uniform, having arrived in an open car accompanied by two Fianna Éireann ADCs to take up duty. After the surrender she refused a British offer of transport but marched her detachment away. Tried and sentenced to death, commuted to life imprisonment. Detained at Aylesbury until general amnesty of June 1917. Led Thomas Ashe funeral cortège with revolver slung at waist. Became a convert to Catholicism August 1917. Arrested in May 1918 for alleged part in supposed 'German Plot'. Deported and imprisoned in Holloway. Elected for St Patrick's Division, Dublin, December 1918, becoming the first woman elected to Parliament. Refused to take her seat. Member of the First Dáil and first Minister for Labour April 1919. Imprisoned in Cork and Mountjoy during her Ministry. Minister for Labour in May 1921 Dáil.

MARREN, M.J.: Mount Irwin, Gurteen, Co. Sligo. Capt Killavil Coy and later Comdt 3rd (Ballymote) Bn, Sligo Bde. Prominent in many actions including the attack on RIC Barracks at Collooney, the Ratra ambush, an attack on the Black and Tans at Keash Hill and several train raids. Imprisoned. Drowned while bathing at Strandhill a few days after his release and the day after the Truce 12 July 1921.

MARSHALL, John: Bandon, Co. Cork. Intelligence agent for West Cork Bde. His home was used by Tom Barry to escape during the Bandon fight 23 February 1921. RIC Const Perrier was shot dead in the incident.

MARTIN (Miss): Ballinalee, Co. Longford. Her house was surrounded to trap Sean MacEoin 7 January 1921. RIC Insp McGrath was killed as MacEoin fought his way out.

MARTIN, Frank: *See McGee.*

MARTIN, Hughie: *See McGuinness, C.J.*

MASON, Susan: Brendan Rd, Dublin. Private and confidential secretary to Collins. Endured an enormous workload under extremely difficult conditions, forced to move location frequently, to carry despatches under cover, etc.

MAXWELL, John (Sir): Maj Gen. Sent with plenary powers from the British Parliament to command British Forces here. Arrived at North Wall 0200 hours on Friday 28 April 1916 and ordered immediate closing in on the Volunteers. He had exacted the surrender by the following evening. Introduced repressive measures here. Wrote to Dr O'Dwyer, Bishop of Limerick, asking him to transfer clergy sympathetic to the rebellion. Recalled 13 November.

(Names with prefixes Mc and Mac are both alphabetized as Mac.)

MEAGHER, Miss: *See Fox.*

MEE, Jeremiah: Const RIC: *See Smyth, Brice-Ferguson.*

MELLOWS, Herbert: Brother of Liam (*below*). Arrested and deported after the Easter Week Rebellion. Released but re-arrested February 1917 and again deported.

MELLOWS, Liam: Castletown, Co. Wexford. Deported with Ernest Blythe before Easter Week. Returned to attempt a rebellion in Galway. An IRB member of the committee of the Irish Volunteers. With HQ in Kilineen, mobilized 1000 Galway Volunteers and led minor actions in Clarinbridge, Oranmore and Athenry. After the Rebellion, moved through Limerick and Cork disguised as a nun. He sailed via England to New York where he became recognized as leader of the '1916 Exiles'. He negotiated on arms importation from Germany to Ireland. Worked with John Devoy on the *Gaelic American*. Returned to Dublin 1921. Appointed Director of Purchases in succession to the imprisoned Joe Vize and held that appointment at time of Truce.

MEREDITH, James Creed: KC. Chaired the board of barristers that drew up the Rules of Court for Republican Courts June 1920.

MIDLETON (Viscount-Lord): The Grange, Midleton, Co. Cork. Gave evidence before the Royal Commission into the Easter Week Rebellion, stressing his frequent pleas to repress sedition in Ireland prior to the Rebellion. Was spokesman for the Southern Unionists in 1921. Accepted de Valera's invitation to a Dublin conference on 4 July 1921 and brought his terms for a Truce to Lloyd George.

MILLING, J.C.: Magistrate shot in Westport, where he later died, 29 March 1919.

MILLS: Maj. Commanded the Regular Army backup troops at Croke Park on Bloody Sunday afternoon 21 November 1920. Reported adversely on behaviour of Black and Tans there.

MILROY, Sean: Tyrone. Member of the Sinn Féin Executive 1917. Member of the organizing committee for the National Council of 1917. Seconded Cathal Brugha's Constitution 1917. Defeated in the East Tyrone election April 1918. Arrested April 1918 for alleged part in the supposed 'German Plot'. Deported and imprisoned in Lincoln Jail. Drew a cartoon of a man with a key similar to that of prison gate as part of escape plan. (The key broke when inserted by Boland and Collins. Allegedly de Valera used another key manufactured inside.) He escaped with de Valera and Sean McGarry 3 February 1919. Interned at Ballykinlar 1921.

MITCHELL, Sean: Cloon, Co. Leitrim. Appointed Vice-Comdt Leitrim Bde at Gorvagh August 1918. Bde Comdt 1919, replacing Ned O'Brien. Organized reprisals after Selton ambush. (See Connolly, Sean)

MOLONEY, Con: Tipperary. Helped organize South Tipperary Bde during Treacy's imprisonment. 2 i/c Tipperary Bn, Bde Adj and Acting Comdt at times. Present at the raided Bde conference known as the 'Blackcastle Races' 12 September 1920. Delivered an oration at Sean Treacy's interment in Kilfeakle Cemetery. (See Chronology, 12 September 1920)

MOLONEY, Thomas Francis (Rt Hon.): Lord Justice. One of three Commissioners appointed to inquire into the Sheehy Skeffington, McIntyre and Dickson deaths at Portobello. (See Simon, John)

MONAGHAN, Alf: Belfast. Assisted Liam Mellows in the Galway area during the Easter Week Rebellion. Brother of Charles (below).

MONAGHAN, Charles: Belfast. Member of the party sent to implement Casement's arms-landing plan. Despite escaping from the car, he was drowned at Ballykissane Pier, Co. Kerry, 21 April 1916. (See Keating, Con; McInerney, Thomas; Sheehan, Donal)

MONAHAN, Peter: Bandon, Co. Cork. Scottish soldier of Irish parents in the Cameron Rgt of the BA posted to Cobh after the Great War. Deserted and joined the West Cork Bde December 1920. Assisted with explosives and was involved in most of the Bde's major activities. KIA at Crossbarry 19 March 1921.

MONTEAGLE (Lord): Chairman of the PR (proportional representation) Society 1920. Advocated national self-government within the Empire and decried partition 1920.

MONTEITH, Robert: Former BA Capt dismissed from the Ordnance Survey, Phoenix Park, for associations with the Volunteer movement. Accompanied Casement from Germany and landed at Banna Strand with him 1916.

MOONEY, Patrick: Commanded 2nd (Trim) Bn Meath Bde 1919. Active throughout the struggle. Led the attack on Ballivor Barracks 31 October 1919. With Sean Hayes, Vice-Comdt Meath Bde, he led the attacking section at Trim Barracks attack 30 September 1920. Assistant Training Officer Div Staff 1st Eastern Div 1921. (See Dunne, Barney)

MOORE, Maurice: Cobh, Co. Cork. Executed in Cork 28 February 1921.

MORAN, Patrick: Crossna, Boyle, Co. Roscommon. Member of Jacob's garrison Easter Week 1916. Imprisoned Knutsford and Wormwood Scrubs. Later Capt D Coy 11th Dublin Bn. Despite having an alibi, he was hanged for alleged part in the assassination of a British officer on Bloody Sunday 21 November 1920. So sure was he of his innocence being established that he chose to forgo his place in the Kilmainham jailbreak of March 1921. Hanged at Mountjoy 14 March 1921. (*See Whelan, Thomas*)

MORELAND, George: *See Stapleton.*

MORRIS, M.C.: Lt 11th East Surrey Rgt. Ordered the arrest of Sheehy Skeffington on Portobello Bridge and had him escorted to the barracks Easter Tuesday 1916.

MORRISSEY, John: *See Grealy, John.*

MORRISSEY, Paddy: Appointed by IRA HQ to command Leitrim units after Sean Connolly's death.

MORRISSEY, Sean: Clonmel, Co. Tipperary. With Frank Drohan, conveyed purchased arms from Waterford in preparation for Easter Week. Survived an RIC check. Assisted Drohan in all Clonmel activities.

MOYLAN, Sean: Comdt Newmarket Bn Cork No 2 Bde and Bde Commander 1918. Used a cannon taken from Ross Castle, Killarney, and equipped for use. Assisted Liam Lynch in the capture of Gen Lucas. Commanded the ambush party at Tureengarriffe 28 January 1921 and at Clonbanin 5 March 1921 where British casualties included Col Comdt H.R. Cumming. Was captured by the Gloucesters 16 May 1921. (*See Armstrong-Holmes, Philip*)

MULCAHY, Arthur: Currabeha Co. Cork. Was taken from his home and shot by Black and Tans 22 March 1921. Dying body cast into a military truck. On making inquiries about his whereabouts next day his father and sister were shown his mutilated body in a shed near barracks. At his funeral people were also harassed.

MULCAHY, Paddy: *See McCormick, Michael.*

MULCAHY, Richard: Waterford. 2 i/c to Thomas Ashe at Ashbourne attack Easter Week 1916. Arrested after the Rebellion and interned at Frongoch until December 1916. On his return, became Comdt 2nd Dublin Bn. Comdt Dublin Bde 1917. Director of Training October 1917. Appointed COS by the National Executive of the Volunteers March 1918, a position which he held throughout the war, although some sources point out that he was deputy to Brugha, who remained COS until March 1919. Elected for Clontarf Div, Dublin, 1918. Minister for Defence in First Dáil from January to April 1919 when he became Assistant Minister for Defence. With Cathal Brugha, brought Volunteers under Dáil control. Narrowly escaped capture on a number of occasions.

MULCAHY, Thomas: Mourne Abbey, Co. Cork. Executed in Cork Jail 28 April 1921.

MULLIGAN, Mick: Clonfin, Co. Longford. Coy Comdt Granard Coy. Suggested Clonfin as an ambush position and surveyed the area for the ambush there 2 February 1921. Participated in that and many other actions.

MULLINS, Billy: Tralee, Co. Kerry. Sworn into IRB by Pearse. Said to have carried message from Casement in Kerry to Pearse and Connolly in Dublin on Good Friday before Easter Week Rebellion. Arrested after his return and imprisoned at Frongoch. Released December 1916 but re-arrested January 1917 and deported. Imprisoned for illegal drilling, he went on hunger-strike in Cork Jail and Dundalk before being released. Other imprisonments and hunger-strikes followed. Bde QM Kerry No 1 Bde and member of Flying Column.

MULLOY, Fergus B.: Allegedly the last British spy who attempted to contact Collins during the war. He worked in the Pay Office at Parkgate and promised arms and passes to Batt O'Connor, Collins's driver. After initial promises to acquire arms proved fruitless he offered to take Liam Tobin, Cullen and Frank Thornton inside Dublin Castle to obtain information. They refused but requested assistance in executing a British Col instead. This officer vacated his house soon afterwards and Mulloy was found dead in Wicklow St March 1920.

MUNRO: Governor of Mountjoy Jail during the hunger-strike of April 1920. Involved in a battle of wits with Peadar Clancy for its duration.

MURPHY: Glan, Co. Clare. Fifteen-year-old member of Fianna Éireann killed by Crown Forces at his home 14 August 1919.

MURPHY, Con: Rathmore, Co. Kerry. Executed 1 February 1921 for alleged possession of firearms and ammunition. (*See Lynch, Patrick*)

MURPHY, Humphrey: Prominent member of Kerry No 2 Bde and appointed its Comdt after a period as QM. He attended the meeting at Kippage at which 1st Southern Div was formed 26 April 1921. (*See Rice, J.J.*)

MURPHY, James: Killarney St, Dublin. Youth arrested with Patrick Kennedy at Talbot St, Dublin, 9 February 1921. Taken to Dublin Castle and found dying in a field at Clonturk Park, Drumcondra, on the following morning. Before dying he told how he and Kennedy were taken to the field and their heads covered with buckets before being shot. Black and Tans were court-martialled but acquitted. (*See Kennedy, Patrick; King, 'Tiny'*)

MURPHY, Jim ('Spud'): Clonakilty, Co. Cork. Member of West Cork Bde. Bn Column Leader 2nd (Clonakilty) Bn 1921. Led a party who shot a constable dead at Clonakilty 27 July 1920. In action at Kilmichael, Burgatia and Crossbarry. Trapped in a public house in Rosscarbery in June 1921, he ended a long siege by escaping and making his getaway by boat.

MURPHY, Joe: Cork. Untried and unsentenced, endured a 79-day hunger-strike. Died in Cork Jail 25 October 1920. ★

★ Joe Kenny, Con Neenan and Michael Fitzgerald also on hunger-strike. The world's longest hunger-strike ever survived lasted 94 days, from 11 August to 12 November, at Cork Jail. The survivors were: Michael Burke, John Crowley, Peter Crowley, Thomas Donovan, Sean Hennessy, Joseph Kelly, Michael O'Reilly, John Power and Christopher Upton.

MURPHY, Richard: South William St, Dublin. KIA within Clanwilliam House during the battle of Mount St Bridge 27 April 1916. His body was burned in the house when it was set on fire.

MURPHY, Seamus: Comdt Galway Bde 1917 pending release from prison of Larry Lardner, who was elected as Connaught member of the IRB Supreme Council 19 November 1917. Led attack on Loughgeorge Barracks May 1920. Other Bde actions took place at Castlehackett, Oranmore, Roxboro and Ardrahan.

MYERS: Dublin. Lt in charge of the Dublin Fire Bde Easter Monday and Tuesday 1916 while its Capt was not present. He denied Gen Maxwell's allegations that the brigade had been fired upon by Volunteers although Purcell, the Capt, supported them.

MYLES, Jerry: Tralee, Co. Kerry. Volunteer Kerry No 1 Bde. KIA at Castlemaine 1 June 1921. (*See O'Connor, Tom*)

NATHAN, Matthew (Rt Hon Sir): Lt Col. Under-Secretary to the Lord-Lt of Ireland 1916. Gave evidence before the Royal Commission of Inquiry into the Easter Week Rebellion. The Commission found that, in the absence of Birrell, he had not sufficiently impressed on the Chief Secretary the need for more active measures to remedy the situation in Ireland prior to the Rebellion.

NATIONALITY: IRB-funded journal that replaced the suppressed *Sinn Féin*. Edited by Arthur Griffith and Sean T. O'Kelly, no Dublin printer would handle it, so it was printed in Belfast. It was followed by *Éire* and *Scissors and Paste*.

NEENAN, Con: *See footnote to Murphy, Joe.*

NEILAN, Mattie: Kilcolgan, Co. Galway. Participated in Easter Week activities in Galway. Imprisoned in Frongoch. A student in University College, Galway, 1917 to 1919, he was forced to go on the run.

NELIGAN, David: Templeglantine, Co. Limerick; Booterstown, Dublin. Det G Div DMP 1919-20. British Secret Service 1921. Agent for Collins in Dublin Castle. Informed Eamonn Broy of Det Insp Redmond's intention of capturing Collins after the Hoey and Barton killings. Broy in turn alerted Collins. He volunteered for secret service and memorized the oath of allegiance, passwords, *etc.*, and passed them on. He feigned a rift with Broy to further their effectiveness. As a result, he remained the last agent in the Castle after Broy's and McNamara's arrests in 1921.

NEWBURY, W.E.: Capt Queen's Rgt. Killed at 92 Lr Baggot St, Dublin, Bloody Sunday morning 21 November 1920. His dead body was seen hanging from a window for many hours.

NICHOLLS: *See Rennie.*

NÍ RIAN, Eilis: Listreena, Lenamore, Co. Longford. Appointed to Dáil staff 1920. Att Ard Craobh of C na mB and became a member of its executive 1920. Assisted Countess Markievicz, Joe McGrath and Joseph McDonagh during their terms of office in the Ministry of Labour. Arranged safe movement of men on the run in the city and looked after the welfare of relatives of imprisoned or deceased Volunteers.

NIXON: *See McCartney.*

NOLAN, George (George Brent): Galway. Returned from New York to take part in the struggle. Acted as despatch rider for Collins. Escaped to Canada.

NORWAY, A.H.: Secretary of the Post Office in Ireland. Defended his employees before the Royal Commission of Inquiry into the Easter Week Rebellion. He told how the complete staff were turned out of the building by Volunteers with the exception of a female telegraphist who remained to nurse a wounded sergeant.

NOYK, Michael: Baggot St, Dublin. Solicitor. Defended the men arrested in connection with the abortive Tolka Bridge ambush November 1920. Rendered legal assistance at the purchasing of accommodation for the Dáil and the Irish Volunteers HQ. Solicitor at Dublin Republican Courts during the Black and Tan period. As Sean MacEoin's solicitor, agreed to smuggle a gun to him in Mountjoy so that he could shoot his way free. The plan was abandoned.

NUNAN, Sean: Returned from England for Easter Week Rebellion. Arrested after it, brought back to England and tortured. Pressure brought to bear on him and on his brother to join BA. Was one of four clerks of the First Dáil and caller of its roll (Diarmuid O'Hegarty, Risteard Ó Foghladha and Patrick Sheehan were the others). Toured USA furthering the National Loan in 1919, as a secretary to de Valera, and married a co-worker for the effort, Anne Ryan.

NYHAN, John ('Flyer'): Clonakilty, Co. Cork. Bn Engineer 2nd (Clonakilty) Bn West Cork Bde. Staff Capt, No 1 Cork Bde. Arrested March 1920 and imprisoned in Cork, Belfast and Wormwood Scrubs. Released, June 1920. In action at Ring Coastguard Station and Clonakilty. One of the selected snipers who opened the Kilmichael ambush. Fought with the Flying Column until his capture at Shannonvale 26 December 1920. Imprisoned at Ballykinlar.

Ó BAOIGHILL, E.: Capt, Vice-Comdt 4th (Killybegs) Bn South Donegal Bde 1919. A raid on Rossan Point Coastguard station by members of Donegal Flying Column was planned for 27 June 1920. On 1 June, Ó Baoighill became aware of the imminent arrival of British reinforcements in the area. He immediately mustered a tiny party and led a raid on his own initiative. Some arms were captured.

Ó BEIRNE, Joseph: Leitrim. Killed by Crown Forces at Selton ambush 13 March 1921.

O'BRENNAN Family: Tullamore, Co. Offaly. Seamus: Lt Irish Volunteers. Member of GPO garrison Easter Week Rebellion. Town Councillor for Dublin. Imprisoned Wormwood Scrubs. Lily: Member of Erskine Childers' propaganda staff at Rathgar 1921. Accompanied the Treaty delegation to London. Ned, Frank & Alo: Volunteers.

Ó BRIAIN, Barra: Dublin. On active service in Carlow, Cork and Dublin areas during the period 1920-21.

Ó BRIAIN, Liam: Dublin & Galway. F Coy 1st Bn Dublin Bde. Fought at a number of locations in St Stephen's Green zone during Easter Week Rebellion, having returned from the Midlands where he distributed MacNeill's countermanding order. Promoted to Cpl during the week. Imprisoned in Richmond Barracks after his arrest, then at Wandsworth and Frongoch. Defeated in the Mid-Armagh election of 1918 but only by 2000 votes in an area where he was a complete stranger. Interned in Belfast 1919 and 1920. Wrote for *New Ireland*. Republican Judge for Galway/Connemara 1920. Arrested and imprisoned in Galway. Interned in the Curragh 1921.

O'BRIEN, Art: Acted as Ambassador in London during the entire struggle. President of the Irish Self-determination League formed in England March 1919. Member of the Truce Observation subcommittee 1921. Presented the Irish Treaty delegates to Lloyd George 11 October 1921. (*See 'Jameson'*)

O'BRIEN, Daniel: Liscarroll, Co. Cork. Volunteer captured 10 May 1921 at Aughrim, Liscarroll. Executed at Cork 16 May 1921.

O'BRIEN, Denis: Castlelack, Bandon, Co. Cork. Arrested early 1920. Released June 1920. In action at Kilmichael.

O'BRIEN, Eamonn: Galbally and Ardrahan, Co. Tipperary. Volunteer Capt and leader of the Galtee Bn which mobilized on Easter Sunday 1916 in preparation for a rebellion. Assisted the 'Big Four' after Soloheadbeg and participated in the Knocklong rescue. Went 'on the run'. Escaped to the USA via Cork and Dublin.

O'BRIEN, John: Warder in Mountjoy prison. Involved in communication between staff and hunger-strikers in 1920. Resigned in protest against some deceptions used to try to break the strikers.

O'BRIEN, M.J.: Neale, Co. Mayo. Adj South Mayo Bde. KIA near Tourmakeady, Co. Mayo, 3 May 1921 while attending to his wounded Bde Commander. (*See Maguire, Tom*)

O'BRIEN, Ned: *See Mitchell, Sean.*

O'BRIEN, Patrick: Liscarroll, Co. Cork. QM Cork No 2 Bde after capture of Jeremiah Buckley in August 1920. Succeeded Sean Moylan as Vice-Comdt 1921. Became Comdt Cork No 4 Bde when No 2 Bde was divided in 1921. Flying Column member and sometime leader. Injured in action at Milford Barracks 3 November 1920. In action at Clonbanin March 1921 when Col Comdt Cumming was killed. Led Rathcoole ambush 16 June 1921.

O'BRIEN, Patrick: Irish Parliamentary Party Whip. His death caused the Kilkenny by-election of August 1917 which was won by W.T. Cosgrave.

O'BRIEN, Seamus: Morriscastle, Kilmuckridge, Co. Wexford; Rathdrum, Co. Wicklow. Took part in Easter Week Rebellion at Enniscorthy and was imprisoned with Collins. In charge of Wicklow Bde which comprised 4th Bn led by Jack Smith and 5th Bn led by Matt Kavanagh. Killed during an attack on an RIC patrol at Rathdrum 12 February 1920.

O'BRIEN, Tom: Dripsey, Co. Cork. Executed 28 February 1921 at Cork.

O'BRIEN, William: Clonakilty, Co. Cork. Deported after Easter Week Rebellion. Interned in Reading and Frongoch. Released by amnesty. General Secretary of the ITGWU, and closely connected with the struggle. Member of the Anti-Conscription Conference. President of Trade Union Congress 1918. With Thomas Johnson, prepared a draft on social and democratic issues for the First Dáil 1919. Labour member of the 'National Cabinet' of April 1918. Arrested and deported January 1920. Imprisoned in Wormwood Scrubs and released having undergone a hunger-strike.

O'BRIEN, William: Mallow, Co. Cork. MP. Proprietor of *Cork Free Press* and renowned orator, yet his speech at Cork's City Hall after Easter Week was drowned by catcalls and songs. A member of the All for Ireland League that preached 'conference, conciliation and consent'. Yielded to Sinn Féin in 1918 election having warned Parliament that conscription would forever turn Irish people away from Westminster. Represented the All for Ireland League at the 'National Cabinet' of 1918.

O'CALLAGHAN, Daniel: Dripsey, Co. Cork. Executed 28 February 1921 at Cork.

O'CALLAGHAN, James (Rev Fr): Clogheen, Co. Cork. In reprisal for an ambush of RIC members at Blackpool the previous day, died some time after being shot by Crown Forces during a raid on his lodgings at Alderman Roche's home in Cork, 15 May 1921. Fr O'Flynn assisted him during his last hours.

O'CALLAGHAN, Leo: *See Sullivan.*

O'CALLAGHAN, Michael: Greenane, Co. Tipperary. IRB, Gaelic League member who favoured action in Tipperary during Easter Week. Was mobbed by British sympathizers on Easter Monday. Shot two members of the RIC at Moanow, Kilross, in the early hours of the following morning, the only such fatalities outside Dublin. He escaped to the USA.

O'CALLAGHAN, Michael: Elected Mayor of Limerick 1920. His home was subjected to numerous raids during office and after. Received a death notice and was killed at his home in his wife's presence March 1921. His wife attempted to save him and was herself injured. She refused to attend the inquiry into her husband's death. She was later elected in the 'Partition Election' of May 1921.

O'CAOIMH, Padraig: Roscommon and Cork. Leading personality in the GAA. Joined the Irish Volunteers in 1916 and served in 1st Cork Bde, attaining the rank of Capt. Arrested in 1920 and imprisoned until after the Treaty.

O'CARROLL, Richard: Camden St, Dublin. General Secretary, Brick and Stoneworkers' Union. Active during Easter Week Rebellion. Informed his wife that he had been deliberately shot while facing a wall with hands raised after his surrender 26 April. He died nine days later.

O'CONNELL: Coachford, Co. Tipperary. Const RIC shot dead with Const McDonnell in Soloheadbeg ambush, the first casualty of the war proper.

O'CONNELL (Rev Fr): PP Ballineen, Co. Cork. Confessor for members of Tom Barry's Flying Column before Crossbarry when he also blessed the Volunteers.

O'CONNELL, Christy: Eyeries, Co. Cork. Section Commander West Cork Bde Flying Column and Column Leader 1921. In action at Eyeries, Rosscarbery, Castletownbere and in events preceding Union Hall 1921. Commanded the flanking section (Section Seven) covering the Bandon approach at Crossbarry where his men turned the British attack.

O'CONNELL, Jack: *See Clancy, Patrick*.

O'CONNELL, Jack: Cobh, Co. Cork. Only survivor of Clonmult ambush, where he replaced Diarmuid Hurley as OC.

O'CONNELL, J.J. ('Ginger'): Sligo; Dublin. Comdt Irish Volunteers. Supported MacNeill's countermand before Easter Week Rebellion. Assistant Director of Training 1920. Disseminated information on guerrilla warfare. Succeeded Dick McKee as Director of Training 1920. One of a group who planned the burning of the Custom House. Assistant COS of IRA at time of Truce 1921. (See Stack, Austin)

O'CONNELL, Morgan (Sir): Lakeview, Killarney, Co. Kerry. Gave evidence before the Royal Commission of Inquiry into the Easter Week Rebellion, saying that the government had appointed Peace Commissioners who were unfit for the task and who attended Petty Sessions solely for the purpose of carrying out 'the most open and flagrant jobbery'.

O'CONNELL, Richard: Caherconlish, Co. Limerick. Comdt Mid-Limerick Bde's ASU. Combined with East Limerick Column for Dromkeen ambush 3 February 1921.

O'CONNELL, William: Drumconrath, Co. Meath. Sgt RIC. Awarded the King's Medal for conspicuous gallantry for his action during the Ashbourne attack 28 April 1916.

O'CONNOR, Art: Commissioner of Land Courts 1920. Minister for Agriculture (outside the Cabinet) August 1921.

O'CONNOR, Batt: Brendan Rd, Drumcondra, Dublin. Collins's driver. Negotiated the purchase of 6 Harcourt St for use as a National Loan HQ and constructed a secret recess for confidential documents there. His wife played a significant role in intelligence arrangements.

O'CONNOR, Johnny 'Blimey': Established wireless communications between GPO and other Volunteer locations, Easter Week Rebellion. (*See McEllistrim, Tom*)

O'CONNOR, Rory: Produced the 'Castle Order' showing plans for strong action by authorities against nationalist organizations. The authenticity of the order has been disputed. It helped sway MacNeill to initial consent regarding Easter Week Rebellion. Fought and was wounded during the Rebellion. Resigned from the IRB in protest against its not dispensing with secrecy. Director of Engineering with the IRA 1918. Directed operations in England including the Manchester Jail rescue of 1919 and the burnings in Liverpool 1920. Co-planner with Dick

McKee of the Mountjoy escape of Walshe, Patrick Fleming and Béaslaí 1919. Assisted the government in the control of food supplies and local administration.

O'CONNOR, Tom: Keel, Co. Kerry. Led the ambush at Castlemaine with the assistance of Tadhg Brosnan of Castlegregory, a prominent leader in Kerry No 1 Bde Flying Column. Three members of the Crown Forces were killed and one Volunteer, Jerry Myles.

O'CONNOR, Tommy and John: Members of North King Street garrison during the Easter Week Rebellion. Both interned. Tommy later imprisoned in Atlanta while actively campaigning on behalf of Devoy, McCartan, etc. He attempted to maintain communication between Devoy and Clan na Gael.

Ó CUILL, Micheál: Scrahanard, Carriganima and Cork City. Councillor. B Coy Cork City Volunteers. Irish language enthusiast. Fianna Éireann and C na mB organizer. Wrote under pen-name 'Muisire'. Close associate of MacCurtain and MacSwiney. Refused to accept MacNeill's countermand, took train to Dublin and had to walk from Sallins. Consequently, he has been described as 'The Man Who Walked To Dublin'. Imprisoned Richmond Barracks, Lewes and Frongoch before 1917 amnesty. Warned MacCurtain of pending raids before the Lord Mayor's execution. Arrested on board the mailboat en route to Holyhead to attend Terence MacSwiney's removal. Released again after intervention of a colleague, Barry Egan.

O'DALY, Paddy: *See Daly, Paddy*.

O'DOHERTY, Joseph: Derry. Member of the Executive which planned the Easter Week Rebellion. Sean MacDermott sent him to Derry to organize Volunteers there. Held at Kilmainham after Rebellion. Elected for North Donegal to the First Dáil.

O'DOHERTY, Liam: Comdt 5th Dublin Bn. Responsible for studying the architectural structure of the Custom House during the planning of its burning.

O'DONAGHUE, Joseph: Ballinacargy, Co. Westmeath; Limerick. Taken away by 12 policemen during the night of 6/7 March 1921. His dead body was found at Jonesborough Ave, Limerick, next day. It was assumed that the 'Cairo Gang', having failed to kill the Bishop of Killaloe, were responsible. (*See Clancy, George; Fogarty, Michael; O'Callaghan, Michael*)

O'DONNELL, Peadar: Meenmore, Co. Donegal. ITGWU organizer. Has been described as the greatest agitator of his generation. Recruited some of Derry city's unemployed for permanent IRA service in Donegal. Was QM of 1st (Dungloe) Bn Donegal West Bde and later commanded the Bde.

O'DONNELL, Philly: *See Wyse, Joe*.

O'DONOGHUE, Florrie: Cork. Active during Easter Week Rebellion. Adj and IO Cork No 1 Bde. Active in the formation of the Bde's Flying Column and in many station attacks and ambushes. Div Adj 1st Southern Div April 1921. Succeeded P.S. O'Hegarty as member of the Supreme Council of the IRB for Munster.

O'DONOGHUE, Patrick: Greenley, Manchester. Collins contact there.

Assessed prospects for successful jailbreaks. Housed Collins and Boland before the de Valera rescue. Accompanied them to Lincoln and drove escapees to Newark, there prevailing upon a fellow taxi-driver to continue with thcm to Sheffield. Played a major part in the arrangements for the Manchester Jail escape of November 1919. Arrested in Manchester 1920.

O'DONOVAN, James: Roscommon. Imprisoned at Mountjoy and Kilmainham and participated in hunger-strike. Released but re-arrested and interned at Newbridge, Co. Kildare, from where he escaped. He experimented with explosives and invented the 'Irish Wallflower' and 'Irish Cheddar' devices. Received a hand injury while experimenting. Director of Chemicals with the IRA 1921.

O'DRISCOLL, Michael: Snave, Bantry. Lt in Coomhola Coy. In action at Crossbarry and Kilmichael.

O'DUFFY, Eoin: Castleblayney, Co. Monaghan. Joined the IRA in 1917. Elected Ulster member of IRB Supreme Council 19 November 1917. Bde Commander at the taking of Ballytrain Barracks 14 February 1920 when a substantial haul of weapons was taken. Jailed in Belfast, he commanded all Ulster and Connaught prisoners there in 1920. Director of Organization for a period 1921 and Deputy COS at time of Truce. First Commissioner of the Civic Guards.

O'DWYER (Most Rev Dr): Bishop of Limerick. Refused to comply with a request from Gen Maxwell to transfer clergy sympathetic to the Rebellion. (*See* Hayes, Rev Fr; Wall, Thomas, Rev Fr)

O'DWYER, Eamonn: Ballagh, Co. Tipperary. Housed Treacy's Easter Week meetings. Went to Limerick on Wednesday to study the position there and report back. Captured by RIC Saturday of that week. Imprisoned in Clonmel. Released January 1917. Later re-imprisoned. Subjected to forced feeding while on hunger-strike in Mountjoy.

O'DWYER, George: Capt Coon Coy IRA Kilkenny 1918, Commander of Flying Column 1920. Comdt Kilkenny Bde 1921. Led the Uskerty Wood ambush 2 May 1921.

O'DWYER, Liam: Eyeries, Co. Cork. Mobilized during Easter Week Rebellion. Prominent in organizing and training in Eyeries, Lauragh, Tahilla, Ardgroom and other areas. Led decoy parade during arms raid on Eyeries RIC barracks. Active at Ballycrovane Coastguard Station and other arms raids. Imprisoned Cork and Wormwood Scrubs 1919 and 1920. Comdt 6th (Beara) Bn West Cork Bde 1920-21.

O'FARRELL, Elizabeth: Dublin. Carried Pearse's instructions concerning the Easter Week Rebellion to the country. Conveyed his intention of surrendering to Brig Gen Lowe on Saturday 29 April. Brought surrender order to other garrisons. (*See* Grennan, Sheila)

Ó FATHAIGH, Padraig: Galway. His ambush and capture by the RIC at Kinvara Presbytery led to the firing of the opening rounds of the Easter Week Rebellion in Galway.

O'FLAHERTY, Sam: *See footnote to Sweeney, Joseph A.*

O'FLANAGAN, Michael (Rev Fr): Cloonfower, Castlereagh, Co. Roscommon; 14 Herbert Park, Dublin. Member of the organizing committee for the National Council. Spoke at election meetings, on one occasion leading supporters through a line of troops with fixed bayonets. Was Joint Vice-President of Sinn Féin with Arthur Griffith October 1917. Read the opening prayers at the First Dáil session 21 January 1919. Was reprimanded by the Hierarchy. Executive member of the Irish Agricultural Organization Society and Vice-President of the Gaelic League. Republican Court Judge. Participated in peace negotiations in 1920 and 1921. Took certain actions not approved by Sinn Féin standing committee and considered by some commentators to have been harmful. Went to USA and to Australia from where he was deported.

O'FLYNN, James Christopher (Rev Fr): Celebrated Cork Asylum Chaplain. Arrested in Dublin Easter Monday 1916 and released after interrogation. Provided shelter for prominent Cork Sinn Féin sympathizers in danger of being arrested, and was transferred to the North Cathedral in October 1920. Celebrated Requiem Mass for Terence MacSwiney 1 November 1920. Under Black and Tan fire, he administered the last rites to four RIC members blown to pieces by IRA in Quarry Lane 14 May 1921. (*See O'Callaghan, James*)

Ó FOGHLADHA, Risteard: *See Nunan, Sean.*

O'HANLON: *See Dillon, John.*

O'HANLON, John: Lackagh, Co. Galway. Shot dead in the presence of his family by Black and Tans 2 October 1920. His funeral cortège was also fired on.

Ó hANNAGÁIN, Donncadha: Mitchelstown, Co. Cork. Comdt East Limerick Bde Flying Column. Led the combined North Cork and East Limerick contingents in an ambush at Glencurrane 17 December 1920. Assisted Tom Barry at Kildorrery. Led the Grange ambush of 8 November 1920 and the Dromkeen ambush of 3 February 1921.

Ó h-ANNRACHÁIN, Micheál: New Ross, Co. Wexford; Carlow. Engaged in clerical duties at Volunteer HQ in Dawson St, Dublin, and was QM of the movement. Was a member of Jacob's factory garrison during Easter Week Rebellion. Court-martialled and sentenced to death. Executed at Kilmainham 4 May 1916.

O'HANRAHAN, Jim: Inistiogue, Co. Kilkenny. IRA. Comdt active in the Kilkenny area. Arrested November 1920 when Ernie O'Malley was discovered in his home during his organizational tour of that area.

O'HEGARTY, Diarmuid: Prominent in re-organization of Volunteers after Easter Week. Vice-Comdt 1st (Dublin) Bn Irish Volunteers. Elected to the Executive of the IRB 19 November 1917. Chief Clerk of the First Dáil. Arrested in Harcourt St, Dublin, 1919. Director of Organization IRA 1920. One of three assistant secretaries to Erskine Childers for the Treaty delegation. (*See Chartres, John; Lynch, Fionan; Nunan, Sean*)

O'HEGARTY, Sean and P.S.: Cork. Sean: Succeeded Terence MacSwiney as Comdt Cork No 1 Bde after Mac-Swiney's arrest August 1921. P.S.: Munster member of the Supreme Council of the IRB and close to Collins whom he swore into the movement in London. He later found himself growing closer to Griffith because of his non-violent outlook.

Ó h-EIDIN, Frank: Athenry, Co. Galway. Capt of the local Company of Volunteers that occupied Athenry Town Hall and attacked the RIC barracks during the Easter Week Rebellion 1916.

O'HIGGINS, Brian: Carrigaholt, Co. Clare. Arrested for alleged part in supposed 'German Plot' May 1918. Deported. Elected for West Clare December 1918. Founded the District Arbitration Courts in West Clare 1919.

O'HIGGINS, Kevin: Stradbally, Co. Laois. Joined Sinn Féin while a student. Imprisoned in 1918 for making a speech condemning conscription. Elected for Sinn Féin as MP for Laois (Queen's County). Active in the war. Minister outside the Cabinet assisting W.T. Cosgrave as Minister for Local Government 1921.

Ó h-IGHNE, M.: Glencolumcille, Co. Donegal. Took on marauding Black and Tans in Malinbeg area of Donegal 28 February 1921 but was himself shot dead.

O'KELLY, J.J. ('Sceilg'): Valentia, Co. Kerry. Editor of The Catholic Bulletin arrested 24 February 1917 after comment on the by-election in Roscommon. Deported. Read the 'Message to the Free Nations of the World' in Irish at the First Dáil session 21 January 1919. Minister for Culture outside the Cabinet in the First Dáil.

O'KELLY, Sean T.: Wellington St and Rutland St, Dublin. Volunteer Capt, Staff Officer to Pearse in the GPO during Easter Week Rebellion. Sent by Sean MacDermott to order Maurice Collins to release Bulmer Hobson. Deported and imprisoned. Elected Sinn Féin MP for Mid-Dublin 1918. Member of the committee that prepared the establishment of and constitution for the First Dáil. First Ceann Comhairle at April session of the Dáil 1919. Sent by government to open an Irish office in Paris in order to arrange Dáil representation at the peace conference and to promote the cause of independence 1919. Visited Rome and USA also.

O'KELLY de GALLAGH, Gerald Edward (Count): Portumna, Co. Galway. Sent by Arthur Griffith to further the cause of Irish independence at the League of Nations in Switzerland. Representative at the Department of Trade's consulate in Berne 1919.

O'LEARY, Jerry: Ten-year-old spectator shot dead in Croke Park during afternoon of Bloody Sunday 21 November 1920.

O'LEARY, John (Jackie): Comdt 6th (Firmount) Bn Cork No 1 Bde. Led Dripsey action and participated at Blarney Barracks action.

Ó LOCHLANN, Colm: Student in University College, Dublin under MacNeill. Helped convince him that the 'Castle Order' (q.v.) was a forgery. Picked up news of Aud's scuttling and, with Sean Fitzgibbon, conveyed it to The O'Rahilly. Awaited the occupants of the car which had the accident at Ballykissane Pier, requiring wireless expert Con Keating from the party to put Cahirciveen Wireless Station out of action.

O'LOUGHLIN, F. (Rev Fr): Army Chaplain at Portobello Barracks, Dublin. Was present at the exhumation of Sheehy Skeffington, Dickson and McIntyre and read the service at their reinterment. Gave evidence that Coade was a member of his Parish Sodality and was returning from one of its meetings when shot.

O'MAHONEY (Dr): RAMC. Held prisoner at the GPO at the outbreak of hostilities Easter Week. Assisted in the treatment of the wounded, including James Connolly.

O'MAHONEY, Dan: Comdt Kerry No 2 Bde which covered the mid-county and had its HQ in Killarney. The Bde had a Flying Column. O'Mahoney ordered the attack on Brosna RIC barracks.

O'MAHONEY, P.: See Whelan, Pax.

O'MAHONY, Patrick: Berrings, Co. Cork. Section Commander, 1 Cork Bde. Participated in Dripsey ambush and other engagements. Executed Cork Barracks 28 February 1921.

O'MAHONEY, Sean: Republican deputy for Fermanagh-Tyrone. Member of National Assembly August 1921. The only member of the Second Dáil who represented a northern constituency only.

Ó MAILLE, Padraic: Resisted arrest during 'German Plot' round-up. Still on the run in 1919 when he attended Dáil sittings.

O'MALLEY, Christopher.: Dublin. Member of Jacob's garrison, Easter Week Rebellion. Worked with Peadar Clancy in effecting the escape from Strangeways prison of Béaslaí, Stack, *etc.*, and worked on Mountjoy escapes with Rory O'Connor. Bde Adj of ASU Dublin Volunteers 1921.

O'MALLEY, Ernie: Castlebar, Co. Mayo; Dublin. Organizer of Volunteers and of many of their actions throughout the country using alias 'Bernard Stewart'. Participated in Easter Week Rebellion and in Tipperary actions at Hollyford (co-leader with Seamus Robinson), Drangan (injured by burns) and Rear Cross (injured by grenade). Capt HQ Staff South Tipperary Bde 1920. In action at Union Hall, Cork, and at Ballytrain, Monaghan. Captured while preparing for an attack on Inistiogue, Co. Kilkenny, December 1920. Imprisoned at Kilmainham from where he escaped with Teeling and Simon Donnelly September 1921. President of the first Land Court in East Limerick. Div Commander 2nd Southern Div, comprising Kilkenny, Limerick and portion of Tipperary 1921.

OMAN, William: Dublin. Citizen Army. Bugler who sounded the 'Fall In' at Liberty Hall for the start of the Easter Week Rebellion 1916. Participated in the action, at one stage being the sole occupant of the High St position.

O'MARA, James: Limerick. Director of Elections for Sinn Féin December 1918. Was called to USA by de Valera to direct the Dáil Loan campaign there October 1919. Was a trustee (with de Valera and Dr Fogarty) of the First

Dáil External Loan January 1920. Resigned from the Loan organization allegedly because of friction with de Valera.

O'MARA, Stephen: Alderman, later Mayor of Limerick. Member of the National Council Organising Committee 1917. Helped to promote Dáil Loan in USA 1919. Republican Judge. Arrested and imprisoned 1920.

O'MEARA, Seamus: Athlone, Co. Westmeath. Led an unarmed party to an ambush position at Crush Bridge with the intention of attacking Ballymore RIC Barracks but the plan to have arms delivered for the action went awry. Arrested and imprisoned in Galway and Mountjoy March 1920. Led a hunger-strike and was released after eight days. Active in raids on Athlone Tax and Revenue Office and Streamstown RIC Barracks, and Faheran ambush 19 October 1920, which was led by James Tormey.

Ó MUIRI, Sean: Cushendall, Co. Antrim. Active in National and Labour movements. Comdt Antrim Bn IRA. Participated in attacks on RIC barracks. Arrested 1920 and interned at Crumlin Rd, Belfast, and Rath Camp, Curragh, from where he was released after the Truce 1921.

Ó MUIRTHILE, Sean: Member of the Supreme Council of the IRB 1916. Particularly active with Diarmuid O'Hegarty in its revitalization. With Cathal Brugha's encouragement this pair were also prominent in re-organizing the Volunteers after the Easter Week Rebellion. Assisted Neil Kerr with arrangements for de Valera's secret passage to USA.

O'NEILL, Dick: Sailor. Throughout the war, assisted in arranging passage of key personnel. Attended to de Valera during his passage to USA.

O'NEILL, Ignatius: Milltown Malbay, Co. Clare. An ex-Irish Guardsman. Led 4th Bn Mid-Clare Bde personnel at Rineen ambush 20 September 1920 when three British soldiers were killed. They captured and burned Ruan RIC Barracks 14 October 1920.

O'NEILL, J.: See McGrath, John.

O'NEILL, Laurence (Rt Hon.): Dublin. Alderman. Refused to act as Crown Prosecutor at Easter Week trials but opted to be Counsel for the Defence. Lord Mayor of Dublin. Attempted to dissuade Thomas Ashe from persisting with his hunger-strike 1917. Intervened after Ashe's death and obtained terms from the Chief Secretary for Ireland, Henry Duke, which ended the strike. Convened the Mansion House Conference of 18 April 1918 which formed the 'National Cabinet' (see *Chronology*). Defended the right of the RIC to be present. Made incessant demands on behalf of the Mountjoy hunger-strikers April 1920. Arranged distribution of monies from the White Cross Fund, established in the USA for the relief of victims of the War of Independence, 1921. (See 'White Cross Fund,')

O'NEILL, Richard: Dunmanway, Co. Cork. 3 West Cork Bde. One of the nominees for reception of arms from the *Aud* at Banna Strand. Arrested 1919. Imprisoned in Cork and Wormwood Scrubs. Under the assumed name of Hurley, he worked on the construction of Kilworth Military Camp, Fermoy.

O'RAHILLY, Alfred: Listowel, Co. Kerry; Cork. Joined Sinn Féin 1916. As a member of Cork Corporation, proposed both MacCurtain and MacSwiney for Lord Mayor. Imprisoned Spike Island January-June 1921. Advised the Treaty delegation on constitutional issues.

O'RAHILLY (The): Herbert Park and Stillorgan Rd, Dublin; Ballylongford, Co. Kerry; England; USA. Foundermember of the Volunteers. Accused Pearse of attempting to start the Easter Week Rebellion without authority. Conveyed MacNeill's countermanding order to Limerick. When the Rebellion went ahead, arrived by car at the GPO to take part. Led the first party out of the GPO 28 April and was shot dead in Moore Street. (See Collins, Michael)

O'REILLY (Sgt): See Harris, Thomas.

O'REILLY, Joe: Bantry, Co. Cork. Close associate of Collins' in London, during Easter Week Rebellion, and in Stafford and Frongoch. Became his devoted accomplice, attending to his every need, carrying out confidential work and keeping constant vigil and track of his movements.

O'REILLY, Michael: See footnote to Murphy, Joe.

O'REILLY, Patrick & Stephen: Dublin. Brothers. When relatives arrived at George V Hospital to identify an IRA Capt, Patrick O'Reilly, they were horrified to discover the remains of his brother Stephen also. Some sources described Stephen as Assistant Adj of the Dublin Bde. Both were killed at the burning of the Custom House operation 25 May 1921.

O'REILLY, Sean: Lr Gardiner St, Dublin. 2 i/c of Citizen Army troops in City Hall area Easter Week Rebellion. Took command when Sean Connolly was killed and was himself killed a few hours afterwards, at 1800 hours 24 April 1916.

O'REILLY, W.M.: 2nd Dublin Bn. Commanded Imperial Hotel garrison Easter Week. Vice-Comdt Dublin Bde. Comdt of North Camp, Frongoch, until removed to Reading when his fellow prisoners refused to work. Attended meeting which proposed the holding of a National Convention of re-organization of the Volunteers 1917. IRA Director of Training for a period 1918.

O'RIORDAN, Sean: Kilmallock, Co. Limerick. Bn Commander 1st Galtee Bn. Led the Kilmallock contingent at the attack on Ballylanders RIC Barracks 26 April 1920 when a large quantity of arms was seized and the barracks burned. Arrested 12 May. (See Malone, Tomás)

O'ROURKE, Dan: Tarmon, Co. Roscommon. National Teacher. Comdt South Roscommon Bde 1920. In charge of the operation against Frenchpark Barracks 2 October 1920. This was a reprisal for the loss of Michael Glavey, Patrick Glynn and Michael Keane who were ambushed by the 9th Lancers having burned Ballinlough Barracks. Black and Tans raided O'Rourke's schoolhouse while he was teaching his class but he escaped under fire. Was succeeded as Bde Comdt by F. Simon 1921.

O'SHANNON, Cathal: Randalstown, Co. Antrim. Member of Gaelic League and IRB. Mobilized Volunteers at Coalisland for Easter Week Rebellion. Arrested and interned at Frongoch and Reading. Released by general amnesty of 1917. Editor of *The Voice of Labour*. Irish Labour Party delegate to the International Labour Conference at Berne February 1919. Arrested in London 1920. Imprisoned at Mountjoy but released after a 17-day hunger-strike. Vice-President of the Irish Labour Party 1921. (*See Johnson, Thomas*)

O'SHEA Patrick: Castlegregory, Co. Kerry. Volunteer instructed by Austin Stack to organize pilots to bring the *Aud* into Fenit harbour. While attending to this and to the organizing of signal lights he actually came across Roger Casement in the custody of police.

O'SHEE, Poer: County Insp RIC. Among the party that roused Listowel RIC to mutiny 19 June 1920. (*See Smyth, Brice-Ferguson*)

O'SHEIL, Kenn: Special Commissioner for Land Courts 1920. Helped draft the Rules and Constitution for the Republican Courts June 1920.

Ó SIOCHFHRADHA, Padraig (An Seabhac): Burnham, Dingle, Co. Kerry. Volunteer organizer and Comdt 2nd (Dingle) Bn No 2 Kerry Bde. Gaelic League organizer and teacher. Imprisoned on a number of occasions.

O'SULLIVAN Brothers: Pat and Mick. Kilnamartyra, Co. Cork. With Dan Harrington and others, went to Millstreet 23 April 1916 in anticipation of being armed. The *Aud* incident prevented this. Pat, then Coy Capt, Ballyvourney Coy, and Harrington disarmed two members of the RIC at Béal na nGleanna 8 July 1918. Both brothers in action in unsuccessful attacks on Inchigeela Barracks, January and March 1920, and in ambushes at Geata Bán, 15 July 1920, and Slippery Rock, August 1920. During 1921 they were in action at Coolcahera, Coomnaclohy and in an attempt to sink Gen Strickland's craft at Cork Marina.

O'SULLIVAN, Dermot: Dublin. Sentenced to death for association with the abortive 'Drumcondra Ambush'. Reprieved. (*See Bryan, Thomas; Flood, Frank; Kenworthy; Ryan, Bernard*)

O'SULLIVAN, Gearoid: Cork. Took part in Easter Week Rebellion as member of GPO garrison. Member of Dublin Bde staff. Elected to the Supreme Council of the IRB 19 November 1921. Close associate of Collins. Narrowly avoided arrest on a number of occasions. AG of the IRA 1919-21.

O'SULLIVAN, John L: Carrigroe, Clonakilty, Co. Cork. Volunteer. Cork No 3 Bde. Participated in many operations including those at Rosscarbery and Union Hall.

O'SULLIVAN John L: Milltown, Co. Cork. Captured early 1921 and interned at Spike Island.

O'SULLIVAN, Michael: Mitchelstown, Co. Cork. One of a pair of sentenced Volunteers who applied for a Writ of Prohibition. At an appeal heard by the House of Lords 16 June 1921, Military Courts and executions were found to be illegal. (*See Clifford, Patrick; Comyn, Michael*)

O'SULLIVAN, Patrick: Cobh, Co. Cork. Executed at Cork Jail 28 April 1921.

O'SULLIVAN, Ted: Bantry, Co. Cork. Comdt 5th Bantry Bn West Cork Bde 1919. Vice-Comdt West Cork Bde 1920-21. Led attack on Durrus Barracks 31 March 1920 in which a constable was killed. Served with Flying Column at Rosscarbery and Dunmanway.

O'SULLIVAN, Tom: Comdt South Wexford Bde 1921. Head centre of Wexford IRB.

PAORA, Siobhán (Bean an): 21 Henry St, Dublin. Acting Joint Treasurer, with Duggan, of Sinn Féin from 8 April 1919.

PARTRIDGE, William P.: Member of Dublin Corporation active during Easter Week. Participated in a shop-burning mission with Fred Ryan, who was killed 27 April 1916. Sent by Connolly to supervise the landing of weapons at Tralee prior to Rebellion. Arrested and sentenced to 25 years' penal servitude. Released April 1917. (*See Casement, Roger*)

PAUL, Patrick: Comdt 1 Bn, East Waterford Bde.

PEARSE, Margaret: (Same addresses as Padraic, *below*.) Mother of Padraic Pearse. Active in Sinn Féin electioneering campaigns. Herself elected May 1921, 'The Partition Election'. (*See McGuinness, Joe*)

PEARSE, Padraic: Great Brunswick St; Newbridge Ave; Sandymount Ave; Lisreaghan Tce; Rathfarnham, Dublin. IRB. Member of Military Council (with Plunkett and Ceannt). C-in-C of the Easter Week Rebellion. First President of the Irish Republic. Signatory and reader of the Proclamation. Met Connolly at 1100 hours Easter Monday at Liberty Hall. Joined him in leading the first contingent to the GPO at 1200 hours. Fought in GPO. Surrendered to Gen Lowe at 1530 hours Saturday 29 April 1916. First leader to be executed at Kilmainham 3 May 1916. (*See MacNeill, Eoin; O'Farrell, Elizabeth*)

PEARSE, William: (Same addresses as above.) Padraic's brother. Capt and Staff Officer GHQ Irish Volunteers. Acted as ADC to his brother. Arrested, court-martialled and sentenced to death. Executed at Kilmainham 4 May 1916.

PEARSON, William: Ex-BA Col. Doctor. Accompanied Edward McLysaght to a shed near Westland Row Church to examine Conor Clune's 13 wounds. His report was at variance with a claim that Clune was fired upon while attempting to escape from custody.

PEEK, Alfred (Sir, Bart): Capt. DSO. Commanded the 9th Lancers Squadron, Strokestown, Co. Roscommon. Threatened the burning of every house within five miles if one of his men was killed. His own will and letter decrying the IRA seized in a mail robbery. Shot dead in Scramogue ambush, Co. Roscommon, 23 March 1921. Some sources claim he was escorting arrested Black and Tans, who had misbehaved, for trial, and that colleagues of the arrested men, knowing of the planned ambush, tricked him into being on the escort himself. (*See Tennant*)

'PEEL': Alias for an Irishman who was a Lt Col in the BA and who worked closely with the 'Cairo Gang'. Participated in a number of assassinations including that of John A. Lynch. From his room in 22 Mount St he heard the IRA shooting on Bloody Sunday morning 21 November 1920. He barricaded his room door and made his escape when Black and Tans arrived on the scene.

PERCEVAL: Maj. Large landowner of Templehouse, Ballymote, Co. Sligo. His staff, informed of an impending raid for arms by Sligo Bde members, protected the mansion throughout the night but the attack took place next morning. Some sources claim that the conviction of Frank Carty for this raid on the evidence of Mrs Perceval was a case of mistaken identity.

PERCIVAL: Maj Essex Rgt. Ambushed near Newcestown, Co. Cork, October 1920. Particularly aggressive against West Cork Bde. Fought against them at Crossbarry and elsewhere, his HQ being in Kinsale. Awarded the OBE and DSM for his part in the war.

PEROLZ, Marie: Cork. Carried Pearse's despatch to the Cork leaders on Easter Monday announcing that the Rebellion was, after all, going ahead. She returned with the communication saying that Cork would do its duty.

PERRIER, Frederick: RIC Const shot dead as he was escaping capture during the second Bandon attack 23 February 1921. (See Barry, Tom; Marshall, John)

PHELAN, Johnny: See Wyse, Joe.

PILKINGTON, William: Sligo. Prominent member of Sligo Bde. Charged with unlawful assembly and sentenced to six months in prison, having refused to accept bail 7 April 1919. Charged again with J.J. Clancy a week later when both refused to recognize the court. He later commanded the Sligo Bde. Both he and P. McDonnell are credited with the command of the 3rd Western Div in 1921.

PLUNKETT, Edward John Moreton Drax (Eighteenth Baron of Dunsany): See Dunsany, Lord.

PLUNKETT, George Noble (Count): Director of National Museum and father of Joseph Mary Plunkett (below). Arrested and interned for protesting against the treatment of Easter Week Rebellion prisoners. Called upon to resign from the RDS. Refused to take his seat when elected to Parliament for North Roscommon 3 February 1917 and was arrested and deported for his alleged part in the supposed 'German Plot' May 1918. Minister for Foreign Affairs 1 April 1919. Delegate to Paris Peace Conference May 1919. Minister of Fine Arts August 1921. (See McGuinness, Joe)

PLUNKETT, Horace (Sir): Gloucestershire, England; Dunsany, Co. Meath. Son of Lord Dunsany. Founded the Irish Dominion League to press for Home Rule within the Commonwealth. Built up the co-operative agriculture movement. These installations were targets for Black and Tan raids and Plunkett unsuccessfully pressed for investigations into their destruction.

PLUNKETT, Joseph Mary: Kimmage Rd, Dublin. Son of Count Plunkett (above); brother of Philomena (below). Member of IRB and Volunteers. Director of Operations for Easter Week Rebellion. Although severely ill on the Friday, he left his nursing home to fight in the GPO. He conducted the liaison with Casement concerning the arms importation and was a signatory of the Proclamation. Executed at Kilmainham, having been married in his cell there, 4 May 1916. (*See Gifford, Grace*)

PLUNKETT, Philomena: Joseph's sister. Conveyed a letter to John Devoy in USA from the Military Council of the Volunteers requesting a change of timing for the arms landing because of the imminence of a full moon Easter 1916. Devoy cabled details of the change to Germany but the *Aud* had already put to sea. (*See von Igel, Wolf*)

POTTER: Cahir, Co. Tipperary. Dist Insp RIC captured by the IRA 22 April 1921. His release was promised if Thomas Traynor's life was spared. He was shot dead 27 April after Traynor's hanging 26 April 1921. His wife had received a letter saying he had been tried, convicted and sentenced to death by the IRA. His diary indicated that he had not been ill-treated.

POWER, George: Adj Cork No 2 Bde 1919. Vice Comdt 1920. Succeeded the captured Sean Moylan as Comdt in 1921. Assisted Liam Lynch in the capture of Gen Lucas. In action at Fermoy 7 September 1919. With Maurice Twomey he helped to incorporate the Post Offices into the Bde's intelligence system. Acted as Liaison Officer with Crown Forces during the Truce.

POWER, John: *See footnote to Murphy, Joe.*

PRENDERGAST, Nicholas: Former BA Capt, ex-Christian Brother. Drowned by Black and Tans at Fermoy, Co. Cork, December 1920. (*See Dooley*)

PRICE: Capt Middlesex Rgt. Shot dead Bloody Sunday morning 21 November 1920 at 28 Upr Pembroke St.

PRICE: Lt BA. Killed during the struggle preceding Treacy's death in Talbot St, Dublin, 14 October 1920.

PRICE, Eamonn: Director of Organization GHQ Staff of the IRA at the time of the Truce in 1921.

PRICE, Ivor: Maj. County Insp RIC. Became IO at Irish Military HQ on commencement of Easter Week Rebellion. He acted as intermediary between the military authorities, the DMP, the RIC and the Under-Secretary of State. Made a Companion of the DSO for his conduct.

PURCELL, Thomas P.: Capt of Dublin Fire Bde who commanded the Bde from the Wednesday of Easter Week. He was awarded a Bronze Medal by the British Fire Prevention Committee in recognition of his conduct. Confirmed Gen Maxwell's allegation of the Bde's being fired upon by Volunteers while engaged in firefighting. (*See Myers*)

QUIGLEY, James: Navan, Co. Meath. County Surveyor court-martialled for alleged collusion with Thomas Ashe at Ashtown ambush in that he signalled movements of police he had observed by scouting on his motor-cycle. Acquitted.

QUIGLEY, Mai: Sean Treacy's fiancée. Their wedding had been fixed for 25 October 1920, eleven days after his death.

QUINLISK, H. (sometimes 'Quinn'): Ex-Cpl Royal Irish Regiment. Served with Casement's Bde in Germany. Returned to Ireland and was for a period in receipt of Sinn Féin funds until Collins realized he was of little use and became aggravated by his persistence. On 11 November 1919, Quinlisk wrote to the Under-Secretary offering to tell all he knew about Sinn Féin. He was granted an interview at Dublin Castle of which Collins was duly informed by his own contacts. After numerous blunders acting as a double-agent, he followed Collins to Clonakilty. Volunteers intercepted a coded telegram. This led to their seizing a despatch confirming Quinlisk's double dealings. Cork Volunteers requested permission to dispense with him finally. This was granted and they duly executed him 18 February 1920.

QUINN: See Quinlisk.

QUINN (Miss): See Lynch, Diarmuid.

QUINN, Ellen: Kiltartan, Co. Galway. Shot in the stomach by Black and Tans while nursing her baby on the day Kevin Barry was hanged, 1 November 1920. Attended to by Rev John Considine while bleeding to death for seven hours. Sir Hamar Greenwood was notified of the incident but ignored it.

REDDINGTON, Tom: Galway. Active organizer of Volunteers in Longford. Comdt Longford Bde 1919-21.

REDMOND, Aidan: See Gleeson, Frank.

REDMOND, John: Ballytrent, Co. Wexford. Father of William (below). Leader of the Irish Parliamentary Party. Opposed the Easter Week Rebellion. Convened a convention to draft a constitution for Ireland within the Empire 1917. Witnessed the dying of his party's power before his death 6 March 1918.

REDMOND, William: Son of John (above). Won his father's Waterford seat March 1918. Re-elected in December 1918. He was refused an inquiry into repressive measures in Ireland in the House of Commons 21 February 1921.

REDMOND, William C. Forbes: Belfast. Assistant Commissioner of Police RIC. Drafted from Belfast December 1919 to counter Collins's 'Twelve Apostles' by re-organizing Dublin Castle Det Div. He chose James McNamara, one of Collins's agents, as his confidant. Involved with 'Jameson' in arranging a meeting with Collins soon after arrival. Neligan warned Collins through Broy. Redmond was shot dead at the Standard Hotel, Dublin, a few days later, 21 January 1920. (See Daly, Paddy)

REGAN, Scottie: See Brady, James.

REILLY: Roskeen, Co. Tipperary. Const RIC. A member of the party that arrested Sean Hogan at Meagher's of Annfield. One of Hogan's escorts at Knocklong; survived that attack. As witness for the prosecution in the Knocklong case, he was kidnapped in Armagh on the eve of the trial 6 July 1920. Extensive searches failed to locate him in time for the hearing on 7 July. He was held and freed unharmed at 0300 hours 8 July.

REILLY, John & Joseph: Derrinkeher and Miskawn, Co. Leitrim. Distinguished, respectively, as 'Little' and 'Big'. Members of Leitrim Bde IRA.

Were among six killed in action when ambushed by Crown Forces at Selton, Co. Leitrim, 11 March 1921. The ambush was said to have resulted from an informer's work. (*See Connolly, Sean*)

REILLY, Mick: *See 'Twelve Apostles'.*

RENNIE: Cambridge graduate who arrived with the BA in 1917. Demobbed in 1920, he joined the RIC and later became a member of the Secret Service. He and his superior, Nicholls, were extremely active against the IRA.

REYNOLDS, George: Ringsend, Dublin. Officer in charge of Clanwilliam House during the battle of Mount St Bridge 27 April 1916. KIA there and his body burned in the fire that followed.

REYNOLDS, Mollie: C na mB, on duty in GPO during Easter Week Rebellion. Gave clerical assistance to the anti-conscription campaign. Assisted Liam Mellows 1919-21.

REYNOLDS, William: Ballyhooleen, Co. Cork. Involved in arms raids and participated in the burning of Ballyfeard RIC Barracks, July 1919, and attacks on Ballinhassig Barracks, Co. Cork, November 1920, June and July 1921.

RICE, J.J.: Comdt 5th (Kenmare) Bn No 2 Kerry Bde. Represented bde, along with Humphrey Murphy, at the Kippagh meeting when 1st Southern Div was formed.

RICE, William: *See Flood, Robert.*

RING: Const RIC. A member of the party that arrested Sean Hogan at Meagher's of Annfield. One of Hogan's escorts at Knocklong. Survived that attack.

ROBBINS, Frank: 39 North William St, Dublin. Sgt, later Lt Citizen Army. Member of St Stephen's Green garrison 1916. Assisted the evacuation to College of Surgeons. Arrested and imprisoned Knutsford and Frongoch. Sought greater co-operation between Citizen Army and Volunteers. (*See Donnelly, Michael; Robbins, Frank*)

ROBERT, Michael: *See McElligott, Michael.*

ROBINSON, Seamus: Dublin; Ballagh, Co. Tipperary. Occupied premises of Hopkins and Hopkins, Sackville St (later O'Connell St), Dublin, during Easter Week Rebellion. Commanded South Tipperary Bde. Supported Treacy in posting a proclamation ordering all British police and military out of South Tipperary in defiance of GHQ of IRA. One of the 'Big Four'. Led the Soloheadbeg ambush. Took part in Knocklong rescue of Sean Hogan. Operated with Collins in Dublin. Took part in the first attempted ambush of Lord French at College Green and at the more ambitious Ashtown ambush. Wounded and burned at actions in Hollyford. Took part in actions at Drangan, Rehill Rifle Range and other Flying Column operations.

ROBINSON, William: Eleven-year-old spectator trampled to death in Croke Park when Black and Tans raided a Gaelic football game on afternoon of Bloody Sunday, 21 November 1920.

ROCHE: Tipperary. Sgt RIC. Extremely active against South Tipperary Bde. Was transferred to Dublin, possibly to track down Treacy, whose body he was said to have gloatingly identified. Was shot dead in Parliament St 17 October 1920 having been pointed out to Collins's squad by the detective accompanying him. (*See Daly, Paddy*)

RODGERS, Alphonsus: Scarriff, Co. Clare. Full-time member of East Clare Flying Column 1920. Shot dead while a prisoner of the RIC in what became known as the Killaloe Murders 17 November 1920.

ROSBOROUGH, James: Maj Royal Irish Rifles. Temporarily i/c of Portobello Barracks during Easter Week Rebellion. His evidence was taken at the Sheehy Skeffington-McIntyre-Dickson inquiry and the Bowen-Colthurst court-martial.

ROWE, William: Head Const RIC. Killed while attempting to arrest Thomas Kent of Bawnard, Castlelyons, Co. Cork on 2 May 1916. (*See Kent Brothers*)

ROYNANE, Patrick: Mourne Abbey, Cork. Executed in Cork Jail 28 February 1921.

RUSSELL, Sean: Dublin. Imprisoned Knutsford and Frongoch. Staff Officer IRA HQ Staff 1919. D/Mun 1921. Arranged the quarry raids for gelignite.

RUSSELL, Thomas: Dingle, Co. Kerry; Clare. Irish-language teacher whose meeting was raided by Crown Forces and all present driven out on to the streets of Kilrush 28 March 1918. Died two days later of bayonet wounds.

RUTTLEDGE, G.B.: County Insp Galway West Riding. Gave evidence before the Royal Commission of Inquiry into Easter Week Rebellion. Awarded the King's medal for his coping with the Rebellion without any back-up troops.

RUTTLEDGE, P.J.: Westport, Co. Mayo. Prominent in the organization of Republican Courts in North Mayo while a TD. He, Tomás Mac Camhthaoil, East Mayo, and Conor Maguire, South Mayo, did the organizing in their own districts but sat elsewhere.

RYAN: Alleged informer on McKee and Peadar Clancy. Executed by the IRA within a fortnight of their deaths.

RYAN, Anne: *See Nunan, Sean.*

RYAN, Bernard: Dublin. Volunteer. Participant in the abortive 'Drumcondra ambush' at Clonturk Park, Dublin. Hanged Monday 14 March 1921. (*See Flood, Frank*)

RYAN, Frank & Moss: Elton, Co. Limerick. Said to have drilled and borne arms while schoolboys at St Colman's College, Fermoy, Co. Cork. Active in war while university students.

RYAN, Fred: 4 High St, Dublin. Citizen Army. One of the first occupants of the College of Surgeons after the evacuation of St Stephen's Green during Easter Week Rebellion. Sent by Mallin to set fire to a Harcourt St shop, hoping the blaze would spread to the Russell Hotel. Was shot dead while carrying out these instructions 27 April 1916. (*See Partridge, William P.*)

RYAN, James (Dr): Tomcoole, Co. Wexford. Performed duties of medical officer in GPO during Easter Week

Rebellion, treating James Connolly among others. Arrested and interned at Frongoch until the 1917 amnesty. Won for Sinn Féin in South Wexford at the 1918 general election. Interned in Spike Island 1920 and 1921. Elected to Dáil for South Wexford 1921.

RYAN, Thomas: Wexford. Shot dead while whispering the Act of Contrition into the dying Michael Hogan's ear at Croke Park, Bloody Sunday afternoon 21 November 1920.

RYNNE, Michael: Captain, Dublin Bde. Active in a number of operations with the Bde.

SADLIER: Maj BA. 3rd Cashel Bn. Accidentally shot by a member of his own command at Cloneen, Co. Tipperary, 13 June 1921, although some reports claim he committed suicide.

SALMON, Joseph: Feakle, Co. Clare. Killed 22 September 1920 while assisting an old man from a licensed premises during the raid by Crown Forces on Lahinch, Co. Clare, in retaliation for the loss of six RIC constables at Milltown Malbay.

SANDBACH, A.E.: Maj Gen BA. Commanded the troops in the Dublin area during Easter Week Rebellion. Ordered closure of licensed premises all day Saturday 6 May 1916 and thereafter at all times except 2-5 pm. Imposed curfew from Sunday 13 May.

SATCHWELL, Joe: *See Bergin, John*.

SAURIN, Frank: *See Intelligence Section*.

SAVAGE, James: Longford. Active in intelligence operations for Longford Bde IRA. Forged and distributed vouchers for food, *etc.*, to his fellow prisoners in Ballykinlar Camp 1921.

SAVAGE, Martin: Streamstown, Ballisodare, Co. Sligo. Lt 2nd Dublin Bn Irish Volunteers. Fought in GPO during Easter Week Rebellion. Arrested and imprisoned in Knutsford until the 1917 amnesty. KIA when shot in the throat by one of Lord French's escort during the Ashtown ambush 19 December 1919.

SAVILLE: *See 'Hardy'*.

SCALLY, Toby: *See Bergin, John*.

SCANLON, Daniel: Ballybunion, Co. Kerry. Volunteer shot dead in Ballybunion during celebrations for de Valera's East Clare election victory July 1917. Stones had been thrown through the windows of the RIC barracks during a parade, resulting in fire being opened from the barracks when the parade returned. (*See Lyons*)

SCANLON, Michael: Galbally, Co. Limerick. Comdt 1st Bn East Limerick Bde. Arrested 27 October 1920 and brought to Limerick from Kilmallock, where he was a teacher. He jumped from the truck as it halted and reached a hide-out in Thomas St where he was later discovered and shot dead.

SCISSORS AND PASTE: *See Nationality*.

SCOTT, J.: Fourteen-year-old spectator shot dead by a ricochet bullet in Croke Park when Black and Tans raided a Gaelic football match on Bloody Sunday afternoon 21 November 1920.

SCULLY, Liam: Glencar, Co. Kerry. Capt. Member of East Limerick Bde IRA. Participated in attack on Ballylanders RIC Barracks 27 April 1920 and was KIA during the successful attack on Kilmallock 28 May 1920.

SEARS, William: MP. Sentenced to six months' imprisonment for a speech delivered in South Mayo 1918. He was carried as a hostage in a military truck during Crown Forces operations in the Cork area and threatened with death if the truck was attacked by the IRA.

SEERY, Patrick: Cluain-Ui-Thaidhg, Co. Westmeath. Died 1 June 1920 of wounds received during an attack on the RIC barracks in Clara, Co. Offaly.

SHANAHAN, P.: Tipperary. Lived in Dublin. Having been imprisoned in Mountjoy during 1917, operated a team of vigilant newsboys, etc., to give protection in safe premises to the 'Big Four' during their Dublin operations.

SHAW, Frederick (Sir): Maj Gen/Lt Gen. Succeeded Sir Bryan Mahon as British C-in-C in Ireland 1918-20. Banned meetings and marches July 1918. Sought martial law for Ireland.

SHAW, George Bernard: 3 Upr Synge St, Dublin. Writer. Wrote to *Daily News* condemning 1916 executions. Wrote a speech for Roger Casement and wrote to the *Manchester Guardian* in his defence.

SHEEHAN, Donal: Rollinson's Bridge, Newcastlewest, Co. Limerick. Drowned in the car that went over the pier at Ballykissane, Co. Kerry, 21 April 1916, while about to rendezvous with Roger Casement. (*See Keating, Con; McInerney, Thomas*)

SHEEHAN, Patrick: One of four clerks of the First Dáil session January 1919. (*See Nunan, Sean*)

SHEEHY, J.J.: Tralee, Co. Kerry. Active with ASU of Kerry No 1 Bde.

SHEEHY SKEFFINGTON, Francis: Bailieboro, Co. Cavan; 23 Longwood Ave, Dublin. Advised against the Easter Week Rebellion. Organized anti-looting patrols during the week. Arrested 25 April 1916 and taken to Portobello Barracks. Shot dead with McIntyre and Dickson the following morning. (*See Coade, J.; Sheehy Skeffington, Hanna; Simon, John*)

SHEEHY SKEFFINGTON, Hanna: 23 Longwood Ave, Dublin. Herself and her seven-year-old son arrested when her house was raided two days after her husband's death (*above*). She insisted on an inquiry into the shooting of her husband. Refused any compensation. After a speechmaking tour of USA she was deported and imprisoned at Holloway 1918. With Alderman Tom Kelly, she was Acting Co-Secretary of Sinn Féin while leading executive members were imprisoned or abroad 1919. (*See Simon, John*)

SHIELDS, Arthur: 12 Vernon Ave, Clontarf, Dublin. Abbey Theatre actor active in GPO during Easter Week Rebellion. This and Sean Connolly's death prevented the opening of a double bill at the Abbey on Tuesday 25 April 1916. Consequently *The Spancel of Death*, by Mayo Fenian T.H. Nally, in which Shields was to have appeared, was never produced and no script survived. Interned at Frongoch for a short term.

SHEILS, Patrick: Derry. First Mountjoy hunger-striker to be released April 1920.

SHORTT: Succeeded Duke as Chief Secretary for Ireland 1918-19.

SIMON, F.: *See O'Rourke, Dan.*

SIMON, John (Sir): KC. Presided over British Government's Commission of Inquiry into the killings at Portobello 1916. The Simon Commission's report was apologetic and recommended compensation to relatives. (*See Sheehy Skeffington, Francis and Hanna; Coade, J.; Dickson, Thomas; McIntyre, Patrick; Moloney, Thomas*)

SINN FÉIN: *See* Nationality.

SKINNIDER, Margaret: Glasgow schoolteacher who took holidays to participate in the Easter Week Rebellion. Arrived at the College of Surgeons on a bicycle. Received bullet wounds at the Harcourt St burning incident. (*See Ryan, Fred.*) Survived. Wrote *Doing My Bit for Ireland* 1917.

SLATTERY, Jimmy: Bodyke, Co. Clare. Involved in the Castle mail robbery of 1919. Lost an arm at the burning of the Custom House May 1921. (*See 'Twelve Apostles'*)

SLOAN, James: Moate, Co. Westmeath. Shot at Ballykinlar Camp 14 January 1921 by a sentry.

SMITH, Compton: Maj Royal Welsh Fusiliers. Held as a hostage by Cork No 1 Bde and shot 28 April 1921 in retaliation for the shooting of six Volunteers.

SMITH, Frederick (Sir): *See Birkenhead, Lord.*

SMITH, Jack: *See O'Brien, Seamus.*

SMITH, Matt: Mill St, Cavan. 2 i/c 3rd (Cavan) Bn IRA 1919. Imprisoned in 1921 for possession of Republican Justice's Oath of Office.

SMITH, Michael ('Tiger'): Dublin. Redmondite leader who joined Volunteers. Fought during Easter Week Rebellion. Helped fashion the shears used to cut the bolts in Kilmainham for the O'Malley-Teeling-Donnelly escape.

SMITH, Patrick: Kilbride, Bailieboro, Co. Cavan. Comdt Cavan Bde. Captured and sentenced to death after court-martial 1921. Truce occurred before sentence was carried out.

SMITH, T.H.: Landlord of 119 Morehampton Road, Donnybrook, Dublin. Shot there on Bloody Sunday morning 21 November 1920.

SMITH, Thomas: Acting Insp Gen of the RIC and one of the prominent people named by a coroner's jury as being guilty of the murder of Tomás MacCurtain. Lloyd George and Lord French also named.

SMUTS, Jan Christian (Gen): *See Casement, Thomas.*

SMYTH (Miss): Balbriggan, Co. Dublin. When she could receive no response from RIC to her pleas for dealing with disturbances in Balbriggan, she called in the Republican Police. This caused the incidents that sparked off the 'Sack of Balbriggan' 20 September 1920.

SMYTH, Brice-Ferguson: Lt Col King's Own Scottish Borderers. Div Police Commissioner for Munster 1920. Advocated brutal measures in address to the RIC at Listowel, Co. Kerry, 16 June 1920. This caused Const Mee to hand him cap, belt and sword and call him a murderer. Smyth ordered Mee's arrest on the spot but nobody complied. The incident became known as the 'Listowel Mutiny'. Smyth was shot dead by six

Volunteers who entered Cork City and County Club 17 July 1920.

SMYTH, 'Dog': Det. The first member of G Div RIC to be executed 31 July 1919 in Collins's campaign against policemen prominent in IRA arrests.

SMYTH, G.: Maj BA. Said to have requested an Irish posting to avenge his brother Brice-Ferguson Smyth (*above*). Shot dead in 'Fernside fight' when Breen and Treacy were escaping capture.

SMYTH, Michael: Co. Kildare. Led Athgarvan Coy during Easter Week Rebellion. Arrested and imprisoned Richmond Barracks, Wormwood Scrubs, Wandsworth and Frongoch. Adj North Kildare Bn 1917. Comdt 2nd Kildare Bn 1920. Comdt 7th Bde 1921. Arrested on a charge of possessing arms just before the Truce.

SOMERVILLE, H.F.: Maj BA. Commanded British troops in the Custom House and North Wall areas during the Easter Week Rebellion. He was made a Companion of the DSO and was mentioned in despatches in connection with his conduct.

SPINDLER, Karl: Officer of the Imperial German Navy. Capt of the *Aud*, which had set out from Germany as the *Libau* to carry arms for the Easter Week Rebellion. Despite tracking by the BN, he arrived on time but was unaware of the change in plan. After a long wait in Tralee Bay he finally turned tail for Spain. He was apprehended by the British destroyer *Bluebell* and taken to Cobh (then Queenstown). The *Aud* and her contents were blown up there by her crew. (*See Casement, Roger*)

SPRING-RICE, Mary (Hon.): Mount-Trenchard, Foynes, Co. Limerick. Daughter of Lord Mounteagle. Although of Ascendancy background, assisted the IRA in West Limerick throughout its campaign. She undertook the carrying of despatches to GHQ in Dublin and made a boat available at all times for use of men on the run in crossing the Shannon to Clare.

'SQUAD, The': *See 'Twelve Apostles'*.

STACK, Austin: Tralee, Co. Kerry. Comdt Kerry Bde, responsible for the planned reception of arms from the *Aud* prior to Easter Week Rebellion. Arrested and imprisoned at Dartmoor. Insubordinate there and in Mountjoy September 1917. With Darrell Figgis, was Joint-Secretary of Sinn Féin while imprisoned. Was moved to Dundalk and released after hunger-strike 17 November 1917. Elected North Munster member of the Supreme Council of the IRB 19 November 1917. Reimprisoned to complete his sentence April 1918. Returned for Kerry in the 1918 election. Imprisoned Belfast December 1918 where he removed John Doran to the political prisoners' wing. Escaped from Manchester Jail 1919. As Minister for Justice outside the Cabinet in 1920, set up the Republican Courts and appointed judges. Was Deputy COS of the IRA and Minister for Home Affairs 1921. Accompanied de Valera on his meetings with Lloyd George July 1921.

STAFFORD, Thomas (Sir): *See McCabe, Alec*.

STAINES, Michael: Staff Officer GHQ Irish Volunteers 1916. One of Connolly's stretcher-bearers during his evacuation from the GPO Easter

Week. Assisted in re-organization of Volunteers 1917 and was elected to Supreme Council of the IRB 19 November 1917. Elected TD and alderman. An RIC constable tailed and shot at Phoenix Park gates in 1920 was said to have been mistaken for him. Arrested at a meeting of Dublin Corporation and imprisoned December 1920. Released July 1921. Involved in peace discussions with Archbishop Clune.

STAPLETON, William (alias 'George Moreland'): Dublin. Guard Commander at Jacob's factory during Easter Week Rebellion 1916. Arrested and imprisoned Knutsford and Frongoch. One of Collins's 'Twelve Apostles'. Accompanied Paddy Daly on the Roche execution operation. Commanded the party at the execution of Capt Newbury, Bloody Sunday morning 21 November 1920, and of the McKee/Clancy informer. Participated in the Sean MacEoin rescue bid from Mountjoy. (*See Dalton, Emmet; Leonard, Joe*)

STENNING, Frederick: Bandon, Co. Cork. Land League activist shot dead near Bandon April 1921.

STEWART, Bernard: *See O'Malley, Ernie.*

STODART, Holden: Victoria Villas, Blackrock, Co. Dublin. Corps Superintendent Co. Dublin Order of Malta Bde. Shot Wednesday 26 April 1916 while approaching a wounded soldier in Baggot St. Had offered the Bde's services to the military authorities at the outbreak of hostilities.

STRICKLAND, Peter (Sir): Maj Gen BA. Div Commander Southern Div. On 18 December 1920 he conducted an inquiry into the burning of Cork city. The inquiry was boycotted and became known as the 'Strickland Farce'. His report was suppressed by the British Cabinet. As Military Governor of Cork January 1921, he threatened to court-martial anyone housing IRA personnel or possessing arms. Before Crossbarry, he conducted a mammoth search-and-sweep operation.

SULLIVAN: Head Const RIC. After the Fermoy attack by Cork No 2 Bde (7 September 1919) he was instructed to arrest Daniel Hegarty, Brian Kelly, Leo O'Callaghan, Edward Waters and Owen Harold on a charge of murdering Pte Jones, King's Light Infantry Rgt, during that action. He refused, was dismissed after 40 years' service and ordered to vacate the barracks, where he lived with his family, within 16 days.

SULLIVAN, Alexander Martin: Belfield, Drumcondra, Co. Dublin. Last King's Sergeant in Ireland. His life was threatened in 1916 because of his opposition to Sinn Féin. He opposed all physical force and only out of a sense of duty did he defend Roger Casement. Became a member of the British Recruiting Council.

SSUPPLE: *See Maher, Jerry.*

WAN, Paddy & Tony: Belvedere Ave, North Circular Rd, Dublin. Brothers. In action at King St and GPO respectively during Easter Week Rebellion. Tony close to The O'Rahilly when he was shot. He was arrested but was considered too young for deportation. Paddy deported.

SWANZY: Dist Insp RIC. One of the prominent persons named by a Coroners' Jury as being guilty of the murder of Tomás MacCurtain. Transferred to Lisburn from Cork after the incident. Shot dead in Lisburn 22 August 1920.

SWEENEY, Bernard: Comdt South Leitrim Bde which engaged in actions at Garadice, Eslin, Fenagh, Ranthogue and Kesh. His officers included Michael Mahon of Drumshanbo, John McGreevy, Pat Whelan and Pat Guckian of Carrick-on-Shannon.

SWEENEY, Joseph A.: Burtonport, Co. Donegal. Member of the GPO garrison Easter Week. Elected for West Donegal 1918. Comdt West Donegal Bde 1919. Youngest member of the First Dáil. OC 1st Northern Div 1921.*

TANGNEY, John: Castleisland, Co. Kerry. RIC. Const stationed in Tipperary, Cork and Limerick until he resigned 1 July 1920. He gave evidence before the American Commission on Conditions in Ireland where he outlined the gradual phasing-in of regulations permitting the use of firearms for acts of aggression within the force.

TANNAM, Liam: Member of GPO garrison Easter Week Rebellion. One of James Connolly's stretcher-bearers during his evacuation.

TANSEY, Owen: See Hunt, Jim.

TEELING, Frank: Wounded in Bloody Sunday morning operation and about to be shot when Gen Crozier intervened 21 November 1920. Court-martialled and sentenced to death. Escaped from Kilmainham Jail 13 February 1921. (See O'Malley, Ernie)

TENNANT: Lt. Died from wounds received at Scramogue ambush, Co. Roscommon, 23 March 1921. (See Peek, Alfred)

TENNANT, H.J. (Rt Hon): See Vane, Francis.

THORNTON, Frank: Leader of the Liverpool Volunteers who fought in Dublin during Easter Week Rebellion. Brought supplies from Liberty Hall to GPO, then returned to Liberty Hall garrison, Easter Monday. Member of Collins's Intelligence Section. Volunteer organizer in Louth. Planned the rescue of Traynor from Dundalk Jail, abandoned due to the hunger-strike's success. Participated in the attempted ambush of Lord French at Ashtown. Captured, held for ten days and freed, unrecognized, by the 'Cairo Gang', one of the events that led to the Bloody Sunday morning killings 21 November 1921. (See Mulloy)

THORNTON, Michael: Comdt East Connemara Bde 1919 and re-appointed by Gen Mulcahy in the re-organization of the Galway area September 1920.

TOBIN, Liam: Volunteer. Fought in Easter Week Rebellion. Imprisoned on a ten-year sentence but released in the 1917 amnesty. On release, was appointed IO for the Dublin Bde. A close associate of Collins, he built up a detailed intelligence portfolio on all

---

* Other early Donegal Bde Commanders were Joe Doherty (North), Sam O'Flaherty (East) and Joe Ward (South). Actions took place at Loughanure (claimed to have been among the first uses of road trenching), Dungloe, Meenamore, Falcarragh, Drumquin, Mountcharles, Ballyshannon, Burtonport, Clonmany and Bundoran.

British agents. Participated in the Dame St/College Green abortive ambush of Lord French. Had numerous narrow escapes. Involved in exposing 'Jameson'. Assistant D/Int 1921. (*See Intelligence Section; Mulloy, Fergus*)

TOBIN, Richard: Surgeon. Attended to the wounded James Connolly in prison before his execution.

TORMEY, James & Joseph: Moneen, Moate, Co. Westmeath. Brothers. James: Commanded the ASU 1st Bn Athlone Bde. Killed while leading an ambush at Cornafulla 2 February 1921. Joseph: Shot dead by a sentry at Ballykinlar Camp 14 January 1921.

TRAYNOR: Sgt RIC. With five constables and his wife assisting, he withstood a four-hour attack by Volunteers on Newtownhamilton Barracks, Co. Antrim, 1919.

TRAYNOR, Oscar: Dublin. Took part in Easter Week Rebellion. Arrested and imprisoned Frongoch and Knutsford. Released by amnesty but re-imprisoned Dundalk 1918. In charge of Custom House burning 25 May 1921. Succeeded Dick McKee as Comdt Dublin Bde November 1921.

TRAYNOR, Thomas: Tullow, Co. Carlow. Volunteer officer arrested after the shooting of an Aux at Brunswick St (now Pearse St), Dublin. Badly beaten by 'Igoe Gang', tried and sentenced to death. Hanged at Mountjoy 26 April 1921. (*See Potter*)

TREACY, Sean: Solohead, Co. Tipperary. Member of IRB. One of the 'Big Four'. His farmhouse was fashioned to conceal guns, documents, *etc*. Attempted to promote the Easter Week Rebellion in Tipperary. Arrested 21 August 1917 for, among other things, parading in Volunteer uniform as a guard of honour for de Valera's visit. Sentenced to six months' imprisonment at Cork and Mountjoy. Joined the hunger-strike there on 22 September 1917. Released June 1918. Although main Volunteer organizer in South Tipperary, refused command of its Bde and became Vice Comdt to Seamus Robinson. Was present at 'Blackcastle Races' 12 September 1920. In action at Soloheadbeg ambush and Knocklong rescue. Moved to Dublin 1919 and was in action at the Ashtown ambush of Lord French. Returned to Tipperary January 1920. Was in action against Hollyford, Kilmallock and Drangan Barracks. He left a party raiding the rifle range at Reehil and, singlehanded, attacked a patrol at Cahir June 1920. Wounded in the attack on Rear Cross Barracks 11 July 1920. Ambushed the patrol in which Gen Lucas was travelling at Oola 29 July 1920. Operated in Dublin from September 1921. Escaped capture, with Breen, by fighting his way out of 'Fernside', Drumcondra. He was tracked down, however, and shot dead in Talbot St, Dublin, 14 October 1920. (*See Brunswick, Sean*)

TRODDEN, Eamonn: 68 Falls Rd, Belfast. Member of IRB and IRA. His home was raided and his family threatened with being burned out after the shooting of policemen in the riots of 20 September 1920. He was taken out and shot dead 25 September.

TUDOR: Gen. Chief of Police Forces in Ireland 1920. Police advisor to the Chief Secretary for Ireland. Recommended the recruitment of the Auxiliaries 1920. Was present at the 'Listowel Mutiny' 19 June 1920. Commanded Dublin Aux Divs 1921. Assisted the Truce Observation Committee 1921. (*See Smyth, Brice-Ferguson*)

TUOHY, Denis: Kerry. Member of RIC who resigned after Easter Week Rebellion and joined Volunteers. Became IO Cross Roads Coy Kenmare Bn. Arrested 1 May 1921 by Auxiliaries and Black and Tans. He seized a grenade to fling at his captors and dashed for freedom, overpowering four guards. He was overtaken, however, and brought to Kenmare and interrogated. Alleged to have been tortured.

'TWELVE APOSTLES' (or 'The Squad'): A squad of specially selected men operating for Michael Collins's Intelligence Department, mainly in execution of British intelligence agents and policemen arrogant in their harassment of IRA personnel. Mick McDonnell was the first leader and Paddy Daly (later leader) the first vice-leader. 'The Squad' were selected, from time to time from Benjamin Barrett, Frank Bolster, J. Brennan, Ned Breslin, Ben Byrne, Eddie Byrne, Vincent Byrne, Sean Caffrey, James Connolly, James Conroy, Jim Conway, Sean Doyle, Pat Drury, John Dunne, Paddy Flanagan, Paddy Griffin, Jack Hanlon, Mick Kennedy, Tom Keogh, Joe Leonard, Pat McCrea (driver), Mick Reilly, Jimmy Slattery, William Stapleton and Johnny Wilson. (*See Intelligence Section, some of whom were also used.*)

TWOMEY, Maurice: Fermoy, Co. Cork. Adj Fermoy Bn 1919. Adj and IO Cork No 2 Bde 1920. (*See Power, George*)

UA BUACHALLA, Domhnall: Maynooth, Co. Kildare. Led a contingent of Volunteers from Maynooth to Dublin to take part in the Easter Week Rebellion. Arrested and imprisoned until the amnesty of 1917. Elected MP for Kildare 1918 and was a member of the First Dáil. (*See Colgan, Patrick*)

UPTON, Christopher: *See footnote to Murphy, Joe.*

VANE, Francis (Sir): Maj Munster Fusiliers. Was on recruiting duties in Ireland at the outbreak of the Easter Week Rebellion. Volunteered for duty and was attached to the Royal Irish Rifles at Portobello, where he was second senior officer. Brought the 'Portobello Murders' to light and condemned the Castle authorities for not arresting Bowen-Colthurst when informed of the crimes. He was allegedly informed by his Commanding Officer at Portobello that higher authority would be intervening in the case. When nothing still happened he reported the facts to Rt Hon H.J. Tennant and then went to London to complain to Lord Kitchener. He gave evidence before the Commission of Inquiry into the affair. (*See Coade, J. Dickson, Thomas; Sheehy Skeffington, Francis; Simon, John*)

VAUGHAN'S HOTEL: Proprietor, Mrs Vaughan of Clare. Situated at Parnell Square, Dublin. In two ownerships, was the constant meeting place for Michael Collins and his associates. (*See McGuire*)

VICARS, Arthur (Sir): Former Ulster King-of-Arms and Custodian of the Crown Jewels at Dublin Castle, an office which he vacated after the jewels disappeared in 1907. He was taken from his home at Kilmorna Castle, Listowel, 14 April 1921, and shot dead, allegedly for informing. His mansion was then destroyed by fire.

VIZE, Joseph: Former BN officer who operated for the IRA from Glasgow up to 1918. IRB member. Director of Purchases IRA. Worked with Neil Kerr on importations. Active in Breen/Treacy protection after 'Fernside fight'. (*See Mellows, Liam*)

VON IGEL, Wolf: Official of the German Embassy in USA whose New York office was raided by Secret Service agents April 1916. Devoy's message concerning arms from Germany was discovered. (*See Plunkett, Philomena*)

WALL, Charlie: Drumcollogher, Co. Limerick. Brother of Sean and Thomas (*below*). Commanded the West Limerick Bde during its involvement in keeping lines of communications open for the expected arrival of arms from the *Aud*. (*See Casement, Roger*)

WALL, Sean: Bruff, Co. Limerick. Comdt East Limerick Bde. Brother of Charlie and Thomas. Participated in attack on Kilmallock RIC Barracks 28 May 1920. Chairman of first Limerick Sinn Féin County Council 25 June 1920. (*See Malone, Tomás; Scully, Liam*)

WALL, Thomas (Rev Fr): Drumcollogher, Co. Limerick. Founded one of the first Volunteer companies outside Dublin. Mentioned in Maxwell's letter to the Bishop of Limerick. Member of Sinn Féin Executive October 1917. (*See O'Dwyer, Most Rev Dr*)

WALLACE, Peter: Roskeen, Co. Tipperary. RIC Sgt. Led the party who arrested Sean Hogan at Meagher's of Annfield. In charge of Hogan's escort when attacked at Knocklong. He wounded the escaping Treacy but was himself fatally shot.

WALSH: *See Deed, Con.*

WALSH, D.P. (Dr): Imprisoned in Birmingham, Leeds and Manchester 1919. Escaped from latter with Stack and others October 1919. Despatch handler for Intelligence Section. Took part in the operations to protect Treacy and Breen after the 'Fernside fight'.

WALSH, Maurice: *See Crowley, Daniel.*

WALSH, Michael: *See McCormick, Michael.*

WALSH, Richard: Balla, Co. Mayo. IRB and IRA member. Arms procurer for the latter in England. Succeeded in getting in a considerable amount of equipment in 1920.

WALSHE: *See O'Connor, Rory.*

WARD, Joe: *See footnote to Sweeney, Joseph A.*

WATERS, Edward: *See Sullivan.*

WEAFER, Patrick: Enniscorthy, Co. Wexford. Participated in Easter Week Rebellion in Dublin and KIA at the Imperial Hotel (now Clery's) 27 April 1916. His body was burned in the Sackville St (O'Connell St) fire.

WEBB: Capt BA. Said by Crozier to have been the only officer in the Kilkenny area who was able to control the Black and Tans.

WHELAN, Pat: *See Sweeney, Bernard.*

WHELAN, Pax: Dungarvan, Co. Waterford. With P. O'Mahoney and George Lennon, occupied Dungarvan Post Office during Easter Week Rebellion. Lennon was Vice Comdt and led a Flying Column in 1920 while Whelan was in overall command of the Decies (West Waterford) Bde. The most significant actions of the Bde were at Pilltown, Brown's Pike and Ardmore September 1920.

WHELAN, Thomas: Galway. Hanged with Patrick Moran at Mountjoy 14 March 1921 for alleged part in Bloody Sunday morning operations.

WHITE: Insp. *See Cassidy, Martin,*

WICKHAM, Charles: Lt Col. Div Commissioner of the RIC in Ulster. A captured document bearing his signature suggested a build-up of British troops during Truce negotiations, contrary to agreement.

WILSON, Alexander: Lt. One of the officers on duty at Portobello on night of 'Portobello Murders'. He was sent with an urgent query to the Adj by another officer and on dashing back with a reply he heard the shootings. (*See Bowen-Colthurst, J.C.; Coade, J.; Dickson, Thomas; McIntyre, Patrick; Sheehy Skeffington, Francis*)

WILSON, Henry (Sir): Currygrane, Edgeworthstown, Co. Longford. Gen. CIGS and close associate of Lloyd George. Field Marshall and Baronet 1919. Urged coercion in Ireland and established the 'Cairo Gang'. Was said to have threatened to resign if Kevin Barry was not hanged. He pressed Lloyd George to introduce the Conscription Bill for Ireland. Shot dead in London 22 June 1922.

WILSON, Johnny: *See 'Twelve Apostles'.*

WILSON, Lee: Capt BA. Dist Insp of the RIC in Gorey, Co. Wexford. Perpetrator of ill-treatment to Easter Week prisoners. He received a violent death on 15 June 1920, allegedly in retribution for his former deeds.

WIMBORNE (Rt Hon Lord): Resigned his appointment as Lord-Lt, held only since February 1915, after the Easter Week Rebellion. The Royal Commission of Inquiry into the Rebellion exonerated him. Reappointed Lord-Lt 14 August 1916.

WINTER, Ormonde (Sir): Appointed Director of British Intelligence 1920. Known as 'The Holy Terror'.

WOODS, Seamus: QM Belfast Bde 1919. Prominent in the Bde's activities. Named by some sources as OC 3rd Northern Div in 1921. Acted as Liaison Officer with Crown Forces during the Truce.

WORSWICK, B.: 2nd Lt King Edward's Horse. (*See Lucas, A.L.*)

WORTHINGTON-EVANS, Lamington (Sir): British Secretary of State for War 1921-22. Member of the Truce Observation sub-committee. Treaty signatory.

WYSE, Joe: QM Decies Bde. Succeeded in importing arms on a number of occasions. Active with Mick Mansfield, Bde engineer, and his brothers; Philly O'Donnell, Bde Adj; Johnny Phelan, IO.

YEATS, W.B.: Sandymount Ave, Dublin; London; Sligo. Writer. Wrote to Lord Haldane, member of British Cabinet, in October 1918 expressing Irish feelings on the Conscription Bill. Spoke passionately at Oxford Union in winter 1920 to a motion of no confidence in British government's Irish policy. Honoured the executed leaders of Easter Week Rebellion in poetry.

THE IRISH REPUBLICAN AND NON-COMBATANT DEAD

List of active personnel executed, killed in action or otherwise deceased in connection with the War of Independence, together with some non-combatant fatalities closely associated with significant incidents of the war. Names are followed by home addresses and death-dates.

ADAMS, J., Cork St, Dublin, 25-4-1916

AHERNE, J., Cobh, Co. Cork, 20-2-1921

AHERNE, J., Midleton, Co. Cork, 20-2-1921

AHERNE, J., Ballyrichard, Co. Cork, 16-6-1920

AHERNE, L., Midleton, Co. Cork, 20-2-1921

AHERNE, M., Ballyrichard, Co. Cork, 15-5-1921

ALLEN, A., Cork, 26-6-1917

ALLEN, S., Bank Place, Tipperary, 28-2-1921

ALLEN, T., Hill of Down, Co. Meath, 29-4-1916

ALLMAN, D., Headford Jct., Ballymacelligott, Co. Kerry, 21-3-1921

ARCHER, T., Kilflynn, Co. Kerry, 6-11-1920

ASHE, T., Kinnard, Lispole, Co. Kerry, 25-9-1917

ASHE, T. M., Kinnard, Lispole, Co. Kerry, 23-3-1921

ATHY, J., Maree, Oranmore, Co. Galway, 16-9-1920

BAILEY, J., Headford Jct., Ballymacelligott, Co. Kerry, 21-3-1921

BALGRIFE, J., Ballykeran, Co. Westmeath, 31-12-1920

BARRY, K., 8 Fleet St, Dublin, 1-11-1920

BARRY, R., Midleton, Co. Cork, 15-5-1921

BARRY, T., Cork, 15-11-1921

BAXTER, M.E., Thurles, Co. Tipperary; Bawnboy, Co. Cavan, 11-3-1921

BEALEN, P., Loan, Castlecomer, Co. Kilkenny, 17-5-1916

BEGLEY, J., Castle Rd, Bandon, Co. Cork, 3-12-1920

BEIRNE, J., Corracramph, Co. Leitrim, 11-3-1921

BERGIN, J., Nenagh, Co. Tipperary, 19-4-1921

BLAKE, M., Co. Limerick, 20-11-1920

BLAKE, T., Alphonsus Ave, Limerick, 28-1-1921

BOLAND, J., Aughamore, Co. Mayo, 29-5-1921

BOURKE, W.F., James St, Dublin, 25-4-1916

BOYLE, J., 21-11-1920

BREEN, P., Tempo, Co. Fermanagh, 12-12-1920

BREENE, S., Kilmihil, Co. Clare, 18-4-1920

BRENNAN, D., Co. Limerick, 9-11-1920

BRETT, T., Drombane, Co. Tipperary, 18-6-1920

BRODERICK, D., Ballymacelligott, Co. Kerry, 24-5-1921

BROSNAN, M., Castleisland, Co. Kerry, 8-11-1920

BROWN, J., Kilmeena, Co. Mayo, 23-5-1921

BROWNE, B., Fealsbridge, Co. Kerry, 28-1-1921

BROWNE, J., Ballymacelligott, Co. Kerry, 18-4-1918

BRYAN, T., Dublin, 14-3-1921

BUCKLEY, B., Midleton, Co. Cork, 27-8-1920

BUCKLEY, D., Macroom, Co. Cork, 8-6-1921

BURKE, J., Cork, 18-7-1920

BURKE, L., Ballyhooley, Co. Cork, 28-5-1921

BURKE, M., Athlone, Co. Westmeath, 22-10-1920

BURKE, T., Dungarvan, Co. Waterford, 9-7-1921

BURKE, W., Easter Week 1916

BURNS, P., Cork, 4-6-1921

BYRNE, A. J., 27-4-1916

BYRNE, J., Scar, Co. Wexford, 12-10-1920

BYRNE, J., Gracefield, Ballylynan, Co. Laois, April 1920

BYRNE, J., Wicklow, Easter Week 1916

BYRNE, L., Summerhill, Dublin, 24-4-1916

BYRNE, S., Wicklow, 27-4-1916

BYRNES, R., Limerick, 16-4-1919

CANNING, W., Ballymaclane, Magilligan Pt, Co. Derry, 12-12-1920

CANTILLION, J., Ardfert, Co. Kerry, 8-11-1920

CANTY, G., Newcestown, Co. Cork, 9-5-1921

CAREW, D., Golden Gdns, Dundrum, Tipperary, 9-4-1921

CAREY, D., Nenagh, Co. Tipperary, 25-11-1920

CARMODY, E., Ballylongford, Co. Kerry, 22-11-1920

CAROLAN, Prof., 'Fernside', Drumcondra, Dublin, 12-10-1920

CARROLL, P., Dublin, 14-10-1920

CARTY, M., Aughaderry, Loughglynn, Co. Roscommon, 2-6-1921

CASEMENT, R., Sandycove, Dublin, 3-8-1916

CASEY, P., Grange, Co. Limerick, 28-2-1921

CEANNT, E., Ballymore, Glenamaddy, Co. Galway, 8-5-1916

CLANCY, D., Kanturk, Co. Cork, August 1921

CLANCY, G., Limerick, 7-3-1921

CLANCY, H., Limerick, 1-5-1921

CLANCY, M., Ballyluskey, Co. Tipperary, 6-3-1921

CLANCY, P., Allenbridge, Newmarket, Co. Cork, 17-8-1920

CLANCY, P., Ballylanders, Co. Tipperary, 17-8-1920

CLANCY, P., Cranny, Co. Clare, 21-11-1920

CLANCY, P., Ballyluskey, Co. Tipperary, 1-12-1920

CLARK, P., Slane, Co. Meath, 25-4-1916

CLARKE, T., Fairview, Dublin, 3-5-1916

CLIFFORD, J., Derry, 6-10-1920

CLOONAN, P., Galway, 5-4-1920

CLUNE, C., Quin, Co. Clare, 21-11-1920

COADE, J., Dublin, 25-4-1916

COEN, W., Ballinrobe, Co. Mayo, 31-10-1921

COFFEY, J., Enniskeene, Co. Cork, 14-2-1921

COFFEY, P., Enniskeene, Co. Cork, 14-2-1921

COGAN, J., Stonefield, Oldcastle, Co. Meath, 21-7-1920

COLBERT, C., Monalena, Athea, Co. Limerick, 8-5-1916

COLEMAN, J., North Wall, Cork, 18-11-1920

COLEMAN, R., 32 St Peter's Rd, Phibsborough, Dublin, 7-12-1918

COLEMAN, S., Broad St, Cork, 18-11-1920

COLLINS, Belfast, 19-5-1921

CONNOLE, T., Ennistymon, Co. Clare, 22-9-1920

CONNOLLY, J., Monaghan, 12-5-1916

CONNOLLY, J., Tullaghan, Kinlough, Co. Leitrim, 14-9-1920

CONNOLLY, J., Bandon, Co. Cork, 1-10-1920

CONNOLLY, J., Whitegate, Co. Clare, 17-11-1920

CONNOLLY, M., Whitegate, Co. Clare, 17-11-1920

CONNOLLY, S., 107 Philipsburgh Ave., Dublin, 24-4-1916

CONNOLLY, S., Ballinalee, Co. Longford, 11-3-1921

CONNOLLY, T., Fearmagerk, Kilbrittain, Co. Cork, 16-2-1921

CONNOLLY, W., Upperchurch, Co. Tipperary, 27-6-1921

CONNOR, J., Barrowhouse, Athy, Co. Kildare, 25-5-1921

CONROY, J., Rathconnor, Co. Roscommon, 15-11-1920

CONRY, J., Tarmon, Castlerea, Co. Roscommon, 6-4-1921

CONWAY, J., Rock St, Tralee, Co. Kerry, 1-11-1920

CONWAY, M., Ennistymon, Co. Clare, 21-7-1920

CONWAY, M., Holycross, Bruff, Co. Limerick, 27-12-1920

CORBETT, W., New Rd, Tipperary, 30-9-1920

CORCORAN, J., Cranford, Gorey, Co. Wexford, 25-4-1916

CORCORAN, S., Kiltimagh, Co. Mayo, 1920

CORRIGAN, C., Glasgow, Scotland; Nth Frederick St, Dublin, 28-4-1916

CORRINGHAM, J., Dublin, 14-10-1920

COSGRAVE, E., 65 Lr Dominick St, Dublin, Easter Week 1916

COSGRAVE, J., Eswary, Camlough, Co. Armagh, 13-6-1921

COSTELLO, E.J., Lurgan, Co. Armagh, 25-4-1916

COSTELLO, S., Athlone, Co. Westmeath, 26-4-1916

COUNIHANE, M., Bodyke, Co. Clare, 28-1-1920

COUNIHANE, M., Limerick, 1-7-1920

COYLE, H., 32 Leinster Ave, Dublin, 28-4-1916

CREEDON, E., Mallow, Co. Cork, 15-2-1921

CRENIGAN, J., Roganstown, Swords, Co. Dublin, 28-4-1916

CROMIAN, J., 18 Fingal Place, Dublin, 24-4-1916

CROWLEY, C., Bantry, Co. Cork, 25-6-1920

CROWLEY, D., Cork, 23-3-1921

CROWLEY, D., Dunmanway, Co. Cork, 7-6-1921

CROWLEY, P., Kilbrittain, Co. Cork, 4-2-1921

CROWLEY, T., Cork, 26-11-1920

CROWLEY, T., Dunmanway, Co. Cork, 15-12-1920

CUNNINGHAM, A., Park View, Pigeon Hse Rd, Ringsend, Dublin, Easter Week 1916

CUNNINGHAM, J., Dublin, 15-10-1920

CURTIN, T., Kilrush, Co. Clare, 6-12-1920

CUSACK, R., Ballycotton, Co. Cork, 3-7-1921

DAHILL, T., Dungarvan, Co. Waterford, 9-7-1921

DALTON, J., 5 Clare St, Limerick, 15-5-1920

DALTON, P., Coole East, Athea, Co. Limerick, 12-5-1921

DALY, C., Ballinascarthy, Co. Cork, 19-3-1921

DALY, C., Cork, 29-6-1921

DALY, C. J., Glasshill Rd, Cork, 1-3-1921

DALY, J., Tyrrellspass, Co. Westmeath, 2-7-1920

DALY, J.E., Limerick, 4-5-1916

DANAHER, L., Co. Limerick, 9-11-1920

DANIEL, Kanturk, Co. Cork, August 1921

DARCY, C., Gloucester St, Dublin, 24-4-1916

DARCY, L., Headford, Co. Galway, 24-3-1921

DARCY, M., Cooraclare, Co. Clare, 1919

DEASEY, P., Kilmacsimon Quay, Bandon, Co. Cork, 28-11-1920

DEASY, S., Kilaclug, Co. Cork, September 1920

105

DEASY, W., 23-3-1921

DELANEY, C., Dublin Hill, Cork, 18-12-1920

DELANEY, J., Dublin Hill, Cork, 12-12-1920

DELANEY, W., Roscrea, Co. Tipperary, 18-12-1920

DENNEHY, D., Midleton, Co. Cork, 20-2-1920

DENNEHY, T., Cork, 23-3-1921

DERMODY, M., Threecastles, Co. Kilkenny, 21-2-1921

DESMOND, D., Midleton, Co. Cork, 20-2-1921

DESMOND, M., Midleton, Co. Cork, 20-2-1921

DEVANEY, J., Pallas, Co. Clare, 26-1-1921

DEVANEY, T., Toomevara, Co. Clare, 26-1-1921

DEVITT, M., Cahersherkin, Ennistymon, Co. Clare, 24-2-1920

DICKSON, T., Dublin, 26-4-1916

DIGNAM, Lr Ormond Quay, Dublin, Easter Week 1916

DINEEN, M., Kilcorney, Co. Cork, 24-6-1921

DOHERTY, J., Co. Derry, 28-12-1920

DOHERTY, M., Mayor St, Dublin, 1918

DONNELLAN, B., Loughrea, Co. Galway, 8-5-1916

DONNELLY, E., Croom, Co. Limerick, June 1920

DONOGHUE, J., Bandon, Co. Cork, 3-12-1920

DONOVAN, M., Bandon, Co. Cork, 10-6-1921

DONOVAN, P., Culnigh, Timoleague, Co. Cork, 21-1-1921

DONOVAN, T., Glengoole, Co. Tipperary, 31-10-1920

DORAN, J., Camlough, Co. Armagh, 12-1-1921

DORGAN, P., Mourne Abbey, Cork, 14-2-1921

DORMAN, S., Cork, 25-5-1921

DORRINS, E., Church Rd, East Wall, Dublin, 25-5-1921

DOUGAN, F., Co. Armagh, 26-10-1920

DOWLING, T., Arklow, Co. Wicklow, 4-5-1920

DOWNEY, M., Limerick, 3-5-1921

DOYLE, P., Milltown, Dublin, 27-4-1916

DOYLE, P., Ballinagare, Co. Roscommon, 20-10-1920

DOYLE, P., 1 St Mary's Place, Dublin, 14-3-1921

DOYLE, S., 159 Emmet Rd, Inchicore, Dublin, 19-9-1920

DOYLE, S., 55 Amiens St, Dublin, May 1921

DOYLE, T., Dolphin's Barn, Dublin, 25-11-1920

DUFFIN, D., 64 Clonard Gardens, Belfast, 23-4-1921

DUFFIN, P., 64 Clonard Gardens, Belfast, 23-4-1921

DUFFY, P., Castleblaney, Co. Monaghan, 4-6-1918

DUFFY, S., Monaghan & Limerick, 1-5-1921

DUGGAN, M., Broadford, Co. Limerick, 26-11-1920

DUNFORD, J., Kilnafrehan, Dungarvan, Co. Waterford, 9-7-1921

DUNFORD, W., Kilnafrehan, Dungarvan, Co. Waterford, 9-7-1921

DUNNE, J., Ballintray, Ferns, Co. Wexford, 5-7-1920

DUNNE, T., Loughlinstown, Dublin, 20-5-1920

DURR, P., Ballintubber, Co. Roscommon, 8-1-1921

DWAN, J., Lr Gardiner St, Dublin, 25-4-1916

DWYER, E., Ballydavid, Co. Tipperary, 18-10-1920

DWYER, F., Ballydavid, Co. Tipperary, 18-10-1920

DWYER, T., The Ragg, Co. Tipperary, 30-3-1920

EDMONDS, M., Tipperary, 16-12-1920

EGAN, M., Scarriff, Co. Clare, 17-11-1920

EGAN, T., Galway, 24-10-1920

ENNIS, E., 5 Dromard Ave, Sandymount, Dublin, 27-4-1916

FAHY, M., Kilkee, Co. Clare, 20-3-1920

FALVEY, B., Ballymurphy, Upton, Co. Cork, 16-2-1921

FARRELL, J., Ballymurphy, Borris, Co. Carlow, 18-4-1921

FARRELL, P., Parnell St, Dublin, 25-4-1916

FARRELL, P., Longford, 2-5-1921

FARRELL, T., Dublin, 10-8-1920

FAY, M., Rathvilly, Co. Carlow, 18-4-1921

FEENEY, P., Ballinrobe, Co. Mayo, 3-5-1921

FEERY, T., Ballycommon, Co. Offaly, 9-7-1920

FINN, J., Auburn, Co. Westmeath, 2-11-1920

FINN, S., Rathkeale, Co. Limerick, 30-3-1921

FITZGERALD, F., Scar, Co. Wexford, 12-10-1920

FITZGERALD, J., Gortivicary, Co. Waterford, 19-3-1921

FITZGERALD, L., 173 Pearse St, Dublin, 14-3-1921

FITZGERALD, M., Fermoy, Co. Cork, 17-10-1920

FITZGERALD, M., Minard West, Co. Kerry, 22-3-1921

FITZGERALD, T., Gaggin, Bandon, Co. Cork, 29-8-1920

FLEMING, J., Cork, 7-12-1920

FLEMING, R., Drangan, Co. Tipperary, 6-3-1921

FLEMING, T., Castleisland, Tralee, Co. Kerry, 10-7-1921

FLOOD, Barracks St, Dundalk, Co. Louth, 1920

FLOOD, F., 30 Summerhill Parade, Dublin, 14-3-1921

FLYNN, J., Ballymacelligott, Co. Kerry, 10-7-1921

FLYNN, M., Mullingar, Co. Westmeath, 25-10-1920

FLYNN, P., Tarmon, Co. Roscommon, 23-11-1920

FLYNN, P., Mourne Abbey, Co. Cork, 15-2-1921

FOGARTY, P., Clontarf, Dublin, 18-4-1920

FOLEY, C., Cork, 6-3-1921

FOLEY, E., Galbally, Co. Tipperary, 7-6-1921

FOX, F., 92 Durham St, Belfast, 15-8-1921

FOX, J., 74 Thomas St, Dublin, and Co. Meath, 25-4-1916

FRAHILL, S., Limerick, 2-5-1921

FREANEY, P., Thomastown, Co. Kilkenny, 11-4-1921

FURLONG, M., Summerhill, Co. Wexford, 15-10-1920

GALVIN, J., Main St, Bandon, Co. Cork, 3-12-1920

GALVIN, M., Macroom, Co. Cork, 20-9-1920

GALVIN, M., Crampton Buildings, Dublin, 9-4-1921

GARVEY, M., Ballyrath, Co. Armagh, 26-10-1920

GAVIN, P., Curragh, Co. Kildare, 13-2-1919

GAYNOR, S., Springfield Rd, Belfast, 26-9-1920

GEOGHEGAN, G., Cork St, Dublin, 26-4-1916

GIBBONS, J., Balbriggan, Co. Dublin, 21-9-1920

GILL, P., Corlara, Co. Leitrim, 10-9-1920

GLAVEY, M., Ballinlough, Co. Roscommon, 14-9-1920

GLAVIN, J., Cobh, Co. Cork, 20-2-1921

GLEESON, A., Liverpool, 1918

GLEESON, C., Upperchurch, Co. Tipperary, 23-5-1921

GLEESON, F., Fairview, Dublin, 14-5-1920

GLEESON, J., Scar, Co. Wexford, 12-10-1920

GLEESON, M., Meelick, Co. Galway, 15-6-1921

GLEESON, W., Thurles, Co. Tipperary, 26-10-1920

GLYNN, P., Aughaderry, Loughglynn, Co. Roscommon, 14-9-1920

GLYNN, T., Drumshinnagh, Cootehall, Co. Roscommon, 9-4-1921

GRANT, P., Mullabane, Co. Armagh, 4-7-1920

GRIFFIN, M., Gurteen, Co. Galway, 15-11-1920

GROGAN, J., Feakle, Co. Clare, 29-6-1921

HACKETT, J., Knocknagashel, Co. Kerry, 27-12-1920

HACKETT, P., Rathkenny, Drangan, Co. Tipperary, 6-3-1921

HALLIHANE, M., Midleton, Co. Cork, 20-2-1921

HALPIN, S., Drogheda, Co. Louth, 9-2-1921

HAND, T., Skerries, Co. Dublin, 5-12-1920

HANLEY, P., Cork City, 17-11-1920

HARRIS, T., Bruree, Co. Limerick, 29-7-1920

HARTNETT, P., Abbeyfeale, Co. Limerick, 20-9-1920

HARTNETT, W., Emly, Co. Limerick, 8-8-1920

HASSETT, P., Killimer, Co. Clare, 21-3-1921

HAWLEY, T., Tralee, Co. Kerry, 22-3-1921

HAYDEN, J., Gortford, Gliter, Cookstown, Co. Tyrone, 17-5-1921

HAYES, J., Knockarden, Co. Tipperary, 4-3-1921

HEAD, D., Seville Place, Dublin, 25-5-1921

HEALY, E., Lismore, Co. Waterford, February 1921

HEALY, J., Abbeyfeale, Co. Limerick, 20-9-1920

HEALY, S., Phibsborough, Dublin, 24-4-1916

HEALY, T., Duagh, Co. Kerry, 1921

HEFFERNAN, W., Castlemartyr, Co. Cork, 27-1-1920

HEGARTY, D., Clanflusk, Co. Cork, 21-1-1921

HEGARTY, L., Ballyvourney, Macroom, Co. Cork, 5-9-1920

HEGARTY, R., Garryvoe, Co. Cork, 20-2-1921

HENNESSY, P., Milltown Malbay, Co. Clare, 23-3-1920

HENNESSY, T., Threecastles, Co. Kilkenny, 21-2-1921

HENNESSY, T., Limerick, 1-5-1921

HERLIHY, D., Nadd, Co. Cork, 9-3-1921

HERLIHY, J., Ballymacelligott, Co. Kerry, 12-11-1920

HEUSTON, S., Dublin, 8-5-1916

HICKEY, J., Dun Laoghaire, Co. Dublin, 14-12-1920

HICKEY, J., Knocknagashel, Co. Kerry, 26-12-1920.

HICKEY, L., Main St, Thurles, Co. Tipperary, 10-3-1921

HICKEY, L., Rathmore, Co. Kerry, June 1921

HOFFMAN, F., Farmer's Bridge, Tralee, Co. Kerry, 10-11-1920

HOGAN, J., Fanningstown, Co. Limerick, June 1920

HOGAN, M., Grangemockler, Co. Tipperary, 21-11-1920

HOGAN, P., Longfield, Co. Tipperary, 3-3-1921

HOGAN, W., Dillon's Cross, Cork, 29-6-1921

HORAN, J., Limerick, 1-5-1921

HOULIHAN, S., Ballyduff, Co. Kerry, 31-10-1920

HOWARD, S., 26 Temple Cottages, Broadstone, Dublin, 2-5-1916

HOWARD, T., Glenbrohane, Co. Limerick, 2-5-1921

HOWETT, Galway, January 1921

HOWLEY, J., Oranmore, Co. Galway, 4-12-1920

HOWLEY, T., Ballina, Co. Mayo, 29-5-1921

HUGHES, P., Roscommon, 29-8-1920

HURLEY, C., Kilbrittain, Co. Cork, 19-3-1921

HURLEY, D., Bandon, Co. Cork, 28-5-1921

HURLEY, F., Laragh, Co. Cork, 9-5-1921

HURLEY, S., Drinagh, Co. Cork, 28-4-1916

HURTON, D., Ardmore, Co. Waterford, 9-11-1921

HYMAN, J., Emly, Co. Limerick, 22-12-1920

HYNES, J., Shanagolden, Co. Limerick, 26-8-1920

JORDAN, P., Islandeady, Co. Mayo, 19-5-1921

JOYCE, J.J., Midleton, Co. Cork, 20-2-1921

KAVANAGH, E., Oxford Rd, Ranelagh, Dublin, 25-4-1916

KEALY, J., Kilkenny, 9-5-1916

KEANE, J., Dromin Hill, Co. Limerick, 3-1-1920

KEANE, M., Ballinlough, Co. Roscommon, 14-9-1920

KEANE, R., Hymenstown, Co. Tipperary, 3-3-1921

KEANE, T., Limerick, 4-6-1921

KEATING, C., Cahirciveen, Co. Kerry, 21-4-1916

KEATING, P., Comeragh, Kilmacthomas, Co. Waterford, 19-3-1921

KEELY, J., Main St, Rathfarnham, Dublin, 24-4-1916

KELLEHER, T., Clonbroney, Co. Longford, 18-5-1921

KELLY, H., Ballygawley, Co. Sligo, 17-10-1920

KELLY, J., Dublin, 25-4-1916

KELLY, M., Glaslough St, Monaghan, 20-10-1920

KENNEDY, P., Annascaul, Co. Kerry, 19-8-1920

KENNEDY, P., Dublin, 9-2-1921

KENNELLY, J., Mooneen, Moybella, Co. Kerry, 10-3-1921

KENT, R., Castlelyons, Coole, Co. Cork, 4-5-1916

KENT, T., Castlelyons, Coole, Co. Cork, 9-5-1916

KEOGH, G., Elm Grove, Ranelagh, Dublin, 27-4-1916

KEOGH, M., Leighlinbridge, Co. Carlow, 24-4-1916

KERR, N., Pigeon Hse Rd, Ringsend, Dublin, 3-9-1920

KIELY, T., Mallow, Co. Cork, 9-3-1921

KILDEA, M., Woodlawn, Co. Galway, 17-11-1920

KILLIAN, L., Crith, Co. Roscommon, 21-8-1921

KILLOURY, D., Moymore, Co. Clare, 5-5-1921

LACEY, J., Augharea, Athy, Co. Kildare, May 1921

LAIDE, R., Ballymacelligott, Co. Kerry, 18-4-1918

LARKIN, T., Rosegreen, Co. Tipperary, 6-3-1921

LATIMER, Co. Leitrim, April 1921

LAWLESS, J., Balbriggan, Co. Dublin, 20-9-1920

LAWLESS, T., Portlaoise, Co. Laois, 21-1-1921

LAWLOR, J., Main St, Waterford, 2-12-1920

LAWLOR, J., Ardfert, Co. Kerry, 1-1-1921

LEDLIE, S., Pleuna St, Belfast, 11-7-1921

LEE, T., Fethard, Co. Tipperary, 4-3-1921

LEEN, J., Ballymacelligott, Co. Kerry, 25-12-1920

LEHANE, D., Lahinch, Co. Clare, 22-9-1920

LEHANE, J., Ballymakeera, Co. Cork, 1-11-1920

LEHANE, P., Lahinch, Co. Clare, 26-9-1920

LEONARD, R., Pallasgreen, Co. Limerick, 31-12-1920

LINNANE, P.J., Lahinch, Co. Clare, 22-9-1920

LOOBY, J.J., Dualla, Co. Tipperary, 20-12-1920

LOOBY, L., Dualla, Co. Tipperary, 19-12-1920

LOOBY, T., Shrough, Ardvillane, Co. Tipperary, 1-3-1921

LOONEY, M., Burnfort, Co. Cork, 17-2-1921

LOUGHNANE, H., Gort, Co. Galway, 6-12-1920

LOUGHNANE, P., Gort, Co. Galway, 6-12-1920

LOUGHNANE, W., Thurles, Co. Tipperary, 10-3-1921

LOUGHRAN, P., Dungannon, Co. Tyrone, 17-6-1920

LUCY, C., Cork, 10-11-1920

LUMLEY, R., Rear Cross, Co. Tipperary, 4-7-1920

LYNCH, Milltown Malbay, Co. Clare, 22-9-1920

LYNCH, C., Milltown Malbay, Co. Clare, 25-10-1920

LYNCH, J., Kilmallock, Co. Limerick, 22-9-1920

LYNCH, M., Ballyvourney, Macroom, Co. Cork, 5-9-1920

LYNCH, P., Dublin, Easter Week 1916

LYNCH, P., Hospital, Co. Limerick, 14-8-1920

LYNCH, P., Golden, Co. Tipperary, 10-11-1920

LYNCH, R., Dungarvan, Co. Waterford, 9-7-1921

LYONS, J., Duagh, Co. Kerry, 1921

LYONS, J., Coachford, Co. Cork, 28-2-1921

LYONS, T., Kinapagh, Co. Mayo, 21-11-1920

McANEANEY, M., Balleady, Co. Monaghan, 30-6-1921

McANEANEY, T., Corlealackagh, Co. Monaghan, 30-6-1921

McATEER, P., Faughilotra, Co. Antrim, 5-6-1921

McBRIDE, A., Cardigan Drive, Cliftonville, Belfast, 12-6-1921

MacBRIDE, J., Westport, Co. Mayo, 5-5-1916

McCAN, P., Ballyowen House, Dualla, Co. Tipperary, 6-3-1919

McCANN, J., Quay Lane, Rush, Co. Dublin, 22-11-1920

McCARRON, J., Ballybofey, Donegal, 2-6-1921

McCARRY, P., Ballycastle, Co. Antrim, 17-7-1921

McCARTHY, C., Ballinadea, Cork, 16-2-1921

McCARTHY, C., Coore, Milltown Malbay, Co. Clare, 15-6-1921

McCARTHY, J., Thurles, Co. Tipperary, 30-3-1920

McCARTHY, M., Dunmanway, Co. Cork, 28-11-1920

McCARTHY, P., Meelin, Co. Cork, 22-11-1920

McCARTHY, P., Killarney, Co. Kerry, 29-6-1921

McCARTHY, S., Norfolk St, Belfast, 8-5-1921

McCARTHY, T., Cork, 28-2-1921

McCARTHY, W., Lixnaw, Co. Kerry, 26-3-1921

McCLEAN, M., Schull, Co. Cork, 8-12-1920

McCORMACK, J., Julianstown, Co. Meath, 28-4-1916

McCREESH, P., Aughnaduff, Co. Armagh, 6-6-1920

MacCURTAIN, T., Blackpool, Cork, 20-3-1920

McDERMOTT, S., Kiltyclogher, Co. Leitrim, 12-5-1916

McDERMOTT, S., Blacklion, Ballinagard, Co. Roscommon, 19-4-1921

MacDONAGH, T., Cloughjordan, Co. Tipperary, 3-5-1916

McDONAGH, T., Cloonloo, Co. Sligo, 1-9-1920

McDONNELL, T., Corrunna Cross, Cork, 21-7-1920

McDOWELL, W., 10 Merchant's Quay, Dublin, 24-4-1916

McELLIGOTT, M.R., Listowel, Co. Kerry, 19-2-1921

McENERY, D., Monegay, Co. Limerick, 27-3-1921

McENTYRE, S., Lagan, Belturbert, Co. Cavan, 3-6-1921

McEVER, T., Dunmore, Co. Galway, 2-5-1921

McEVILLY, S., Castlebar, Co. Mayo, 19-5-1921

McEVOY, C., 73 Gloucester St, Dublin, 6-11-1921

McFADDEN, S., Springfield Rd, Belfast, 26-9-1920

McGOWAN, J., Portahard, Frenchpark, Roscommon, 23-12-1920

McGRATH, D., Corruna Cross, Co. Cork, 21-7-1920

McGRATH, J., Rathclarin, Co. Cork, 16-2-1921

McGRATH, M., Polebery, Waterford, 7-1-1921

McGRATH, W., Cork, 18-7-1920

McGREAL, M., Craughwell, Co. Galway, 15-6-1921

McINTOSH, J., Portlaoise, Co. Laois, 22-6-1921

McINTYRE, P., Dublin, 26-4-1916

McKEE, D., Finglas, Co. Dublin, 21-11-1920

MACKEN, F., Main St, Rathfarnham, Dublin, 28-4-1916

MACKEN, P., 13 Nassau Place, Dublin, 26-4-1916

McKINGNEY, H., Newry, Co. Down, 7-4-1921

McLEAN, M., Lowertown, Schull, Co. Cork, 8-12-1920

MacMACKIN, B., Drogheda, Co. Louth, 29-5-1917

McMAHON, J., Ballymacelligott, Co. Kerry, 12-11-1920

McMAHON, M., Scarriff, Co. Clare, 17-11-1920

McNALLY, J., Cranagh, Co. Tyrone, 6-7-1921

McNAMARA, W., Doonbeg, Co. Clare, 24-12-1920

McNEICE, F., Tartaraghan, Loughall, Co. Armagh, 15-8-1920

McSWIGGIN, J., Magherafelt, Co. Derry, 20-11-1920

MacSWINEY, T., Cork, 25-10-1920

MADIGAN, T., Shanagolden, Co. Limerick, March 1921

MAGEE Brothers, Cornogs, Newry, Co. Down, June 1921

MAGEE, J., Boher, Cooley, Co. Louth, 13-5-1921

MAGEE, M., 20 Ostman Pl., Arbour Hill, Dublin, 21-1-1921

MAGNIER (Canon), Dunmanway, Co. Cork, 15-12-1920

MAGUIRE, M., Ardfert, Co. Kerry, 5-10-1920

MAHER, P., Galbally, Co. Tipperary, 7-6-1921

MALLIN, M., Emmet Hall, Inchicore, Dublin, 8-5-1916

MALONE, M., Sth Circular Rd, Dublin, 27-4-1916

MALONEY, E., Limerick, 27-12-1920

MALONEY, J., Croom, Co. Limerick, June 1920

MALONEY, P.J., Tipperary, 1-5-1921

MANNING, P., 4 Broadstone Ave, Dublin, 28-4-1916

MARRON, B., Co. Monaghan, 1-9-1920

MARRON, P., Co. Monaghan, 1-9-1920

MEANY, P., Tomard, Co. Carlow, 21-5-1920

MEHIGAN, J., Cork, 23-11-1920

MONAGHAN, C., Belfast, 21-4-1916

MONAHAN, P., Bandon, Co. Cork, 19-3-1921

MONDS, J., South Park, Castlerea, Co. Roscommon, 6-4-1921

MOORE, H., Derry, 26-10-1920

MOORE, M., Cobh, Co. Cork., 28-2-1921

MORAN, J., Church St, Enniscorthy, Co. Wexford, 9-2-1921

MORAN, M., Tuam, Co. Galway, 24-11-1920

MORAN, P., Crossna, Boyle, Co. Roscommon, 14-3-1921

MORRIS, P., Co. Tyrone, 10-6-1921

MORRISON, D., Belfast, 27-12-1921

MORRISSEY, C., Cork, 21-11-1920

MORRISSEY, D., Cork, 26-11-1920

MORRISSEY, J., Athlone, Co. Westmeath, 20-2-1921

MOY, F., Bridgend, Co. Donegal, 16-10-1920

MOYNIHAN, A., Gneevguilla, Co. Kerry, 1921

MULCAHY, A., Currabeha, Co. Cork, 22-3-1921

MULCAHY, J., Nicker, Co. Limerick, 31-7-1920

MULCAHY, T., Mourne Abbey, Co. Cork, 28-2-1921

MULCAHY, W., Cork, 26-11-1920

MULHOLLAND, T., John St, Dundalk, Co. Louth, 16-4-1920

MULLAN, J., Killucan, Co. Westmeath, 13-12-1920

MULLANE, J., Cork, 23-3-1921

MULLOOLY, M., Kiltrustan, Strokes-, Co. Roscommon, 24-3-1921

MULVIHILL, M., Lixnaw, Co. Kerry, 28-4-1916

MULVOY, S., Galway, 10-9-1920

MURPHY, Glan, Co. Clare, 14-8-1919

MURPHY, A., Watkins Bdgs, The Coombe, Dublin, 24-3-1921

MURPHY, C., Rathmore, Co. Kerry, 1-2-1921

MURPHY, C., Timoleague, Co. Cork, 11-5-1921

MURPHY, D., Cork, 23-3-1921

MURPHY, F., Bandon, Co. Cork, 5-12-1920

MURPHY, J., Cork, 25-10-1920

MURPHY, J., 22 Killarney St, Dublin, 12-2-1921

MURPHY, J., Longford, 26-5-1921

MURPHY, J., Bandon, Co. Cork, 22-6-1921

MURPHY, M., Dundalk, Co. Louth, 21-6-1919

MURPHY, P., Blarney St, Cork, 29-6-1921

MURPHY, R., South William St, Dublin, 27-4-1916

MURPHY, T., Ballylanders, Co. Limerick, 1-1-1921

MURPHY, T., Foxrock, Dublin, 30-5-1921

MURPHY, W., Ballincollig, Co. Cork, 27-6-1921

MURRAY, D., 35 Lr Mt Pleasant Ave, Rathmines, Dublin, 25-4-1916

MYLES, J., Castlemaine, Co. Kerry, 1-6-1921

NAIGHRAN, P., Dungannon, Co. Tyrone, 17-6-1920

NOLAN, E., Askamore, Co. Wexford, 12-8-1920

NUNAN, P., Ardprior, Buttevant, Co. Cork, 28-9-1920

O'BEIRNE, J., Selton, Co. Leitrim, 13-3-1921

O'BOYLE, C., Oughtmeen, Dungloe, Co. Donegal, July 1921

O'BRIEN, D., Liscarroll, Co. Cork, 16-5-1921

O'BRIEN, J., Cork, 19-7-1920

O'BRIEN, J., Nenagh, Co. Tipperary, 4-11-1920

O'BRIEN, J.P., Coolacappa, Co. Limerick, February 1921

O'BRIEN, M., Shercock, Co. Cavan, 5-12-1920

O'BRIEN, M., Duke St, Dublin, 8-9-1921

O'BRIEN, M.J., Neale, Co. Mayo, 3-5-1921

O'BRIEN, P., Co. Tipperary, 26-12-1920

O'BRIEN, S., Morriscastle, Kilmuckridge, Co. Wexford, 12-2-1920

O'BRIEN, T., Nenagh, Co. Tipperary, 5-11-1920

O'BRIEN, T., Dunhill, Co. Waterford, 7-1-1921

O'BRIEN, T., Dripsey, Co. Cork, 28-2-1921

O'BRIEN, W., Rathmore, Co. Kerry, 30-5-1921

O'BRYAN, T., Sean MacDermott St, Dublin, 14-3-1921

O'CALLAGHAN, M., Limerick, 7-3-1921

O'CALLAGHAN, P., Dripsey, Co. Cork, 28-2-1921

O'CARROLL, P., Manor St, Dublin, 16-10-1920

O'CARROLL, S., Gibson St, Belfast, 30-11-1920

O'CARROLL, T.C., Camden St, Dublin, 5-5-1916

O'CONNELL (Miss), Ardfert, Co. Kerry, 15-11-1920

O'CONNELL, E., 7 Broadlane, Cork, 17-11-1920

O'CONNELL, J., Derrygallon, Co. Cork, 17-8-1920

O'CONNELL, L., Glantane, Co. Cork, 14-10-1920

O'CONNOR, J., Killarney, Co. Kerry, 18-12-1920

O'CONNOR, P., Rathmore, Co. Kerry, 28-4-1916

O'CONNOR, P., Co. Tipperary, 19-12-1920

O'DONNELL, T., Rosclare, Newport, Co. Mayo, 19-5-1921

O'DONOGHUE, J., Cork, 3-12-1920

O'DONOGHUE, J., Ballinacargy, Co. Westmeath, 6/7-3-1921

O'DONOVAN, P., Timoleague, Co. Cork, 17-1-1921

O'DRISCOLL, P., Mohana, Skibbereen, Co. Cork, 7-2-1921

O'DWYER, D., 7 Walworth Rd, Sth Circular Rd, Dublin, 20-3-1921

O'DWYER, E., Ballydavid, Co. Tipperary, 19-10-1920

O'DWYER, F., Ballydavid, Co. Tipperary, 19-10-1920

O'DWYER, R., Limerick, 2-2-1920

O'DWYER, T., 'The Ragg', Baileduff, Co. Tipperary, 30-3-1920

O'FLANAGAN, P., Hardwicke St, Dublin, 29-4-1916

O'GRADY, J., Ormond Way, Dublin, 29-4-1916

O'HALLORAN, P., Limerick, 30-1-1921

O'HANLON, B., Dundalk, Co. Louth, 14-3-1921

O'HANLON, J., Lackagh, Galway, 2-10-1920

Ó hANNRACHÁIN, M., New Ross, Co. Wexford, 4-5-1916

O'HARE, H., Newry, Co. Down, 22-10-1921

O'HARE, J.F., Needham St, Newry, Co. Down, 5-10-1921

O'HERLIHY, J., Ovens, Co. Cork, 11-10-1920

Ó h-IGHNE, M., Glencolumcille, Co. Donegal, 28-2-1921

O'KEEFE, J., Ballinvoher, Co. Tipperary, 5-2-1921

O'LEARY, J., Dublin, 21-11-1920

O'LEARY, J., Corrin Leap, Co. Cork, 19-3-1921

O'LEARY, T., Milltown Malbay, Co. Clare, 20-4-1920

O'LOUGHLIN, J., Cormackstown, Thurles, Co. Tipperary, 5-4-1921

O'LOUGHLIN, J., Milltown Malbay, Co. Clare, 14-4-1921

O'LOUGHLIN, M., Killinan, Co. Tipperary, 26-11-1920 or 14-12-1920

O'MAHONEY, D., Copeen, Co. Cork, 15-2-1921

O'MAHONEY, J., Copeen, Co. Cork, 10-12-1920

O'MAHONY, P., Berrings, Co. Cork, 28-2-1921

O'MALLEY, T., Islandready, Castlebar, Co. Mayo, May 1921

O'MEARA, F., Tipperary, 27-1-1921

O'MEARA, J., Ballyhone, Emly, Co. Tipperary, 28-6-1921

O'NEILL, A., Dublin, 1920

O'NEILL, J., Limerick, 20-11-1920

O'NEILL, J., Kilbrittain, Co. Cork, 16-2-1921

O'RAHILLY (The), Ballylongford, Co. Kerry, 28-4-1916

O'REGAN, D., Castlefreke, Co. Cork, 8-12-1920

O'REILLY, D., Granassig, Co. Cork, 24-1-1921

O'REILLY, P., Granassig, Co. Cork, 24-1-1921

O'REILLY, P., Dublin, 25-5-1921

O'REILLY, R., Dublin, 24-4-1916

O'REILLY, S., Lr Gardiner St, Dublin, 24-4-1916

O'REILLY, S., Dublin, 25-5-1921

O'REILLY, S., Cloghoe, Newry, Co. Down, 4-7-1921

O'REILLY, T., 43 Geraldine St, Dublin, 27-4-1916

O'REILLY, T., Cloghoe, Newry, Co. Down, 4-7-1921

O'RIORDAN, W., Cullane, Limerick, 2-5-1921

O'ROURKE, J., Waterford, 27-5-1921

O'ROURKE, M., Sean MacDermott St, Dublin, 17-10-1920

O'SHEA, M., Granagh, Co. Limerick, March 1921

O'SULLIVAN, C., Midleton, Co. Cork, 20-2-1921

O'SULLIVAN, J., Limerick, 30-7-1920

O'SULLIVAN, J., Rossmore, Co. Cork, 28-11-1920

O'SULLIVAN, M., Cork, 23-3-1921

O'SULLIVAN, P., Raheen, Upton, Co. Cork, 18-2-1921

O'SULLIVAN, P., Cobh, Co. Cork, 28-4-1921

O'SULLIVAN, S., Sallins, Co. Kildare, 4-5-1921

O'SULLIVAN, T., Rathmore, Co. Kerry, 19-5-1921

O'TOOLE, P., Brown St, Carlow, 8-2-1921

OWENS, J., The Coombe, Dublin, 24-4-1916

OWENS, W., Loughlinstown, Co. Dublin, 10-12-1920

PATTERSON, M., Ballybough, Dublin, April 1921

PEARSE, P.H., Rathfarnham, Dublin, 3-5-1916

PEARSE, W., Rathfarnham, Dublin, 4-5-1916

PHELAN, J., Liverpool, England, 16-2-1921

PIGGOT, J., Limerick, 15-8-1921

PLUNKETT, J.M., 26 Upr Fitzwilliam St, Dublin, 4-5-1916

POWER, F., Cork, 28-2-1921

PRENDERVILLE, J., Castleisland, Co. Kerry, 10-7-1921

PURCELL, M., Dundrum, Co. Tipperary, 30-5-1921

QUAINE, J., Cork, 10-5-1921

QUINLAN, D., Hollyford, Co. Tipperary, 13-2-1921

QUINLAN, J., Limerick, 27-12-1920

QUINN, E., Kiltartan, Co. Galway, 1-11-1920

QUINN, J., 2 Hammond St, Blackpitts, Dublin, 24-4-1916

QUINN, J., Dungarvan, Co. Waterford, 9-7-1921

QUIRKE, S., Cork, 10-9-1920

RAFFERTY, T., Lusk, Co. Dublin, 28-4-1916

RAFTER, S., Enniscorthy, Co. Wexford, 12-9-1918

REDMOND, M., Dublin, 26-4-1916

REGAN (Mrs), Callan, Co. Kilkenny, December 1920

REIDY, M., Ballymacelligott, Co. Kerry, 25-12-1920

REILLY, C., Newmarket, Co. Cork, 23-3-1921

REILLY, J.J., Derrincahir, Co. Leitrim, 11-3-1921

REILLY, J.J., Miskawn, Co. Leitrim, 11-3-1921

REYNOLDS, C., Woodview Tce, Rathfarnham, Dublin, 1-4-1921

REYNOLDS, G., Ringsend, Dublin, 27-4-1916

RIORDAN, S., Kilfinan, Co. Limerick, 10-12-1920

ROBINSON, W., Dublin, 21-11-1920

ROCHE, M., Scar, Co. Wexford, 12-10-1920

RODGERS, A., Scarriff, Co. Clare, 17-11-1920

ROURKE, P., Lissycasey, Co. Clare, 22-5-1921

ROYNANE, P., Mourne Abbey, Co. Cork, 28-2-1921

RUSSELL, T., Dingle, Co. Kerry, 30-3-1918

RYAN, B., 7 Royal Canal, Dublin, 14-3-1921

RYAN, F., 4 High St, Dublin, 27-4-1916

RYAN, J., Limerick, 3-5-1921

RYAN, J., Woodstock, Carrigtwohill, Co. Cork, 15-5-1921

RYAN, M., Curraghduff, Co. Tipperary, 25-10-1920

RYAN, M., Ballymurphy, Borris, Co. Carlow, 18-4-1921

RYAN, P., Limerick, 2-5-1921

RYAN, P., Knockfine, Co. Tipperary, 6-6-1921

RYAN, T., Wexford, 21-11-1920

RYNNE, J., Kilcrummin, Ballinamore, Co. Leitrim, 11-3-1921

SALMON, J., Feakle, Co. Clare, 22-9-1920

SAUNDERS, J., Limerick, 28-5-1920

SAVAGE, M., Ballisodare, Co. Sligo, 19-12-1919

SCALLY, J., Portnahinch, Lanesboro, Co. Longford, 11-5-1921

SCANLON, D., Ballybunion, Co. Kerry, 11-7-1917

SCANLON, M., Kilmallock, Co. Limerick, 5-11-1920

SCOTT, J., Dublin, 21-11-1921

SCULLY, L., Glencar, Co. Kerry, 28-5-1920

SEERY, P., Cloneyheigue, Co. Westmeath, 1-6-1920

SHANAHAN, R., Castleisland, Co. Kerry, 10-7-1921

SHANAHAN, W., Doughmore, Co. Clare, 24-12-1920

SHANNON, E., Aughaderry, Co. Roscommon, 17-6-1921

SHEAHAN, J., Coilbwee, Co. Kerry, 26-5-1921

SHEEHAN, D., Newcastlewest, Co. Limerick, 21-4-1916

SHEEHAN, D., Holycross, Bruff, Co. Limerick, 27-12-1920

SHEEHY SKEFFINGTON, F., Dublin, 26-4-1916

SHERIDAN, T., Co. Cavan, 27-5-1920

SHERLOCK, J., Skerries, Co. Dublin, 27-10-1920

SHIELDS, P., Newry, Co. Down, 25-12-1920

SHORTIS, P., Ballybunion, Co. Kerry, 28-4-1916

SLATTERY, W., Lisobyhane, Emly, Co. Tipperary, 31-12-1920

SLOAN, J., Legan, Moate, Co. Westmeath, 14-1-1921

SMALL, M., Upperchurch, Co. Tipperary, 4-7-1920

SMYTH, M., Co. Donegal, 27-12-1920

SNODDY, E., Quinagh, Co. Carlow, 5-1-1921

SPRIGGS, D., Blarney St, Cork, 8-7-1921

STAINES, L., Balangare, Co. Roscommon, 2-11-1918

STARR, P., Silver St, Nenagh, Co. Tipperary, 1-5-1921

STAUNTON, Kilmeena, Co. Mayo, 19-5-1921

STENNING, F., Bandon, Co. Cork, April 1921

STODART, H., Victoria Villas, Blackrock, Co. Dublin, 26-4-1916

STUDERT, P., Kilkee, Co. Clare, 3-7-1919

SULLIVAN, J., Clonakilty, Co. Cork, 28-11-1920

TAYLOR, G., Glencar, Co. Kerry, 1921

THOMPSON, P., Lisnadaragh, Finea, Co. Westmeath, 6-10-1920

TIERNEY, P., Ardee, Co. Louth, 1920

TOBIN, D., Ballinalackin, Co. Limerick, 1-1-1921

TOBIN, M., Ballineen, Co. Cork, 9-11-1920

TOLAN, M., Ballina, Co. Mayo, 14-4-1921

TORMEY, J., Moneen, Moate, Co. Westmeath, 14-1-1921

TORMEY, J., Moneen, Moate, Co. Westmeath, 2-2-1921

TRAHEY, P., Cork, 23-11-1920

TRAYNOR, J.J., 3 Shannon Tce, Kilmainham, Dublin, 24-4-1916

TRAYNOR, T., Tullow, Co. Carlow, 26-4-1921

TREACY, S., Solohead, Co. Tipperary, 14-10-1920

TRODDEN, E., 68 Falls Rd, Belfast, 25-9-1920

TULLY, H., Cloneyquinn, Co. Roscommon, 11-5-1921

VAUGHAN, J., Cloonsuck, Castlerea, Co. Roscommon, 17-6-1921

WADE, H., Limerick, 27-12-1920

WALL, S., Limerick, 16-5-1921

WALL, T., Tralee, Co. Kerry, 2-11-1920

WALSH, E., Lr Dominick St, Dublin, 24-4-1916

WALSH, J., Ballymacelligott, Co. Kerry, 1920

WALSH, M., Longford, April 1919

WALSH, M., Ring, Dungarvan, Co. Waterford, 15-5-1919

WALSH, M., Old Malt House, Galway, 20-10-1920

WALSH, P., Manor St, Dublin, 29-4-1916

WALSH, P., Tubrid, Kilkenny, 18-5-1921

WALSH, P., Listowel, Co. Kerry, n.d.

WALSH, R., Scar, Co. Wexford, 12-10-1920

WALTON, M., Co. Tipperary, 19-12-1920

WATERS, E., Nadd, Co. Cork, 9-3-1921

WATTERS, J., Barrack St, Dundalk, Co. Louth, 17-6-1921

WATTERS, P., Barrack St, Dundalk, Co. Louth, 17-6-1921

WEAFER, P., Enniscorthy, Co. Wexford, 27-4-1916

WEEKES, A., Norwich, England, 28-4-1916

WEIR, E., Knockalaughta, Ballintubber, Co. Roscommon, April 1921

WHELAN, J., Ballyroan, Co. Laois, 20-12-1920

WHELAN, P., Dublin, 27-4-1916

WHELAN, S., Cork, 3-7-1921

WHELAN, T., Galway, 14-3-1921

WHITE, P., Donabate, Dublin, 18-4-1921

WHOOLEY, T., Ballineen, Co. Cork, 22-3-1921

WHYTE, P., Meelick, Co. Clare, 1-6-1921

WILSON, P., Swords, Co. Dublin, 26-4-1916

WYNNE, P., Culeenboy, Co. Roscommon, April 1921

THE CROWN DEAD

Order of details, when given: name, rank, affiliation, place of action leading to death and date of death. Where no county name is given, it means that information was not given in the original documentation and could not be determined by other means.

[No complete list of Crown Forces casualties has ever been issued. The following is a representative list and is by no means complete.

Because many Auxiliaries were retired British Army personnel who continued using their rank and unit, they appear along with regular troops, Black and Tans, and others under the heading MILITARY.

British government policy and the exigencies of manpower prevented the demilitarization of the RIC during the War of Independence and so they became legitimate targets to the IRA. Again, the Constabulary List and Directory for the period does not elaborate on the causes of death during the period so the lists of casualties classified as RIC, Special Constabulary and DMP that follow are also incomplete.]

MILITARY

ACHESON, Maj, Army Service Corps, Dublin, April 1916

ADAMS, Lt, 1 Royal Fusiliers, Headford, Co. Galway, 21-3-1921

AIMES, Lt, Rifle Bde, Dublin, 21-11-1920

AIRY, Capt, 1 Manchesters, Macroom, Co. Cork, 21-7-1920

ALLAT, Col, Dublin, April 1916

ANGLISS, Lt, Dublin, 21-11-1920

APPLEFORD, Dublin, 24-6-1921

BAGALLAY, Capt, 5th Wales Borderers, Dublin, 21-11-1920

BAKER, Dvr (RASC), Att 1st Essex Rgt, Crossbarry, Co. Cork, 19-3-1921

BALL, Aux, Dublin, 5-12-1920

BANKS, Sth Staffordshire Rgt, Dublin, April 1916

BANTING, Sth Staffordshire Rgt, Dublin, April 1916

BARKS, L/Cpl, Sherwood Foresters, Dublin, April 1916

BARNES, Cdt, RAF, Kilmichael, Co. Cork, 28-11-1920

BARNES, Pte, Royal Norfolk Rgt, Belfast, September 1920

BARRATT, Sherwood Foresters, Dublin, April 1916

BARRETT, Cpl, Sth Staffordshire Rgt, Dublin, April 1916

BARRY, Maj, Cork Detention Barracks, 8-4-1921

BATEMAN, Pte, Oxfordshire Rgt, Cratloe, Co. Clare, 18-11-1920

121

BAYLEY, Cdt, RAF, Kilmichael, Co. Cork, 28-11-1920

BAYLISS, Pte, Oxfordshire Rgt, Oola, Co. Limerick, July 1920

BEARD, Sect/Ldr, Dublin, 14-3-1921

BEATTIE, L/Cpl, 2nd Hampshire Rgt, Cork, 28-2-1921

BEATTIE, Capt, Northamptonshire Rgt, Templemore, Co. Tipperary, 1920

BELL, Cpl, Border Rgt, Ballinrobe, Co. Mayo, 8-3-1921

BENNETT, Sgt (RASC), Att 1st Essex, Annesbagh, 22-10-1920

BENNETT, Temp Capt, Royal Artillery, Dublin, 21-11-1920

BETTERIDGE, Lt, RAF, Fethard, Co. Tipperary, 19-6-1921

BLISSETT, Sherwood Foresters, Dublin, April 1916

BLUNDELL, Lancers, Dublin, April 1916

BOAST, Lt, Dublin, 28-12-1919

BOURNE, Sth Staffordshire Rgt, Dublin, April 1916

BOWCOTT, Sth Staffordshire Rgt, Dublin, April 1916

BOWDEN, Sgt, Royal Engineers, Cork, 28-2-1921

BOWER, Capt, Dublin, 27-10-1921

BOYDE, Temp Cdt, Newmarket, Co. Cork, 17-6-1921

BRACKENBURY, Sgt, Lincolnshire Rgt, Glengoole, Co. Tipperary, 24-1-1921

BRADFORD, Sherwood Foresters, Dublin, April 1916

BRADSHAW, Cdt, Royal Field Artillery, Kilmichael, Co. Cork, 28-11-1920

BRENNAN, Capt, Royal Irish Rgt, Dublin, April 1916

BRINDLEY, Nth Staffordshire Rgt, Dublin, April 1916

BROSNAN, Sgt Maj, Royal Irish Fusiliers, Dublin, 24-4-1916

BROWNE, Lt, Sherwood Foresters, Dublin, April 1916

BROWNE, Pte, RAF, Dublin, 28-3-1921

BURKE, Bman, 2nd Hampshire Rgt, Youghal, Co. Cork, 31-5-1921

BURKE, Sgt, Royal Dublin Fusiliers, Dublin, April 1916

BUSHE, Aux, Macroom, Co. Cork, 25-2-1921

BYRNE, Royal Dublin Fusiliers, Dublin, April 1916

CALVERT, Lt, Royal Irish Rifles, Dublin, April 1916

CAMERON, Gnr, Royal Marine Artillery, Ballincollig, Co. Cork, 5-7-1921

CARR, Royal Irish Rgt, Dublin, April 1916

CARTLIDGE, Gnr, Royal Field Artillery, Dublin, April 1916

CAVANAGH, Royal Irish Rgt, Dublin, April 1916

CAWLEY, Pte, 1st Essex Rgt, Crossbarry, Co. Cork, 19-3-1921

CHAPMAN, Sherwood Foresters, Dublin, April 1916

CHAPMAN, Aux, Cork, 11-12-1920

CHICK, Sth Staffordshire Rgt, Dublin, April 1916

CHRISTIAN, Sgt, Intelligence Section, Dublin, 14-10-1920

CLAYTON, Capt, Clonfin, Co. Longford, 22-11-1920

COBBALD, Army Service Corps, Dublin, April 1916

COLLINS, Sth Staffordshire Rgt, Dublin, April 1916

COMPTON-SMYTH, Maj, Royal Welsh Fusiliers, Cork, 28-4-1921

CORDWELL, Hussars, Dublin, April 1916

CORNWALL, Sgt, Nth Staffordshire Rgt, Dublin, April 1916

CORNWALLIS, Capt, 17th Lancers, Ballyturin, Co. Galway, 15-5-1921

COXON, Royal Dublin Fusiliers, Dublin, April 1916

COYLE, QMS, Royal Irish Rifles, Dublin, April 1916

CRAFER, Pte, 1st Essex Rgt, Crossbarry, Co. Cork, 19-3-1921

CRAKE, Capt, Bedfordshire Rgt, Kilmichael, Co. Cork, 28-11-1920

CRAVEN, Lt/Comdr, Sussex Rgt, Clonfin, Co. Longford, 2-2-1921

CROCKETT, Lt/Col, Royal Ennis Fusiliers, Dublin, April 1916

CRUMMERY, Pte, Northamptonshire Rgt, Thomastown, Co. Tipperary, 28-10-1920

CULLEN, Royal Irish Fusiliers, Dublin, April 1916

CUMMING, Col Comdt, East Lancashire Rgt, Clonbanin, Co. Cork, 5-3-1921

DAFFEN, Lt, Sherwood Foresters, Dublin, April 1916

DAVENPORT, Sherwood Foresters, Dublin, April 1916

DIEIRICHSEN, Capt, Sherwood Foresters, Dublin, April 1916

DIXEY, Sherwood Foresters, Dublin, April 1916

DIXON, Sherwood Foresters, Dublin, April 1916

DIXON, Lt 2nd Suffolk (Att 1st Essex) Rgt, Ballinhassig, Co. Cork, 20-10-1920

DIXON, Capt, Tooreen, Co. Cork, 24-10-1920

DOWLING, Maj, Grenadier Guards, Dublin, 21-11-1920

DUFFY, Royal Irish Rgt, Dublin, April 1916

DUGGAN, Royal Irish Rifles, Dublin, April 1916

ELLIOTT, Sherwood Foresters, Dublin, April 1916

ELLIS, Royal Dublin Fusiliers, Dublin, April 1916

ELLIS, Sgt, Lincolnshire Rgt, Mitchelstown, Co. Cork, 17-2-1920

EVANS, Boy, 2nd Hampshire Rgt, Youghal, Co. Cork, 31-5-1921

FARNWORTH, Sherwood Foresters, April 1916

FARRELL, Aux, Dublin, 14-3-1921

FAULKNER, Temp Cdt, Tubbrid, 12-3-1921

FIELDING, Pte, Buttevant, Co. Cork, April 1921

FITZGERALD, Capt, Dublin, 21-11-1920

FLYNN, Royal Irish Rgt, Dublin, April 1916

FORTH, Sherwood Foresters, Dublin, April 1916

FOX, Sth Staffordshire Rgt, Dublin, April 1916

FUGGLE, L/Cpl, Northamptonshire Rgt, Templemore, Co. Tipperary, 1920

GAMBLE, QMS, Royal Irish Rgt, Dublin, April 1916

GAMMON, Bman, 1st Buffs, Lacabally, 27-11-1920

GARNIN, Aux, Dublin, 21-11-1920

GARVIS, Cdt, Dublin, 21-11-1920

GIBBS, Sgt, 17th Lancers, Mallow, Co. Cork, 28-9-1920

GILL, Pte, 2nd Hampshire Rgt, Cork, 28-2-1921

GLAISTER, Dublin, April 1916

GLASSOP, Lt, RAF, Fethard, Co. Tipperary, 19-6-1921

GLEANE, Cdt, RAF, Kilmichael, Co. Cork, 28-11-1920

GOSS, Sherwood Foresters, Dublin, April 1916

GRAHAM, Capt, Northumberland Fusiliers, Kilmichael, 28-11-1920

GRANT, Maj, Coolavokig, Co. Cork, 1921

GRAY, Lt, Sherwood Foresters, Dublin, April 1916

GRAY, RASC, 1st Essex Rgt, Crossbarry, Co. Cork, 19-3-1921

HALL, Dvr, RASC, Churchtown, 27-8-1920

HALL, Cpl, 1st Buffs, Lacabally, 27-11-1920

HAMBLEDON, Lt, Northamptonshire Rgt, Nenagh, Co. Tipperary, 4-11-1920

HANNA, Royal Irish Rifles, Dublin, April 1916

HARE, Sgt, Royal Dublin Fusiliers, Dublin, April 1916

HARRISON, Army Service Corps, Dublin, April 1916

HAWKEN, Lt, Sherwood Foresters, Dublin, April 1916

HEADLAND, Sgt, Lancers, Dublin, April 1916

HERROD, Sgt, South Wales Borderers, Navan, Co. Meath, 16-5-1921

HESTERMAN, Boy, 2nd Hampshire Rgt, Youghal, Co. Cork, 31-5-1921

HEWETT, Cpl, 2nd King Edward's Horse, Dublin, 27-4-1916

HILL, L/Cpl, 2nd Hampshire Rgt, Cork, 18-6-1921

HOBBS, L/Cpl, Northamptonshire Rgt, Tipperary, 28-10-1920

HODNETT, L/Cpl, RASC, Cork, 28-2-1921

HOLBROOK, Sherwood Foresters, Dublin, April 1916

HOLLAND, Sherwood Foresters, Dublin, April 1916

HOOPER-JONES, Cdt, Northumberland Fus, Kilmichael, Co. Cork, 28-11-1920

HOTBLACK, Capt, 1st Essex Rgt, Crossbarry, Co. Cork, 20-3-1921

HOUGHTON, Aux, Sussex Rgt, Clonfin, 2-11-1920

HOYLE, Cpl, Sherwood Foresters, Dublin, April 1916

HUGHES, Lancers, Dublin, April 1916

HUGHES, Sgt, Castleconnell, 17-4-1921

HUGO, Maj, (late Indian Army), Kilmichael, 28-11-1920

HUMPHRIES, Royal Dublin Fusiliers, Dublin, April 1916

HUMPHRIES, Sth Staffordshire Rgt, Dublin, April 1916

HUNTER, Lt, Lancers, Dublin, April 1916

JAMES, Yeomanry, Dublin, April 1916

JAYS, Aux Const, Leap, Co Cork, 21-11-1920

JEFFS, Sherwood Foresters, Dublin, April 1916

JOBBERT, Sth Staffordshire Rgt, Dublin, April 1916

JOHNSTONE, Maj, Glenties, Co. Donegal, 28-8-1920

JONES, Pte, King's Light Infantry, Fermoy, Co. Cork, 7-9-1919

JONES, Pte, Ballinhassig, Co. Cork, 22-10-1920

JONES, Cdt, Suffolk Rgt, Kilmichael, Co. Cork, 28-11-1920

KEENLYSIDE, Capt, 1st Lancashire Fusiliers, Dublin 21-11-1920

KING, Aux, Drangan, Co. Tipperary, 3-6-1920

KING, Pte, 2nd Hampshire Rgt, Youghal, Co. Cork, 4-11-1920

KITCHEN, Sherwood Foresters, Dublin, April 1916

KNIGHT, Pte, 1st Essex Rgt, Bandon, Co. Cork, 23-2-1921

KNOX, Royal Inniskilling Fusiliers, Dublin, April 1916

LAMBERT, Col Comdt, Athlone, 19-6-1921

LEEN, Lancers, Dublin, April 1916

LEIGH, Pte, 2nd Hampshires, Youghal, Co. Cork, 1-11-1920

LENDRUM, Capt, Doonbeg, Co. Clare, 22-9-1920

LLEWELLYN, Yeomanry, Dublin, April 1916

LUCAS, 2nd Lt, King Edward's Horse, Dublin, 28-4-1916

LUCAS, Royal Dublin Fusiliers, Dublin, April 1916

LUCAS, Cdt, Royal Sussex Rgt, Kilmichael, Co. Cork, 28-11-1920

McCALL, L/Cpl, 2nd Hampshires, Youghal, Co. Cork, 31-5-1921

McCLELLAND, Royal Irish Rifles, Dublin, April 1916

McCORMACK, Capt, RVC, Dublin, 21-11-1920

McCREERY, Lt, 17th Lancers, Ballyturin, Co. Galway, 15-5-1921

McCULLOUGH, Capt, RAMC, Dublin, 25-4-1916

McKINNON, Maj, Tralee, Co. Kerry, 17-4-1921

MacLEAN, Lt, Dublin Rifle Bde, 21-11-1920

MADDOX, L/Cpl, 1st Essex Rgt, Bandon, Co. Cork, 26-7-1920

MADELL, L/Cpl, 1st Essex Rgt, Courtmacsherry, Co. Cork, 14-5-1921

MALONE, Aux, Ballybay, Co. Monaghan, 1-1-1921

MARTIN, Dvr, RASC (Att 1st Essex Rgt), Crossbarry, Co. Cork, 19-3-1921

MILLER, Sherwood Foresters, Dublin, April 1916

MINCHIN, Pte, Lincolnshire Rgt, Mitchelstown, Co. Cork, 17-12-1920

MONTGOMERY, R.S. Rgt, Dublin, 21-11-1920

MOORE, Leinster Rgt, Dublin, April 1916

MORRIS, Aux, Dublin, 21-11-1920

MORTON, Royal Irish Rifles, Dublin, April 1916

MUIR, Ballylongford, Co. Kerry, 20-12-1920

MULHERN, Royal Irish Rifles, Dublin, April 1916

MULRANEY, Hussars, Dublin, April 1916

MULVEY, Army Service Corps, Dublin, April 1916

NEILAN, Royal Dublin Fusiliers, Dublin, April 1916

NEWBURY, Capt, Queens Rgt, Dublin, 21-11-1920

NEWLAND, Lancers, Dublin, April 1916

NOLAN, Royal Irish Rifles, Dublin, April 1916

O'GORMAN, Hussars, Dublin, April 1916

O'LOUGHLIN, Temp Const, Tralee, Co. Kerry, 21-4-1921

OSBORNE, Lancers, Dublin, April 1916

PARKER, L/Cpl, Oxfordshire Rgt, Oola, Co. Limerick, July 1920

PARKER, Lt, Northamptonshire Rgt, Thomastown, Co Tipperary, 28-10-1920

PEARSON, Cdt, Green Howards Rgt, Kilmichael, Co. Cork, 28-11-1920

PEEK, Capt, 9th Lancers, Scramogue, Co. Roscommon, 23-3-1921

PERCEVAL, Bman, 1st Kings Own, Dublin, 2-7-1921

PERRY, Lt, Sherwood Foresters, Dublin, April 1916

PINFIELD, Lt, Hussars, Dublin, April 1916

PRICE, Lt, Dublin, 14-10-1920

PRICE, Capt, Middlesex Rgt, Dublin, 21-11-1920

PRINGLE, Temp Cdt, Castleconnell, Co. Limerick, 17-4-1921

[PRIVATE] (1), Ballybrack, 8-6-1921

[PRIVATE] (1), Inchicore, Dublin, 17-5-1921

[PRIVATES] (3), Camp, Co. Kerry, 15-5-1921

PURSER, Lt, Army Service Corps, Dublin, April 1916

RAMSAY, Lt, Royal Irish Rgt, Dublin, April 1916

REID, Pte, 1st Essex Rgt, Annesbagh, 22-10-1920

REYNOLDS, Sgt, Lincolnshire Rgt, Mullinahone, Co. Tipperary, 11-7-1921

RICHARDSON, F/Lt, RAF (1st Essex), Newcestown, Co. Cork, 9-10-1920

ROBERTSON, Lt, 1st Essex Rgt, Newcestown, Co. Cork, 12-10-1920

RODGERS, Sherwood Foresters, Dublin, April 1916

RODGERS, Pte, Bruree, Co. Limerick, 30-7-1920

ROPER, Dvr, November 1920

RYAN, Cpl, Dublin, 5-2-1921

SADLIER, Maj, 3rd Cashel Bn, Cloneen, Co. Tipperary, 13-6-1921

SANDY, Aux, Newmarket, Co. Cork, 17-6-1921

SAUNDERS, Sth Staffordshire Rgt, Dublin, April 1916

SCARLETT, Lancers, Dublin, April 1916

SEAFIELD, Maj, Macroom, Co. Cork, 25-2-1921

SHEPHERD, Sgt, Lancers, Dublin, April 1916

SHEPHERD, Pte, 1st Essex Rgt, Bandon, Co. Cork, 14-5-1921

SHERMAN, Lt, Royal Horse Artillery, Ballyvourney, Co. Cork, 18-8-1920

SHERWOOD, Sth Staffordshire Rgt, Dublin, April 1916

SHORTER, Temp Cdt, Newmarket, Co. Cork, 17-6-1921

SHORTT, Northamptonshire Rgt, Thomastown, Co. Tipperary, October 1920

SIBLEY, Sherwood Foresters, Dublin, April 1916

SIMMONS, Boy, 2nd Hampshire Rgt, Youghal, Co. Cork, 31-5-1921

SMITH, Hussars, Dublin, April 1916

SMITH, Pte, Lincolnshire Rgt, Fethard, Co. Tipperary, 19-6-1921

SMYTH, Lt Col, Kings Own Scottish Borderers, Cork, 17-7-1920

SMYTH, Maj, 12-10-1920

SOUCHON, Lt, 17th Lancers, Galway, 2-10-1921

SPACKMAN, Pte, Oxfordshire Rgt, Cratloe, Co. Clare, November 1920

SPEED, Sth Staffordshire Rgt, Dublin, April 1916

SQUIBBS, Pte, 2nd Hampshire Rgt, Cork, 8-10-1920

STAVES, Pte, Lincolnshire Rgt, Glengoole, 24-1-1921

STEWARD, Pte, 1st Essex Rgt, Crossbarry, Co. Cork, 19-3-1921

STUBBS, L/Cpl, 1st Essex Rgt, Bandon, Co. Cork, 23-2-1921

TAYLOR, Aux, Clonfin, Co. Longford, 2-11-1920

TAYLOR, Cdt, RAF, Kilmichael, Co. Cork, 28-11-1920

TEMPEST, QMS, Sth Staffordshire Rgt, Dublin, April 1916

TENNANT, Lt, 9th Lancers, Scramogue, Co. Roscommon, 23-3-1921

THOMPSON, Royal Dublin Fusiliers, Dublin, April 1916

THOMPSON, Capt, 1st Manchesters, Ballincollig, Co. Cork, 22-11-1920

TOOGOOD, 2nd Lt, Lincolnshire Rgt, Fethard, Co. Tipperary, 19-6-1921

TREACY, Royal Irish Rgt, Dublin, April 1916

TUNNICLIFFE, Sherwood Foresters, Dublin, April 1916

TYLER, Sherwood Foresters, Dublin, April 1916

WAINRIGHT, Capt, Royal Dublin Fusiliers, Kilmichael, Co. Cork, 28-11-1920

WALKER, Lancers, Dublin, April 1916

WALTON, L/Cpl, Hussars, Dublin, April 1916

WARMINGTON, Maj, Royal Irish Rgt, Dublin, April 1916

WARNER, Sherwood Foresters, Dublin, April 1916

WARNES, Cdt, Dublin, 24-6-1921

WASHINGTON, Pte, Wellington Rgt, Dublin, 20-9-1920

WASHINGTON, Bman, 2nd Hampshires, Youghal, Co. Cork, 21-5-1921

WATCHORN, Royal Dublin Fusiliers, Dublin, April 1916

WATTS, A/Sgt, 1st Essex Rgt, Crossbarry, Co. Cork, 19-3-1921

WEBSTER, Cdt, Black Watch Rgt, Kilmichael, Co. Cork, 28-11-1920

WHICHELOW, Cpl, 2nd Hampshire Rgt, Youghal, Co. Cork, 31-5-1921

WHITE, Maj, 12-10-1920

WHITEAR, Bman, Cork, 28-2-1921

WHITEHEARD, Pte, Doonbeg, Co. Clare, 22-9-1920

WILDE, Dublin, 21-11-1920

WILDON, L/Cpl, Leicestershire Rgt, Castlerea, Co. Roscommon, 7-4-1921

WILKINS, Pte, 1st Essex Rgt, Crossbarry, Co. Cork, 19-3-1921

WILSON, Royal Irish Rifles, Dublin, April 1916

WILSON, Capt, Dublin 1919/20

WOARD, Sherwood Foresters, Dublin, April 1916

WOODCOCK, Col, Lancashire Fusiliers, Dublin, 21-11-1920

WORSWICK, Lt, King Edward's Horse, Dublin, 28-4-1916

WRIGHT, Sth Staffordshire Rgt, Dublin, April 1916

RIC

ADAMS, Const, Pallasgreen, Co. Limerick, 3-2-1921

AGAR, Const, Ballivor, Co. Meath, 31-10-1919

AHERNE, Sgt, Bandon, Co. Cork, 25-7-1920

ANDERSON, Sgt, Balbriggan, Co. Dublin, 21-5-1921

ARMSTRONG-HOLMES, Div Comdr, Tureengarriffe, Co. Kerry, 28-1-1921

BECKETT, Const, Newport, Co. Tipperary, 20-5-1921

BEGLEY, Const, Granard, Co. Longford, 27-4-1921

BELL, Const, Pallasgreen, Co. Limerick, 3-2-1921

BENSON, Const, Tralee, Co. Kerry, May 1921

BERGIN, Const, Ennis, Co. Clare, 5-3-1921

BESANT, Const, Cashel, Co. Tipperary, 4-3-1921

BLAKE, Dist Insp, Ballyturin, Co. Galway, 15-5-1921

BLOXAM, Sgt, Cork, 21-1-1921

BLYTHE, Const, Carrowkennedy, Co. Mayo, 2-6-1921

BOLGER, Const, Cork, 14-12-1919

BOOTH, Const, Ballinalee, Co. Longford, 20-5-1921

BOURKE, Const, Pallasgreen, Co. Limerick, 3-2-1921

BOWLES, Const, Rosscarbery, Co. Cork, 31-3-1921

BOYD, Const, Cappagh White, Co. Tipperary, 17-1-1921

BOYLAN, Const, Kilmilkin, 23-4-1921

BOYNE, Const, Kildorrery, Co. Cork, 10-4-1921

BRADFORD, Const, Mooncoin, Co. Kilkenny, 19-6-1921

BRADY, Sgt, Lorrha, Co. Tipperary, 3-9-1919

BRADY, Sgt, Rush, Co. Dublin, 29-4-1920

BRADY, Dist Insp, Ratra, Co. Roscommon, 11-9-1921

BRANDISH, Sgt, 22-3-1921

BRENNAN, Const, Dundalk, Co. Louth, 21-8-1920

BRETT, Const, Cork, 1920

BREWER, Const, Hospital, Co. Limerick, 5-7-1921

BRICK, Const, Timoleague, Co. Cork, 10-5-1920

BRIDGES, Const, Drumcollogher, Co. Limerick, May 1921

BROWN, Const, Carrowkennedy, Co. Mayo, 2-6-1921

BROWNE, Const, Rathmore, Co. Kerry, 4-5-1921

BROWNE, Const, Newport, 20-5-1921

BRUCK, Const, Rosscarbery, Co. Cork, 28-2-1921

BUDD, Const, Killadysert, Co. Clare, 26-5-1921

BURKE, Const, Dunmore, Co. Galway, 19-7-1920

BURKE, Det Insp, Balbriggan, Co. Dublin, September 1920

BURKE, Sgt, Swarteragh, Co. Derry, 5-6-1921

BUSTROCK, Const, Glen of Aherlow, Co. Tipperary, 13-9-1920

BUTLER, Sgt, Newport, 18-5-1921

CAMPBELL, Const, Mullinahone, Co. Tipperary, March 1921

CAMPBELL, Const, Dundalk, Co. Louth, 18-6-1921

CARBOY, Const, Castlemartyr, Co. Cork, 27-10-1920

CAREY, Const, Dunmore, Co. Galway, 19-7-1920

CARROLL, Sgt, Kilmihill, Co. Clare, 18-4-1920

CARROLL, Const, Limerick, 11-6-1920

CARROLL, Sgt, Kilmichael, Co. Cork, 28-11-1920

CARTER, Const, Ballinhassig, Co. Cork, February 1921

CARTER, Const, Letterkenny, Co. Donegal, 18-5-1921

CARTY, Sgt, Ruan, Co. Clare, 13-1-1921

CASELY, Const, Killorglin, Co. Kerry, 31-10-1920

CHEVE, Const, Cork, 3-10-1920

CLAPP, Const, Rathmore, 4-5-1921

CLARKE, Head Const, Cork, November 1918

CLARKE, Const, Lanesborough, Co. Longford, 4-7-1920

CLARKE, Dist Insp, Glenwood, Co. Clare, 20-1-1921

CLARKE, Const, Clonmany, Co. Donegal, 10-5-1921

CLARKE, Const, Cliffoney, Co. Sligo, 27-6-1921

CLEARY, Const, Ashbourne, Co. Meath, April 1916

COLEMAN, Sgt, Midleton, Co. Cork, 15-5-1921

COLLERY, Sgt, Castlemaine, Co. Kerry, 1-6-1921

COMPSTON, Const, Cullyhanna, 9-11-1920

CONLON, Const, Belfast, 8-7-1921

COONEY, Const, Granard, Co. Longford, 2-11-1920

COONEY, Const, Kilworth, Co. Cork, 1-6-1921

COOPER, Const, Belfast, 11-3-1921

CORMER, Const, Rathdrum, Co. Wicklow, 8-7-1921

COUGHLAN, Const, Cork, 15-5-1921

COUGHLAN, Const, Cork, 20-5-1921

COUGHLIN, Sgt, Carrowkennedy, March 1921

COULTER, Const, Fivemiletown, Co. Tyrone, 29-5-1921

CREAN, Sgt, Innishannon, Co. Cork, 25-4-1920

CREEDON, Const, Tallow, Co. Waterford, 2-7-1921

CREIGHTON, Const, Cork, May 1921

CRONIN, Const, Castlemartyr, Co. Cork, 27-10-1920

CRONIN, Sgt, Tullamore, Co. Offaly, 30-10-1920

CROOKS, Const, Belfast, 11-3-1921

CULLEN, Const, Cork 3-5-1921

CURTIN, Sgt, Ruan, Co. Limerick, 13-1-1921

CUTHBERTSON, Const, Arva, 1-5-1921

DALTON, Det Officer, Dublin, 20-4-1920

DAY, Const, Milltown, 27-6-1921

DELANEY, Const, Tullow, Co. Waterford, 8-9-1920

DEVEREUX, Const, Keadue, March 1921

DOHERTY, Sgt, Feakle, Co. Clare, 7-10-1920

DOHERTY, Const, Carrowkennedy, Co. Mayo, 2-6-1921

DOOGE, Const, Belmullet, Co. Mayo, 15-6-1920

DOOGE, Const, Glenwood, Co. Clare, 20-1-1921

DORAN, Const, Kinnitty, Co. Offaly, 18-5-1921

DOWLING, Const, Keadue

DOWLING, Carrowkennedy, Co. Mayo, 2-6-1921

DOYLE, Const, Pallasgreen, Co. Limerick, 3-2-1921

DRAY, Const, Midleton, Co. Cork, 28-12-1920

DUCKHAM, Const, Macroom, Co. Cork, 3-7-1921

DUDDY, Const, Scartacrooka, Co. Waterford, 3-3-1921

DUFFY, Const, Carlow, 3-4-1921

DUNNE, Const, Timoleague, Co. Cork, 10-5-1920

DUNNE, Const, Kinnitty, Co. Offaly, 18-5-1921

DUNPHY, Sgt, Limerick, 19-5-1920

DUPREE, Const, Gorey, Co. Wexford, 7-5-1921

DYNE, Const, Rathmore, Co. Kerry, 4-5-1921

ELTON, Const, Castletownroche, Co. Cork, 18-3-1921

ENRIGHT, Const, Knocklong, Co. Tipperary, 13-5-1919

EVANS, Const, Killorglin, Co. Kerry, 31-10-1920

FAHEY, Const, Foynes, Co. Limerick, 14-7-1920

FALLON, Sgt, Ballymote, Co. Sligo, 3-11-1920

FINN, Const, Newport, 9-4-1920

FINNEGAN, Const, Thurles, Co. Tipperary, 20-1-1920

FINNERTY, Sgt, Balbriggan, Co. Dublin, 14-4-1920

FITZGERALD, Const, The Marrough, 4-7-1921

FLAHERTY, Const, Kill, Co. Kildare, 21-8-1920

FLOOD, Const, Killoskehan, Co. Tipperary, 29-9-1920

FLOOD, Const, Templemore, Co. Tipperary, 29-11-1920

FLYNN, Sgt, Timoleague, Co. Cork, 10-5-1920

FOLEY, Const, Deelis, Co. Kerry, 16-4-1920

FOODY, Const, Pallasgreen, Co. Limerick, 3-2-1921

FOODY, Sgt, Ballina, Co. Mayo, 7-7-1921

FORBES-REDMOND, Asst Comdr, Dublin, 21-1-1920

FRENCH, Const, Carrowkennedy, Co. Mayo, 2-6-1921

GARVEY, Sgt, Cork, 11-5-1920

GAUGHRAN, Const, Tullow, Co. Waterford, 8-8-1920

GLOVER, Const, Belfast, 10-6-1921

GORMLEY, Const, Ashbourne, Co. Meath, 28-4-1916

GORMLEY, Const, Kilmichael, Co. Cork, 28-11-1920

GRADOCK, Sgt, Athlone, 21-8-1920

GRANT, Const, Abbeydorney, Co Kerry, March 1921

GRAY, Insp, Ashbourne, Co. Meath, 28-4-1916

GREENE, Const, Balbriggan, Co. Dublin, 2-2-1920

GREER, Const, Dublin, 23-2-1921

HALLIDAY, Sgt, Ballyfermot, Dublin, 30-3-1920

HARMON, Const, Rineen, Co. Clare, 20-9-1920

HARRINGTON, Const, Cork, 11-5-1920

HARTE, Const, Rineen, Co. Clare, 20-9-1920

HAYES, Const, Cork, 23-5-1921

HAYTON, Const, Pallasgreen, Co. Limerick, 3-2-1921

HEALY, Const, Toomevara, Co. Tipperary, 16-3-1920

HEANUE, Const, Pouladuff, Co. Tipperary, 4-3-1920

HEFFREN, Const, Belfast, 26-1-1921

HEGARTY, Const, Stanooden, 22-1-1921

HETHERINGTON, Const, Ballisadare, Co. Sligo, 19-4-1921

HEWITT, Const, Doolin, Co. Clare, 8-7-1921

HICKEY, Const, Ashbourne, Co. Meath, 28-4-1916

HIGGINS, Sgt, Derry, 1-1-1921

HIGGINS, Const, Culleens, Co. Mayo, 3-7-1921

HILL, Const, Oola, Co. Limerick, 2-7-1921

HILLYER, Const, Rathmore, 4-5-1921

HODGKINSON, Const, Bruff, Co. Limerick, 27-12-1920

HODNETT, Const, Rineen, Co. Clare, 22-9-1920

HODSON, Const, Bruff, Co. Limerick, 26-12-1920

HOEY, Det Const, Dublin, 12-9-1919

HOEY, Const, Dublin 23-2-1921

HOEY, Const, Dublin, 28-6-1921

HOLLAND, Sgt, Cullyhanna, Co. Armagh, 16-6-1920

HOLMAN, Const, Kilworth, Co. Cork, 1-6-1921

HOPKINS, Const, Ballindine, Co. Mayo, 9-5-1921

HORAN, Const, Loughrea, Co. Galway, 30-10-1920

HOUGH, Const, Bantry, Co. Cork, 25-8-1920

HOWLETT, Const, Ballylongford, Co. Kerry, 22-21921

HUGHES, Const, Donegal, 22-2-1921

HUGHES, Sgt, Maynooth, Co. Kildare, 21-2-1921

HUNT, Dist Insp, Thurles, Co. Tipperary, 23-6-1919

HURLEY, Const, Kilross, 25-4-1916

HURLEY, Const, Ashbourne, Co. Meath, 28-4-1916

HURLEY, Const, Tureengarriffe, Co. Kerry, 20-1-1921

HYNES, Sgt, Rineen, Co. Clare, 20-9-1920

JAYS, Const, Leap, Co. Cork, 21-11-1920

JOHNSTONE, Sgt, Oola, Co. Limerick, 2-7-1921

JOLLY, Const, Abbeyfeale, Co. Limerick, 5-6-1921

JONES, Const, Bunclody, Co. Wexford, 22-12-1920

KEANE, Sgt, Kilmallock, Co. Limerick, 28-5-1920

KEANE, Const, Macroom, Co. Cork, 25-2-1921

KEARNEY, Head Const, Newry, Co. Louth, 21-11-1920

KEARNES, Const, Derry, 6-11-1920

KEARNY, Const, Ballyturin, Co. Galway, 15-5-1921

KELLEHER, Dist Insp, Granard, Co. Longford, 21-10-1920

KELLY, Const, Rineen, Co. Clare, 20-9-1920

KELLY, Const, Ballisadare, Co. Sligo, 19-4-1921

KENNA, Const, Innishannon, Co. Cork, 15-5-1921

KENNY, Const, Derry, 1-1-1921

KENWARD, Const, Upton, Co. Cork, 19-3-1921

KENYON, Const, Ballymahon, Co. Longford, 18-5-1921

KERINS, Const, Bandon, Co. Cork, 23-2-1921

KICKEY, Sgt, Dungarvan, Co. Waterford, 19-3-1921

KING, Const, Culleens, Co. Mayo, 3-7-1921

KINGSTON, Const, Pallasgreen, Co. Limerick, 3-2-1921

KINGSTON, Sgt, Cappagh White, Co. Tipperary, 8-5-1921

KINSELLA, Const, Kilmallock, Co. Limerick, March 1921

LAFFEY, Const, Grange, Co. Waterford, 25-10-1920

LAHIFF, Dublin, April 1916

LARKIN, Recruit Const, Athlone, 2-11-1920

LOONEY, Const, Bandon, Co. Cork, 15-5-1921

LOUGHEED, Const, Ruan, Co. Clare, 18-10-1920

LUCAS, Sgt, Templemore, Co. Tipperary, 25-10-1920

LYNCH, Const, Grange, Co. Waterford, 25-10-1920

LYNCH, Const, Balbriggan, Co. Dublin, 12-3-1921

McCARTHY, Const, Newport, 9-4-1920

McCAUGHEY, Dist Insp, Castlemaine, Co. Kerry, 1-6-1921

McCORMACK, Sgt, Rathmore, 4-5-1921

McCORMICK, Const, Castlemaine, Co. Kerry, 1-6-1921

McDONAGH, Const, Dublin 23-2-1921

McDONAGH, Sgt, Mountfield, 21-5-1921

McDONALD, Sgt, Goold's Cross, Co. Tipperary, 10-5-1920

McDONNELL, Const, Soloheadbeg, Co. Tipperary, 21-1-1919

McELHILL, Head Const, Kilbeggan, Co. Westmeath, 12-6-1921

McFADDEN, Sgt, Kilrush, Co. Clare, 23-4-1921

McGEE, Const, Castlebellingham, Co. Louth, 24-4-1916

McGOLDRICK, Const, Innishannon, Co. Cork, 25-5-1920

McGRATH, Dist Insp, Ballinalee, Co. Longford, 7-1-1921

McHALE, Const, Ashbourne, Co. Meath, 28-5-1916

McKENNA, Sgt, Listowel, Co. Kerry, 3-4-1920

McKENNA, Const, Falcarragh, Co. Donegal, March 1921

McKEOWN, Grange, Co. Waterford, 25-10-1920

MACKESY, Const, Glen of Aherlow, Co. Tipperary, 13-11-1920

McLEAN, Const, Skibbereen, Co. Cork, May 1921

McNAMARA, Const, Glengarriff, Co. Cork, 24-8-1920

McROWE, Const, Ashbourne, Co. Meath, 28-5-1916

MADDEN, Const, Abbeydorney, Co. Kerry, 21-10-1920

MAGUIRE, Const, Rineen, Co. Clare, 22-9-1920

MAGUIRE, Sgt, Kilmallock, Co. Limerick, 6-3-1921

MAGUIRE, Const, Newport, 23-5-1921

MAHONEY, Const, Abbeyfeale, Co. Limerick, 18-9-1920

MALONE, Const, Ballybay, 1-1-1921

MARTIN, Const, Kilmallock, Co. Limerick, 28-5-1920

MASTERSON, Const, Newcastle West, Co. Limerick, 17-7-1920

MAUNSELL, Sgt, Inchigeela, Co. Cork, 21-8-1920

MAXWELL, Const, Cloughjordan, Co. Tipperary, 3-11-1920

MEADE, Const, May 1921

MILAN, Const, Glen of Aherlow, Co. Tipperary, 13-11-1920

MILES, Const, Tureengarriffe, Co. Kerry, 28-1-1921

MILLAR, Const, Dublin, 28-4-1916

MILLAR, Const, Pallasgreen, Co. Limerick, 3-2-1921

MILLAR, Const, Dublin

MILLING, Const, Belfast, 30-3-1919

MITCHEL, Const, Mountjoy, 7-6-1921

MOLLAGHAN, Const, Pallasgreen, Co. Limerick, 3-2-1921

MOLLOY, Sgt, Glenwood, Co. Clare, 20-1-1921

MORAN, Const, Glenwood, Co. Clare, 20-1-1920

MORGAN, Const, Ballyduff, Co. Kerry, 31-10-1920

MORONEY, Det Sgt, Derry, 15-5-1920

MORRIS, Const, Glenwood, Co. Clare, 20-1-1921

MORTON, Const, Kilmallock, Co. Limerick, 28-5-1920

MUGGINS, Const, Carrick-on-Shannon, Co. Leitrim, 18-4-1921

MULHERN, Sgt, Bandon, Co. Cork, 1920

MULLEN, Const, Drumlish, Co. Longford, 27-8-1920

MULLEN, Const, Midleton, Co. Cork, 29-12-1920

MULROONEY, Head Const, Ballyfermot, Dublin, 30-3-1921

MUNNELLY, Const, Drumquin, Co. Tyrone, 26-8-1920

MURPHY, Const, Ballyvourneen, Co. Limerick, 4-8-1919

MURRAY, Sgt, Ballinacarrigy, Co. Westmeath, 7-5-1921

MURREN, Sgt, Milltown, 27-6-1921

MURTAGH, Const, Cork, 19-3-1920

MYLES, Const, Tureengarriffe, Co. Kerry, 28-1-1921

NATHAN, Const, Limerick, 15-8-1920

NEAZOR, Sgt, Rathkeale, Co. Limerick, 10-3-1920

NEENAN, Const, Allihies, Co. Kerry, 12-2-1920

NOONAN, Const, Killoskehan, Co. Tipperary, 29-9-1920

NUNAN, Const, Templemore, Co. Tipperary, 29-11-1920

NUTLEY, Const, Bansha, Co. Tipperary, 15-5-1921

OATES, Const, Tourmakeady, Co. Mayo, 3-5-1921

O'BRIEN, Const, Limerick, 6-3-1919

O'BRIEN, Const, Ballymote, Co. Sligo, 15/16-2-1921

O'CONNELL, Const, Soloheadbeg, Co. Tipperary, 21-1-1919

O'CONNOR, Const, Drimoleague, Co. Cork, 1-2-1921

O'DONOGHUE, Sgt, Cork, 17-11-1920

O'FLAHERTY, Const, Derry, 16-10-1920

O'GORMON, Const, Derry, 2-12-1921

O'HANLON, Const, Kilrush, Co. Limerick, 21-8-1920

O'KEEFE, Insp, Granard, Co. Longford, 31-10-1920

O'LEARY, Const, Inche's Cross, 13-11-1920

O'REGAN, Sgt, Tourmakeady, Co. Mayo, 3-5-1921

O'REILLY, Sgt, Kill, Co. Kildare, 21-8-1920

O'RIORDAN, Sgt, Illaunbawn, 5-8-1920

O'ROURKE, Sgt, Kilross, 25-4-1916

O'SULLIVAN, Dist Insp, Listowel, Co. Kerry, 20-1-1921

PERRIER, Const, Bandon, Co. Cork, 23-2-1921

PERRY, Const, Grange, Co. Waterford, 25-10-1920

PHELAN, Const, Rathmore, 4-5-1921

PIERCE, Const, Pallasgreen, Co. Limerick, 3-2-1921

POTTER, Const, Knockcroghery, Co. Roscommon, 26-8-1920

POTTER, Dist Insp, Tipperary, 26-4-1921

POWER, Const, Tourmakeady, Co. Mayo, 3-5-1921

PREDERVILLE, Const, Youghal, Co. Cork, 3-12-1920

QUINN, Const, Belfast, 26-1-1921

QUIRKE, Const, Cappoquin, Co. Waterford, 29-11-1920

QUIRKE, Const, Castlemaine, Co. Kerry, 1-6-1921

REDDING, Const, Killirooskey, 29-5-1921

REDMOND, A/Comdr, Dublin 21-1-1920

REDMOND, Const, Dungarvan, Co. Waterford, 19-3-1921

REID, Const, Bruff, Co. Limerick, 27-12-1920

REILLY, Const, Callan, Co. Kilkenny, 12-3-1921

REVELLE, Det Sgt, Dublin, 8-4-1920

REYNOLDS, Const, Clifden, Co. Galway, 15-3-1921

RIPPENDALE, Const, Leap, Co. Cork, 21-10-1920

ROCHE, Sgt, Dublin, 17-10-1920

ROCK, Const, Toomevara, Co. Tipperary, 16-3-1920

ROGERS, Const, Fedamore, Co. Limerick, 13-4-1921

ROURKE, Sgt, Lisvarrinane, Co. Tipperary, April 1916

ROWE, Head Const, Castlelyons, Co. Cork, 2-5-1916

RUNDLE, Const, Leap, Co. Cork, 21-10-1920

RYAN, Const, Hugginstown, Co. Kilkenny, 8-3-1920

RYLE, Const, Cork, 20-5-1921

SATCHWELL, Const, Mountcharles, 22-2-1921

SCULLY, Const, Cork, 11-3-1920

SHANAGHER, Sgt, Ashbourne, Co. Meath, 28-4-1916

SHANLEY, Const, Kildorrery, Co. Cork, 27-6-1921

SHANNON, Const, Swanlinbar, Co. Cavan, 17-12-1920

SHAW, Const, Fyhora, 1-5-1921

SHEA, Sgt, Rosscarbery, Co. Cork, 31-3-1921

SHELSTER, Const, Barnlough, Co. Tipperary, 2-7-1921

SHORTALL, Const, Cork, 4-1-1921

SKEATH, Const, Cabinteely, Co. Dublin, May 1921

SMITH, Sgt, Drumcondra, Dublin, 30-7-1919

SMITH, Const, Glenwood, Co. Clare, 20-1-1921

SMITH, Const, Pallasgreen, Co. Limerick, 3-2-1921

SMITH, Const, Castlemartyr, Co. Cork, 1-5-1921

SMYTH, Dist Insp, Ashbourne, Co. Meath, 28-4-1916

SMYTH, Det Sgt, Dublin 31-7-1919

SMYTH-BRICE, Div/Comdr, Cork, 17-7-1920

SOMERS, Const, Banteer, Co. Cork, 8-3-1921

STANLEY, Const, Feakle, Co. Clare, 7-10-1920

STEPHENSON, Det Insp, Carrowkennedy, Co. Mayo, 2-6-1921

STERLAND, Const, Cork, 8-5-1921

STEWART, Const, Ballinalee, Co. Longford, 20-5-1921

STOKES, Sgt, Rear Cross, Co. Limerick, 13-7-1920

STOREY, Head Const, Castleisland, Co. Kerry, 8-5-1921

STUCTON, Det Officer

SWANZY, Dist Insp, Lisburn, Co. Antrim, 22-8-1920

SWEENEY, Const, Clifden, Co. Galway, 15-3-1921

SWEETMAN, Sgt, Mooncoin, Co. Kilkenny, 19-6-1921

TALTON, Det Sgt, 1920

TAYLOR, Const, Ballinalee, Co. Longford, 10-12-1920

TAYLOR, Const, Stanooden, 22-1-1921

THORPE, Const, Midleton, Co. Cork, 29-12-1920

TOBIN, Sgt, Dualla, Co. Tipperary, 2-7-1920

TURNER, Const, Ballybrack, 10-11-1920

VAUSTON, Const, Monboro, 2-2-1921

WALLACE, Sgt, Knocklong, Co. Tipperary, 13-5-1919

WALSH, Const, Dublin, 20-2-1920

WALSH, Const, Clonmel, Co. Tipperary, 20-12-1920

WALSH, Const, Churchtown, 12-2-1921

WATKINS, Const, Kildorrery, 8-7-1920

WHARTON, Det, Dublin, 10-11-1919

WHELAN, Const, Carnmore, April 1916

WIGGINS, Const, Limerick, 8-4-1921

WILL, Const, Rathmore, Co. Kerry, 11-7-1920

WILLIAMS, Dist Insp, Gorey, Co. Wexford, 15-6-1920

WOODS, Const, Ballybrack, 10-11-1920

WOODWARD, Const, Kildorrery, 10-4-1921

YOUNG, Sgt, Ashbourne, Co. Meath, 28-4-1916

PART II

The Civil War
1922-1923

A-Z

ADAMSON, George: PT. Brig Gen. After being involved in early confrontation, shot dead by AT troops in Athlone 24 April 1922. ATs claimed that he was one of theirs and was shot by PTs. (*See Fitzpatrick*)

ADARE, Sean (also Adaire and O'Daire): PT. Comdt. QM. Shot dead when *The Ballinalee* was captured by AT ambush, 13 July 1922, at Rockwood, Co. Sligo.

AHERNE, Leo (Dr): PT. Comdt Gen. OC Medical Corps. Examined body of Collins when it was brought to Imperial Hotel, Cork.

AIKEN, Frank: AT. Comdt 4 Northern Div (three brigades: Armagh, North Louth, South & West Down) March 1922. Initially neutral. Did not attend the banned Army Convention (*see Chronology 26/27 March 1922*), but remained under Dáil Ministry for Defence. In May-June, his Div made sorties into Northern Ireland and killed seven Protestants in Altnaveigh, Newry, in retaliation for killing of Catholics in Belfast. Attempted to placate PT and AT elements in his Div. Visited Limerick to persuade Liam Lynch to end hostilities. While absent, his troops in Dundalk Barracks received orders to attack AT posts (*see Hogan, Dan*). On his return, he countermanded these, and concealed all his troops' weapons, and then went to Dublin to explain that he would not attack AT positions. On 16 July 1922, he and his men, still unarmed, were captured by 5 Div PT troops. Colleagues mined Dundalk Jail and he and 100 men escaped 27 July. With Brig McKenna and about 250 ATs, he recaptured the barracks 14 August. In the town square he called for a truce but Dan Hogan's PT troops soon moved in and Aiken withdrew. Fought on AT side thereafter. Allegedly one of the 'prominent Cork citizens' who proposed peace terms to Emmet Dalton, 18 August 1922. Appointed to AT Executive 16 October 1922. Succeeded Liam Lynch as AT COS and member of AT Council 20 April 1923. On 27 April 1923, signed, on foot of de Valera's Proclamation of the same date, an order suspending all aggressive operations from noon, 30 April 1923. WI.

ALBERT, Aloysius Augustine (Rev Fr): Gave general absolution to Four Courts garrison. Advised a surrender and finally negotiated it with PT HQ. WI. (*See Poblacht na hÉireann War News*)

ALLEN, William: AT. *See McDonagh, Paddy.*

ANDREWS, C.S. ('Todd'): AT. Active organizer. Ernie O'Malley's clerk in Four Courts. Wounded in action in Dublin fighting and hospitalized in the Mater Hospital. Transferred to Portrane Mental Hospital for convalescence, he was captured there but quickly escaped. Detailed to bomb Dublin from the air, had the Baldonnel raid (*see Chronology, July 1922*) been successful. Staff Officer to D/Organization, Sean Dowling, and later to Liam Lynch. Captured in Knockmealdown Mountains 20 April 1923. Imprisoned in Cork and Newbridge, where he became Camp Adj. WI.

ANGELA (Sister): Bon Secour Hospital, Glasnevin. Smuggled comforts to Mountjoy prisoners.

ARCHDALE, E.M.: Signatory, on behalf of the Government of Northern Ireland, to Collins-Craig Agreement, 30 March 1922.

ARCHER, Liam: PT. Col. OC Independent Corps of Signals which operated over 60 stations that provided communications between all active units. WI.

ARGENTA: Prison ship in Belfast Lough in which Northern nationalists were interned.

ARVONIA, SS: Irish sea packet commandeered by Provisional Government, 7 August 1922, for sea-borne landing at Westport.

ASHE, Gregory: AT. Adj Dingle Bn.

AYLWARD: Allegedly one of the 'prominent Cork citizens' who proposed peace terms to Emmet Dalton 18 August 1922.

AYLWARD, Jack: AT. *See Cooney, Sean.*

AYRES (Fr): Oblate Priest. Gave spiritual assistance during Tralee fighting, August 1922.

BAGWELL, John: PT. Senator. His Marlfield, Clonmel, home and art collection were burned 9 January 1923. Kidnapped in Dublin 30 January 1923, leading to threats of reprisals by Comdt Gen Dan Hogan.

BALFE: PT. Capt. OC Carrick-on-Suir garrison. Taken prisoner when Tom Barry captured the town. Released unharmed after a few days.

BALLINALEE, THE: PT armoured car captured at Rockwood 13 July 1922 and re-captured at Ballintrillick/Glencar, Co. Sligo, 20 September 1922. Involved in a number of actions (renamed *Lough Gill* when in AT hands).

BANKS, Joseph: AT. Vol 3 Western Div. KIA Ballintrillick/Glencar, Co. Sligo, 20 September 1922 when PTs re-captured *The Ballinalee*.

BARRETT, Frank: AT. Comdt Gen. OC 1 Western Div. Member of AT Executive. Signatory of Proclamation of 29 June 1922 (*see Chronology*) Active in Clare. Allegedly one of the 'prominent Cork citizens' who proposed peace terms to Emmet Dalton 18 August 1922. WI.

BARRETT, Richard: AT. Four Courts garrison. Imprisoned after surrender. Executed in Dublin 8 December 1922 in reprisal for shooting of Sean Hales. WI.

BARRY, Denis: AT. Comdt. Imprisoned Cork and Newbridge. Died from hunger-strike, Newbridge, 20

November 1923. Rev Dr Cohalan refused to accept the remains in Cork. (*See Kent, David*)

BARRY, Kathleen: AT. C na mB. Assisted in Dublin Bde HQ in O'Connell Street, June 1922. (*See Markievicz, Constance*)

BARRY, Tom: AT. Comdt Gen. Involved in early Limerick occupations. Commanded the *Upnor* operation 31 March 1922. Member of AT Army Executive, 18 June 1922, when he proposed declaring war on Britain. Initially carried, the proposal was later defeated. Signatory of Proclamation of 29 June 1922 (*see Chronology*). Captured when trying to gain access to Four Courts disguised as a nurse, the first prisoner of the CW. Imprisoned in Mountjoy, Kilmainham and Gormanston Camp, from where he escaped September 1922. Captured Carrick-on-Suir, 9 December, then Callan, Mullinavat and Thomastown. Prevailed on Liam Lynch to hold Executive meeting 23 March 1923. His motion, that the Executive recognize that continued resistance would not further the cause of independence, was defeated by one vote. AT Council member, April 1923. WI. (*See Harty, Most Rev Dr; Russell, Charles*)

BARRYMORE (Lord): His Fota House was held by AT troops in defending Cork.

BARTON, Robert: AT. TD. Active in attempts to prevent CW. Although a Treaty signatory, he supported de Valera during CW. Bde staff officer, Dublin Bde, during the fighting in the city June/July 1922. Elected to Dáil June 1922 but did not take seat. Member of AT Council of State 25 October 1922. Imprisoned in Portobello Barracks, Mountjoy, and Curragh, where he endured hunger-strike. WI. (*See Childers, Robert Erskine*)

BÉASLAÍ, Piaras: PT. Maj Gen. Propagandist and press censor. Toured United States promoting support for Treaty. Coined the term 'Irregulars' for AT troops. WI.

BELL, Martin: PT. Field paymaster. Toured areas of action, paying troops. (*See King, Patrick*)

BENNETT, Louie: Member of anti-war delegation June 1922. (*See Gonne, Maud*)

BENSON, Henry: AT. Capt 3 Western Div. KIA Ballintrillick/Glencar, Co. Sligo, 20 September 1922 when PTs re-captured *The Ballinalee*.

BERGIN, J.J.: PT. Comdt. Assistant to John Hearne.

BIG FELLOW, THE: PT armoured car called after Collins's nickname.

BIRKENHEAD, F.E. 'Galloper' Smith (Lord): British Lord Chancellor. Supported the efforts of Griffith and Collins in his Commons speeches and welcomed the attack on the AT forces in Dublin.

BISHOP, Stanley: PT. Capt. Took over Griffith Barracks from Harpur May 1922. Comdt July 1922, when he led one of three columns, with armour and artillery, converging on Blessington. In action in Kerry area later.

BLYTHE, Ernest: PT. TD. Minister for Trade & Commerce (1919-22). Non-Cabinet Trade position January-September 1922. Minister for Local Government (August-December 1922).

Minister for Local Government & Public Health (December 1922-September 1923). Made persistent calls for military courts which were finally established in October 1922. Appointed Vice-President, Executive Council of IFS, 1923. WI.

BOFIN Brothers: AT. Edward & Paul. Arrested 25 March 1923 in the Arigna Mountains. Paul had escaped from Sligo Jail 17 October 1922 with nine others. The brothers were condemned to death but their sentences were commuted to penal servitude.

BOLAND, Gerry: AT. TD. In action in Blessington July 1922. Imprisoned in Kilmainham during 1923 strike. Stood as Republican candidate for Roscommon in place of his brother Harry (*below*) and was elected 27 August 1923. WI.

BOLAND, Harry: AT. TD. Sinn Féin secretary. Dismissed as Irish Envoy in Washington February 1922. Dáil Peace Committee member May-June 1922. AT organizer in Leinster. Re-elected for Roscommon June 1922. Director of Operations July 1922. In action in Blessington July 1922. Surrounded in Grand Hotel, Skerries, Co. Dublin, 31 July 1922 and shot attempting to escape. Died 2 August in St Vincent's Hospital, Dublin. WI.

BOLSTER, Frank: PT. Close associate of Collins. GHQ staff-officer. In action in Cork and Kerry. WI.

BOYD: *See Macready, Nevil*. WI.

BOYLAN, Sean: PT. Comdt 1 Eastern Div (nine brigades: Meath, Kildare, Westmeath) March 1922. Signatory of Army document of 1 May 1922. WI.

BOYLE, Neil Plunkett: AT. Comdt. OC of unit known as 'The Plunkett Column'. On 15 May 1923, after the cease-fire, he was shot dead in an action near Valleymount, Co. Wicklow.

BRACKEN, Peadar: AT. Comdt Offaly Bde, Att HQ until June 1922. Active organizer. WI.

BRADY, Kay: Gave use of her house in Leeson Street, Dublin, for AT staff meetings.

BRADY, Patrick: PT. Pte. WIA in Enniscorthy fighting. He requested to speak to Frank Carty, who responded when called, and came, under PT escort, with a priest.

BRADY, Terence: AT. Former PT Pte. Captured after AT attack on PTs in Leixlip. Tried for treachery by court-martial. Convicted and executed in Portobello Barracks, Dublin, 8 January 1923.

BREEN, Dan: AT, although disapproving of CW. Negotiated with Mulcahy at outset and appealed for army unity. Signatory of Army document of 1 May 1922. Elected in June 1922 election when he was nominated by both sides. Engaged in sporadic actions around Clonmel. Defended Nine Mile House against PT troops but later withdrew. Captured, while asleep, in the Glen of Aherlow. Imprisoned in Limerick and Mountjoy, where he endured hunger- and thirst-strikes until released. WI.

BREEN, Martin ('Sparky'): AT. Comdt. From August 1922, OC No 1 Tipperary Bde Column drawn mainly from old Tipperary 4 Bn with elements from 2, 3, 7 and 8 Bns. Operated in Glen of Aherlow, Knockgraffon, Rosegreen, Drangan and Slievenamon (Kilfeacle) areas. Joined with Barry and Lacey in the attack on Carrick-on-Suir Barracks 9 December 1922. KIA 16 January 1923 when, on leaving his home, he was called upon to halt by PTs but chose to fight. A companion, Capt Denis Ryan, was wounded and died on 4 June.

BREEN, Simon: PT. Captured when Annacarthy Barracks was overrun and burned 30 April 1922.

BRENNAN, Austin: PT. Commanded the Clare section in Limerick in support of his brother, Michael (*below*).

BRENNAN, J.P., Dr: AT. Head of Medical Services. Attended to wounded in O'Connell St fighting.

BRENNAN, Michael: PT. Comdt Gen. Comdt I Western Div (Clare & South Galway) March 1922. His occupation of Limerick after departure of British in February 1922 was resented strongly by predominantly AT troops. On 1 July Lynch took Adare Barracks and a portion of Limerick city, then requested a truce from Brennan. He agreed, but was unable to have it approved by the government. Despatched troops to Kerry to assist Fenit landing. Engaged in numerous actions. GOC Limerick Command April 1923. WI. (*See* Hogan, Seamus; Ó hAnnagáin, D.)

BRENNAN, Patrick: PT. Comdt. OC Kildare Bde. Deployed his illarmed troops in Wicklow to isolate Dublin, July 1922.

BRENNAN, Patrick: AT. Acting Brigadier, 1 Eastern Div.

BRENNAN, Robert: Leading AT propagandist. Had attempted to organize a united front at the Irish Race Convention in Paris in January 1922. WI.

BRENNAN-WHITMORE, W.J.: PT. Comdt. WI.

BRESLANE: AT. Comdt. Met Col Prout in Kilkenny 4 May 1922 to discuss army unity.

BRESLIN: PT. Capt. Injured in Ballyseedy explosion. (*See Chronology, 7 March 1923*)

BRESLIN, Peadar: AT. Teller at Convention 18 June 1922. QM Four Courts Garrison. After surrender, remained behind with O'Malley to burn arms. Imprisoned. Shot dead during escape bid from Mountjoy 10 October 1922.

BROSNAN, Michael: AT. Executed in Tralee 20 January 1923 for unlawful possession of arms.

BROSNAN, Tadhg: AT. OC 4 Castlegregory Bn, Kerry No 1 Bde. Active in Limerick, Clare and Kerry after Fenit landing.(*See Chronology, July-Aug.1922*)

BROWNE, Jimmy: *See* McMonagle, James.

BROY, Eamonn: AT. Despite aiding Collins during War of Independence and Treaty negotiations, he supported de Valera during CW. WI.

BRUGHA, Cathal: AT. TD. Vigorous in opposition to Treaty. Four Courts garrison and Hamman Hotel. Ordered his garrison to surrender in O'Connell Street, Dublin, 5 July 1922. Last out, he himself refused to surrender, was shot and died two days later. WI.

BUCKLEY, Dan: AT. Stood down when Sean Gaynor became OC 3 Southern Div and remained his 2 i/c.

BUCKLEY, Sean: AT. Hunger-striker in Kilmainham, October 1923. WI.

BURKE, Frederick.: AT. Executed in Roscrea 13 January 1923 for unlawful possession of arms and ammunition.

BURKE, Luke: Alias Henry, Keenan. Keady, Co. Armagh man executed in Mullingar Barracks, 13 March 1923 for a bank robbery in Oldcastle. (*See Greery, Michael*)

BURKE, Martin: AT. Executed in Athlone 20 January 1923 for unlawful possession of arms and ammunition.

BURKE, William: PT. Captured when Annacarthy Barracks, Co. Tipperary, was overrun and burned 30 April 1922.

BURNS, Peter: AT. Vol 3 Western Div. KIA Ballintrillick/Glencar, Co. Sligo, 20 September 1922.

BURNS, Todd: AT. Vol 3 Western Div. KIA Ballintrillick/Glencar, Co. Sligo, 20 September 1922.

BUTLER (Canon): Involved in mediation in Sligo confrontation. (*See Coyne, Brian*)

BYRNE: Methodist pacifist who endured a lone hunger-strike in Mountjoy until his release December 1922.

BYRNE, Ben: PT. Col. On staff of Dalton's Imperial Hotel, Cork.

BYRNE, Daniel: AT. Early casualty, killed when attempting to make safe a shotgun attached to gelignite in Gorey, Co. Wexford, RIC Barracks.

BYRNE, Joseph: AT. Executed in Portlaoise 27 January 1923 for unlawful possession of a revolver.

BYRNE, Joseph: PT. Led part of attack on Breen's Nine Mile House, Co. Tipperary, stronghold, July 1922.

BYRNE (Most Rev Dr): Archbishop of Dublin. Attempted to prevent CW developing.

BYRNE, Terence: PT. KIA Nenagh 29 June 1922. (*See Houlihan, William*)

BYRNE, Vincent: PT. Lt. OIC Bank of Ireland guard. Resisted early AT demand to evacuate bank. Promoted in the field to Capt. Ambushed in York Street June 1922. OC Government buildings. WI.

CAFFERKY, J.: AT. Capt. Adj Sligo Bde.

CAGNEY, Patrick (Dr): Examined Collins's body at Shanakiel Hospital, Cork.

CAHILL, Patrick: AT. His early dismissal (1921) from Kerry No 1 Bde for Andy Cooney caused considerable friction that carried on into CW. Engaged in defence of Tralee with detachments of the Bde's 9 Bn. WI.

CAHILL, William: PT. Comdt. Assistant to Henry Conner.

CALLAGHAN, Patrick: PT. Comdt. In charge of troops when *The Ballinalee* was captured by AT ambush 13 July 1922 at Rockwood.

CAMPBELL John J.: AT leanings but not committed at time of death, 14 July 1922, in Dundalk when 4 Northern Div was surrounded and he was shot trying to escape.

CAMPION, Edward: AT. Early occupant of Clonalis House, Co. Roscommon. Evacuated it after PT attack and operated in Mayo area.

CAREW, Thomas: PT. Col. Occupied Annacarthy Barracks, Co. Tipperary, 29 April 1922. Seriously injured there when ATs attacked next day. A cease-fire permitted his removal to hospital, after which the garrison surrendered. In action in Kilkenny.

CARNEY, Frank: In Portobello Barracks, June 1922, as Supplies Officer, disobeyed orders and refused to release supplies to British officer from Phoenix Park depot. Resigned with others in his stores.

CARNEY, Tom: AT. Brig Gen. Active in Mayo area. On 9 September 1922 captured a significant number of PTs in an attack on Swinford barracks, carried out to rescue Tomás Mac Cathmaoil, being held prisoner there. Sgt Frank Neary, PT, was killed in the action.

CARRIG, Louis: PT. Comdt. Senior staff officer, legal section at GHQ, November 1922.

CARROLL, Patrick: AT. Lt 3 Western Div. KIA Ballintrillick/Glencar, Co. Sligo, 20 September 1922 when PTs re-captured *The Ballinalee*.

CARTY, Frank: AT. Prominent leader in Sligo/Mayo area. Used a Vol posing as a priest to mislead PTs and successfully seized 30 rifles, one machine gun, some revolvers and ammunition in Tubbercurry. In co-operation with Michael Kilroy, maintained frequent sea-patrol from Roonagh Point to Clare Island to Mulranny. WI. (*See Brady, Patrick*)

CARTY, Frank: AT. South Wexford Bde Adj and Training Officer 3 Eastern Div. After a bridge-blowing success in Ferns, he attacked PT stronghold in Enniscorthy Castle. Seized the castle but was later captured after a PT counter-attack. Endured hunger-strike. Led attempt to burn Portlaoise Prison 29 August 1922. (*See Gallagher, Sean*)

CASEY, Charles: PT. Lt Comdt. Staff officer GHQ Legal Section November 1922. Prosecuting counsel who served charges on Ernie O'Malley in Mountjoy Hospital wing.

CASEY, Con: AT. Adj 1 Eastern Div in Drogheda. Organizer 1 Southern Div (Kerry). Attended Army Convention 26 March 1922. Organizer in 1 Southern Div. Captured 1 November 1922. Tried by court-martial and sentenced to death in Tralee, December 1922. PTs circulated notices threatening his immediate execution if hostilities against them continued in the area. Sentence commuted to 10 years penal servitude. Imprisoned Tralee, Mountjoy and Newbridge where he endured hunger-strike. Ordered off it. Hospitalized in Curragh, then interned in its Hare Park until final release June 1924. (*See Moroney, Matthew; O'Connor, Jeremiah*)

CASSIDY: PT. Sgt. In action during severe fighting in Collooney, Co. Sligo, 15 July 1922. He was injured by machine-gun fire from the Protestant church but immediately shelled and destroyed the AT outpost by direct artillery fire.

CASSIDY, Peter: AT. Executed at Kilmainham Jail, Dublin, 17 November 1922 for unlawful possession of a revolver. James Fisher, John Gaffney and Richard Twohig were executed the same day, the first such executions of the CW.

CHAMBERLAIN, Austen: MP. Participated in discussions concerning the draft constitution for the IFS.

CHARTRES, John: PT. Dismissed from a Provisional Government post in Germany, July 1922, for allowing publication of an article supporting ATs in a journal for which he held editorial responsibility.

CHILDERS, Robert Erskine: AT. TD. Director of Propaganda. Issued numerous proclamations and bulletins calling for opposition to PT forces. Involved in Dublin fighting. Captured at Glendalough House, the home of his cousin Robert Barton, 10 November 1922. Convicted by court-martial for unlawful possession of a pistol. Shook hands with members of firing party before his execution 24 November 1922. WI.

CHUDLEIGH, Maj: Handed over Viceregal Lodge to Comdt T. Gunne, 14 December 1922.

CHURCHILL, Winston Leonard Spencer (Rt Hon Sir): Countersigned the Collins–Craig agreement of 30 March 1922 on behalf of British government. Was prejudicial to the proposed 'Pact Election' by declaring in May 1922 that evacuation of British troops would cease and that the Provisional Government would receive no further assistance from Britain. Declared 23 June that continuation of occupation of the Four Courts would be a violation of the Treaty. Discussed draft constitution with Collins, disagreeing with it and with concessions to ATs. Threatened renewed British action after assassination of Wilson. Spoke bitterly about Childers after his arrest. WI. (*See Macready, Nevil*)

CLANCY: PT. Lt. In charge of party that sealed off Lynch's escape route and forced him and his party to expose themselves to PT fire, resulting in Lynch's death, 10 April 1923.

CLANCY (Sr): PT. Early member of Army Nursing Service.

CLARE, Patrick: AT. Charged with possessing revolver near home of Mulcahy. Death sentence commuted to 10 years imprisonment. Imprisoned in Curragh.

CLARKE, Kathleen: TD. Chairman of Dáil Peace Committee, May–June 1922. Applied to the AT supreme court to have the Ceann Comhairle, Eoin MacNeill, convene the Dáil. The hearing was fixed for 11 August, when a conditional order was made absolute. AT court was powerless to put it into effect. WI. (*See Crowley, Diarmuid*)

CLEARY, Sean: AT. Taken prisoner by PTs at Castle Blake, near Cashel, Co. Tipperary, 16 April 1923. (*See Kennedy, Patrick*)

CLERY, Arthur: Prof. With Dr Con Murphy and Count Plunkett, protested to the Pope about bishops who refused sacraments to AT forces. WI.

CLIFFORD, J. (Billy): *See Dandy Six.*

CLIFFORD, John: AT. Executed in Tralee 20 January 1923 for unlawful possession of weapons and ammunition.

CLIFFORD, Madge: AT. C na mB. Typist at GHQ. Assisted Lynch in early days of Four Courts occupation. Secretary to ACS September 1922.

COATES, David: PT. Capt. In charge of armoured transport in Cork area, August 1922.

COFFEY, Stephen: AT. Escaped from explosion at Countess Bridge, Killarney, 7 March 1923. (*See Chronology*)

COFFEY, Tadhg: AT. Avoided explosion at Countess Bridge, Killarney, by escaping 7 March 1923. (*See Chronology*)

COGHLAN, Dan: PT. Col. Former BA officer who was decorated by British and French establishments for work in graves registration of First World War victims. At outbreak of CW Collins prevailed on him to return from England and join PTs. He was close to Collins and was a pallbearer at his funeral.

COHALAN, D.F. (Most Rev Dr): Bishop of Cork. Welcomed PT troops to city. At close of conflict, stated that 'Republicanism in Ireland for the past twelve months has been a wicked and insidious attack on the Church and on the souls of the faithful committed to the Church by the law of the Catholic Church.' WI. (*See Barry, Denis*)

COLIVET, M.P.: AT. TD. Member of de Valera's Council of State appointed 25 October 1922.

COLLINS: PT. KIA in attack on Cappard House, Abbeyleix, 28 July 1922.

COLLINS, Herbert: AT. Executed in Athlone 20 January 1923 for unlawful possession of weapons and ammunition.

COLLINS, John: PT. Col. In action in Kilkenny and Carrick-on-Suir areas.

COLLINS, Michael: PT. TD. Chairman of Provisional Government. CIC of PT forces from 13 July 1922, after resigning Dáil Finance Ministry. Met Craig, January and March 1922, in attempts to end unrest in NI, end Belfast Boycott and agree on Boundary Commission findings. Signed formal pact on these issues 30 March 1922. With Churchill, signed authority for transfer of power from Britain to Saorstát Éireann 1 April 1922. Signatory of Army document of 1 May 1922. Member of Army Reunification Committee, which arranged a temporary truce 4 May 1922. Chairman of committee that drafted the 1922 Constitution. Made election pact with de Valera in May/June 1922 but repudiated it before polling day. Survived attack on his car in Stillorgan 18 August 1922. Began tour of inspection in Munster 20 August. KIA at Béal na mBláth 22 August. Various reports suggest he was about to meet Dan Breen (who had cleared the meeting with Lynch) or other influential ATs with a view to ending the CW. WI. (*See McGrath, Joseph; Pact Election, Chronology, 1 January 1922*)

COLLINS, Michael: PT. NCO. Seriously injured when he rushed an AT machine-gunner at Rochestown during PT advance on Cork.

COLLINS, Sean: PT. Michael's brother. Captured by ATs a few days after Béal na mBláth ambush, but released.

COLLISON, John: PT. Comdt 3 Southern Div. Involved in early Limerick operations. Active in Laois-Offaly area. KIA when ambushed leading a party to deal with a mine reportedly laid at Tonduff, Abbeyleix, 28 July 1922. WI.

COLUMB, Patrick: PT. Capt Company Adj Mullingar Military Barracks.

Shot dead 27 April 1922 when attacking an AT stronghold in which PT prisoners were detained. Authoritative sources claim that he was shot by the man he replaced as Barrack Adj, at Sean MacEoin's request.

COMERFORD, Máire: AT. C na mB. Carried despatches between Four Courts and Dublin Bde HQ in O'Connell Street. Made liaison with PT leaders for transfer of wounded from Four Courts. Continued despatch work in the provinces throughout CW. Arrested after involvement in attempt to kidnap W.T. Cosgrave January 1923 (see McGrath, Paddy). Imprisoned in Mountjoy, where she was shot in the leg, and in North Dublin Union, from where she escaped. Re-arrested and imprisoned in Kilmainham. Endured hunger-strike. Released. WI.

COMYN, Michael: KC. Made application on behalf of Kathleen Clarke.

CONLON, Peter: PT. Led attack on Passage East after sea landing 8-9 August 1922.

CONNELL, Seamus: PT. Col. Active in Sligo-Leitrim-Fermanagh area.

CONNER, Henry: PT. Comdt. Appointed to conduct military courts in Limerick October 1922.

CONNOLLY, George: AT. Four Courts garrison.

CONNOLLY, James: AT. Capt. OC of Finner Camp. KIA during PT takeover 29 June 1922.

CONNOLLY, Joseph: AT. In action in Gresham Hotel during Dublin fighting.

CONNOLLY, Katie: AT. Member of Barry's Hotel garrison during Dublin fighting.

CONNOLLY, Louis: PT. Capt. ADC to MacEoin during Sligo confrontation.

CONNOLLY-O'BRIEN, Nora: AT. Set up medical aid posts during Dublin fighting. Replaced Margaret Skinnider as Stack's assistant. Captured and imprisoned in her Hume St office. Imprisoned Mountjoy November 1922. Won a *habeas corpus* case and was released August 1923.

CONROY, Harry: AT. Col Comdt. IO Western Command.

CONROY, J. (Sonny): PT. Capt. 2 i/c to Comdt James McGuinness in push from Fenit to Tralee August 1922.

CONROY, William: AT. Executed in Birr 26 January 1923 for unlawful possession of weapons and burglary.

CONSIDINE, Brendan: AT. Arranged capture of Gogarty.

CONWAY, Christopher (Kit): PT/AT. Served in National Army in the Curragh, Co. Kildare, and in Clonmel and Cahir, Co. Tipperary. Kept in contact with his former AT comrades in 3 Tipperary Bde, passing on information that helped them avoid capture. Eventually deserted autumn 1922, moved to Dublin and joined ATs there. WI.

COONEY: PT. Vol. Member of armoured car crew at Béal na mBláth when Collins was killed 22 August 1922.

COONEY, Andrew: AT. His taking over Kerry No 1 Bde from Paddy

Cahill in 1921 caused lasting friction in Kerry, and affected resistance to Fenit landing. Illness forced his return to Dublin. Comdt 1 Eastern Div with HQ in Drogheda March 1922. Involved in abortive plan to capture Baldonnel. Assisted in capture of armoured car, *The Mutineer*, for Four Courts garrison. Imprisoned, Mountjoy where he organized escape attempt. WI.

COONEY, Sean: AT. Arranged mine-laying for Mollsheen Cross ambush. Guided by Jack Lonergan. Jack Aylward, Ned McNamara and 'Buck' O'Reilly also involved in planning and execution of the ambush. (*See Dalton, Paddy*)

COPE, Alfred W: Assistant Under-Secretary. Met Griffith, Ernie O'Malley and Emmet Dalton in Dublin 23 June 1922 to discuss continuing occupation of the Four Courts. With Macready, supervised withdrawal of British troops. He was instrumental in equipping PTs with artillery pieces. WI. (*See Woods, Tony*)

CORBETT: PT. Lt. Member of Collins escort who was replaced 20 August 1922 by Capt Joe Dolan at Limerick.

CORCORAN, Bill: PT. Captured when Annacarthy Barracks was overrun and burned 30 April 1922.

CORRIGAN: Chief State Solicitor whose house was blown up 29 January 1923.

CORRY: PT. Vol. English-born driver of Collins's car at Béal na mBláth.

COSGRAVE, Philip: Brother of W.T. Cosgrave. Governor of Mountjoy Prison. Stopped troops firing on escapees led by Andy Cooney. Carried mail from and to Ernie O'Malley.

COSGRAVE, W.T.: PT. TD. Minister for Local Government, January-September 1922. Acting Chairman of Provisional Government 12 August 1922, after Griffith's death. Chairman and Minister for Finance 23 August-6 December President of the Executive Council of the IFS October 1922. His home was gutted January 1923. Founded Cumann na nGaedheal political party March 1923. WI.

COSTELLO, Michael J.: PT. Comdt, later Col Comdt. Served at HQ No 3 Bde, Southern Command (Roscrea). Active in Tipperary-Offaly-Laois area. Took firm decisions, even depriving Cumann na mBan despatch carriers of their bicycles. His troops were successful in rounding up AT parties attacking trains, laying ambushes, etc. D/Int October 1923. WI.

COTTOR, Frank: AT. Four Courts garrison. Manufactured bombs there.

COUGHLAN, F.X.: PT. OC E Coy, 4 Dublin Bn, all but four of whom supported the Treaty. Involved in organizational duties in greater Dublin area. WI.

COURTNEY, T.C.: PT. Maj. 2 i/c Corps of Engineers, formed March 1923.

COUSINS, Thomas: PT. Lt. In action at Spencerstown, Co. Wexford, 9 January 1923, when two ATs were killed.

COYLE, Eithne: AT. C na mB. Carried despatches. Arrested November 1922. Imprisoned in Mountjoy and North Dublin Union.

COYNE, Brian (Most Rev Dr): Bishop of Elphin. Rose from his sickbed and attempted to negotiate a PT surrender in Sligo July 1922. PTs refused, so he remained at their Courthouse HQ to discourage AT attack until he arranged an exchange of prisoners. When this was expedited 15 July, ATs withdrew. (*See Devins, Seamus*)

COYNE, Thomas: PT. Lt/Comdt. Staff officer, legal section at GHQ, November 1922.

CRAIG, James (First Viscount Craigavon): Prime Minister of NI. Signatory to Collins-Craig Agreement, 30 March 1922, promising to protect Northern Catholics in return for boundary settlement. WI. (*See Collins*)

CREANE, John: AT. Executed in Wexford 13 March 1923 for unlawful possession of a revolver.

CROFTS, Thomas: AT. Comdt Gen Cork No 3 Bde. Member of AT Executive. Close associate of Liam Lynch. Surrounded after Fenit landing but fought his way out. Pressed for executive meeting to discuss ceasefire. Member of ambush party at Béal na mBláth who left the scene before the Collins convoy arrived. Present at Nire Valley meeting 24 March 1923. Comdt 1 Southern Div after Lynch's death.

CRONIN: PT. Col Comdt. Div QM 3 Southern Div February-April 1923. On QMG's staff. WI. (*See McCarthy, Owen Felix*)

CROWLEY, Daniel: Train fireman, scalded to death when ATs derailed a train at Liscahane Bridge, Ardfert, 19 January 1923. (*See Driscoll, Tom; Riordan, Patrick*)

CROWLEY, Diarmuid: Supreme Court Judge. On 19 July 1922 granted Count Plunkett's application of *habeas corpus* for liberation of his son, Seóirse. Also issued warrants for arrest of Richard Mulcahy and Colm Ó Murchadha. These acts led to Eamonn Duggan, Minister for Home Affairs, rescinding Court authority. Granted conditional order to Kathleen Clarke. Arrested and imprisoned after this incident. WI.

CULHANE, Sean: AT. Early associate of Lynch's.

CULLEN, Tom: PT. Went to London to examine possibility of rescuing Reginald Dunne and Joseph O'Sullivan from imprisonment. Collins's bodyguard, although not at Béal na mBláth. WI.

CUMMIN, Joseph: PT. Comdt North Wexford Bde (N. Wexford & S. Wicklow) March 1922.

CUNNANE, Frank: AT. Executed in Tuam, Co. Galway, 11 April 1923, for unlawful possession of a rifle and ammunition.

CUNNINGHAM, Joe: PT. Comdt. Active in Donegal area.

CUNNINGHAM, Patrick: AT. Executed in Birr, Co. Offaly, 26 January 1923, for unlawful possession of weapons and burglary.

CURRAN, Frank: PT. *See Murphy, Michael*.

CUSACK, John: AT. KIA in Four Courts 30 June 1922, immediately prior to the garrison's surrender.

CUSTOM HOUSE, THE: PT Whippet armoured car.

DAHILLE, Jim: AT. Vol. *See Sadlier Brothers.*

DALTON, Emmet: PT. Maj Gen. GOC Eastern Command. Director of Training March-August 1922. Later, Director of Operations. Advised and was in charge of artillery fire on Four Courts 28 June 1922. Was in overall command of Leinster operations July 1922. Conceived and co-ordinated sea-borne attacks and commanded Dublin troops landing in Passage West from the *Arvonia* and *Lady Wicklow*. With Tom Ennis, led the attack on Cork. After occupation, ordered city banks to open, thus lifting economic blockade of the south. Pressed on to Union Hall and Youghal. Notified Collins of peace proposals received from 'prominent Cork citizens' 18 August 1922. On request, supplied the names. Escorted Collins on his fateful tour of Munster and was alongside him at Béal na mBláth when Collins was killed. WI. (*See Aylward; Barrett, Frank; O'Neill, Ignatius; Aiken, Frank*)

DALTON, Paddy ('Big Paddy'): AT. OC No 2 Column, 3 Tipperary Bde and Bde Vice Comdt. Bde Comdt for a short spell. Originally took over Clonmel Barracks from the departing British. Planned and participated in ambush at Mollsheen's Cross, Woodroof, Co. Tipperary, 4 October 1922. KIA Donohill 26 October 1922, on the Cahir-Clonmel road.

DALY, Charles: AT. Comdt Gen. Comdt 2 Northern Div (four brigades, Tyrone and Derry) March 1922. Imprisoned in Drumboe Castle for eight months. Executed in Drumboe 14 March 1923 for unlawful possession of weapons and ammunition.

DALY, Charles: AT. Cousin of above. With others, burned part of Tralee Barracks before it fell into PT hands, 2 August 1922. WI. (*See Sheehy, J.J.*)

DALY, Daniel: Railway engine driver shot dead by ATs at Tralee station 23 January 1923. Other railway staff received threats but continued working. (*See Lynch, Daniel*)

DALY, James: AT. Executed in Tralee 20 January 1922 for unlawful possession of weapons and ammunition.

DALY, Madge: AT. C na mB member active in escape plans for ATs in Limerick Prison.

DALY, Paddy (Also O'Daly): PT. Maj Gen. On 1 February 1922, as a Capt, led first uniformed troops (ASU) into Beggarsbush Barracks. Commanded Portobello Barracks. Surrounded Four Courts. Refused to grant terms when receiving its garrison's formal surrender. I/c of Dublin Guard at Fenit landing. Captured Tralee and Castleisland. GOC Kerry Command 1 February 1923. Reprimanded for unnecessary commandeering of private cars and conduct unbecoming an officer when, with two other officers, he manhandled two Kenmare women. Accounts of his being relieved of his command for ill-treatment of prisoners are not borne out by official documents bearing his signature.

DALY, Paddy (Nap): AT. 1 Tralee Bn, later 9 Bn Kerry No 1 Bde. Involved in resistance to Fenit landing.

DALY, Tom: AT. Active in Kerry. Captured at Kilcummin 22 August 1922. Imprisoned Mountjoy. Endured hunger-strike. One of the last prisoners to be released.

'DANDY SIX': PT. Officers of 1 Western Div who refused to accept Tralee AT orders and moved to Listowel: J. Clifford, Jack Flavin, James Lyons, Harold Reid, Stephen Scannell and Thomas Slattery.

DANNY BOY: Later called *Tom Keogh*. PT armoured car widely used in Limerick, Cork and Kerry. (See *Murphy, Humphrey*)

DAVIN, Jerome: AT. Comdt 1 Bn 3 Tipperary Bde. With Con Scanlon, Comdt 5 Bn, Capt Tom Quinlan and eleven others, was captured in search-and-sweep operations in Newcastle, Ardfinnan area, Co. Tipperary, mid-February 1923.

DAVIN'S: AT. Rosegreen. South Tipperary Bde meeting-centre.

DAVIS, M.: AT. Leader in Athlone area. Captured after a raid by boat on Quaker Island, Lough Ree. (See *Masterson, B.*)

DAVITT, Cahir: PT. Maj Gen. Judge-Advocate General. WI.

DEASY, Liam: AT. Comdt Gen. Close supporter of Lynch. Member of Executive Council. Wavered during disputes leading to CW. Signatory of AT Proclamation of 29 June 1922 (see *Chronology*). Adj 1 Southern Div under Lynch and later its Comdt. Realized early on that AT position was impossible. In action in Tipperary and Limerick. Held meeting of senior AT officers and de Valera at Béal na mBláth 22 August 1922. Visited the ambush site but was not there during shooting of Collins. He sent a formal report to Lynch after the event. As D/COS was captured at Tincurry 18 January 1923 and imprisoned in Clonmel and Arbour Hill. Tried by court-martial 20 January and sentenced to death the following morning. Requested stay of execution in order to negotiate an end to hostilities. Signed a dictated document calling on his AT Executive collegues to surrender (see *Chronology, 8 January 1923*). They did not, and condemned his action. WI. (See *Russell, Charles*)

DE COURCY, Robert: AT. Div Engineer, 2 Southern Div. Continued with development of a compressed-air gun which, prior to CW, he had demonstrated to Mulcahy, de Valera and others. Captured. Imprisoned Kilmainham. On hunger-strike 13 October 1923.

DEIGNAN, Tom: AT. Comdt East Sligo Bde. Active in Sligo area.

DELVIN, Ted: AT. Active in Donegal area.

DEMPSEY, James: PT. Comdt ASU. Vice Comdt, Kerry Command after Fenit landing. Carried out part of the PT pincer movement on Tralee. Lost an eye in action at Kilgobnit, Killorglin.

DERRIG, Tomás: AT. Comdt Gen. Member of Executive of sixteen from 12 June 1922. Signatory of AT Proclamation of 29 June 1922 (see *Chronology*). Four Courts garrison. Escaped from Jameson's distillery where he had been held after its surrender. In action in Dublin, Wicklow and Wexford, July 1922. Later, Adj General and D/Int, AT forces. Called for assassination of all members of Provisional Government, after passing of Special Powers Resolution. Attended Nire Valley meeting. Captured, in

Dublin April 1923 and wounded in escape attempt, eventually losing an eye. Imprisoned Kilmainham. Endured hunger-strike October 1923. With David L. Robinson, exhorted strike leaders to call it off. WI.

DESART, Dowager Countess of: PT. Senator 6 December 1922.

DESMOND'S HOTEL: Cork location of proposed meeting between Collins and 'prominent citizens' with a view to ending CW.

DESPARD, Charlotte: Sister of Lord French (*see WI*), she added the AT cause to the many she espoused. Member of anti-war delegation June 1922. (*See Gonne, Maud*)

DE VALERA, Eamonn: AT. TD. Drafted alternative 'Document Number Two' to the Treaty. When defeated in Treaty vote, resigned Presidency of Dáil but retained Presidency of Sinn Féin. President of Fine Ghaedheal, formed at Convention of the Irish Race in Paris 27 January 1922. Supported introduction of franchise for women. Appealed to Richard Mulcahy to avert violence in Limerick March 1922. Formed a political party, Cumann na Poblachta 22 March 1922. Made election pact with Collins 20 May 1922. Elected 22 June. Appealed for public denouncement of the Treaty and support for Rory O'Connor and the Four Courts resistance. Re-joined his old 3 Dublin Bn as a private. In action in Dublin, Clonmel, Fermoy. Although the AT political leader, he did not hold any positions of military command. Nominal assistant to Sean Moylan in Directorate of Operations. While supportive, he advised against continuing the impossible struggle and actually met Mulcahy 6 September 1922 in an attempt to find a basis for peace. Was called upon to become President of the Republic and Chief Executive of the State by AT deputies 25 October 1922. He accepted and formed his own cabinet and Council of State. Attended Nire Valley meeting 24 March 1923 and outlined possibilities for peace. On 27 April 1923, signed a proclamation calling for a suspension of all aggressive action. Arrested while speaking at an election rally in Ennis 15 August 1923 and imprisoned in Kilmainham and Arbour Hill until July 1924. WI.

DEVANE, Thomas: AT. Sentenced to death in Tralee December 1922. Notices were circulated, threatening immediate execution if hostilities against PTs continued in the area. He was not executed. (*See Casey, Con; Moroney, Matthew; O'Connor, Jeremiah*)

DEVANNEY, Kathleen: AT. C na mB. Imprisoned Mountjoy.

DEVINS, Seamus: AT. TD. Brig Gen. OC 1 Bde, 3 Western Div. On 14 July 1922 sent ultimatum to PT troops in Sligo to vacate the town, causing a serious confrontation. KIA Ballintrillick/Glencar, Co. Sligo, 20 September 1922 when PTs re-captured *The Ballinalee*. (*See Coyne, Most Rev Dr*)

DILLON, Dr: PT. Assisted Dr Walsh in food-control duties in Galway July 1922.

DINEEN: PT. Comdt. WIA in attack on Blessington 5 July 1922.

DOBYNN, Sean: AT. In action in Waterford-Kilkenny area. Accidentally shot July 1922.

DOCKERY, Michael: PT. Brig Gen. Held Boyle for PT forces. KIA in fierce fighting there 7 July 1922. A female resident of the town was also killed. WI.

DOHENY: AT. Active in Tyrone-Donegal area.

DOLAN, Joe: PT. Capt. Close associate of Collins. Went to London to examine possibility of rescuing Reginald Dunne and Joseph O'Sullivan. A member of Collins's escort at Béal na mBláth. WI. (*See Corbett, Lt*)

DOMINICK, Rev Fr (O'Connor): Assisted Four Courts garrison in material and spiritual matters. WI.

DONNELLY, Simon: AT. Four Courts garrison. Military Police commander. Imprisoned Mountjoy. Shot a PT soldier while attempting to escape from there. WI.

DONOVAN, John: PT. Lt/Comdt. Staff officer Legal Section GHQ November 1922.

DOUGLAS, James: PT. Senator. Intermediary between Cosgrave and de Valera in settlement attempt May 1923. (*See Jameson, Andrew*)

DOWDALL, T.P.: With Fr Duggan, delivered letter from People's Rights Association, Cork, to Collins, seeking cessation of hostilities.

DOWLING, Leo: AT. Former PT Cpl. Captured after AT attack on PTs in Leixlip. Tried by court-martial for treachery. Convicted and executed in Portobello Barracks, Dublin, 8 January 1923.

DOWLING, Sean: AT. Executive member. OC Dublin 4 Bn. D/Operations and D/Organization. His area of operation opposite the Four Courts was not held, due to his men refusing to participate in CW. It was in this area that the PT field gun was deployed. In action in Tramway Office, O'Connell St. Involved in abortive Baldonnel operation (*see Chronology, July 1922*). Present at Nire Valley meeting. WI. (*See Langan, Miss*)

DOWNEY, C.: PT. Lt. Platoon commander during take-over of Wellington (Griffith) Barracks.

DOYLE, Johnny: PT. Capt. Fired the first round of artillery from 18-pounder gun on Four Courts 28 June 1922.

DOYLE, Philip: Jail escapee shot dead by ATs near Killane, Co. Wexford, for attacking a Sgt of the Civic Guard and taking his bicycle. His body was found 21 July 1922.

DOYLE, Tommy: PT. In action in South Leinster and Munster. Accompanied David Moran in many actions. Wounded trying to recover body of Cpl Kelly 9 August 1922 at Redmondstown, Clonmel.

DRISCOLL, Tom: AT. Led party that derailed train at Liscahane bridge, Ardfert, 19 January 1923. (*See Crowley, Daniel; Riordan, Patrick*)

DRUMM, Jack: PT. Lt. Took over Crinkle Castle, Birr, but AT forces captured it. In action in Blue Ball, Geashill and Portlaoise. WIA Killeigh 24 May 1923.

DUBLIN LIZ, THE: PT armoured car.

DUFFY, George Gavan: PT. TD. Minister for Foreign Affairs until 5 July 1922 when he resigned in protest against the suppression of the Supreme

Court. His Dáil proposal that AT prisoners should be given POW status was defeated. Was critical of the 1922 Constitution and of the execution of Childers and others. WI.

DUGGAN, Eamonn: PT. TD. Minister for Home Affairs January-August 1922. Provisional Government signatory to the Collins-Craig agreement, 30 March 1922. Minister without portfolio in Executive Council, 6-14 December 1922. WI.

DUGGAN, Fr Tom: PT. Involved in a number of peace moves. Brought Deasy's surrender dictate to Army Executive January 1923. (*See Dowdall, T.P.*)

DUNNE: AT. Mobilized up to 40 Vols for abortive attack on Baldonnel. (*See Chronology, July 1922*)

DUNNE, Peadar: AT. Severely injured at preliminary compressed-air gun test. WI. (*See de Courcy*)

DUNNE, Reginald: AT. Comdt. With Joseph O'Sullivan, was convicted of the assassination of Sir Henry Wilson 22 June 1922. Tried at Old Bailey 18 July and found guilty. Executed in Wandsworth 10 August.

DWYER, Paddy: PT. WIA in defence of Annacarthy Barracks. WI.

DWYER, Seamus: PT. TD. In action in South Leinster and Tipperary. WI.

EGAN: PT. Capt. Chief Technical Officer, Independent Signal Corps.

ENGLISH, Theo: AT. KIA trying to escape from Castle Blake near Cashel 16 April 1923.

ENNIS: PT. Sgt. Injured in Ballyseedy explosion. (*See Chronology, 7 March 1923*)

ENNIS, Thomas: PT. Gen. OC 2 Eastern Div. Issued order demanding surrender of Four Courts. Planned O'Connell Street attack on AT forces. In action in Kilkenny, Baltinglass and Tuagh, Co. Cork. Led attack on Cork road sector of Passage West after 22 August 1922 landing. Led first PT troops into Cork in an armoured car named *The Manager*. Discussed possibility of cease-fire with Barry, Lynch and Co. Cork clergy. WI. (*See Dalton, Emmet; Russell, Charles*)

ENRIGHT, Daniel: AT. Lt. Executed in Drumboe 14 March 1923 for unlawful possession of a rifle and ammunition.

ENRIGHT, Eamonn: AT. Imprisoned Mountjoy, where he gave lectures to prisoners.

ESMOND, Thomas, Sir: His home, 'Ballynastragh', at Gorey, Co. Wexford, part of which dated from the 14th century, was burned by ATs January 1923.

ETCHINGHAM, Sean: AT. TD. Vehement speaker against the Treaty. Lost his seat in Pact Election 16 June 1922.

FAHY, Frank: AT. TD. WI.

FAHY, T.: AT. Comdt 8 Bn 3 Tipperary Bde. Captured when large haul of arms was discovered and seized at Windgap, Co. Kilkenny, 2 February 1923.

FALLON, Martin: PT. Comdt/Col Comdt. Planned and executed the take-over of Boyle from ATs, imprisoning AT leaders. Acceding to their request to be placed in open arrest, he and his leaders were, in turn, captured and made to leave Boyle. As a result,

MacEoin relieved him of his command but relented. Commanded Sligo courthouse garrison 14 July 1922. From this HQ Fallon later defied AT ultimatum to vacate Sligo.

FARRELL, John: PT. Sgt. Longford associate of MacEoin's. KIA Dooney Rock, Sligo, 13 July 1922 in a dawn ambush when *The Ballinalee* armoured car was captured by ATs.

FARRELLY, Matt: PT. Comdt. Occupied part of Collooney, Co. Sligo, 20 July 1922. Pretending to be an AT officer, he double-marched a contingent of AT troops up to MacEoin's HQ in the town. Later Comdt Gen. Planned and executed ambushes at Rosses Point and Sligo. Commanded *The Tartar*.

FARRELLY, Patrick: AT. Executed in Dublin 30 November 1922 for unlawful possession of a bomb.

FERGUSON, Joseph: AT. Executed in Dundalk 22 January 1923 for unlawful possession of arms and ammunition.

FIGGIS, Darrell: PT. TD. Deputy Chairman of committee that drafted the 1922 Constitution. Wrote a book entitled *The Irish Constitution Explained* the same year. A speech on 25 May 1922 damaged the prospects of the Pact election. WI.

FIGHTING SECOND, THE: PT armoured car active in Dublin.

FINNEGAN, J.P. (Rev Fr): Secretary to Bishop of Meath. Attended Mullingar executions 13 March 1923. (*See* Burke, Luke; Greery, Michael)

FISHER, James: AT. Executed at Kilmainham Jail, Dublin, 17 November 1922 for unlawful possession of a revolver. Peter Cassidy, John Gaffney and Richard Twohig were executed the same day, the first such executions of the CW.

FITZALAN, Edward Talbot (Lord): Lord-Lieutenant of Ireland. Handed over formal control of Dublin Castle to Collins 16 January 1922. Formally dissolved the Parliament of Southern Ireland and announced the Provisional Parliament 27 May 1922. WI.

FITZGERALD, Desmond: PT. TD. Government Publicity Director January-September 1922. Present at embalming of Collins's body. Minister for External Affairs from 23 August 1922. WI.

FITZGERALD, John: Fenit pilot forced at gunpoint to bring the *Lady Wicklow* into harbour 2 August 1922.

FITZGERALD, Michael: AT. Executed in Waterford 25 January 1923 for unlawful possession of arms and ammunition.

FITZGERALD, Paddy Paul: AT. Comdt 9 Bn, No 1 Kerry Bde, formed 30 July 1922. Active in resistance to Fenit landing. Captured at Spa. Imprisoned in Tralee.

FITZGERALD, Seamus: AT. Cork No 1 Bde. In action in Cork.

FITZPATRICK: Comdt. Engaged Ulster Special Constabulary, B-Specials in Clones 11 February 1922. He was shot dead. His colleagues killed four B-Specials, an incident that exacerbated violence against Northern Catholics. (*See Chronology, January 1922*)

FITZPATRICK: AT. Officer in charge of Royal Hotel, Athlone, garrison April 1922. Surrendered to Sean MacEoin, allegedly in disgust over the Adamson shooting.

FITZPATRICK, Michael: AT. Comdt. QM 3 Southern Div towards end of CW.

FITZPATRICK, Sean: AT. Comdt. Adj 3 Southern Div towards end of CW.

FITZPATRICK, Sean: Deputy Governor, Mountjoy Prison.

FLAVIN, Jack: *See Dandy Six.*

FLAVIN, James: AT. Engineer Officer Kerry No 1 Bde.

FLEMING, Patrick: AT. OC 3 Eastern Div (3 Bdes: North & South Wexford & Carlow). In action in Enniscorthy. Imprisoned in Curragh and Mountjoy. WI.

FLOOD, Matthew: AT. In action in Tipperary, Cork. Sometime bodyguard to Liam Lynch. Captured in Araglen 8 April 1923. Imprisoned in Cork and Curragh. WI.

FLOOD, Thomas: PT. Comdt. Assisted in take-over of Wellington (Griffith) Barracks. In action in Dublin, Bruff, Kilmallock and in heavy fighting at Pouldragoon Bridge, Co. Limerick. Led Dublin Guards in attack on Kilmallock. Held Bruree against AT attack August 1922. Occupied Mallow. WI.

FLUSK, Michael: AT. Extremely active in railway disruption in Wexford area.

FLYNN, Jack: AT. OC Killorglin company who conducted sustained attack on PTs there September 1922.

FLYNN, James: PT. Capt. Active in Dublin, Offaly and Laois.

FLYNN, Thomas: AT. Company Adj, Fenit, Co. Kerry. KIA at Spa.

FOGARTY, Michael (Most Rev Dr): Officiated at Griffith's funeral and warned Collins that his life too was in danger. WI.

FORBES Family: AT. Dan: In action at Kinsale, The Rising Sun, Ballinhassig and Half Way. Captured, escaped, re-captured. Dick: In action at Ballinabearna and other locations. Jack: Involved in sniping activities.

FORDE, Michael: Permanent way inspector of Dublin and South-East Railway. Played vital part in keeping lines open.

FORDE, Sean: *See Malone, Tomás.*

FORE, James: Provided men from Clondalkin area for proposed attack on Baldonnel. (*See Mullaney, Patrick*)

FOSTER: PT. Capt. In action in Tipperary under Prout.

FRIEL, Frank: *See O'Friel, F.J.*

FULLER, Stephen: AT. Escaped from Ballyseedy 7 March 1923. PTs did not realize that he had escaped and, because of the impossibility of identification, they released a coffin bearing his name to relatives. (*See Chronology, 7 March 1923*)

FURLONG, John A.: PT. Sgt. KIA near Lisduff, Co. Tipperary, 14 July 1922. As Miss M. Ryan, Comdt Gerry Ryan's sister, placed a wreath on his coffin outside Templemore church on 15 July, she was accidentally shot and died three days later.

FYNES, J.J.: PT. In Passage West landing from the *Arvonia*.

GAFFNEY, John.: AT. Executed at Kilmainham Jail, Dublin, 17 November 1922 for unlawful possession of a revolver. Peter Cassidy, James Fisher and Richard Twohig were executed the same day, the first such executions of the CW.

GALLAGHER, Frank: AT. Assisted Robert Brennan with publicity. Wrote open letter to Dr Byrne, Archbishop of Dublin, criticizing his pastoral's support of PT action. Imprisoned in Mountjoy 1922 and Kilmainham 1923. Endured hunger-strike. WI.

GALLAGHER, Sean: PT. Capt, later Comdt. OC Castle garrison in Enniscorthy which was surrounded by ATs 30 June 1922. He was captured some days later, but participated in a successful counter-attack. A passenger on an ambushed train at Killurin, he dismounted and fired his revolver. Thinking it was a military train, his attackers dispersed. (*See Carty, Frank*)

GALVIN, Denis: PT. Comdt. Active in Tipperary-Limerick-Kerry area.

GALVIN, Sean: AT. Courier who reported death of Collins to Cork No 3 Bde HQ.

GANNON, Bill: AT. Sniper at Four Courts. Attempted to shoot PT gunners at considerable personal risk.

GARVEY, Patrick: AT. Capt. Vice-Comdt 1 Bn No 1 Kerry Bde formed 30 July 1922. In action in resistance to Fenit landings. Captured and imprisoned.

GAYNOR, Sean: AT. Took over Birr Barracks despite presence of 1 Eastern Div elements, who then withdrew. Appointed OC 3 Southern Div, 6 March 1923. WI.

GERAGHTY, Patrick: AT. Executed in Portlaoise 27 January 1923 for unlawful possession of a pistol.

GERRARD, Thomas: PT. Medical Orderly, Portobello Barracks. Delivered notes for Ernie O'Malley.

GIBSON, Thomas: AT/PT. PT Cpl who deserted from Portlaoise Barracks 19 November 1922 taking arms with him. Tried by GCM and convicted. Executed in Portlaoise 26 February 1923.

GILDEA, Charles: Active in Sligo area.

GILHEANY: PT. OC Special Military Area which included Ballyconnell, Ballinamore, Drumshanbo, Arigna.

GILLESPIE, Neil: AT. Vol. Captured early in CW, in Muff, Co. Donegal. Imprisoned in Buncrana, aboard the *Lady Wicklow*, and in Newbridge. Endured hunger-strike.

GILMORE, George: AT. Imprisoned in Mountjoy 1923.

GINNELL, Laurence: AT. Returned Australian. Only AT deputy to attend August 1922 sitting of the Dáil. De Valera had instructed this. Ginnell demanded an explanation of the Dáil's status. When he persisted, he was forcibly removed. Member of AT Council of State. WI.

GLENAVY, First Baron (James Henry Campbell): Elected Chairman of An Seanad 12 December 1922.

GOGAN, Dick: AT. Four Courts garrison. In action in O'Connell Street also. Arrested 1923 and imprisoned in Mountjoy. WI.

GOGARTY, Oliver St John: PT. Dr. Prepared Collins's body for lying in state and filled cavity in skull with wax. Senator 6 December 1922. Kidnapped by ATs 20 January 1923 but escaped by diving into the flooded Liffey. His Renvyle mansion in Connemara was burned a month later.

GOLDEN, Peter: Helped establish the American Association for the Recognition of the Irish Republic. A de Valera supporter, he came to Ireland in August 1922 and met de Valera and Lynch with a view to establishing a cease-fire. Mistaken for Childers, he was arrested, but released, after which he returned to USA. WI.

GONNE, Iseult: Helped her mother, Maud Gonne treating AT sick and wounded.

GONNE, Maud (Madame Gonne MacBride): Established a women's anti-war committee under the chairmanship of Dublin's Lord Mayor in June 1922 and approached both sides, without success. Turned her home into a medical centre. Formed the Women Prisoners' Defence League. Its members gathered at prison gates and helped inmates and relatives in various ways. Arrested 10 April 1923. Imprisoned and endured hunger-strike. WI. (See O'Neill, Laurence)

GOOD: See Walshe, J.

GOODWIN, John & Robert: Brothers who fought on opposite sides at Blessington July 1922.

GORDON, Eleanor: Matron of Shanakiel Hospital. Attended to corpse of Collins and later testified to nature of wounds in skull.

GORDON, Winifred (Una): AT. C na mB member who kept a safe house and carried despatches.

GOUGH: PT. Lt. Member of armoured-car crew at Béal na mBláth.

GRADY, Francis: AT. KIA (after capture, some sources say) at Garrane, Co. Kerry, 11 March 1923.

GRANARD, Earl of: PT. Senator from 6 December 1922. His family seat at Castle Forbes was blown up 12 January 1923.

GREALY, John: AT. Commanded Boyle Barracks initially. Later, active in Sligo-Mayo area. WIA. Arrested October 1922. Imprisoned and endured hunger-strike. WI.

GREANY, Edward: AT. Tried by Committee and executed in Tralee 25 April 1923 for attacking and killing PT troops.

GREER, Rev: Protestant chaplain to Mountjoy prisoners.

GREERY, Michael: Athenry man executed in Mullingar Barracks 13 March 1923 for a bank robbery in Oldcastle. (See Burke, Luke)

GRIFFIN, Joseph: AT. Comdt. Executive member. D/Int. Four Courts garrison. Escaped after surrender. Arrested in Skerries 31 July 1922.

GRIFFIN, Paddy: PT. Commanded an armoured car in Dublin fighting. WI.

GRIFFITH, Arthur: PT. TD. Replaced de Valera as President of Dáil Éireann 10 January 1922. Proclaimed the Army Convention planned for 26 March 1922 and threatened suspension of those who attended. Provisional Government signatory to the Collins-Craig Agreement 30 March 1922. Cancelled Belfast Boycott April 1922. Defied AT threats in Sligo 16 April

1922. Brought draft Constitution to London June 1922. Prorogued the Dáil and suspended the Supreme Court July 1922. Sent uncompromising reply to Cork People's Rights Association, who had forwarded Liam Lynch's terms for a cease-fire to him in August 1922. Died of cerebral haemorrhage 12 August 1922. WI.

GUILMARTIN: AT. Capt. Ambushed MacEoin, his bride and escort near Sligo June 1922. Surrendered to MacEoin after some gunfire.

GUINEY, James: PT. Capt. Member of Fenit landing party 2 August 1922.

GUNNE, Thomas: PT. Comdt. Took over Viceregal Lodge from Major Chudleigh 14 December 1922.

GUNNING, Edward: AT. Vol 3 Western Div. In action in Sligo area.

GUTHRIE (Nurse): AT. C na mB member active in escape plans for ATs in Limerick Prison.

HALES, Sean: PT. TD. Maj Gen. OC Bandon garrison. Visited by Collins before Béal na mBláth ambush 22 August 1922. Attempted to force an official inquiry into the affair. Voted for Emergency Powers. Shot dead in Dublin 7 December 1922. In reprisal, O'Connor, Mellows, McKelvey and Richard Barrett were executed. WI.

HALES, Tom: AT. Brother of Sean (*above*). Comdt 3 Cork Bde. Elected an Executive member 9 April 1922. Resigned later. Signatory of Army Document of 1 May 1922. Called for control of all arms in his area after a number of Protestants were shot during April 1922. Member of ambush party at Béal na mBláth. WI.

HALLINAN (Rev Fr): Administered the Last Rites to Liam Lynch.

HAMMAN HOTEL: AT HQ during Dublin fighting, situated in Sackville (now O'Connell) St.

HANAFIN, William: AT. Unconfirmed fatal casualty of CW.

HAND, William: AT. Vol 3 Western Div. In action in Sligo area.

HANDS': AT safe house in Crookedwood, Co. Westmeath.

HANLON, James: AT. Executed in Tralee 20 January 1923 for unlawful possession of arms and ammunition.

HANNON, D.: PT. Active in round-up operations along Cork-Kerry border October 1922.

HANNON, James: PT. Active in Clare-Limerick area.

HARKIN, Daniel: AT. KIA during PT attack on Rockhill House, Letterkenny. (*See McMonagle, James*)

HARKIN, Paddy: *See McMonagle, James*.

HARPUR, Jack: PT. Capt. Responsible for prisoners in Tralee.

HARPUR, James: PT. Capt. Recruiting officer, 2 Eastern Div. Took over Wellington Barracks 22 April 1922. It was then re-named Griffith Barracks. In action with Dublin Guards in Kilkenny area.

HARRINGTON, Niall C.: PT. Vol. In action against Four Courts garrison and O'Connell Street. Landed at Fenit with Dublin Guards 2 August 1922. Promoted to 2/Lt by O'Duffy for bravery in the field during an ambush at Barraduff, Co. Kerry, the same month. WI.

HARTNEY, Michael: AT. WIA Adare 3 August 1922.

HARTY (Most Rev Dr): Archbishop of Cashel. In July 1922, had got agreement for a cease-fire but news of conditions did not find favour with PT HQ. Dissuaded ATs from attacking Templemore Barracks 16 July 1922. Proposed to Tom Barry in March 1923 that AT arms should be concealed until after an election and then surrendered to whichever government was returned to office.

HATHAWAY, Reginald: AT. British army deserter. Executed in Tralee 25 April 1923 for attacking and killing PT troops.

HAYES, Liam: PT. Col. In action Tipperary-Limerick-Cork. Captured by ATs at Tuagh, Co. Cork, August 1922 and moved to Tipperary.

HAYES, Michael: PT. TD. Prof. Non-Cabinet Minister for Education and Minister for Foreign Affairs from 12 August 1922. Ceann Comhairle of the First IFS Dáil 9 September 1922.

HAYES Brothers: AT. Sean: Comdt 3 Tipperary Bde. Among party who captured PT troops at Annacarthy Barracks and burned the building April 1922. With Liam Lynch's party when Lynch was shot. Jim: 7 Bn 3 Tipperary Bde, KIA in fight with PTs near Cashel, Co. Tipperary.

HEALY, Cahir: Elected as Nationalist MP for Fermanagh-Tyrone November 1922.

HEALY, Maurice: MP. Brother of T.M. (*below*). Law adviser to Cork Employees' Federation. Advised against succumbing to income-tax demand from AT leaders 1 August 1922. Soon afterwards, he was arrested and deported to England for unexplained reasons.

HEALY, T.M.: Governor-General of IFS from 5 December 1922. Thought to have had considerable influence on a junta within Collins's cabinet.

HEALY, William: AT. Executed in Cork 13 March 1923 for murder conspiracy, aiding attack on PT troops, and unlawful possession of a revolver.

HEANEY, Sylvester: AT. Executed in Dublin 8 January 1923 for treachery, by assisting ATs in attack on PT troops at Leixlip and passing them information.

HEARNE, John: PT. Comdt. Appointed Legal Officer to MacEoin in Athlone Command by Collins, April 1922. Appointed to conduct military courts October 1922.

HEASLIP: PT. Comdt, later Col Comdt. Led one of three columns converging on Blessington July 1922. In action during PT attack on Waterford. As OC Clonmel garrison, imposed curfew 13 December 1922.

HEFFERNAN'S: *See Sadlier Brothers.*

HEGARTY: AT. Vice Brigadier, Mayo Bde. Active in Sligo and Mayo.

HEGARTY, Dermot: *See O'Hegarty, Diarmuid.*

HEGARTY, Sean: AT. Executive member. Discussed re-unification of army with Mulcahy in April 1922 and discussed cease-fire in April 1923.

HENDERSON, Leo: AT. Directed the Belfast Boycott on behalf of ATs. Arrested while taking possession of cars imported from Belfast by a Dublin motor trader for use by the Four

Courts garrison. Imprisoned in Mountjoy. This incident prompted the AT kidnapping of J.J. O'Connell and demand for Henderson's release.

HENDRICK, Sean: AT. With Frank O'Connor, assisted Childers to produce news-sheet. Both men moved printing materials around to avoid capture. (*See O'Donovan, Michael*)

HENNESSY, Patrick: AT. Executed in Limerick 20 January 1923 for unlawful possession of ammunition, assisting in destroying railways, and burglary at Ard Solus railway station.

HEWART, Gordon (Sir): English constitutional lawyer. With Hugh Kennedy, KC, met in May 1922 to amend constitutional draft submitted by Provisional Government.

HIGGINS, Michael: PT. Lt/Comdt. Adj No 2 Sligo Bde.

HIGGINS, Patrick (Rev Fr): In car with MacEoin and his bride when it was ambushed near Sligo. (*See Guilmartin*)

HOGAN, 'Chummy': AT. Four Courts garrison.

HOGAN, Dan: PT. Comdt Gen. Appointed Comdt 5 Northern Div by Dalton when Aiken was in Limerick negotiating. Arrested in Northern Ireland and held for a short period. Commanded one of two forces surrounding and capturing Dundalk Barracks 17 August 1922. D/Int March-July 1923. GOC Dublin Command April 1923. WI. (*See McCurtain, Sean P.*)

HOGAN, Michael: PT. Col Comdt. 1 Western Div. Led detachment of troops landing at Tarbert from Kilrush, August 1922. Occupied Tarbert, Ballylongford (where he took six prisoners), and Listowel. Linked up with Dublin Guards to take Castleisland and Tralee. Eventually commanded North Kerry forces. His troops were involved in shoot-out at Dumfort caves, the last major CW action in Kerry April 1923. GOC Claremorris Command April 1923. WI.

HOGAN, Patrick: AT. Executed in Wexford 13 March 1923 for unlawful possession of a revolver.

HOGAN, Patrick J.: PT. TD. Minister for Agriculture throughout CW. His 1923 Land Act helped to bring rural areas behind the government.

HOGAN, Seamus: PT. Comdt Gen. Conveyed arms from Dublin to Michael Brennan during Limerick confrontation. Assisted Brennan there and was in action in Killaloe and Nenagh.

HOLLAND, Daniel: AT. Member of ambush party at Béal na mBláth 22 August 1922.

HORAN, Eamonn: PT. After PT capture of Tralee, advertised in *The Kerry People* 4 August 1922 seeking recruits for the 'Official IRA', and formed a separate column to reinforce PT advance to link up with Cork units.

HORNIBROOK: *See O'Neill, Michael.*

HORNICK, John & Margaret: Non-participant and his twelve-year-old sister shot by a PT sentry at Palace East, Co. Wexford, 3 March 1923.

HOULIHAN, Brian: PT. Capt Dublin Guards. KIA Knockeen, Co. Kerry, after capture of Castleisland following Fenit landing August 1922. WI.

HOULIHAN, Garry: AT. In action in O'Connell Street, Dublin, July 1922.

HOULIHAN (or Holohan), William: PT. Col. Comdt Nenagh Bde. In June 1922 placed James Nolan in charge of police there. Nolan occupied the police barracks but declared for ATs. Houlihan arrested him after the shooting of Terence Byrne but sympathetic officers manipulated his escape from custody.

HOWLETT, William: PT. Vol. Prominent and daring in attack on Waterford. KIA there 22 July 1922.

HUGHES, Thomas: AT. Executed in Athlone 20 January 1923 for unlawful possession of arms and ammunition.

HUMPHREYS, Ellen Mary: AT. Mother of Emmet, Richard and Sheila (*below*). Provided accommodation for Ernie O'Malley's HQ. Arrested after his capture. Imprisoned in Mountjoy, North Dublin Union and Kilmainham. Participated in Easter Week commemoration parade in Kilmainham. (*See Plunkett, Grace*)

HUMPHREYS, Emmet: AT. Son of Ellen Mary (*above*) and brother of Richard and Sheila (*below*). Arrested at AT HQ July 1922. Imprisoned in Mountjoy.

HUMPHREYS, Richard: AT. Son of Ellen Mary (*above*) and brother of Emmet (*above*) and Sheila (*below*). Arrested November 1922 when Humphreys' home was raided and Ernie O'Malley captured.

HUMPHREYS, Sheila: AT. Daughter of Ellen Mary and sister of Emmet and Richard (*above*). C na mB organizer. Arrested after O'Malley's capture. Imprisoned in Mountjoy, North Dublin Union and Kilmainham. Involved in escape attempts. Released after 31-day hunger-strike November 1923.

HUNT, Jim: PT. Active in Sligo area. A member of MacEoin's escort during his April 1922 visit there and a member of the PT courthouse garrison during negotiations. WI.

HUNT, Matthew: PT. Non-combatant. He and James O'Connor (PT) were taken from their homes in Tubbercurry, Co. Sligo, 5 November 1922 and shot dead by ATs. Frank Scanlon, fearing the same fate, fled and was shot in error by PTs.

HURLEY, James: AT. Cork leader in action against PT attack on Waterford 19 July 1922.

HURLEY, Jim: AT. Member of ambush party at Béal na mBláth. WI.

HURLEY, Nora: AT. C na mB. Active in Tralee fighting.

HURLEY, Sean: PT. Capt. Mid-Limerick Bde QM. Took over positions in Limerick February 1922. Local ATs placed him under arrest for this action and he went on hunger-strike. This led to the early troubles in the city.

HYDE, Sean: AT. Executive member. Attended April 1923 meeting in Poulacapal, near Mullinahone, and was among those appointed to meet de Valera and some of his cabinet members in Dublin. The latter meeting resulted in de Valera's call for cessation of AT aggressive action. Helped carry the wounded Liam Lynch before Lynch insisted on being left. WI.

HYLAND, Joseph: PT. Capt. OC Armoured Car Corps formed 14 September 1922. WI.

HYLAND, Mollie: AT. C na mB. Prominent activist. On office staff at Suffolk Street, Dublin, from where the campaign for prisoners' release was conducted.

IMPERIAL HOTEL: Pembroke St, Cork HQ of Emmet Dalton.

INGRAM: PT. Sgt. Sean MacEoin's driver. Under fire, cranked his touring car in Sligo.

INNISFALLEN, SS: Brought Collins's body from Cork to Dublin.

JACKSON: PT. Sgt. Assisted in takeover of Wellington (Griffith) Barracks. KIA Kerry.

JACOB, Rosamund: Member of anti-war delegation June 1922. (*See Gonne, Maud*)

JAMES (Rev Fr): Paced to and fro in front of PT artillery piece in Athlone to prevent its being fired during Adamson incident.

JAMESON, Andrew: PT. Senator. Intermediary between Cosgrave and de Valera in settlement attempt May 1923. (*See Douglas, James*)

JEFFERS, Daniel: AT. Coy Capt B Coy 1 Kerry Bn. In action opposing Fenit landings and PT push for Tralee. Captured 1 February 1923.

JOHNSON, Thomas (Dr): TD. Leader of Labour Party. Organized a general strike of 75,000 workers 24 April 1922 as a protest against the slide towards militarism and possible CW. The only male member of anti-war delegation June 1922. Strongly criticised executions of ATs December 1922. Opposed Special Powers Bill September 1922. Supported de Valera's peace proposal May 1923. WI. (*See Gonne, Maud*)

JOHNSTON, John: AT. Vol 3 Western Div. In action in Sligo area.

JOHNSTON, Joseph: AT. Executed in Dublin 19 December 1922 for unlawful possession of arms and ammunition.

JORDAN, John: PT. CQMS, later Lt, Army Medical Service.

JOYCE, Richard: AT. Prominent activist and fighter in western Galway.

JOYCE, Stephen: AT. Executed in Athlone 20 January 1923 for unlawful possession of a rifle and ammunition.

'KATMANDU': *See Phelan Brothers.*

KEANE: PT. Brig. Led a force of 200 against Rathkeale, Askeaton, Foynes and Newcastle West. In action at capture of Adare.

KEARNEY, John: AT. Capt. Active in Tipperary. Captured and imprisoned in Clonmel, Kilkenny and Kildare. Endured hunger-strike.

KEARNEY, Peadar: Prison censor, Portlaoise prison, but AT leanings caused him to resign. WI.

KEARNS, James: AT. Active in Mayo area. Held Westport with a small garrison until PT sea landing, then abandoned it to continue guerrilla campaign in mountains.

KEARNS, Linda: AT. C na mB. Assisted in Dublin Bde HQ in O'Connell Street June 1922. WI.

KEATING, Thomas: AT. Comdt 2 Bn Waterford Bde. KIA 19 April 1923 at Coolnasmear, Co. Waterford.

KEATINGE, T.J.: PT. Sgt. Medical NCO i/c medical personnel on board the *Lady Wicklow*.

KEAVENEY, James: AT. Vol. 3 Western Div. In action in Sligo area.

KEENAN, Henry: See Burke, Luke.

KELLEHER, Tom: AT. Comdt Gen 1 Southern Div. Captured in Tuagh, Co. Cork, after a fight August 1922. Imprisoned in Cork and Curragh. Released after AT capture of prisoners at Ballymakeera. WI. (See *O'Sullivan Brothers*)

KELLER, Edward: AT. Lt. The first member of Four Courts garrison captured.

KELLIHER, Thomas: AT. Member of ambush party at Béal na mBláth 22 August 1922. WI.

KELLY: PT. Cpl. In action in Tipperary. KIA in ambush at Redmondstown 9 August 1922 during push for Clonmel.

KELLY (Fr): Attended at Mullingar shootings, 13 November 1923. (See *Burke, Luke; Greery, Michael*)

KELLY, Colm: AT. Executed in Birr 26 January 1923 for unlawful possession of a rifle and ammunition and burglary in Tullamore.

KELLY, Patrick: PT. Director of Engineers. Wounded attempting to disarm mines and explosives in the Four Courts basement when PT forces seized portion of the building June 1922.

KENNEDY, Andrew: AT. In action in Tipperary. In action resisting PT attack on Waterford 19 July 1922.

KENNEDY, Hugh: PT. TD. Law Officer to Provisional Government January-December 1922, when he became Attorney General to Saorstát Éireann. (See *Hewart, Gordon*)

KENNEDY, Pat (Mrs): AT. C na mB. Active in Tralee fighting.

KENNEDY, Patrick ('Cashin'): PT. Lt. Led attack on Castle Blake, near Cashel, 16 April 1923. KIA there. (See *Cleary, Sean; English, Theo; Moran, David; Somers, Edward*)

KENNELLY, T.J.: PT. Having surrendered PT post in Listowel 30 June 1922 signed an agreement with AT Humphrey Murphy decrying CW.

KENT, David: AT. TD. Recited prayers at Denis Barry's funeral when no clergyman officiated. (See *Coholan, Rev Dr*)

KEOGH, Tom: PT. Col Comdt. Close associate of Collins. In action in Dublin, Wexford, Limerick, Kerry and Cork. He was killed by a mine in a road bridge at Carrigaphooca, leading a sweep from Macroom to Killarney August 1922. WI.

KERRIGAN, P.: PT. WIA at Spa, Co. Kerry, during advance from Tralee 18 October 1922.

KERRY, Earl of: PT. Senator from 6 December 1922.

KIDNEY, Madge: AT. C na mB. Active in Tralee fighting.

KIELY, Gerard: AT. Capt. KIA Lisvarnan, Glen of Aherlow, February 1923 when he and Dan Breen were trapped. Breen escaped.

KILCOYNE, Thomas. PT. Comdt. In action in Passage West, Co. Cork, after sea-borne landing. WI.

KILKELLY: AT. Comdt. Took command of Eglinton Barracks, Galway. Attacked Renmore Barracks. In action in Abbey St and Bohermore before leaving the city and surrounding it. Captured August 1922.

KILLEEN, Jack: AT. Comdt. Became OC of No 2 Column 3 Tipperary Bde just after it had attacked a PT victory march in Clonmel. On 16 August 1922 ambushed PTs under Capt Mullaney, moving towards Cahir, at Kilmurray, killing three PTs and wounding nine. Led ambushes at Redmondstown 21 August and Mullinarinka Cross 28 August. Captured near Kilcash 14 September 1922. (*See Thornton, Frank*)

KILROY, Michael: AT. TD. Comdt Gen. Comdt 4 Western Div (North and West Mayo, portion of Galway & Sligo). Attended convention on 26 March 1922 (*see Chronology*). Member of Executive of sixteen from April 1922. Signatory of Proclamation of 29 June 1922. Active in many actions in the west. Built a bomb and mine factory and manufactured armoured cars, including *Queen of the West,* from boilers taken from Mulranny Hotel. Captured 12 September 1922. Maintained frequent sea patrol from Roonagh Point to Clare Island to Mulranny. Imprisoned in Athlone and Mountjoy. Tony Lawlor, his great adversary, appealed for his safety. Elected as Republican TD for South Mayo 27 August 1923. Comdt of prisoners. Began hunger-strike. Called it off, after forty-one days, on 23 November 1923. WI.

KING (Dr): PT. Capt. Army Medical Service.

KING, Patrick: PT. Comdt. Toured areas of action, paying troops. (*See Bell, Martin*)

KIVLEHAN, M.: Uninvolved civilian killed when PTs attacked AT Police HQ in Wine Street, Sligo, 6 July 1922.

LACEY, Denis: AT. Comdt Gen. Tipperary leader. In action at Annacarthy. Captured Urlingford 5 July 1922. Co-ordinated AT counter-attack against PTs in Waterford 19 July 1922. Commanded Carrick-on-Suir garrison and defended it and Clonmel. Later, led numerous ambushes in Knockmealdown Mountains. Assisted Tom Barry in re-taking Carrick-on-Suir December 1922. In Ballydavid, Glen of Aherlow, on 18 February 1923 refused call to surrender when surrounded in a house at Castledavid, and was shot dead attempting to assist a wounded comrade. WI. (*See McCormack*)

LADY WICKLOW, SS: Irish sea packet commandeered by Provisional Government August 1922 for seaborne landing at Fenit.

LALOR, Francis: AT. Victim of unauthorized execution at Orwell Bridge, Dublin, 28 December 1922.

LAMBERT, Robert: AT. Attacked train in which AT prisoners, including Frank Carty, were being conveyed to Dublin at Killurin, Co. Wexford. Three PT soldiers were killed but the attack failed.

LANGAN (Miss): Wealthy houseowner who provided accommodation for Sean Dowling.

LANGAN, Thomas: AT. Vol. KIA Ballintrillick/Glencar, Co. Sligo, 20 September 1922 when PTs re-captured *The Ballinalee.*

LARKIN, John: AT. Brig Gen. Communications officer. Executed in

Drumboe 14 March 1923 for unlawful possession of arms and ammunition.

LAVERY, John (Sir): Painted a portrait of Collins lying in state.

LAW, Andrew Bonar (Rt Hon): British Prime Minister from 23 October 1922 to 22 May 1923. WI.

LAWLOR, Patrick: PT. *See Walshe, J.*

LAWLOR, Tony: PT. Comdt General. In action against Four Courts. With Daly, accepted the surrender of that garrison from Ernie O'Malley. Suppressed mutinous behaviour in Athlone. MacEoin's leading field officer in the West, especially in Sligo and Mayo, he was mainly responsible for overcoming dogged AT resistance there. Wounded in ambush in Ox Mountains September 1922. (*See McMahon, Peadar; Morrissey, Paddy*)

LEADER (Mrs): Proposed cease-fire motion by women electors of Cork 2 August 1922. (*See Thompson, Mrs*)

LEAHY, James. AT. OC Templemore initially and considered to be PT. He entertained the crew of an armoured car travelling to Limerick with Capt William Stapleton and two Black and Tans included. On its return from Limerick three days later he seized it but released the PTs. Comdt Gen Dermot MacManus later entered barracks by ladder at the rear and removed parts, then came to the front gate, called for Leahy and tried to get him to release the car. He refused so MacManus returned to Beggarsbush. Another PT officer took the parts and deserted with them. Eventually, Leahy and Ernie O'Malley brought the car to the Four Courts, where it was named *The Mutineer.*

LEHANE, Sean: AT. Comdt 1 & 2 Northern Divisions. Donegal leader who received arms intended for impeding the authorities in Northern Ireland. Planned a mining operation along the border. Later, he was ordered to move to the midlands and finally was in action in Munster. Was in Béal na mBláth area on eve of Collins's death. Moved to midlands September 1922. AT Executive member from 16 October 1922. Imprisoned in Mountjoy and sentenced to death. Favoured signing a document which would save prisoners from execution under certain terms, February 1923, and was reproached by the hospitalized Ernie O'Malley for doing so.

LEMASS, Noel: AT. Capt. IO. Captured in Glencullen but escaped from custody. Re-captured 3 July 1923. Suspected of tampering with Collins's mail, he was allegedly kidnapped and killed by CID. Body found in Dublin mountains 12 October 1923. WI.

LEMASS, Sean: AT. TD. Lt, later Capt. Adj of Four Courts garrison. Escaped from Jameson's Distillery where he had been held after its surrender. In action at Blessington, Enniscorthy, Baltinglass. Director of Communications from July 1922. Captured in December 1922 and imprisoned in Mountjoy and Curragh Camp. Released in December 1922. WI.

LENNON, Sean: PT. SM. In action during Adamson incident. Manned Lewis gun in attack on AT convoy at Golden 29 July 1922.

LENNON, Thomas: AT. Executed in Dundalk 22 January 1923 for unlawful possession of arms and ammunition.

LENNOX, Patrick: Train driver. Refused to obey AT order to allow train to run free into Tralee station December 1922. ATs released the train themselves but shunter Jerome O'Connor averted disaster by sending it into a siding.

LEONARD, Joe: PT. Close associate of Collins. Wounded when forcing an entry to Four Courts. In action in Kilkenny. WI.

LIDWELL, Frederick: Assistant to Joseph T. Mooney.

LILLIS, James: AT. Executed in Carlow 15 January 1923 for attack on PT troops and unlawful possession of arms and ammunition.

LILLIS, James: PT. Capt. Adj Carlow Bde. Took over Carlow Barracks from British.

LLEWELLYN DAVIES, Moya: Collected intelligence for Collins. Present at embalming of Collins's body by Gogarty.

LLOYD GEORGE, David (First Earl Lloyd George of Dwyfor): British Prime Minister until 23 October 1922. After assassination of Henry Wilson, he issued threats directly to Collins 22 June 1922 about the AT holding of the Four Courts, claiming His Majesty's government's 'right to expect that the necessary action will be taken by your government without delay'. Critical of draft Constitution and exerted pressure for change. WI.

LOGUE, Michael (Cardinal): With Episcopal College, issued a pastoral denying absolution and the sacraments to ATs on same date that Special Emergency Powers became operative, 15 October 1922. WI. (*See Luzio, below*)

LONERGAN, Jack: AT. *See Cooney, Sean*.

LOUGHLIN, Paddy: AT. *See Sadlier Brothers*.

LUCEY, Con: AT. Director of Medical Services.

LUZIO, Monsignor: Italian prelate sent by the Holy See to meet Cardinal Logue and intervene in CW. Met Sinn Féin deputation 10 April 1923 and had interviews with de Valera and Cosgrave.

LYDON, John: PT. Sgt. Fenit-born member of Dublin Guards whose local knowledge was of considerable help to the success of the Fenit landing 2 August 1922. KIA at Spa, Co. Kerry, 18 August 1922.

LYNCH, Daniel: Engine driver fired at when talking to Dan Daly at Tralee railway station 23 January 1923. Escaped with injuries.

LYNCH, Fionan: PT. TD. Comdt Gen. Minister for Education, January-August 1922. Member of General Staff. On Collins's escort at a proscribed meeting in Killarney April 1922. In action in Killarney April 1922. Ambushed at Roberts Glen, on way to reinforce Tom 'Scarteen' O'Connor, under pressure from Kerry No 2 Bde in South Kerry, August 1922. Non-cabinet Minister for Fisheries, 6 December 1922 to 29 December 1923. WI.

LYNCH, James (Dr) & Family: From 8-10 August 1922, after Passage landings, they turned their home near Rochestown into a virtual field dressing station for both sides.

LYNCH, Liam: AT. IRB Supreme Council member. Gen. Comdt 1 Southern Div (ten brigades: Cork, Kerry, Waterford, west Limerick). Signatory of demand for Army Convention 11 January 1922. Member of AT Executive. COS (*but see McKelvey, Joseph*). Initially attempted to bring about unity and ordered AT evacuation of a number of Dublin strongholds. Called an army convention for 26 March 1922 without Mulcahy's consent. It adjourned until 9 April when he was chairman. Member of Army Reunification Committee, which arranged a temporary truce 4 May 1922. Instigator and signatory of Proclamation of 29 June 1922 (*see Chronology*). Just after the opening of shelling of Four Courts, he was apprehended by PTs in both Dublin and Castlecomer, Co. Kilkenny, but was allowed continue his journey southward. In action in Limerick, Tipperary and Cork. On 30 November 1922, issued orders concerning the shooting on sight of TDs who voted for the Emergency Powers Bill. WIA during a PT search-and-sweep operation in the Knockmealdown Mountains 10 April 1923. Removed by ambulance to St Joseph's Hospital, Clonmel, where he died later. WI. (*See Hyde, Sean; Prout, John; Ryan, Tommy*)

LYONS, Brigid: PT. Medical officer at Model School, Marlborough St, during Dublin fighting July 1922. WI.

LYONS, James: *See 'Dandy Six'*.

LYONS, Timothy ('Aeroplane'): AT. Severely injured while being taken prisoner from a cave at Clashmealcon, Co. Kerry, 18 April 1923. The rope used to haul him up broke or was cut deliberately.

(Names with prefixes Mc and Mac are both alphabetized as Mac.)

McAULEY, Charles (Dr): AT. Medical officer to Four Courts garrison.

MacBRIDE, Maud Gonne: *See Gonne, Maud*.

MacBRIDE, Sean: AT. Assistant Director of Organization. Attended 11 June 1922 Executive meeting. Four Courts garrison and the first to publicly suggest its occupation after the defeat of Tom Barry's 18 June proposition. Captured there and imprisoned in Mountjoy and Newbridge. Made a number of escape attempts. Went on hunger-strike 1923. Escaped while being moved to Kilmainham with Michael Price and Daithi O'Donoghue. With Eoin O'Duffy, gradually dispersed western sector of AT line of defence. WI.

McCABE, Alex: PT. Col Comdt. Leader of troops in Sligo area. A member of Sean MacEoin's escort during his April 1922 visit there. Converted the *SS Tartar* into an armoured cruiser to combat AT troops who manned a ferryboat. Captured Ballymote from ATs 8 July 1922. Introduced curfew in Sligo 17 July 1922. WI.

McCARTHY: PT. Lt. Resigned after Ballyseedy incident 6 March 1923 and published an account of what occurred.

McCARTHY, Con: AT. Lt. *See Radford, Bernard*.

McCARTHY, Liam: PT. Comdt. In action in Tipperary-Kilkenny area, particularly at Mullinahone, Windgap and Kilmaganny. Led frontal attack on Breen's Nine Mile House stronghold July 1922. (*See Byrne, Joseph*)

McCARTHY, Owen Felix (Dr): Resident Medical Superintendent Cork Asylum. Institution was commandeered by Comdt Cronin, PT, for 150 AT prisoners from 10-14 August 1922.

McCARTHY, Patrick: AT. In action in Mayo-Sligo area. A member of Clonalis Castle garrison when it was attacked by PT troops.

McCARTHY, Richard (Rev Fr): Mediator in Limerick.

McCARTHY, Trant: PT. Comdt. Appointed to conduct military courts in Kerry October 1922.

MAC CATHMAOIL, Tomás: AT. See Carney, Tom.

McCLEAN, William: PT. Capt. Led part of a pincer movement during the fight for Tralee.

McCONVILLE: PT. Capt. In action during a number of operations in Wexford December 1922.

McCORLEY, Roger: PT. Col Comdt. Belfast leader who criticized early failure to take action in North. In action in Curragh and Kerry, particularly Kenmare, 27 December 1922.

McCORMACK: PT. OC Thurles garrison. Seriously wounded in ambush by Denis Lacey's troops at Kilfeacle, Co. Tipperary, 18 August 1922.

McCORMACK, Michael: PT. Col. OC Salvage Corps which obtained materials from former British barracks for miscellaneous purposes.

McCORMACK, Sean: PT. Capt. Moate man shot dead in ambush by 30 AT troops at Glasson, Athlone, 25 August 1922, while attending to a colleague, Rhatigan.

McCORMICK, Michael: PT Comdt 3 Southern Div (five brigades: Laois, Offaly, portion of Tipperary). Authorized a number of strong measures against ATs. WI.

McCREA, Patrick: PT. Close associate of Collins. HQ driver. WI.

McCULLAGH'S: Dublin music store bombed by ATs, 29 December 1922.

MacCURTAIN, Austin: PT. Col Comdt 3 Southern Div. Laois-Offaly area. KIA when ambushed leading a party to deal with a mine reportedly laid at Tonduff, Abbeyleix, Co. Laois, 28 July 1922.

McCURTAIN, Sean P.: PT. Col. Early deputy to Sean MacEoin in Midland Div. During a cross-border raid to kidnap prominent Unionists as hostages for the release of Dan Hogan in February 1922 he was arrested on Cavan-Fermanagh border. Sentenced to ten years imprisonment in Peterhead, Scotland, in March. While serving sentence, he was elected for Cumann na nGaedheal in Tipperary 27 August 1923 and was still treated as a member of the NA.

McDONAGH, Joseph: AT. TD. Imprisoned in Mountjoy. Refused to sign permission for appendicitis. Moved to Mater Hospital and died there 25 December 1922. WI.

McDONAGH, Paddy: AT. Comdt 3 Tipperary Bde. With Capt William Allen, was surrounded in Ballydavid 18 February 1923. Joined by Denis Lacey, he came under fire at Ashgrove House and was wounded. He died next day in Tipperary Hospital.

MacDONNELL, Andrew: AT. Comdt South Dublin Bde. Signed call for 26

March 1922 convention in the Mansion House. Four Courts garrison. Escaped from Jameson's distillery where he had been held after its surrender. Occupied positions in Dublin and Wicklow July 1922. In action in Blessington. Captured. Imprisoned in Mountjoy.

McDONNELL, Matthew: AT. Four Courts garrison. Wounded there.

McELDUFF, James: AT/PT. Originally 1 Bde 2 Northern Div. Active in Donegal area, including the take-over of Raphoe Masonic Hall and back-up, including mine-preparation, for cross-border sorties. He visited a PT officer, was accused of desertion and was temporarily imprisoned. Eventually joined NA November 1923.

McELLISTRIM, Tom: AT. OC 7 Limerick City Bn. Elected as Republican TD for Kerry 27 August 1923. WI.

MacENTEE, Sean: AT. TD. Spoke relentlessly, warning of a permanent partition resulting from the Treaty. Led an attempt to break into Mountjoy from a house in Glengariff Parade and allow escape of AT prisoners. WI.

MacEOIN, Seamus: PT. Capt. Laid ambush at Glasson, near Athlone, and almost opened fire on his brother, Sean, who was returning unexpectedly with his bride from their honeymoon June 1922.

MacEOIN, Sean: PT. TD. Comdt Midland Div (Longford, Leitrim, Fermanagh). Took over and re-named Custume Barracks, Athlone. Authorized and co-ordinated raids into Northern Ireland February 1922, when 40 Unionists and Special Constables were seized and held as hostages for release of Monaghan IRA prisoners. Led Sligo preparation for visit from Griffith 16 April 1922. Member of Army Reunification Committee which arranged a temporary truce 4 May 1922. OC Western District Command from 5 July 1922. GOC Athlone Command from April 1923. Conducted vigorous campaign in the west and mid-west. WI. (*See* Ingram; MacEoin, Seamus; and Morrissey, P.)

McEVILLY, Thomas: PT. Vol. 3 Western Div. In action in Sligo area.

McEVOY, M.: PT. Lt. Very active in 3 Southern Div area.

McGARRY, Sean: PT. TD. Comdt. Home burned 10 December 1922 and his son of seven years died later from burns received. His electrical fittings shop was bombed the following month. WI.

McGINLEY, J.P. (Dr): PT. TD. Prominent Donegal activist. WI.

McGLYNN, Michael: AT. Staff Capt. Involved in scouting duties during Fenit landing and aftermath. In action at Castleisland.

McGOLDRICK, Martin: AT. Vol 3 Western Div. In action in Sligo area.

McGOWAN, Bernard: AT. Vol 3 Western Div. In action in Sligo area.

McGRATH, Joseph: PT. TD. Non-cabinet Minister for Labour in January-September 1922 Dáil. Minister for Labour, Industry and Commerce and Economic Affairs in Provisional Government August-September 1922. Minister for Industry and Commerce, Executive Council, December 1922 to

September 1923. D/Int with rank of Major General, June 1922. Attempted to stop Collins going on the tour of inspection that led to his death. Member of Army Council 28 September 1922. WI.

McGRATH, Martin: AT. Comdt. OC 6 Bn Kilkenny Bde. Active in South Leinster. Escorted Lynch's party through his area during his final journey to attend the Nire Valley conference.

McGRATH, Paddy: With Máire Comerford, was preparing for kidnapping of W.T. Cosgrave when arrested at Loughlinstown, Co. Dublin. Imprisoned in Mountjoy and endured hunger-strike.

McGRATH, Thomas: AT. Drowned while attempting to escape when surrounded at Clashmealcon caves 16 April 1923.

McGUINAN, James: PT. Comdt. 2 i/c Dublin Guards aboard the *Lady Wicklow* at Fenit landing 2 August 1922.

McGUINNESS, James: PT. Comdt. In action in Dublin June 1922. Led advance from Tralee after Fenit landing. Captured the town. Advanced to Castleisland. Taken prisoner temporarily after receiving a head wound in an ambush at Droum, near Killarney.

McGUINNESS, Joe: PT. TD. Dáil Peace Committee member May-June 1922. WI.

McINERNEY, James: AT. Executed in Tralee 25 April 1923 for attack on PT troops in which some of them were killed.

McKELVEY, Joseph: AT. Comdt Gen. Comdt 3 Northern Div (three brigades: North Down, Belfast, Antrim). ACOS April 1922. Elected COS by Executive members favouring war 18 June 1922 until Lynch fully supported the action, 27 June. Signatory of Proclamation of 29 June 1922 (*see Chronology*). Operated from Four Courts. Authorized kidnapping of J.J. O'Connell. Imprisoned in Mountjoy 30 June after surrender of Four Courts. Executed in Dublin 8 December 1922 in reprisal for shooting of Sean Hales. WI.

McKENNA, Kathleen: Secretary in Dáil Publicity and Press Room, Merrion St, 1922. WI.

McKENNA, Patrick: AT. Brig. Commanded a small number of Dundalk troops earmarked for operations in Northern Ireland. Although AT, he accepted Aiken's authority initially. KIA when a mine was being dismantled and exploded during the AT recapture of Dundalk Barracks 14 August 1922.

McKEON, Kit: AT. Capt. Initially OC Custume Barracks. Shot dead in Moate. Some say soon after Adamson incident April 1921, others 3 December 1922.

McKEOWN, Thomas: AT. Executed in Dundalk 13 January 1923 for unlawful possession of a revolver and ammunition.

MACKEY: AT. Capt. Active in Limerick fighting July 1922.

MACKEY, Dominic: PT. Capt. In action in taking of Waterford from ATs and in advance to Clonmel.

McLEAN: PT. Capt. Led a party into Tralee from Bothar Buidhe approach after Fenit landings.

MacLOCHLAINN, Joe: PT. Col. Son of Johnny Sean (*below*). Active in Donegal area.

MacLOCHLAINN, Johnny Sean: PT. Prominent Donegal organizer.

McLYNN, Joseph: AT. Vol. 3 Western Div. In action in Sligo area.

MacMAHON (Rev Fr): RC chaplain to Mountjoy prisoners.

McMAHON, Cornelius: AT. Executed in Limerick 20 January 1923 for unlawful possession of ammunition and for assisting in destroying railway and burglary at Ard Solus railway station.

McMAHON, M.C.: AT. Demanded hand-over of Mullingar Post Office from Sean MacEoin 27 April 1922.

McMAHON, Peadar: PT. Capt, later Maj Gen. With Tony Lawlor took over guns from British June 1922 for attack on Four Courts. Deployed them in Green Street. GOC Curragh Command February 1923. WI.

MacMAHON, Sean: PT. General. Member of Army Reunification Committee which arranged a temporary truce 4 May 1922. QMG until appointed COS 15 September 1922. Member of Army Council from 28 September 1922. WI.

McMAHON, Thomas: AT. AT Prisoners' OC, Newbridge.

MacMANUS, Dermot: PT. Comdt Gen. In early actions at Templemore and against Four Courts, being one of the first to penetrate the building. Involved in negotiations and operations in Athlone, Clare and particularly Limerick. Commanded two vessels for a successful sea-borne landing at Kenmare 11 August 1922. Later Provost Marshal, Southern Command, and Deputy Governor of Mountjoy. (*See Leahy, James; O'Connor, Tom 'Scarteen'; and Ó hAnnagáin, Donncadha*)

McMENAMIN, William T.: PT. Comdt. Appointed to conduct military courts, Stranorlar, Co. Donegal, October 1922.

McMONAGLE, James: PT. Lt. OC Letterkenny forces stationed in Garda barracks. On 22 July 1922 he organized attacks on Rockhill House and Ballymacool, occupied by ATs under Capts Paddy Harkin and Jimmy Browne.

McNAMARA, Ned: AT. *See Cooney, Sean.*

McNAMARA, Patrick: PT. Col. Active in Kilkenny and Carrick-on-Suir areas.

MacNAMARA, Patrick: AT. Executed in Roscrea 15 January 1923 for unlawful possession of a rifle and ammunition.

McNEELY (Dr): Chaplain to Donegal Command June 1922. Bishop of Raphoe 1923.

MacNEILL, Brian: AT. Comdt Adj 4 Western Div. Son of Eoin (*below*). KIA Ballintrillick/Glencar, Co. Sligo, 20 September 1922 when PTs re-captured *The Ballinalee*.

MacNEILL, Eoin: PT. TD. Ceann Comhairle of Dáil up to 9 September 1922. Minister without Portfolio in Provisional Government, January–August 1922; Minister for Education, August–September 1922 and in Executive Council of Saorstát Éireann, from August 1922. Father of a PT Capt and of the AT Brian (*above*). WI.

McNEILL, Hugo: PT. Col. Captured AT battle plans and passwords for proposed re-occupation of Dublin 5 August 1922, leading to capture of 200 ATs. Used air power when attacking Dundalk August 1922.

MacNEILL, Niall: PT. Brig Gen. Led push through north Wicklow and Wexford July 1922.

McNEILUS, Donncha: AT. Active in Donegal area.

McNULTY: PT. Comdt. Led one of three columns converging on Blessington July 1922.

McNULTY, John (alias Joseph Murphy): AT. Executed in Dublin 13 January 1923 for unlawful possession of a revolver and ammunition.

McPARTLAND, James: Non-combatant. Shot dead when motoring with his sister at Chaffpool, Sligo, 5 November 1922, and failed to stop at PT checkpoint.

McPEAKE, John ('Jock'): PT/AT. Machine-gunner in armoured car, *The Slievenamon*, on Collins's escort at Béal na mBláth. Deserted with the vehicle to the AT side 2 December 1922. Arrested in Glasgow July 1923 and tried in Ireland for its theft, receiving six years imprisonment. Imprisoned in Portlaoise and endured hunger-strike. (See O'Sullivan Brothers)

MACREADY, Nevil (Sir): CIC British Forces remaining in Ireland. Met Gen Boyd in Dublin 24 June 1922 to discuss plans for British action against AT forces. Initially refused to sanction hand-over of artillery to PTs, but Cope persuaded Churchill to override the decision. WI. (See O'Neill, Ignatius)

MacSIMONS, P.: PT. Comdt Gen. 2 Western Div. Attacked Newport Barracks, Co. Mayo, 27 August 1922.

McSWEENEY, Maimie: AT. C na mB. Active in Tralee fighting.

McSWEENEY, W.J.: PT. Maj Gen. First OC of Air Corps and D/Military Aviation, established in 1922.

MacSWINEY, Mary: AT. TD. C na mB. Assisted in Dublin Bde HQ in O'Connell Street June 1922. Administered AT HQ in Cork. Member of AT Council of State from 25 October 1922. Arrested later and imprisoned in Kilmainham. WI.

MacSWINEY, Sean: AT. Executive member from 16 October 1922.

MAGUIRE, John: AT. Executed in Tuam, Co. Galway, 11 April 1923 for unlawful possession of a rifle and ammunition.

MAGUIRE, Tom: AT. TD. Brig. Comdt 2 Western Div (north Galway, south & east Mayo, south Roscommon). Executive member from 9 April 1922. Active in Mayo-Sligo area. Captured in Headford October 1922. Imprisoned in Athlone. Escaped 10 June 1923. WI.

MAHON, Bryan (Sir): PT. Senator. His home at Ballymore Eustace, Co. Kildare was burned February 1923.

MALLEY, Cecil: AT. Brother of Ernie O'Malley (only Ernie used the O'Malley form) and Charles (*below*). Commanded Gresham Hotel garrison during Dublin fighting July 1922. Captured while cutting railway lines August 1922. Imprisoned Portlaoise and Mountjoy.

MALLEY, Charles: AT. Brother of

Ernie O'Malley (only Ernie used the O'Malley form) and Cecil (*above*). KIA Dublin July 1922.

MALLIN, Seamus: AT. Death sentence for possession of a revolver commuted to life imprisonment November 1922.

MALONE, Tomás (Alias Sean Forde): AT. Comdt Gen. Comdt Mid-Limerick Bde. While about to take over Limerick for the Provisional Government 18 February 1922 he declared for ATs whereupon PH HQ detailed Michael Brennan to forestall him. After Four Courts shelling, he advocated immediate organized response against PTs. Captured in Nenagh July 1922. Moved to Portlaoise, he was visited by Collins with a view to participation in peace moves. Escaped in a refuse wagon 13 July 1923. WI.

MANAGER, THE: PT armoured car used in push for Cork. (*See Ennis, Thomas*)

MANGAN, Patrick: AT. Executed in Dublin 19 December 1922 for unlawful possession of arms, bomb equipment and ammunition.

MANNION, Patrick: AT. Comdt. KIA Mount Street Bridge. Inquest returned a verdict of murder.

MARKHAM, Thomas: British civil servant and confidante of Collins. Examined files left by British in Dublin Castle. Alleged to have discovered the identity of a spy, Thorpe, and reported it to Collins in August 1922, just before Collins's assassination.

MARKIEVICZ, Constance (Countess): AT. President of C na mB. Proposed its rejection of the Treaty, making it the first national organization to do so. Defeated for a Dublin seat in June 1922 election. Sailed to United States with Kevin Barry's sister Kathleen and was later joined by Austin Stack and J.J. O'Kelly to raise funds there. Won Dublin Borough South seat August 1923. Arrested for collecting petitions for release of hunger-strikers. Imprisoned and went on hunger-strike herself. WI.

MARRINAN: PT. Early member of Nursing Service.

MASTERSON, B.: PT. Capt. Garrison adj in Athlone. Led a raid by boat on Quaker Island in Lough Ree and, under fire, landed and captured ten ATs. (*See Davis, M.; and Walshe, Thomas*)

MAYO, Earl of: PT. Senator from 6 December 1922. His Co. Kildare home was burned 29 January 1923.

(Names with prefixes Mc and Mac are both alphabetized as Mac.)

MEADE, Maurice: AT. 2 Bn 3 Tipperary Bde. Active on Tipperary-Cork border. Captured by PTs in Mitchelstown, Co. Cork, 18 February 1923.

MELIA, James: AT. Executed in Dundalk 22 January 1923 for unlawful possession of arms and ammunition.

MELLOWS, Liam: AT. TD. Comdt Gen. QMG. Signatory of demand for Army convention, 11 January 1922. Opposed Barry's motion to declare war on Britain, 18 June 1922. Member of Army Reunification Committee, which arranged a temporary truce 4 May 1922. Signatory of Proclamation of 29 June 1922 (*see Chronology*). Four Courts garrison. With Rory O'Connor, led out troops after surrender. Imprisoned in Mountjoy. Published a call in the *Irish Independent* 21 September 1922 for a government to replace the Provisional Government. Nominated as Minister for Defence in de Valera's nominal government. Executed in Dublin in reprisal for shooting of Sean Hales 8 December 1922. WI.

MILES, Gerry: AT. In action in Kilkenny-Tipperary area July 1922.

MILROY, Sean: PT. Accompanied Griffith to Sligo meeting 16 April 1922. On platform with Collins in Killarney 22 April 1922. WI.

MITCHELL, Walter: AT. Offaly No 2 Bde. In action against PT convoy near Tullamore October 1922. Captured March 1923 at Tully, Co. Offaly. Imprisoned at Tullamore, Portlaoise and Curragh.

MOLONEY: AT. Waterford leader. Captured at Ardfinnan, Co. Tipperary, 20 February 1923.

MOLONEY, Con: AT. Adj 2 Southern Div. Replacement Army Executive member 16 October 1922. AG and Deputy COS from February 1923. Wounded and captured 7 March in Glen of Aherlow. WI.

MOLONEY, Maria: AT. Secretary in Directorate of Organization.

MOLONEY, Thomas (Sir): Lord Chief Justice of Ireland. Moved his courts from Four Courts to maintain their function.

MONAGHAN, M.: AT. Executed in Tuam, Co. Galway, 11 April 1923 for unlawful possession of a rifle and ammunition.

MONKS: PT. Vol. Member of armoured car crew at Béal na mBláth.

MOONEY, James: AT. Vol. Imprisoned in Mountjoy. Cellmate and orderly to Ernie O'Malley, who acknowledged his assistance to him during several illnesses in prison. Collapsed August 1923. Hospitalized in Mountjoy and St Bricin's Hospital and died shortly afterwards.

MOONEY, Joseph T.: PT. Comdt. Appointed to conduct military courts in Kilkenny October 1922.

MOORE, Brian: AT. Executed in Dublin 19 December 1922 for unlawful possession of arms, bomb equipment and ammunition.

MOORE, Maurice: Col. Engaged in debate with Mulcahy, Minister for Defence, May 1922. PT Senator 6 December 1922. His home, Moore Hall, Ballintober, Co. Mayo, was burned 29 January 1922.

MORAN, David: PT. Lt. In action in Kilkenny April 1922, and in Waterford and Clonmel July 1922. Captured Austin Stack 14 April 1923. Survived numerous ambushes and actions in Tipperary, including that at Castle Blake, near Cashel, 16 April 1923. (*See Kennedy, Patrick*)

MORIARTY, Michael: AT. OC 5 Dingle Bn, Kerry No 1 Bde. In action at Fenit.

MORONEY, Matthew: AT. QM 1 Tralee Bn, Kerry No 1 Bde. Sentenced to death in Tralee December 1922. PTs circulated notices threatening his immediate execution if hostilities against them continued in the area. (*See Casey, Con; O'Connor, Jeremiah*)

MORRIS, Michael: AT. Vol. Accidentally killed when withdrawing from PT attack in Clongeen, Co. Wexford, 29 December 1922.

MORRIS, Tom: AT. Maj. Led successful raid for arms on 'A Specials" Pomeroy Barracks early 1922.

MORRISSEY, Paddy: AT. Athlone Brigadier. Delegate to convention 26 March 1922. Shortly after that, insubordination to Tony Lawlor in Custume Barracks led to his being stripped of his Sam Browne belt and expelled from barracks, with others of like mind, by Sean MacEoin. They then occupied buildings in Athlone. WI.

MORRISSEY, Tom: AT. Four Courts garrison.

MOUTRAY, Anketell: Octogenarian Orange Grand Master among 40 Loyalists captured by the still-intact IRA in a preliminary incident January 1922.

MOYLAN, Martin (sometimes 'Nolan'): AT. Executed for unlawful possession of arms and ammunition, Tuam, 11 April 1923.

MOYLAN, Sean: AT. TD. Comdt Gen. D/Operations. Executive member April 1922. Member of Army Reunification Committee, which arranged a temporary truce 4 May 1922. Appointed to army reunification conference June 1922. Signatory of Proclamation of 29 June 1922 (see Chronology). Backed Lynch at Extraordinary Convention of 18 June 1922. In action in Tullow and South Leinster. Member of AT Council of State 25 October 1922. WI.

MOYLETT, Patrick: Prominent London businessman who acted as mediator between Griffith and members of the British cabinet.

MULCAHY, Paddy (P.A.): PT. Capt, later Col Comdt. Brother of Richard. Commanded a Signal Cadet unit in Portlaoise March-April 1922. Wounded in hip during attack on AT position in Cappard House, Portlaoise, July 1922. In charge of PT troops controlling prisoners at burning of Portlaoise prison 29 August 1922. OC 3 Southern Command October 1922. WI.

MULCAHY, Richard: PT. TD. Brother of Paddy. Gen. COS up to 9 January 1922, when he became Minister for Defence. As such he directed the fight against AT forces. Signatory of Army Document of 1 May 1922. Member of Army Reunification Committee which arranged a temporary truce 4 May 1922. Commander-in-Chief, 23 August 1922 to 17 August 1923. Member of Army Council following Collins's death 28 September 1922. Met de Valera 6 December 1922 but failed to bring about a cessation of hostilities. Introduced Special Emergency Powers which gave enormous scope for suppressing AT activities 10 October 1922. WI. (See Moore, Maurice)

MULLANEY: PT. Capt 3 Tipperary Bde. See Killeen, Jack.

MULLANEY, Patrick: AT. Brig. Kildare Bde. Planned an attack on Baldonnel, with a view to carrying out an AT bombing mission. The action did not materialize (see Chronology, July 1922). Captured 29 June 1922. Imprisoned in Kilcock, Lucan and Curragh. Escaped 20 August 1922.

MULLIGAN, P.J. (Rev Fr): Involved in mediation in Sligo confrontation. (See Coyne, Brian)

MULLINS, Billy: AT. Tralee Bn. Arrested August 1922. Imprisoned in Curragh and endured hunger-strike.

MULVIHILL, Dan: AT. Lynch's staff officer. Present with him when ATs burned Fermoy, the last military barracks held by them, 11 August 1922.

MURPHY, Con (Dr): *See Clery, Arthur.*

MURPHY, Humphrey: AT. Brigadier Kerry No 1 Bde. Signatory of Army Document of 1 May 1922. Proclaimed Collins meeting in Tralee April 1922. Signed agreement with PTs in Listowel June 1922. Virtually controlled vehicular movement in North Kerry July 1922. Planned an attack on Farranfore 6 August 1922 but non-arrival of expected reinforcements forced cancellation. WI. (*See Kennelly, T.J.*)

MURPHY, Humphrey: PT. Major Gen. OC Kerry No 1 Bde. Led main attack on Bruree AT position 30 July 1922 with machine-gun carrier called *Danny Boy*, armoured cars and a field gun. He took the town, then led another attack and captured Kilmallock 5 August 1922. With Eoin O'Duffy, gradually dispersed western sector of AT line of defence.

MURPHY, James: PT. Capt. Involved in takeover of Finner Camp, Co. Donegal, 29 June 1922. Joseph Murray became OC. (*See O'Carroll Brothers [Jack]*)

MURPHY, John: AT. Executed in Kilkenny, 29 December 1922 for unlawful possession of arms and ammunition and for involvement in larceny of property from Shenstown House.

MURPHY, Joseph: *See McNulty, John.*

MURPHY, Michael: Final execution in CW. With Joseph O'Rourke was executed 30 May 1923 for armed robbery in Athenry on 24 May. They were apprehended by Lt Frank Curran and a section of PT troops. (Some accounts disagree on date and on detail, and his affiliations, if any, are unclear.)

MURPHY, Michael: *See O'Hegarty, Sean.*

MURPHY, N.J.: PT. Brig Gen. Surrendered Enniscorthy Barracks to ATs after a fight 5 July 1922.

MURPHY, Thomas: PT. Vol. Shot dead when a 2 Eastern Div parade on Griffith Barracks square was attacked 18 November 1922.

MURPHY, W.R.E.: PT. Gen. GOC Kerry Command until December 1922. In action in Limerick, Clare and Cork. Adopted trench warfare at Kilmallock. First Director of amalgamated Training and Operations section January 1923. Resigned 23 May 1923. Appointed Chief Commissioner of Dublin Metropolitan Police.

MURRAY, Joseph: AT. *See Murphy, James.*

MURRAY, Thomas: AT. Medical Officer, East Mayo Bde.

MURRAY, Thomas: AT. Executed in Dundalk 13 January 1923 for unlawful possession of arms and ammunition.

MURTAGH: Non-combatant killed, as was his horse, in Glasson ambush 25 August 1922. (*See McCormack, Sean*)

MURTAGH, Joseph: PT. Lt. Injured in Ballyseedy explosion 7 March 1923.

MUTINEER, THE: Armoured car, called *Ex-Mutineer* when in PT hands. (See Leahy, James)

MYLES, Gerard: AT. A Coy, Tralee Bn. Led numerous engagements against PTs in Kerry and Tipperary.

NAUS: PT. Col. OC Railway Protection, Road and Maintenance Corps.

NEARY: Allegiance unclear. Taken prisoner at Seskin, near Dromahair, Co. Leitrim, 15 September 1922. Shot two sentries dead and escaped.

NEARY, Frank: PT. *See Carney, Tom*.

NEENAN, Connie: AT. 1 Southern Div. Member of AT force moving through Buttevant, Rathkeale and Adare to reinforce Limerick at outbreak of hostilities.

NELIGAN: PT. Capt. Chief Wireless Insp, Independent Corps of Signals.

NELIGAN, David: PT. Comdt, later Col. Close associate and, at times, bodyguard to Collins. In action with Dublin Guards in Fenit and area. WI.

NEWELL, John: AT. Executed in Tuam, Co. Galway, 11 April 1923 for unlawful possession of a revolver and ammunition.

NOLAN, James: AT. KIA by a mine which he was setting to blow up Nenagh police barracks 29 June 1922. (*See Houlihan, William*)

NOLAN, Martin: PT. Lt. WIA at Spa, Co. Kerry, after Fenit landing.

NOLAN, Martin: *See Moylan, Martin*.

NOLAN, Patrick: AT. Executed in Dublin 19 December 1922 for unlawful possession of arms, bomb equipment and ammunition.

NUGENT, James: AT. Covered final withdrawal of ATs from Clonmel July 1922. OC No 2 Column 3 Tipperary Bde towards end of CW. Participated in Mollsheen's Cross ambush. (*See Dalton, Paddy*)

O'BEIRNE, Frank: AT. Active in Sligo area. Led AT forces in Collooney fighting 15 July 1922. Surrendered with 23 ATs when the force came under artillery fire.

O'BRENNAN, Lily: AT. C na mB. Imprisoned in Kilmainham. Participated in Easter Week commemoration parade there. (*See Plunkett, Grace*)

O'BRIEN: PT. Capt. *See Radford, Michael*.

O'BRIEN, Barry (Ó Bríain, Barra): PT. Took over Beresford Barracks, Curragh, mid-1922. Led forced march from Curragh to participate in Wicklow fighting.

O'BRIEN, Dinny: AT. Four Courts garrison. WIA.

O'BRIEN, Edward: PT. In action in taking of Waterford from ATs and in advance to Clonmel.

O'BRIEN, Elizabeth: AT. C na mB. Active in Tralee fighting.

O'BRIEN, Molly: AT. C na mB. Active in Tralee fighting.

O'BRIEN, Paddy: AT. Captain, later Comdt. Staff Officer to ACOS. Commanded HQ Section, Four Courts garrison. Escaped from Jameson's distillery where he had been held after its surrender. Wounded by shrapnel and evacuated. Persisted in following action to Carlow and Enniscorthy where he was shot 5 July and died 11 July 1922.

O'CALLAGHAN, Donal: AT. TD. Member of de Valera's alternative cabinet April 1923. One of a number called upon by Liam Deasy to agree to surrender.

O'CALLAGHAN, John: AT. Member of ambush party at Béal na mBláth 22 August 1922.

O'CALLAGHAN, Kate: AT. TD. Member of AT Council of State 25 October 1922.

O'CARROLL Brothers: PT. Lts. Active in Donegal area. Jack: Involved in raid on Beleek Barracks. Led the Guard of Honour after PT take-over of Finner Camp from ATs 29 June 1922. He did not take part after this. Jim: IO 3 Western Div. (*See Sweeney, Joseph*)

O'CARROLL, M.: PT. Operations Officer, Special Military area. (*See Gilheany*)

O'CONNELL, J.J. 'Ginger': PT. Gen. ACOS. In action with MacEoin in Sligo 16 April 1922. Kidnapped by AT troops in reprisal for arrest of Leo Henderson. The incident represented a significant factor in the PT decision to attack the Four Courts. Held in Four Courts until its surrender. Took over Curragh Camp from British mid-1922. OC Southern District Command 5 July 1922.

O'CONNELL, John: PT. Vol. Driver of Crossley tender in escort at Béal na mBláth 22 August 1922.

O'CONNELL, Sean: PT. Comdt. Member of Collins's escort at Béal na mBláth 22 August 1922.

O'CONNOR: Comdt. PT. Dublin Guards. With Comdt Gerry Ryan, attacked Golden, Co. Tipperary, 27 July 1922. Two ATs killed, 24 taken prisoner. Ambushed and captured near Kilfeacle January 1923. Next day, his AT guards were in turn ambushed and he escaped.

O'CONNOR, Art: AT. In action in O'Connell Street. Led out surrendered troops from Granville Hotel 5 July 1922.

O'CONNOR, Frank: *See O'Donovan, Michael.*

O'CONNOR, Hanna: AT. C na mB. Active in Tralee fighting.

O'CONNOR, Henry: AT. Fianna Éireann member killed accidentally during an arms raid in Ballycarney, Co. Wexford, 26 April 1922.

O'CONNOR, James: AT. Executed in Dublin 19 December 1922 for unlawful possession of arms, bomb equipment and ammunition.

O'CONNOR, James: PT. *See Hunt, Matthew.*

O'CONNOR, Jeremiah: AT. Sentenced to death in Tralee December 1922. PTs circulated notices threatening his immediate execution if hostilities against them continued in the area. (*See Casey, Con; Moroney, Matthew*)

O'CONNOR, Jerome: *See Lennox, Patrick.*

O'CONNOR, John ('Scarteen'): PT. Vol. Shot dead during raid on his home 9 September 1922. Billeted AT troops in his Kenmare home. Younger brother of Tom 'Scarteen' (*below*).

O'CONNOR, Joseph: AT. Brig Gen. Signatory of Proclamation of 29 June

1922 (see Chronology). Comdt 3 Dublin Bn. In action in Dublin, Tipperary.

O'CONNOR, Joseph: AT. Chaired portion of Executive meeting of 11 June 1922.

O'CONNOR, Matthew: PT. Comdt. Directed the Army Medical Service Authority that issued certificates of fitness to stand trial. It delayed some, *e.g.* Ernie O'Malley.

O'CONNOR, Padraig: PT. Maj Gen. Succeeded W.R.E. Murphy as D/Training and Operations 23 May 1923.

O'CONNOR, Patrick: PT. Lt, later Col. Close associate of Collins.

O'CONNOR, Roger (Dr): Gave medical assistance in Tralee fighting August 1922.

O'CONNOR, Rory: AT. Comdt Gen. D/Engineering. Signatory of demand for Army Convention 11 January 1922. Member of Army Reunification Committee, which arranged a temporary truce 4 May 1922. Signatory of Proclamation of 29 June 1922 (see Chronology). Chairman of Executive. Prominent member of Four Courts garrison. Imprisoned in Mountjoy after surrender. Executed in Dublin 8 December 1922 in reprisal for shooting of Sean Hales. WI. (See Mellows, Liam)

O'CONNOR, Tom ('Scarteen'): PT. Brig Gen. Elder brother of John, above. In action in Kerry. Took Valentia and other areas by sea-borne operations. Led the landing at Kenmare 10 July 1922. Shot dead during raid on his home 9 September 1922. (See MacManus, Dermot; Lynch, Fionan)

O'CONNOR, Tom ('Thady'): PT. Cousin of 'Scarteens' (above). Lay low after shooting of his cousins and later escaped by boat at night and was picked up by a British patrol boat, *Seawolf*.

Ó CUILL, Micheál: Neutral. Secretary of Cork People's Rights Association who contacted Lynch concerning peace and brought Lynch's reply to Collins. Wrote to Collins warning him not to travel via Béal na mBláth. WI.

O'DALY, Paddy: See Daly, Paddy (PT).

O'DONNELL, Lisa: C na mB. Despatch carrier for Oscar Traynor.

O'DONNELL, Peadar: AT. Col Comdt. Member of Executive. Signatory of Proclamation of 29 June 1922 (see Chronology). Four Courts garrison. Imprisoned in Mountjoy, Kilmainham and Curragh. Went on hunger-strike. Escaped 1924. WI.

O'DONNELL, Tom: PT. TD. Friend of de Valera. Voted for the Treaty on 7 January 1922 but voted for de Valera as President on 9 January.

O'DONOGHUE, Daithi: AT. Imprisoned in Mountjoy. Went on hunger-strike. Escaped while being moved to Kilmainham with MacBride and Michael Price.

O'DONOGHUE, Florrie: Neutral, although on 9 April 1922 he was nominated Adjutant General on Army Council selected from AT Executive. Prominent in attempts to prevent CW. Signatory of Army Document of 1 May 1922. Had a meeting with Collins 21 August 1922.

O'DONOVAN, Michael (later Frank O'Connor, author): AT. Twelve-year-old bearer of dispatches in Cork. Assisted in producing AT news-sheet. (*See Hendrick, Sean*)

O'DONOVAN, Seamus: AT. D/Chemicals. Signatory of demand for Army Convention 11 January 1922. First to suggest formation of separate AT army HQ. Arrested but escaped. Active in provision of explosives, grenades, etc. WI.

O'DRISCOLL, Denis: AT. Capt 8 Bn 3 Tipperary Bde. Taken prisoner after heavy fighting in Brownswood area, Co. Waterford, 27 September 1922.

O'DRISCOLL, Neilus: PT. After PT capture of Cork he led advance to Bantry and took the town.

O'DUFFY, Eoin: PT. Gen. COS 10 January-14 September 1922. Insisted on a conciliatory approach to the early Limerick dispute. Member of Army Reunification Committee, which arranged a temporary truce 4 May 1922. Signatory of Army Document 1 May 1922. Also GOC Eastern District Command from 5 July 1922 and GOC South-Western Command. Active in Limerick area July 1922. With Humphrey Murphy, gradually dispersed western sector of AT line of defence. Appointed Commissioner of Civic Guard September 1922. WI.

O'DWYER, George: PT. Brig Gen. OC Kilkenny Bde. Took over Kilkenny Barracks February 1922. Imposed martial law after serious destruction to Castlecomer collieries.

O'DWYER, Seamus: PT. TD. Dáil Peace Committee member May-June 1922.

O'FARRELL, Michael: PT. Blamed for firing across the border on British troops at Pettigo 3 June 1922 and was taken prisoner by them. This led to sharp exchanges between Churchill and Collins.

O'FARRELLY, Agnes: Member of anti-war delegation June 1922. (*See Gonne, Maud*)

O'FLAHERTY, Liam: AT. Member of Communist Party and CW activist.

O'FRIEL, F.J. (Frank Friel): PT. Capt. Orderly officer on board the *Arvonia* when it landed troops at Passage West 7 August 1922. He led first reconnaissance troops ashore in a boat. Promoted in the field to Comdt by Dalton before push to Cork. On Dalton's Cork staff. Assisted matron of Shanakiel Hospital in washing Collins's corpse.

Ó GAORA, Colm: AT. Brig 4 Connemara Bde. Active in Connemara. He and his men endured lack of clothing and provisions during a severe campaign. He made a strong appeal for more adequate AT funding in December 1922.

O'GRADY'S: AT. House in Rochestown, Co. Cork used as a defensive position.

O'HAGAN (Monsignor): Rector, Irish College of Rome. Met Richard Mulcahy, Ernie O'Malley and others in an attempt to bring about cessation of hostilities.

Ó hANNAGÁIN, Donncadha: PT. Comdt Gen. Comdt 4 Southern Div. Close associate of Collins. Signed an agreement with Lynch, with whom he was friendly, whereby neither side would attack the other, in Limerick 4 July 1922. This was annulled the following day by Dermot MacManus but Ó hAnnagáin and Michael Brennan signed another agreement 7 July, whereupon MacManus returned to HQ in Dublin to report to O'Duffy. WI.

O'HEGARTY, Diarmuid: PT. Comdt Gen. Member of Army Reunification Committee which arranged a temporary truce 4 May 1922. Member of Army Council 28 September 1922. D/Int 28 September 1922 to March 1923 when appointed Secretary to Government Executive Council. WI.

O'HEGARTY, Jack: AT. Non-combatant. Brother of P.S. (*below*). Attempted to bring an end to hostilities. WI.

O'HEGARTY, P.S.: PT. Non-combatant. Attempted to bring an end to hostilities. WI.

O'HEGARTY, Sean: AT. With Michael Murphy, attempted to intercept British arms ship leaving Haulbowline March 1922. Drafted and co-signed the 1 May 1922 Army Document. He was allowed the unusual distinction of addressing the Dáil, of which he was not a member, 3 May 1922. Remained a non-combatant throughout CW. WI.

Ó hÉIGEARTAIGH, Diarmuid: *See* *O'Hegarty, Diarmuid.*

O'HIGGINS, Kevin: PT. TD. Minister for Economic Affairs 10 January-9 September 1922. Provisional Government signatory to the Collins-Craig agreement 30 March 1922. Supervisor of British withdrawal and draftee of Constitution. Minister for Home Affairs 22 August-6 December 1922. A strict disciplinarian, he sanctioned a number of executions, yet was critical of some army excesses. WI.

O'HIGGINS, T.F. (Dr): PT. Father of Kevin (*above*). Shot dead in front of his wife and daughter 13 February 1923.

O'KEEFFE, Patrick: PT. On platform with Collins at Killarney 22 April 1922.

O'KEEFFE, Patrick (Paudeen): Deputy Governor, Mountjoy Prison.

O'KELLY, J.J. ('Sceilg'): AT. Conducted fund-raising activities in United States. Member of AT Council of State 25 October 1922. WI.

O'KELLY, Sean T.: AT. Arrested on Baggot Street Bridge, Dublin, 27 July 1922. Imprisoned in Mountjoy and endured hunger-strike. Member of AT Council of State 25 October 1922. WI. (*See Plunkett, George Noble*)

O'LEARY: PT. Capt. In action in Limerick-Clare area July 1922.

O'LEARY, Jeremiah: AT. Bn OC, Ballylongford and Castleisland, Co. Kerry. Captured in Knocknagashel and shot dead at Castleisland Barracks 24 May 1923 after Aiken's cease-fire order.

O'MAHONEY, Patrick: Executed in Ennis 26 April 1923 for unlawful possession of a revolver and for an attack on PT troops in which some were killed.

O'MAHONEY, Sean: AT. TD. Member of AT Council of State 25 October 1922. WI.

Ó MÁILLE, Padraig: PT. TD. Leas Ceann Comhairle of Dáil. Dáil Peace Committee member May-June 1922.

Wounded in Sean Hales shooting in Dublin 7 December 1922.

O'MALLEY, Christopher: PT. Col Comdt. Commanded troops on the *Arvonia,* which landed at Westport 24 July 1922. Captured Westport and pressed inland to link up with MacEoin's troops for action in Mayo-Sligo area. WI.

O'MALLEY, Ernie: AT. Comdt 2 Southern Div (five brigades: Limerick, Kilkenny, part of Tipperary) and later Northern/Eastern Command. Raided Clonmel Barracks 26 February 1922. Member of Army Reunification Committee which arranged a temporary truce 4 May 1922. Secretary of 9 April 1922 army convention. Signatory of Proclamation of 29 June 1922 (*see Chronology*). D/Organization. Active in Limerick confrontation (*see Chronology, 23 February 1922*). Prominent leader in Four Courts. Signed surrender document. Captured but escaped from Jameson's distillery where he had been held after surrender. In action Leinster and Munster. ACOS October 1922. Member of council convened to negotiate settlement. Captured and wounded in Dublin November 1922. Imprisoned in Mountjoy, Kilmainham and Curragh. Endured hunger-strike. WI. (*See Humphreys, Ellen; Leahy, James; Malley, Cecil and Charles; O'Connor, Matthew*)

O'MALLEY, James: AT. Executed in Tuam 11 April 1923 for unlawful possession of a rifle and ammunition.

O'MARA, Stephen (Alderman): Mayor of Limerick. Arranged meeting of opposing officers and also met de Valera regarding the Limerick confrontation March 1922.

Ó MUIRTHILE, Sean: PT. Lt Gen. Involved in discussions concerning the early Limerick confrontation. Reorganized the IRB under the Army Council to prevent its being taken over by ATs. QMG 29 January 1923. WI.

Ó MURCHADHA, Colm: Governor of Mountjoy July 1922. (*See Plunkett, Count*)

O'NEILL, Denis ('Sonny'): AT. Member of ambush party at Béal na mBláth 22 August 1922. Often regarded as the firer of the shot that killed Collins.

O'NEILL, Ignatius: PT gunner. Used 18-pounder to fire at sniper on roof of Four Courts. Shells went through dome and landed at Macready's Royal Hospital HQ. Macready summoned Emmet Dalton and complained that PTs promised not to use them against the British. WI.

O'NEILL, Laurence (Rt Hon.): Lord Mayor of Dublin. Chaired a women's anti-war committee in June 1922 which approached both sides without success. WI. (*See Gonne, Maud*)

O'NEILL, Michael: AT. Captured 29 June 1922. Imprisoned in Kilcock, Maynooth and Curragh.

O'NEILL, Michael: AT. Acting Comdt 3 Cork Bde. When he called to the Hornibrook home, Bandon, Co. Cork, 25 (or 29) April 1922, he was shot dead from within.

O'RAHILLY, Áine: AT. Housed HQ staff. Shot accidentally by Ernie O'Malley when her house was raided to capture him. Imprisoned in Kilmainham. Participated in Easter Week commemoration parade there. (*See Plunkett, Grace*)

O'RAHILLY, Alfred: PT. Prof. Member of 1922 Constitution-drafting committee.

O'RAHILLY, Aodhagán: AT. Son of The O'Rahilly (*see Part One*). As a university student on holidays in Kerry joined ATs in Ventry, Dingle. Posted to 3 Tipperary Bde. Operated as a driver for many of its prominent leaders and was machine-gunner in some actions during the summer of 1922. Participated in the ambush of Frank Thornton. When his holidays expired, he returned to his engineering studies.

O'REILLY, Anthony: AT. Former PT Pte. Executed in Dublin 8 January 1923 for assisting ATs in attack on PT troops at Leixlip and passing them information.

O'REILLY, 'Buck': AT. *See Cooney, Sean*.

O'REILLY, Patrick: AT. Executed in Waterford 25 January 1923 for unlawful possession of arms and ammunition.

O'REILLY, Tom (Skinner): AT. Former close associate of Collins. Sentry and sniper at Four Courts. Attempted to shoot PT gunners at considerable risk to himself. Took ultimatum to surrender from PH HQ despatch rider. (*See Ennis, Tom*)

ORIEL HOUSE: HQ of PT special task force (CID) that dealt with political crimes.

O'ROURKE, Donal: TD. Resigned his seat November 1922 in protest against the election pact not being observed.

O'ROURKE, James: AT. Executed in Dublin 13 March 1923 for participating in attack on PT troops at Jury's Hotel 21 February 1923 and for unlawful possession of arms and ammunition.

O'ROURKE, Joseph: *See Murphy, Michael*.

O'SHANNON, Cathal: Labour Party representative in June 1922 and later peace efforts. Protested at repudiation of the Second Dáil and accused government of irregular arrests and punishments. Opposed the appointment of a Governor-General. WI.

O'SHEA, Martin: AT. Executed in Roscrea 15 January 1923 for unlawful possession of arms and ammunition.

O'SHEA, Patrick: AT. Drowned while attempting to escape when surrounded at Clashmealcon caves 16 April 1923.

O'SHEA'S: AT. Rochestown, Co. Cork house used as a defensive position.

O'SULLIVAN, Andrew: AT. Imprisoned Mountjoy. Endured hunger-strike October 1923.

O'SULLIVAN Brothers: AT. Pat and Mick. Active in Cork. On 2 December 1922 they expedited the acquisition of McPeake and the armoured car *Slievenamon*. Participated in the capture of Ballymakeera from PTs on same day, taking 125 prisoners but releasing them later.

O'SULLIVAN, Gearoid: PT. TD. Major Gen. Adj General. Signatory of Army Document 1 May 1922. Member of Army Reunification Committee which arranged a temporary truce 4 May 1922. Member of Army Council 28 September 1922. WI.

O'SULLIVAN, John L.: PT. Made a river crossing under fire to take Kinsale. Spoke to Collins in Bandon on morning of 22 August 1922. Collins assured him he was about to end the CW. WI.

O'SULLIVAN, Joseph: AT. Vol. With Reginald Dunne, was convicted of the assassination of Sir Henry Wilson 22 June 1922. Tried at Old Bailey 18 July and found guilty. Executed in Wandsworth 10 August.

O'SULLIVAN, Richard: PT. Capt. In action in Wicklow July 1922 and Kerry, where he was 2 i/c to 'Scarteen' O'Connor. Prominent in the capture of Caherciveen and Waterville. Evacuated AT prisoners by boat from the latter.

O'SULLIVAN, Tadhg: AT. OC West Cork Bde. Imprisoned after cease-fire and endured hunger-strike in Curragh.

O'SULLIVAN, Ted: AT. OC Cork No 3 Bn. Persisted in opposing any cessation of hostilities.

O'SULLIVAN, Timothy: AT. Lt. Executed in Drumboe 14 March 1923 for unlawful possession of arms and ammunition.

O'SULLIVAN, Tom: AT. Comdt South Wexford Bde. Prominent in Enniscorthy fighting. WI.

PAGE: AT. Four Courts garrison.

PAUL, Patrick: PT. Comdt, later Col. OC Waterford Bde. Used his intimate knowledge of the area during many actions. Led attack on Waterford and ordered its shelling July 1922. With Prout gradually dispersed eastern sector of AT line of defence. WI.

PEARLE, James: AT. Executed in Wexford 13 March 1923 for unlawful possession of a revolver.

PEARSE, Margaret: AT. TD. C na mB. Prominent activist.

PHELAN Brothers, Michael & John: Owners of the property at Poulacappal, Co. Tipperary, where 'Katmandu' was situated. This hide-out for AT leaders was a small room built at the rear of a cowshed. Secret access was through the shed.

PHELAN, John: AT. Executed in Kilkenny 29 December 1922 for unlawful possession of arms and ammunition and for involvement in theft of property from Shenstown House.

PILKINGTON, Frederick: AT. Vol 3 Western Div. In action in Sligo area.

PILKINGTON, John: AT. Vol 3 Western Div. In action in Sligo area.

PILKINGTON, William: AT. Comdt 3 Western Div (Sligo, North Roscommon, part of Mayo and Leitrim). During Four Courts occupation, on 16 April 1922, issued proclamation forbidding Griffith's public appearance in Sligo. Sean MacEoin, J.J. O'Connell, Alex McCabe, Jim Hunt, Tony Lawlor and others put on a show of force and Griffith spoke. Pilkington's area put up a stubborn resistance to intense PT pressure. Appointed to AT Executive Council 20 April 1923 after Lynch's death. Imprisoned in Mountjoy, Kilmainham and Curragh. Endured hunger-strike. WI.

PLUNKETT, George Noble (Count): AT. TD. Re-elected for Roscommon June 1922. Signatory, with Sean T.

O'Kelly, of AT manifesto explaining their reasoning, sent to Cork newspapers July 1922. On 18 July 1922 instituted a *habeas corpus* application for his son, Seóirse, imprisoned in Mountjoy. Applied for a writ to be served on Gen Mulcahy and the Governor of Mountjoy Prison, Ó Murchadha, ordering them to produce his son. Member of AT Council of State 25 October 1922. WI. (*See Clery, Arthur*)

PLUNKETT, Grace (née Gifford): AT. C na mB. Imprisoned in Kilmainham. On anniversary of Easter Week Rebellion, she and other relatives of those executed on 5 May 1916 marched to the place of execution, unfurled a tricolour and made a speech.

PLUNKETT, Horace (Sir): PT. Senator 6 December 1922. Kilteragh, his Foxrock, Co. Dublin, home, was blown up by a mine 29 January 1923. Valuable works of art were destroyed. WI.

PLUNKETT, Jack: AT. Four Courts garrison. Imprisoned in Mountjoy after surrender.

PLUNKETT, Seóirse: AT. Son of George Noble (*above*). Four Courts garrison. Imprisoned in Mountjoy after surrender, later Kilmainham.

POBLACHT NA hÉIREANN WAR NEWS: AT news-sheet, originally a diary by Rev Fr Albert.

POWELL: PT. Comdt. Div Engineer, 3 Southern Div. Active in Laois-Offaly area. WIA, seriously, when ambushed as he led a party to deal with a mine reportedly laid at Tonduff, Abbeyleix, Co. Laois, 28 July 1922.

POWER, Albert: Sculptor who made Collins's death mask.

POWER, Joseph (Dr): Attended to Liam Lynch's wounds after his capture.

PRICE, Eamonn: PT. Often deputized for Costello in 3 Southern Div actions.

PRICE, Eamonn: PT. Maj Gen. Director of Organization up to September 1922. Director of Military Statistics, Portobello Barracks.

PRICE, Jackie: AT. 1 Tralee Bn, later 9 Bn Kerry No 1 Bde. Involved in resistance to Fenit landing. Captured and imprisoned in Newbridge. Escaped by tunnelling.

PRICE, Michael: AT. Member of Executive. Involved in early activities in Mullingar and Drogheda. QM 1 Eastern Div. Imprisoned in Curragh and Mountjoy where he was involved in tunnelling. Went on hunger-strike. Escaped while being removed to Kilmainham with MacBride and Daithi O'Donoghue October 1921.

PRITCHARD: British officer alleged to have remained on to help Collins with intelligence duties after the Treaty.

PROUT, John T.: PT. Col and Maj Gen. Occupied Kilkenny but initially allowed ATs two positions, confining their activities to policing. Later, ATs occupied the Castle and Prout, with reinforcements from Dublin, dislodged them. Using artillery, he commanded 2 Southern Div in its push through Leinster to Waterford and Tipperary, July-August 1922. GOC Waterford Command February 1923. Personally accompanied ambulance from Clonmel to scene of Liam Lynch's shooting.

QUEEN OF THE WEST: Armoured car manufactured by Michael Kilroy.

QUIGLEY: Not committed at time of death in Dundalk when 4 Northern Div were surrounded and he was shot trying to escape. Not included in either casualty list.

QUINLAN, John: PT. Staff officer to Prout.

QUINLAN, Maurice (Dr): Gave medical assistance in Tralee fighting August 1922.

QUINLAN, Tom: AT. *See Davin, Jerome.*

QUINN, Christopher: AT. He and William Shaughnessy were the only two ATs charged with murder of a PT soldier throughout CW. Both executed in Ennis 2 May 1923 for this and for unlawful possession of a revolver each.

QUINN, M.: Reserve driver in Collins's car at Béal na mBláth.

QUINN, Patrick: AT. QM 4 Northern Div. Captured and imprisoned. Hospitalized in Curragh.

QUINN, Patrick: PT. Pte. KIA with Dublin Guards near Kilfenora 3 August 1922 after Fenit landing.

QUINN, Sean: PT. Col Comdt. Appointed Chief Ordnance Officer 15 May 1922.

QUIRKE, William: AT. South Tipperary Bde. Issued a proclamation threatening the execution of a prominent PT civilian supporter for every execution of an AT. Captured Callan, Thomastown and Mullinavat from PTs. Captured PT armoured rail car and its occupants near Cashel September 1922. Succeeded Paddy Dalton as Vice-Comdt 3 Tipperary Bde December 1922. Supported Tom Barry in capture of Carrick-on-Suir, leading the party that stormed the barracks 9 December 1922. Attended Nire Valley conference.

RADFORD, Bernard: AT. Wounded by a grenade when giving cover to escaping members of Murrinstown, Co. Wexford, column, at Spencerstown 10 January 1923. Operated upon in Wexford hospital but died. In the same action, Lt Con McCarthy, AT, was KIA.

RADFORD, Michael: AT. Comdt 3 Wexford Bn. Took part in attack on Enniscorthy Castle June 1922. Captured by PTs under Capt O'Brien at Sleedagh House, Co. Wexford, 9 January 1923 but escaped with 28 others 2 May. Killed in search-and-sweep operation by PTs in Bridgetown area 21 June 1923, after the cease-fire.

RAFTER: PT. Vol. Second driver of Collins's car. Shot in hip when it was fired on near Stillorgan, Co. Dublin, 18 August 1922.

REID, Harold: *See Dandy Six.*

REIDY, Joseph: PT. Comdt. Appointed to conduct military courts in Roscrea October 1922.

REILLY, Edward: PT. Capt. In action in Tipperary August 1922.

REYNOLDS, David: PT. Col. WIA storming Limerick Castle 18 July 1922. Eventually took command of the city.

GOC Cork Command, February 1923.

REYNOLDS, William: AT. Capt. Participated in arms and explosive dumping. In action at Bandon and Ballinhassig, Co. Cork, September 1922. Captured 4 October. Imprisoned in Kinsale Union, Cork and Newbridge. Endured hunger-strike. WI.

RHATIGAN: Seriously injured by AT troops at Glasson, Athlone, 25 August 1922. (*See McCormack, Sean*)

RICE, J.J.: AT. Comdt Kerry No 2 Bde. Proclaimed Collins's public meeting there 22 April 1922. Defended Kenmare after Fenit landings. Withdrew to the mountains but led a successful counter-attack, capturing weapons and ammunition. Dislodged again. As late as April 1923 he and Ted Sullivan supported Lynch's view that further resistance was possible. WI.

RIGNEY, Patrick: AT. Four Courts garrison. Escaped capture on surrender.

RING, Joseph: PT. Brig Gen. Comdt Westport Bn. Taken prisoner for a while by ATs when he engaged in recruitment for Civic Guard. Commissioner designate of Civic Guard. KIA, Banniconlan, Ox Mountains, 14 September 1922.

RIORDAN, Patrick: Train driver scalded to death when ATs derailed a train at at Liscahane Bridge, Ardfert, Co. Kerry, 19 January 1923. (*See Crowley, Daniel; Driscoll, Tom*)

RIVER LEE, THE: Armour-plated truck used by ATs in Cork.

ROBBINS, Sean: AT. Brig. OC Offaly No 2 Bde.

ROBINSON, David L. ('Deadeye Dave'): AT. In action in Cork and Kerry. Captured with Childers 10 November 1922. Imprisoned in Mountjoy and Kilmainham, where he was jail adj. (*See Derrig, Tomás*)

ROBINSON, Michael: PT. Lt, later Capt. In Athlone action against AT forces on Lough Ree islands. Commander of *The Ballinalee* when it was captured in an ambush at Rockwood 13 July 1922. Escaped capture.

ROBINSON, Seamus: AT. Comdt Gen. OC 3 Tipperary Bde. Executive member of Army Reunification Committee which arranged a temporary truce 4 May 1922. Signatory of Proclamation of 29 June 1922. Appointed Comdt 2 Southern Div, July 1922. In action in Munster, particularly in Carrick-on-Suir and Clonmel and in numerous ambushes in Knockmealdown Mountains. WI. (*See Chronology 9 April 1922*)

RODGERS, Sean: AT. Garrison Adj in Sligo.

ROGERS, John (Monsignor): San Francisco clergyman who persuaded de Valera to meet Mulcahy on 6 September 1922. The meeting bore no fruit.

ROGERS, John Theodore: Master of the *Lady Wicklow*.

ROONEY, Edward: WIA by grenade shrapnel during intense action at Moyderwell Cross, Tralee, August 1922.

ROSE OF TRALEE: Field gun used by PTs in Kerry area.

ROSS, Gibbs: AT. Brig. Comdt. Beara Bde KIA Bantry 30 August 1922.

ROSSES, THE: Sligo-Rosses Point ferry seized and used by ATs.

RUSSELL, C.F.: PT. Maj Gen. OC Railway Protection, Repair and Maintenance Corps, later Corps of Engineers. 2 i/c Air Corps and Director of Civil Aviation, 1922.

RUSSELL, Charles: PT. Col. Fought off an attack on an armoured-train repair party near Farnalee, Co. Tipperary. With Tom Ennis, represented Provisional Government in meeting with Liam Deasy and Tom Barry at Crookstown, Co. Cork 13 October 1922, in an attempt to find a peace formula.

RUSSELL, Patrick: AT. Executed in Roscrea 15 January 1923 for unlawful possession of arms and ammunition.

RUSSELL, Sean: AT. Director of Munitions. Signatory of demand for Army Convention 11 January 1922. Arranged quarry raids for explosives. Imprisoned and went on hunger-strike. WI.

RUTTLEDGE, P.J.: AT. Member of Council and Executive. Dáil Peace Committee member May-June 1922. Signatory of Proclamation of 29 June 1922. Minister for Justice and Council of State member in de Valera's opposition cabinet. Acting President of that cabinet during de Valera's imprisonment, 1923. WI.

RYAN (Miss): *See Furlong, John A.*

RYAN, Denis: AT. *See Breen, Martin.*

RYAN, Gerry: PT. Comdt Brig. In action in Tipperary. Held Thurles and sent reinforcements to PT operations in a number of areas, including Cork. On 29 August 1922, successfully fought off two ambushes on the Tipperary-Cashel road. (*See O'Connor, Comdt; Furlong, John A.*)

RYAN, James: PT. Captured when Annacarthy Barracks was overrun and burned 30 April 1922.

RYAN, James (Dr): AT. TD. Established temporary hospital in Four Courts. He, his staff and the wounded were evacuated before the surrender. Captured. Imprisoned. Endured hunger-strike. WI.

RYAN, Patrick: PT. Captured when Annacarthy Barracks was overrun and burned 30 April 1922.

RYAN, Tommy: PT. Col. Initially Sean MacEoin's QM in Athlone. After some prevarications, joined in attack on Four Courts. Requested and was granted a Tipperary posting and adopted numerous disguises in making his way south. Active in Tipperary-Kilkenny area. Planned the operation that led to Lynch's death. Also present at arrest of Austin Stack 19 April 1923 and the Castle Blake shootings 16 April. (*See Cleary, Sean; English; Kennedy, Patrick Moran; Somers*)

RYAN-LACKEN, Patrick: AT. Active in north Tipperary. Captured. Imprisoned. Endured hunger-strike.

RYNNE, Michael: PT. Capt Involved in the preparations for bombardment of the Four Courts. WI.

SADLIER Brothers: AT. Michael: Comdt 2 Bn 3 Tipperary Bde. In action when PT troops were captured in Annacarthy 30 May 1922. Surrounded by PTs at Heffernan's of Marlhill early on 3 November 1922, he and Paddy Loughlin were being apprehended when a candle was extinguished. Firing took place in the dark and he was shot. Died next day in Cashel hospital. Tom: succeeded Paddy Dalton as OC No 2 Column and on the day Michael was killed engaged PTs at Ballymacarbery in the Nire Valley. Vol Jim Dahille was wounded in the action.

SCANLON, Con: AT. *See Davin, Jerome.*

SCANLON, Frank: *See Hunt, Matthew.*

SCANNELL (Rev Fr): Chaplain to PT HQ in Cork.

SCANNELL, Stephen: *See Dandy Six.*

SCOTT: PT. IO active in Cork.

SEAWOLF: *See O'Connor, Tom (Thady).*

SEXTON, Sean: PT. Lt Comdt. QM No 1 Bde, Western Command. Took on ambushers near Ballinalee with success 7 September 1922.

SHANAHAN, Bryan: AT. In action when PT troops were captured in Annacarty 30 May 1922.

SHAUGHNESSY, William: *See Quinn, Christopher.*

SHEEHAN, Michael: AT. Comdt. QM South Tipperary Bn. In action when PT troops were captured in Annacarthy 30 May 1922. Led Tipperary contingent in Wexford and Wicklow fighting. Participated in resistance to PT attack on Waterford 19 July 1922 and at Carrick-on-Suir, Callan, Mullinavat and Thomastown. Assisted Tom Barry in attack on Carrick-on-Suir 9 December 1922. After Martin Breen's death, he re-organized No 1 Column, 3 Tipperary Bde. Post cease-fire Executive member.

SHEEHY, J.J.: AT. Vice Brigadier, Kerry No 1 Bde, later Brigadier. Commanded Ballymullen Barracks, Tralee, before Fenit landing. Defended Tralee and supervised the burning of part of the barracks on vacating it. Wounded by grenade shrapnel in intense fight at Moyderwell Cross, Tralee, 2 August 1922. Led large contingent of the Bde against Kilmallock. WI.

SHEEHY, Lawrence: AT. Former PT Pte. Executed in Dublin 8 January 1923 for treachery in assisting ATs in attack on PT troops at Leixlip and passing them information.

SHEEHY, Thomas: AT. Capt. OC E (Oakpark) Company 1 Bn Kerry No 1 Bde. OC Fenit garrison opposing Fenit landing. In many actions during CW.

SHEEHY SKEFFINGTON, Hanna: Member of anti-war delegation June 1922. Arrested for collection of petitions for release of hunger-strikers. Imprisoned and went on hunger-strike. WI. (*See Gonne, Maud*)

SHERIDAN, Henry: AT. Vol 3 Western Div. In action in Sligo area.

SHIELS: PT. Vol. WIA after Fenit landing.

SIEMAN: PT. Vol. WIA after Fenit landing.

SIMONS: PT. Gen. Co-ordinator of Sligo operations September 1922.

SKELLY: PT. Vol. Medical services, Beggarsbush Barracks.

SKINNIDER, Margaret: AT. Austin Stack's assistant in Records and

Accounts Department. Arrested and imprisoned in Mountjoy. WI.

SLATTERY, Jimmy: PT. Brig Limerick Bde. His seizure of Castle Barracks, Limerick, sparked the early tension in the city. Commanded westward movement to Kerry, supported by armoured car and artillery piece. Overcame strong resistance at Kilmallock, Adare, Newcastlewest and Rathkeale. WI.

SLATTERY, Thomas: See 'Dandy Six'.

SLIEVENAMON, THE: Rolls-Royce Whippet armoured car, part of Collins's convoy at Béal na mBláth 22 August 1922.

SMALL, Michael: PT. Led a party from Thurles that rescued PT prisoners taken at Urlingford on 5 July 1922. The prisoners and AT guard had been halted at Mary Willie's road junction bar.

SMIDDY, T.A.: PT. Prof. Replaced Harry Boland as 'Envoy Extraordinary from the Elected Government of the Irish Republic to the United States of America'.

SMITH, John: PT. Lt. Motor-cycle scout leading Collins's convoy at Béal na mBláth 22 August 1922. Shot in the neck while helping to move Collins's body.

SMYTH: PT. Comdt. 2 i/c Independent Corps of Signals March 1923.

SOMERS, Edward: PT/AT. Changed sides when Tom Barry captured Callan. KIA at Castle Blake, Cashel, 16 April 1923.

SPOONER, Joseph: AT. Executed in Dublin 30 November 1922 for unlawful possession of a revolver.

STACK, Austin: AT. TD. Minister for Home Affairs until January 1922. Secretary of Sinn Féin. Involved in Dublin fighting. Records and Accounts officer in HQ, later QM. Visited USA on fund-raising mission. Minister for Finance and member of AT Council of State 25 October 1922. Captured 14 April 1923 while bearing a document calling on the AT President to order a cessation of hostilities. Imprisoned in Kilmainham where he led hunger-strike. Suffered ill-health as a result. Re-elected for Kerry 27 August 1923. WI. (*See Moran, David*)

STACK, James: AT. In action in Tipperary, especially Lisduff, July 1922.

STACK, Liam: PT. Comdt Carlow Bde.

STAINES, Michael: PT. TD. Directed Belfast Boycott January-February 1922. WI.

STAPLETON, Daniel: PT. KIA when moving to take surrender of Granville Hotel, O'Connell St, from a white-flag bearer 5 July 1922.

STAPLETON, Edward: Capt 19 Bn, Kerry. KIA, mine explosion, Knocknagashel, Co. Kerry, 6 March 1923.

STAPLETON, William: PT. Capt. Close associate of Collins. WI. (*See Leahy*)

STOPFORD GREEN, Alice: PT. Appointed Senator 6 December 1922.

STUART, Francis: AT. Writer. Imprisoned in Portlaoise and participated in its burning.

SULLIVAN, Andrew: AT. Capt. Died after forty days on hunger-strike, Mountjoy, 22 November 1923.

SULLIVAN, John: AT. Lt 4 Bn, Kerry No 1 Bde. Involved in attempt to halt PTs' progress at Sammy's Rock, Spa, after Fenit landing 2 August 1922. KIA.

SULLIVAN, Ted: AT. Brigadier, West Cork Bde. (See Rice, J.J.)

SULLIVAN'S: Gurranereagh house, meeting-place of 1 Southern Div (AT), where Deasy met de Valera 21 August 1922, the day before the Béal na mBláth ambush.

SWAN, John: PT. Collins's regular driver in Dublin.

SWAYNE: PT. Capt. I/c Kenmare garrison which was re-captured by ATs 9 September 1922.

SWEENEY, John: PT. Vol. Fatally wounded when *The Ballinalee* was captured by AT ambush 13 July 1922 at Rockwood.

SWEENEY, Joseph: PT. Comdt Gen. Comdt 1 Northern Div (Four Bdes, Donegal). Attacked and seized Finner Camp from AT forces 29 June 1922. His forces also seized posts in Ballyshannon, Buncrana, Clonmany and Carndonagh. Later, joined up with Sean MacEoin's force by capturing Kinlough, Tullaghan, Kiltyclogher and Manorhamilton. GOC Donegal Command April 1923. WI.

SWEENEY, Michael: AT. Early victim whose shooting in Grafton Street, Dublin, 21 April 1922 angered AT leaders.

TARTAR, THE: Sligo Steam Navigation Company vessel which was steel-plated and used in PT operations.

TATE: PT. Lt. Reported killing of prisoners at Ballyseedy 7 March 1923.

TAYLOR, Thomas: PT. Capt. Led attack on ATs at Blackcastle, Co. Tipperary, 18 September 1922. Engaged in the search-and-sweep operation that led to Lynch's death.

TEELING, Frank: PT. Lt and Capt. WIA during Limerick fighting 13 July 1922. WI.

THOMPSON (Mrs): Seconded ceasefire motion by women electors of Cork 2 August 1922. (See *Leader, Mrs*)

THORNTON, Frank: PT. Col. IO sent by Joe McGrath to Clonmel 21 August 1922 to ensure that trustworthy PT troops there would protect Collins on his inspection tour. Some sources claimed he had been despatched to shoot de Valera. His driver and another private were killed instantly when their vehicle was ambushed at Redmondstown, Co. Tipperary, by Jack Killeen's column. Thornton remained unconscious for some days before dying. Killeen sent a note by a passing cyclist to closest PT commander, stating where the casualties lay. WI.

THORPE: Alias for a British agent who, allegedly, was a confidante of Collins and a person of some standing in Irish affairs. (See *Markham, Thomas*)

TOBIN, Liam: PT. Col. Alleged London recipient of instructions for Sir Henry Wilson's assassination. IO in Passage West landing 8 August 1922. Often Collins's bodyguard, although not at Béal na mBláth. WI.

TOBIN'S: AT safe house in Tincurry, Co. Tipperary.

TOM KEOGH: PT armoured car. (See *Danny Boy*)

TRAYNOR, Oscar: AT. Comdt Dublin No 1 Bde. Signatory of demand for Army Convention 11 January 1922. Intervened in Limerick dispute. Provided original AT HQ accommodation in the Gaelic League Hall, Parnell Square, Dublin. Occupied the Kildare Street Club, the Ballast Office and the Masonic Hall. Evacuated them at Lynch's behest. Attempted to persuade Four Courts garrison to vacate the building. Provided sniper cover for Four Courts garrison and attempted to counter PT attack on it. Finally ordered its surrender. Commanded O'Connell Street fighting and had positions in Mary's Abbey and Capel Street. Ordered evacuation of Dublin forces for deployment in Wicklow. Arrested, Baggot Street Bridge, Dublin, 27 July 1922. Imprisoned at Dundalk. WI.

TWOHIG, Richard: AT. Executed at Kilmainham Jail, Dublin, 17 November 1922 for unlawful possession of a revolver. Peter Cassidy, James Fisher and John Gaffney were executed the same day, the first such executions of the CW.

TWOMEY, John: Governor of Portlaoise Prison, later of Curragh.

TWOMEY, Maurice: AT. General Staff Officer. Advised return to the south instead of continuing Four Courts occupation. Active in Munster, and was in AT withdrawal from 'Katmandu' when Lynch was shot. Captured in Dublin 6 April 1923. WI.

UA BUACHALLA, Domhnall: AT. Captured 29 June 1922. Imprisoned in Kilcock, Maynooth and Curragh.

UPNOR: British arms ship intercepted by ATs, forced into Ballycotton Bay and arms removed on to eighty commandeered lorries, 31 March 1922. (*See Barry, Tom;* Warrior)

VIZE, Joseph: PT. Leader in Wexford operations. WI.

WALL, Thomas: AT. KIA in Four Courts 30 June 1922 immediately prior to the garrison's surrender.

WALSH (Dr.): Provided liquid yeast in Galway area in order to maintain supplies of bread when the city was surrounded by ATs.

WALSH, J.J.: PT. TD. Postmaster General from April 1922.

WALSH, Michael: AT. Executed in Athlone 20 January 1923 for unlawful possession of arms and ammunition.

WALSH, Sean: Allegedly executed in Kilkenny 17 March 1923, although official records do not corroborate.

WALSHE, J.: PT. Capt. In action in Limerick and Clare July 1922. KIA 2 October 1922 when ambushed at Mollsheen's Cross, Woodruff, Co. Tipperary 2 October 1922. His driver, Pte Patrick Lawlor, was seriously wounded, five others were wounded, two of whom died later. Walshe's 2 i/c, Lt Good, was taken prisoner. (*See Dalton, Paddy*)

WALSHE, Maurice: AT. Fought with Breen in Tipperary.

WALSHE, Thomas: AT. Leader in Athlone area. Captured after a raid by boat on Quaker Island, Lough Ree. (*See Masterson, B.*)

WARRIOR: Tug boat, commandeered by boarding party who raided *Upnor* 31 March 1922.

WEBB, Gertrude: Member of anti-war delegation June 1922. (*See Gonne, Maud*)

WHELAN, Pax: AT. Col Comdt, later Brig Gen. OC 1 Cork Bde, later Waterford Bde. Executive member 12 June 1922. Signatory of Proclamation of 29 June 1922. Held Waterford in July 1922 by raising cantilever bridge and laying mines. PTs crossed upriver and captured the city. Captured and imprisoned in Mountjoy December 1922. Endured hunger-strike from 13 October 1923. WI.

WHITE, Stephen: AT. Executed in Dublin 19 December 1922 for unlawful possession of arms, bomb equipment and ammunition.

WHITE'S: Public house near Clonakilty where Collins held a meeting before being ambushed at Béal na mBláth.

WICKLOW, Earl of: PT. Senator from 6 December 1922.

WILSON, Henry (Sir): General BA. MP for Co. Down. Craig's security advisor. Shot dead in London 22 June 1922. The incident brought exhortations from the British authorities that the Provisional Government should take action against AT forces.

WOODS, Tony: AT. Capt. Early involvement included procuring of arms and an attempt to capture A.W. Cope. Acquired an armoured car when Cope escaped. Among ATs who dislodged PTs from Birr Barracks. Member of Four Courts garrison. Captured after surrender. Imprisoned in Mountjoy and Newbridge. (*See Gaynor, Sean*)

WORTHINGTON-EVANS, L.: Co-untersigned the Collins-Craig agreement of 30 March 1922 on behalf of British government.

WOULFE, James: PT. Vol. Sean Hales' driver.

WYATT: Lincolnshire Rgt. Involved in Pettigo incident. (*See O'Farrell, Michael*)

WYSE POWER (Mrs): PT. Senator from 6 December 1922. Some of her property was bombed 10 December 1922.

WYSE POWER, Charles: PT. Comdt. Appointed to conduct military courts in Cork October 1922.

YEATS, W.B.: PT. Senator from 6 December 1922. WI.

YOUNG, Henry: AT. Vol 3 Western Div. In action in Sligo area.

YOUNG, John: PT. Capt. With Dublin Guards who landed in Fenit 2 August 1922. Killed in Rathmore, Co. Kerry, 13 October 1922.

CIVIL WAR PRO-TREATY CASUALTIES
ARMY OFFICERS, NCOs AND MEN

Order of details, when given: name, rank, division, and cause, place and date of death. This record is incomplete. A total of 122 officers lost their lives. Deaths from natural causes, suicides and accidental shootings are not listed as casualties.

OFFICERS

ADAIR, Sean, Comdt: KIA 13-7-1922.

ADAMSON, George, Brigadier: GSW, Athlone, Co. Westmeath, 25-4-1922.

BEHAN, Michael, Lt, Dublin Guards: KIA, Co. Kerry, 25-4-1923.

BOYLE, John, Capt, 5 Northern Div: KIA, Dooney Rock, Co. Sligo, 14-11-1922.

BROWN, William, Capt, 12th Bn: KIA.

BURKE, Charles, Lt: GSW at Killurin, Co. Wexford, when Dublin mail train on which he was travelling was attacked by ATs. Died two days later, 28-1-1923.

BURKE, James, Capt, 1 Western Div: KIA, Kilmaine Bridge, Co. Kerry, 27-8-1922.

BYRNE, Terence, Capt: GSW 29-6-1922.

CALLAGHAN, Patrick, Comdt, 3 Western Div: KIA, Dooney Rock, Co. Sligo, 13-7-1922.

CALLAGHAN, Peter, Comdt, 1 Eastern Div: no date or cause of death given.

COLLINS, Michael, Commander-in-Chief: KIA, Béal na mBláth, Co. Cork, 22-8-1922.

COLLISON, John, Comdt, 3 Southern Div: KIA, Cappard House, Tonduff, Abbeyleix, Co. Laois,. 28-7-1922

COLUMB, Patrick, Lt, Coy Adjt, Mullingar Military Barracks: KIA, Mullingar, Co. Westmeath, 27-4-1922.

CONDRON, Luke, Capt, Dublin Guards: KIA 2-7-1922.

COOPER, Clement, Lt, Kerry Command: KIA near Cahirciveen, Co. Kerry, 1-9-1922.

CORCORAN, P., Capt: KIA.

COYLE, Patrick, Capt, Kerry Command: KIA, Brosna, Co. Offaly, 27-1-1923.

CREEGAN, Edward, Lt, Kerry Command: KIA near Kanturk, Co. Cork, 20-8-1922.

CRUISE, George Leo, Lt: GSW near Clonmel, Co. Tipperary, 23-1-1923.

CULLEN, Matthew, Lt, 3 Southern Div: KIA near Tullamore, Co. Offaly, 28-8-1922.

DOCKERY, Michael, Brig Gen: KIA, Sligo, 7-7-1922.

DOWNES, Michael, Lt: 30-9-1922.

DUNNE, Michael, Capt, 19 Bn, Kerry Command: killed in mine explosion, Co. Kerry, 6-2-1923.

GANTLY, Capt: KIA Tonduff, Co. Laois, 28-7-1922 (not officially recorded).

GARDINER, James, 2-Lt, 2 Southern Div: GSW 10-12-1922.

HALES, Sean, Brig Gen: GSW, Dublin, 7-12-1922.

HANRAHAN, Joseph G., Capt: GSW, Limerick, 17-10-1922.

HEALY, T., Capt: Glenamoy, Co. Mayo, 16-9-1922.

HIGGINS, S, Capt: Glenamoy, Co. Mayo, 16-9-1922.

HOULIHAN, Brian, Capt, Dublin Guards: KIA.

HOURIHAN, Jeremiah, Comdt, 1 South Div: GSW, Bantry, Co. Cork, 30-8-1922.

JONES, Thomas, Lt: GSW, 24-3-1923.

KANE, Patrick J., 2-Lt, 5th Bn: KIA 25-3-1924.

KEALY, James, Cadet, 3 Southern Div: KIA, Durrow Bridge, Co. Laois, 2-7-1922.

KEANE, Michael, Lt, 23 Bn: GSW 25-12-1923.

KEHOE, Thomas, Col Comdt, Dublin Guards: landmine explosion, Cork, 16-9-1922.

KELLY, John, 2-Lt, Dublin Guards: KIA 17-2-1923.

KENNEDY, James, Lt, 2 South Div: GSW 23-1-1923.

KENNEDY, Patrick, 2-Lt, 25 Bn: 25-4-1923, from WIA 16-4-1923.

KEOGH, Michael, Capt: no details.

KEOGH, Sean, Lt: GSW 17-12-1922.

KEOGH, Tom, Col Comdt: KIA by mine in a road bridge August 1922.

KILKELLY, Patrick, Capt, APM: died from wounds, Claremorris, Co. Mayo, 18-2-1923.

LEAVY, James, Lt: injuries received in car crash 30-12-1922.

LEE, Thomas Joseph, Lt: KIA, Macroom, Co. Cork, 27-8-1922.

LEHANE, Donald, Capt, 1 Western Div: KIA, Killorglin, Co. Kerry, 27-9-1922.

MANDERVILLE, Thomas A., Col Comdt: died from wounds 28-6-1922.

McCORMACK, Sean, Lt: KIA, Glasson, Athlone, Co. Westmeath, 25-8-1922.

McCURTAIN, Austin, Col Comdt, 3 Southern Div: KIA, Tonduff, Abbeyleix, Co. Laois, 28-7-1922.

McDARAGH, John Francis, 2-Lt, Air Corps: result of aeroplane crash, 26-6-1923.

McDERMOTT, Patrick, Lt, 3 West Div: GSW 2-7-1922.

McDONAGH, John Francis, 2-Lt: result of aeroplane crash, 26-6-1923.

McEVOY, L.: no details.

McGARRITY, Peter, Brig, MP: GSW, Dublin, 8-8-1922.

McLOUGHLIN, J., Lt: Gowel, Co. Leitrim, 1-6-1922.

McMAHON, Lt: KIA.

McQUAID, Eugene, Lt: died from wounds 26-2-1923.

MOLONEY, Thomas J., Comdt, Air Corps: result of aeroplane crash, 22-9-1925.

MORAN, P., Lt: Ballina, Co. Mayo, 18-8-22.

MORGAN, Capt: KIA, Co. Kerry.

NAUGHTON, Michael, Capt: died from wounds 28-6-1922.

NEVIN, Timothy, Lt, Air Corps: result of aeroplane crash, 24-1-1924.

NOLAN, Sean, Comdt, unattached: KIA, Navan, Co. Meath, 5-7-1922.

O'CONNOR, Thomas, Brig, Kerry No 1 Bde: KIA, Kenmare, Co. Kerry, 9-9-1922.

O'SHEA, Timothy, Capt, 9 Bn: KIA, Gunane, 5-3-1923.

PEARSON, Capt: KIA, Co. Kerry.

PENDER, Matthew, Cadet, 50 Bn: KIA, Ferns, Co. Wexford, 3-7-1922.

POLLARD, Patrick, Capt, 2 Southern Div: from WIA, 2-6-1923.

POWER, Capt: KIA, Bruree, Co. Limerick.

PRENDERVILLE, Timothy Joseph, 2-Lt, Air Corps: result of aeroplane crash, 21-9-1926.

REDDINGTON, Thomas, Brig: Carriglass, 9-9-1922.

REDMOND, Ignatius (Nacey), Lt: GSW, 'The Kiln', Bunclody, Co. Wexford, 2-11-1922.

RING, J, Brig: Banniconlan 14-9-1922.

RYAN, James: died from wounds 15-4-1923.

SKELLY, Capt: Boyle, Co Roscommon, 2-7-1922.

SKELLY, Michael J, Comdt: Swinford, Co. Mayo, 21-8-1922.

SLATTERY, Thomas, Lt, Kerry Command: KIA, Scartnaglen, Co. Kerry, 11-2-1923.

STAPLETON, Edward, Capt, 19 Bn: killed in mine explosion, Co. Kerry, 6-3-1923.

SWIFT, Michael, Lt: Clooncastle, 12-8-1922.

THORNTON, Hugh, Capt, 2 Eastern Div: killed in mine explosion, 27-8-1922.

WALSH, Thomas: KIA.

WALSHE, J., 2 Southern Div: KIA, 2-10-1922.

WALSHE, Michael Joseph, Brig, Mayo Bde: KIA, Westport, Co. Mayo, 24-11-1922.

YOUNG, John, Capt, Dublin Guards: KIA, Rathmore, Co. Kerry, 13-10-1922.

NCOs AND MEN

ACTON, Patrick (Pte): KIA, Clonagheen, Co. Kerry.

AHEARNE, Michael (Vol): from WIA, Mercy Hospital, Cork.

ALLEN, Ernest (Pte): DOW received in City Hall, Mercier Hospice.

ALLISON, Patrick (Pte): KIA, Graney, Co. Kildare.

ANDERSON, Norman.

ANDERSON, Patrick.

ARGUE, John.

AYLWARD, John (Pte): from WIA, Richmond Hospital, New Ross, Co. Wexford.

AYLWARD, Richard (Pte): GSW, Cork.

BAILEY, Michael (Pte): KIA, Naas Road, 19-10-1922.

BAKER, Michael (Cpl): GSW, St Michael's Hospital, Dun Laoghaire, 22-3-1923.

BALFE, Frank (Sgt): GSW, Boyle, Co. Roscommon, 8-7-1922.

BANNON, Michael (Vol): from WIA, Tubbercurry, Co. Sligo, 25-8-1922.

BARRY, George: explosion, October 1921.

BARRY, Robert (Pte): KIA, 4-8-1922, Kilmallock, Co. Limerick.

BEATTY, John (Vol): KIA, Co. Kerry, August 1922.

BEHAN, Michael (Pte): KIA, Cork, 2-9-1922.

BEHAN, Peter (Pte): KIA, Ferrycarrig, Co. Wexford, 22-10-1922.

BEIRNE, James (Vol): ambushed outside Sligo jail, 3-7-1922.

BERGIN, Joachim (Vol): KIA, Woodroof, Co. Tipperary, 16-8-1922.

BERGIN, Joseph (Pte): discovered dead, Milltown, Co. Kildare, 14-12-1923.

BLACKHALL, James (Vol): Swinford Hospital, Co. Mayo, 10-2-1923.

BLANEY, John (Pte): KIA, Ferbane, Co. Offaly, 5-7-1922.

BRABAZON, James (Pte): from WIA, Clogheen, Co. Tipperary, 6-5-1923.

BRADY, Patrick (Vol): KIA, 18-9-1922.

BRAY, Patrick (Vol): KIA, Ennis, Co. Clare, 20-10-1923 [sic].

BRENNAN, Dan (Pte): GSW, Ballast Office, Dublin, 30-6-1922.

BROWN, Michael (Pte): KIA, Windgap, Co. Tipperary, 15-3-1923.

BROWN, Rick J. (Vol): KIA, Woodroof, Co. Tipperary, 2-10-1922.

BROWN, Thomas (Pte): from WIA, 20-10-1922.

BROWN, Thomas (Pte).

BURKE, James (Pte): from WIA, Cashel, Co. Tipperary, 22-10-1922.

BYRNE (Vol): KIA, Fenit, Co. Kerry, 2-8-1922.

BYRNE, Edward (Pte): KIA, Graney, Co. Kildare, 24-10-1922.

BYRNE, James: 14-10-1922.

BYRNE, Patrick (Pte): KIA, Dunmanway, Co. Cork, 5-10-1922.

BYRNE, Patrick (Sgt): KIA, Cremlin, Monegal, Co. Tipperary, 3-3-1923.

BYRNE, Peter (Sgt): KIA, Buttevant, Co. Cork, 28-10-1922.

CADDIGAN, John (Pte): from WIA, Co. Kerry, 2-11-1922.

CADOGAN (Vol): KIA, Co. Kerry.

CAFFREY, James (Pte): KIA, Fermoy, Co. Cork, 6-1-1923.

CALLAGHAN, Andrew (Pte): GSW, St Bricin's Hospital, Dublin, 20-2-1923.

CAMPION, Michael (Pte): KIA, Killurin, Co. Wexford, 27-7-1922.

CANTWELL, John (Pte): KIA, Riverstown, Clonmel, Co. Tipperary, 24-8-1922.

CANTY, Stephen (Pte): GSW, Ennis, Co. Clare, 21-4-1923.

CAREY, Patrick (Vol): KIA, Bruff, Co. Limerick, 22-7-1922.

CARSON, William D. (Cpl): KIA, Tralee, Co. Kerry, 3-8-1922.

CARTER, John (Pte): KIA, Leenane, Co. Galway, 3-12-1922.

CARTER, John (Sgt): Mayo, 3-12-1922.

CARTY, John (SM): from WIA, Renmore Hospital, Headford, Co. Galway, 9-4-1923.

CASEY, Michael (Vol): from WIA, Rathmore, Co. Kerry, 26-11-1922.

CASSERLY, Joseph (Pte): KIA, Cork, 9-12-1922.

CLARKE, James (Vol): KIA, Powelsborough, Co. Sligo, 30-11-1922.

CLOHERTY, John (Pte): KIA, Tralee, Co. Kerry, 21-8-1922.

COCHRANE, Edward (Cpl): GSW, Amiens St Station, Dublin, 8-8-1922.

COLLINS, William (Cpl): KIA, Srahmore, Co. Mayo, 19-2-1923.

COMBER, Patrick (Pte): KIA, Emly, Co. Tipperary, 23-8-1922.

COMERFORD, Gerald: Brosna, Nenagh, Co. Tipperary, 9-3-1923.

CRONIN, William (Pte): from WIA, Bantry Hospital, Co. Cork, 14-11-1922.

CONNEELY, Thomas (Vol): KIA, Clifden, Co. Galway, October 1922.

CONNOLLY, Thomas (Pte): KIA, Limerick, 29-12-1922.

CONNORS (Vol): KIA, Co. Kerry.

CONROY, Patrick (Pte): KIA, Blennerville, Co. Kerry, 4-11-1922.

CONROY, William (Pte): KIA, Kilmallock, Co. Limerick, 20-7-1922.

CONWAY, Ralph (Pte): explosion, Macroom, Co. Cork, 16-9-1922.

CONWAY, Thomas (Pte): KIA, Cork, 1-9-1922.

COONAN, John (Pte): KIA, Glen of Aherlow, Co. Tipperary, 12-10-1922.

COPELAND, George (Sgt): KIA, Sneem, Co. Kerry, 27-3-1923.

CORCORAN, John (Cpl): KIA, Co. Kerry, 21-10-1922.

CORCORAN, Patrick (Pte): from WIA, Cork, 20-8-1922.

COSTELLOE, Michael (Vol): KIA, Waterford, 18-7-1922.

COTTLE, Albert (Sgt): landmine explosion, Watergrass Hill, Co. Kerry, 13-8-1922.

COYLE, Patrick (Pte): KIA, Castlebar, Co. Mayo, 7-3-1923.

CRABBE, Edward (Sgt Maj): KIA, Erris, Co. Mayo, 16-9-1922.

CRAMPTON, Frank (Pte): KIA, railway station (location unknown), 3-11-1922.

CRAWFORD, Samuel (Pte): Crosshaven, Co. Cork, 24-12-1922.

CRIBBIN, John (Cpl): KIA, Co. Kerry, 25-4-1923.

CUMMINS, Patrick (Vol): GSW, Limerick, 16-11-1922.

CURLEY, John (Vol): KIA, Rochestown, Co. Cork, 9-8-1922.

DALY, M. (Sgt): KIA, Co. Kerry.

DALY, Martin J. (Sgt): KIA, Ballybay, 1-4-1923.

DEASY, John (Pte): KIA, Newport, Co. Mayo, 28-7-1922.

DENNEHY, Daniel (Pte): KIA, 31-10-1922.

DEVOY, John (Sgt): St Vincent's Hospital, Dublin (from WIA at Dundalk, Co. Louth), 20-11-1922.

DIVINEY, Stephen (Pte): GSW, Athenry, Co. Galway, 1-10-1922.

DOHERTY, William (Pte): Claremorris, Co. Mayo, 21-8-1922.

DOLAN, Joseph (Pte): Drumshanbo, Co. Leitrim, 6-9-1922.

DONNELLY, Owen (Pte): explosion, Dundalk Barracks, 14-8-1922.

DONOGHOE, Patrick (Pte): Curragh Hospital, Co. Kildare (from WIA on 19-7-1922), 19-9-1923.

DOYLE, Patrick (Pte): KIA, Crooksling, Co. Dublin, 7-7-1922.

DUFFY, James (Vol): KIA, Castlebar, Co. Mayo, 13-8-1922.

FALLEY, C. (Vol): KIA, Ballyhaunis, Co. Mayo, 6-9-1922.

FARRELL, Michael (Cpl): KIA, Tralee, Co. Kerry, 3-8-1922.

FARRELL, John (Sgt): KIA, Dooney Rock, Co. Sligo, 13-7-1922.

FERGUSON, Matthew (Pte): Killarney Hospital, Co. Kerry (from WIA at Rathmore), 17-12-1922.

FINNEGAN, Michael (Sgt): KIA, Clonmel, Co. Tipperary, 22-8-1922.

FINNEGAN, Michael (Pte): St Bricin's Hospital, Dublin (from WIA at Claremorris, Co. Mayo), 5-1-1924.

FITZGERALD, Cecil (Pte): Killarney, Co. Kerry, 17-8-1922.

FITZGERALD, Edward (Pte): Ballinamuck, Co. Longford, 22-3-1923.

FITZGERALD, John (Pte): GSW, Monaghan, 20-12-1923.

FITZGERALD, Patrick (Pte): Granby Rd, Dublin, 22-12-1922.

FITZSIMONS, John (Sgt): 5-7-1922.

FOGARTY, Dan (Cpl): KIA, Woodroof, Co. Tipperary, 16-8-1922.

FOLEY, P. (Vol): KIA, Woodhouse, Co. Tipperary, 22-10-1922.

FORAN, John (Pte): Mater Hospital, Dublin (from GSW received 22-7-1922), 25-12-1922.

FOSTER, Joseph (Pte): KIA, Nine Mile House, Tipperary, 18-1-1923.

FURLONG, John (Pte): Ballyduff, 14-7-1922. May be same as below.

FURLONG, John (Sgt): KIA, Ballyduff, Thurles, Co. Tipperary, 14-7-1922. May be same as above.

GAFFNEY, Sean (Pte): Mountjoy Prison (shot by prisoner trying to escape), 10-10-1922.

GALLAGHER, Edward (Pte): KIA, 4-5-1923.

GALLAGHER, James (Pte): from WIA, Mountjoy Prison, 11-10-1922.

GALLAGHER, Thomas (Pte): KIA while attending wounded, Ballaneen, Co. Kerry, 4-11-1922.

GALVIN, Laurence (Pte): GSW, 14-12-1922.

GALVIN, M. (Vol): KIA, Co. Kerry.

GALVIN, Michael (Pte): killed by trap mine, Knocknagashel, Co. Kerry, 6-3-1923.

GANNON, John (Pte): KIA, Derryfore, Ballyroan, Co. Laois, 25-4-1923.

GERAGHTY, Patrick J. (Sgt): KIA, Co. Limerick, 17-1-1923. May be same as below.

GERAGHTY, Patrick Joseph (Pte): KIA, Kilfeekhill, Co. Limerick, 17-1-1923. May be same as above.

GETHINGS, Edward (Vol): KIA, Grange, Dundrum, Co. Tipperary, 7-8-1922.

GILCHRIST, Joseph (Pte): 13-10-1922.

GILES, Charles (Pte): Drogheda, Co. Louth, 8-12-1922.

GILLANDERS, T. (Vol): GSW, Monaghan, 18-8-1922.

GILLESPIE, Fred (Sgt): KIA, Tralee, Co. Kerry, 3-8-1922.

GILLIGAN (Vol): KIA, Co. Kerry.

GILSENAN, Peter (Pte): GSW from sniper, Carrick-on-Suir, Co. Tipperary, 9-12-1922.

GOGGIN (Vol): KIA, Co. Kerry.

GORMAN, George (Sgt): GSW, St Bricin's Hospital, Dublin, 18-1-1923.

GORMAN, Edward (Sgt): GSW, Adamstown, Co. Wexford, 24-3-1923.

GRACE, Thomas (Vol): KIA, Linduff, 29-7-1922.

GRAHAN, Christopher (Pte): GSW, St Vincent's Hospital, Dublin, 27-11-1922.

GUINAN, James (Pte): GSW, Bushfield Park, Nenagh, Co. Tipperary, 22-9-1922.

GUNNING, John (Pte): from WIA, 1-3-1923.

HANLEY, Peter (Pte): KIA, Limerick, July 1922.

HANLY, J. (Sgt): Cuckoo Hill, Cahir, Co. Tipperary, 17-9-1922.

HANNAN (Vol): KIA, Co. Kerry.

HANNIFFY, Timothy (Vol): KIA, Renmore Hospital, Galway, 20-7-1922.

HARDING, Patrick (Pte): KIA while aiding wounded comrade under Red Cross flag, Tralee, Co. Kerry, 3-8-1922.

HARTIGAN, Thomas (Vol): KIA, Ballinasloe, Co. Galway, 19-7-1922.

HAYES, Alfred (Vol): KIA, Glasson, Athlone, Co. Westmeath, 22-8-1922.

HEALY, William (Pte): KIA, Cahirciveen, Co. Kerry, 5-3-1923.

HICKEY, Andrew (Pte): KIA, Coolcross, Caherly, Co. Limerick, 18-7-1922.

HOGAN, Peter (Pte): KIA, 16-11-1922.

HOGAN, Michael: from WIA, Castlebar Infirmary, Co. Mayo, 31-8-1923.

HOGAN, Andrew (Pte): GSW, Kilkenny, 7-11-1922.

HOGAN, Thomas (Pte): KIA, Dublin, 13-6-1922.

HOGAN, William (Pte): KIA, Silvermines, Co. Tipperary, 3-1-1923.

HOWLETT, John: KIA, 11-9-1922.

HOWLETT, William (Vol): KIA, Campile, Co. Wexford, 20-8-1922.

HUNT, James (Pte): from WIA, Graney, Co. Kildare, 24-12-1922.

INGHAM, Thomas (Sgt): Bonnyconlon, 14-8-1922.

JOYCE, William (Pte): KIA, Kilmulkin, Co. Offaly, 2-12-1922.

KAVANAGH (Vol): KIA, Co. Kerry.

KEANE, Terence (Cpl): from wounds received while escaping from ATs, Clonaslee, Co. Laois, 17-9-1922.

KEANE, Thomas (Sgt): KIA, Headford Barracks, Co. Galway, 8-4-1923.

KEARNES, Charles (Pte): GSW, Imperial Hotel, Cork, 9-10-1922. Discrepancies in sources as to cause.

KEARNES, James (Pte): Mountjoy Prison, Dublin, 10-11-1922.

KEARNES, Richard (Pte): GSW, Watergrass Hill, Co. Cork, 5-9-1922.

KEARNS, Christopher (Pte): KIA, Ferrycarrig, Co. Wexford.

KEENAN, John, (Capt, Dublin Guards): KIA, 6-11-1922.

KELLY (Cpl): KIA, Redmondstown, Clonmel, Co. Tipperary, 9-8-1922.

KELLY, J. (Vol): KIA, Co. Kerry.

KELLY, Patrick (Pte): Kilrush, Co. Clare, 22-8-1922.

KENNEDY, James (Pte): KIA, Dublin, 22-9-1922.

KENNEDY, John (Sgt): KIA, Dublin, 8-7-1922.

KENNY, John (Pte): KIA, Tralee, Co. Kerry, 3-8-1922.

KENNY, Peter (Pte): KIA, Blessington, Co. Wicklow, 24-8-1922.

KENERICK, James (Pte): from WIA, 30-7-1923.

KEOGH, Patrick (Cpl): KIA, Nenagh, Co. Tipperary, 17-9-1922.

KILMURRAY-McMAHON (Cadet): KIA.

LARKIN, Thomas (Pte): KIA, Tralee, Co. Kerry, 3-8-1922.

LAVERY (Sgt): 20-10-1922.

LEWIS, John (Pte): KIA, Dublin, 30-6-1922.

LOFTUS, Elmer (Cpl): GSW, New Ross, Co. Wexford, 10-4-1923.

LOONEY, John (Pte): 24-9-1923.

LYDEN, John (Pte): KIA, Tralee, Co. Kerry, 11-9-1922.

LYDON, John (Sgt): KIA, Tralee, Co. Kerry, 18-8-1922.

LYNCH, Patrick (Pte): from WIA, Curragh Hospital, Co. Kildare, 12-1-1923.

LYNCH, T. (Vol): KIA, Co. Kerry.

LYNCH (Vol): KIA, Co. Kerry.

LYNN, John (Pte): KIA, Boher Cross, Nenagh, Co. Tipperary, 17-9-1922.

LYONS, James (Pte): from WIA, Renmore Hospital, Galway, 9-4-1923.

LYONS, John (Pte): died after operation, 11-2-1923.

MADDEN, James (Pte): KIA, Co. Cork, 8-8-1922.

MADDEN, John (Pte).

MAGEE, Michael (Pte): KIA, Castleisland, Co. Kerry, 11-9-1922.

MAGUIRE, Patrick (Pte): KIA, Cork, 8-8-1922.

MAHONEY, Daniel (Sgt): KIA, Bruree, Co. Limerick, 28-7-1922.

MAHONEY, Michael (Pte): Mercy Hospital, Cork (from WIA at Macroom, Co. Cork), 22-10-1922.

MAHONEY, J. (SM): KIA, Millstreet, Co. Cork, 2-1-1923.

MALONEY, James (Vol): KIA, Bedford, Co. Kerry, 16-9-1922.

MALONEY, Martin (Vol): GSW, Limerick, 15-9-1922.

MANIFOLD, Thomas (CSgt): GSW, Killaloe, Co. Clare, 18-11-1922.

MANNING, Thomas (Pte): KIA, Ballimackeera, Co. Cork, 16-9-1922.

MARTIN, John (Vol): KIA, Kerry, December 1922.

MARTIN, John (Pte): KIA, Co. Cork, 8-8-1922.

MARTIN, Thomas (Pte): St Vincent's Hospital, Dublin (from WIA 16-1-1923 at Kells, Co. Meath), 16-1-1923.

MARUM, James (Sgt): KIA, Charleville, Co. Cork, 23-10-1922.

McBREEN, Patrick (Pte): KIA, Dundalk, Co. Louth, 15-9-1922.

McCABE (Vol): KIA, Co. Kerry.

McCABE, Patrick (Sgt): GSW, Monaghan, 5-9-1922.

McCAFFREY, Charles (Pte): GSW, Fermoy, Co. Cork, 8-12-1922.

McCAFFREY, Hugh (Vol): Tubbercurry, Co. Sligo.

McCANN, James (Pte): KIA, Cork, 14-9-1922.

McCANN, Thomas (SM): mine explosion, Cork, 24-11-1922.

McCARTHY, Morris (Vol): KIA, Bruff Barracks, Co. Limerick, 4-8-1922.

McCARTHY, Timothy (Pte): KIA, 14-4-1923.

McCARTNEY, John (Vol): KIA, Cavan, 8-5-1922.

McCARTNEY, Peter (Pte): Baggot St Hospital, Dublin, 4-11-1922.

McCLOSKEY, Robert (Pte): GSW, 16-7-1922.

McCURLEY, Joseph (Pte): KIA, High St, Dublin, 23-2-1923.

McDONNELL, James (Pte): GSW, St Bricin's Hospital, Dublin, 29-10-1923.

McDONNELL, Jeremiah (Vol): GSW, Clonakilty, Co. Cork, 18-8-1922.

McDONNELL, Michael (Pte): KIA, Clonakilty, Co. Cork, 26-12-1922.

McELLIN, Patrick (Pte): KIA, Shanmore, Newport, Co. Mayo, 23-11-1922.

McEVOY, Edward (Pte): KIA, Ferrycarrig, Co. Wexford, 9-8-1922.

McEVOY, Thomas (Pte): Graney, Co. Kildare, 1-1-1923.

McGARRY, Patrick (Pte): KIA, Dublin, 29-6-1922.

McGEE (Vol): KIA, Co. Kerry.

McGIVENY, John (Sgt): GSW, Castlemount, Dundalk, 17-10-1922.

McGLYNN, Christopher (Vol): KIA, Abbeyleix, Co. Laois, 7-7-1922.

McGOVERN, James (Pte): KIA, Castlemaine, Co. Kerry, 23-1-1923.

McGRADE, Michael (Pte): KIA, Claremorris, Co. Mayo, 29-11-1922.

McGRANE, Christopher (Pte): KIA, Barraduff, Co. Kerry, 7-3-1923.

McGRATH, William (Vol): KIA, Glen of Aherlow, Co. Tipperary, 18-2-1923.

McGUINNESS, Donald (Cpl): Dublin, 15-3-1923.

McINTYRE, John (Pte): KIA, Tipperary, 30-7-1922.

McKINLEY, Charles (Pte): KIA, Drumkeane, Letterkenny, Co. Donegal, 10-7-1922.

McLOUGHLIN, H. (Vol): KIA, Castlegregory, Co. Kerry, 29-11-1922.

McMAHON, Thomas (Pte): KIA, Enniscorthy, Co. Wexford, 24-7-1922.

McMAHON, Timothy (Vol): bomb explosion, Tralee, Co. Kerry, August 1922.

McMANUS, Michael (Vol): Dowra Barracks, 6-1-1922.

McNAMARA, Matthew (Cpl): KIA, Meelick Tower, Co. Mayo, 10-10-1922.

McNEICE, William (Pte): KIA, Cork, 7-12-1922.

McWILLIAM, Patrick (Pte): KIA, Dundalk, Co. Louth, 15-9-1922.

MEEHAN, Patrick (Vol): 30-7-1922.

MINOGUE, Denis (Sgt): KIA, 14-2-1923.

MOLONEY, John (Pte): KIA, 16-9-1922.

MOLONEY, Martin (Pte): Limerick, 15-9-1922.

MOLLOY, Michael (Pte): GSW, Tallaght Camp, Co. Dublin, 9-6-1923.

MOONEY, Thomas (Pte): GSW, 13-12-1922.

MOORE, Thomas (Pte): Castlebar, Co. Mayo, 17-8-1922.

MORAN, Joseph (Pte): KIA, Leixlip, Co. Kildare, 1-12-1922.

MORAN, Thomas (Pte): St Bricin's Hospital, Dublin (from WIA at Castleisland, Co. Kerry), 14-2-1923.

MORGAN (Cpl): KIA, Co. Kerry.

MORRISSEY, Edward (Pte): from injuries, 24-2-1925.

MOYLES, John (Pte): Ballyhaunis, Co. Mayo, 5-12-1922.

MULHALL (Vol): KIA, Co. Kerry.

MULLIGAN, John (Sgt): GSW, Longford, 8-5-1922.

MULLIN (Vol): KIA, Co. Kerry.

MULLINS, Michael (Pte): KIA, Ballydavis, Co. Laois, 16-1-1923.

MULVANNEY, Edward (Pte): KIA, Cork, 28-9-1922.

MURPHY (Vol): KIA, Co. Kerry.

MURPHY, James (Pte): KIA, 24-10-1922.

MURPHY, John (Pte): KIA, Co. Kerry, 20-9-1922.

MURPHY, Patrick (Pte): KIA, Newport, Co. Mayo, 24-11-1922.

MURPHY, Thomas (Pte): KIA, Wellington Barracks, Dublin, 8-11-1922.

MURPHY, Thomas (Pte): KIA, Emly Barracks, Co. Tipperary, 21-7-1922.

MURPHY, Timothy (Pte): KIA, Kilmallock, Co. Limerick, 16-7-1922.

MURPHY, William (Sgt): KIA, Co. Kerry, 16-9-1922.

MURRAY, Edward (Pte): KIA, 4-5-1923.

MURRAY, James (Pte): KIA, Castledermot, Co. Kildare, 24-11-1922.

MURRAY, John (Vol): GSW, Athlone, Co. Westmeath, 10-10-1922.

MURRAY, Thomas (SM): Lismore, Co. Waterford, 27-9-1922.

NAGLE (Vol): KIA, Co. Kerry.

NEARY, Frank (Sgt): KIA, Swinford, Co. Mayo, 2-9-1922.

NEVIN, William (Pte): KIA, Passage West, Co. Cork, 8-8-1922.

NEWCOMBER, William (Pte): KIA, Athlone, Co. Westmeath, 6-3-1923.

NOLAN, James (Pte): Mercy Hospital, Cork (from WIA at Millstreet, Co. Cork), 5-2-1923.

NOLAN, John (Pte): Dublin, 16-3-1923.

NOLAN, Thomas (Pte): KIA, Ballymakeera, Co. Cork, 5-12-1922.

NOLAN, Thomas (Pte): KIA, Ballymakeera, Co. Cork, 5-12-1922.

NOONE, Edward (Pte): KIA, Cork, 28-9-1922.

NOONE, Edward (Sgt): KIA, Rathmore, Co. Kerry, 28-9-1922.

NUGENT, Patrick (Pte): KIA, Kilmihill, Co. Limerick, 16-1-1923.

O'BRIEN, Bernard (Vol): KIA, Ballinspittle, Kinsale, Co. Cork, 28-3-1923.

O'BRIEN, Patrick (Pte): GSW, Amiens St, Dublin, 27-9-1922.

O'CALLAGHAN (Sgt): KIA, Co. Kerry.

O'CONNOR (Vol): KIA, Co. Kerry.

O'CONNOR, Denis (Vol): KIA, Killorglin, Co. Kerry, 29-9-1922.

O'CONNOR, Gerald (Pte): KIA, Gort, Co. Galway, 8-7-1922.

O'CONNOR, J. (Vol): Moylough, 5-11-1922.

O'CONNOR, James (Pte): KIA, Tralee, Co. Kerry, 3-8-1922.

O'CONNOR, John (Vol): KIA, Kenmare, Co. Kerry, 9-9-1922.

O'CONNOR, L. (Vol): KIA, Co. Kerry.

O'CONNOR, Lee (Vol): mine explosion, Knocknagoshel, Co. Kerry, 6-3-1923.

O'CONNOR, P.: KIA, Co. Kerry.

O'CONNOR, Patrick (Sgt): KIA, 3-3-1923.

O'CONNOR, Patrick (Pte): KIA, Ferrycarrig, Co. Wexford, 21-10-1922.

O'DARE, Joseph (Pte): St Bricin's Hospital, Dublin (from WIA August 1922 at Millstreet, Co. Cork), 19-4-1923.

O'DONNELL, M. (Pte): Clonakilty, Co. Cork, 28-12-1922.

O'DONOGHUE, J. (Sgt): KIA, Cahirciveen, Co. Kerry, 4-9-1922.

O'DONOVAN, Denis (Vol): KIA, Inchigeela, Co. Cork, 2-10-1922.

O'HEHIR, Michael (Pte): KIA, Dublin, 28-7-1922.

O'KEEFE, Bart (Pte): GSW, Limerick Infirmary, 20-6-1923.

O'LEARY, John (Vol): KIA, Macroom, Co. Cork, 2-9-1922.

O'LOUGHLIN, Martin (Cpl): St Bricin's Hospital, Dublin (from WIA in Clare), 4-4-1923.

O'MEARA, Joseph (Vol): KIA, Killarney, Co. Kerry, 27-8-1922.

O'NEILL, Edward (Sgt): GSW, Naas County Home, Co. Kildare, 20-8-1922.

O'NEILL, James (Pte): KIA, Clash, Co. Kilkenny, 16-4-1923.

O'NEILL, Peter (Pte): 29-10-1923.

O'REILLY (Vol): KIA, Co. Kerry.

O'SHEA (Vol): KIA, Co. Kerry.

O'SHEA, Con (Pte): KIA, 30-9-1922.

O'SHEA, David (Pte): KIA, Nenagh, Co. Tipperary, 27-8-1922.

O'SULLIVAN, Dan (Pte): KIA, 22-10-1922.

O'SULLIVAN, David (Pte): GSW, Cork, 19-9-1922.

O'TOOLE, Christopher (Pte): KIA, Passage West, Co. Cork, 8-8-1922.

PENDER, Matthew (Pte): KIA, Ferns, Co. Wexford, 3-7-1922.

PERRY, Patrick (Pte): KIA, Cork, 8-8-1922.

PHELAN, Laurence (Vol): KIA, Woodhouse, Fethard, Co. Tipperary, 22-10-1922.

POMERROY (Pte): GSW, 19-1-1923.

PURCELL, Michael (Vol): KIA, Co. Kerry, 5-8-1922.

QUAIDE (Vol): KIA, Bedford, Co. Kerry, 10-8-1922.

QUAYNE, Jeremiah (Sgt): KIA, Cahirciveen, Co. Kerry, 5-3-1923.

QUAYNE, John (Vol): KIA, Listowel, Co. Kerry, 12-8-1922.

QUIGLEY, Patrick: KIA, 7-10-1922.

QUINN, Patrick (Pte): KIA, Tralee, Co. Kerry, 3-8-1922.

QUIRKE, John (Vol): KIA, Ballinagaddy, Co. Limerick, 26-7-1922.

QUIRKE, Maurice (Pte): KIA, Killurin, Enniscorthy, Co. Wexford, 24-7-1922.

RALEIGH, Michael (Pte): GSW, Adare, Co. Limerick, 5-2-1923.

RAWL, Thomas (Cpl): KIA, Glenamoy, 16-9-1922.

REID, Richard (SM): Dublin, 1-7-1922.

REILLY, Patrick (Pte): KIA, Tralee, Co. Kerry, 22-8-1922.

RIORDAN, John (Vol): mine explosion, Carraigaphooka, Macroom, Co. Cork, 16-9-1923.

RICHARDS, Henry (Sgt): GSW, Sligo Courthouse, 29-6-1923.

ROCHE, Cornelius (Vol): KIA, Woodroof, Co. Tipperary, 16-8-1922.

ROCHE, Michael (Sgt): bomb explosion, Tralee, Co. Kerry, 25-8-1922.

ROCK, Michael (Pte): KIA, Cahirciveen, Co. Kerry, 25-1-1923.

RYAN, Michael (Pte): from WIA, Glen of Aherlow, Co. Tipperary, 20-2-1923.

RYAN, John (SM): KIA, Castleconnel, Co. Limerick, 6-1-1923.

RYAN, Michael (Pte): GSW, 20-2-1923.

SEARLES, Edward (Pte): from WIA, 27-9-1922.

SHEEHAN, Patrick (Pte): KIA, Waterville, Co. Kerry, 26-8-1922.

SHERLOCK, Owen (Pte): GSW, Dundalk, Co. Louth, 25-9-1922.

SKEFFINGTON, James (Sgt): KIA, Town Hall, Sligo, 8-11-1922.

SMYTH, Joseph (Vol): KIA, Athboy Barracks, Co. Meath, 12-9-1922.

SMYTH, Patrick (Pte): KIA, 7-7-1922.

SPELLMAN, Harry (Sgt): KIA, Bunnacranagh, 30-3-1923.

STENSON, Thomas (Pte): bomb explosion, Kenmare, Co. Kerry, 1-5-1923.

STEWART, Joseph (Pte): 2-7-1922.

STRINGER, George (Pte): KIA, Taaffe's Bridge, 22-11-1922.

SULLIVAN, Con (Pte): KIA, Ballinagaddy, Limerick, 26-7-1922.

SULLIVAN, Charles (Pte): Newport, Co. Mayo, 28-8-1922.

SULLIVAN, Daniel (Pte): KIA, 22-10-1922.

SUGRUE, D. (Vol): KIA, Co. Kerry.

SWEENEY, Christopher (Pte): KIA, Waterford, 5-1-1923.

SWEENEY, John (Pte): KIA, Dooney Rock, Co. Sligo, 13-7-1922.

TALTY, John (Pte): KIA, Castlegregory, Co. Kerry, 29-12-1922.

TIERNAN, Thomas (Pte): Ballyhaunis, Co. Mayo, 26-8-1922.

TIQUIN, Patrick (Vol): Ratheabbin, Co. Tipperary, 18-9-1922.

TRAVERS, John (Pte): KIA, Youghal, Co. Cork, 15-12-1922.

TRAYNOR, B. (Sgt): Greenore, Co. Louth.

TRAYNOR, Joseph (Pte): Swinford, Co. Mayo, 4-8-1922.

TRAYNOR, Peter (Pte): KIA, 4-11-1922.

UNIACKE, Thomas (Pte): KIA, Carrick-on-Suir, Co. Tipperary, 9-8-1922.

WALSH, Patrick (Vol): KIA, Galway, 8-7-1922.

WALSHE, George (Pte): KIA, 13-6-1922.

WALSHE, J. (Capt): KIA, Mollsheen's Cross, Woodroof, Co. Tipperary, 2-10-1922.

WALSHE, James (Pte): KIA, Four Courts, Dublin, 13-6-1922.

WALSHE, John (Pte): mine explosion, Ballyvolane, Co. Cork, 26-11-1922.

WALSHE, Michael (Pte): KIA, Barnaderg, Co. Galway, 1-9-1922.

WALSHE, Thomas (Sgt): killed in armoured-car crash, Phoenix Park, Dublin, 17-12-1922.

WARDE, Nicholas (Pte): KIA, Co. Cork, 1-9-1922.

WEBB, Samuel (Cpl): KIA, Dalkey, Co. Dublin, 13-11-1922.

WHITE, Patrick (Pte): from WIA, Geashill, Co. Offaly, 18-1-1923.

WILLIAMSON, W. (Pte): KIA, Crosscarberry, 27-11-1922.

WOODS, Michael (Pte): KIA, Ballineen, Co. Cork, 4-11-1922.

WOODS, Austin (Pte): KIA, Sea View, Newport, 24-11-1922.

WOODS (Vol): KIA, Co. Kerry.

YEATES, James (Pte): GSW, Cork, 14-9-1922.

CIVIL WAR ANTI-TREATY CASUALTIES
ALL RANKS

Order of details, when given: name, rank, cause of death, place of death, date of death. This record is incomplete since a total of 918 NCOs and Men lost their lives. Deaths from natural causes, suicides and accidental shootings are not listed as casualties but these do not account fully for the incompleteness of the record.

BANKS, Joe (Vol): KIA, Ballintrillick-Glencar, Co. Sligo, 20-9-1922.

BENNETT, P.: KIA, Glenbower, Co. Tipperary, 3-12-1922.

BENSON, Harry (Capt): KIA, Ballintrillick-Glencar, Co. Sligo, 20-9-1922.

BLANEY, Seamus: died after period of imprisonment, 8-12-1922.

BOLAND, Harry: GSW, St Vincent's Hospital, Dublin, 2-8-1922.

BOLTON, Thomas: from WIA, September 1922.

BONDFIELD, Robert: Clondalkin, Co. Dublin, 30-3-1923.

BOYLAN, Edward: GSW in escape attempt, Cavan Barracks, 25-7-1922.

BRADY, Patrick: KIA, Waterford, 23-7-1922.

BREEN, Martin: KIA, Tipperary, 16-1-1923.

BREHENY, Harry: GSW, Sligo, 16-2-1923.

BRESLIN, Christopher: killed in custody, Cabra Road, Dublin, 30-4-1923.

BRESLIN, Peadar: GSW while attempting to escape, Mountjoy Jail, Dublin, 10-10-1922.

BRUGHA, Cathal: KIA, O'Connell St, Dublin, 5-7-1922.

BUCKLEY, James: KIA, Carraigaphooca, Macroom, Co. Cork, 15-9-1922.

BUCKLEY, Patrick: mine explosion while in PT custody, Ballyseedy Cross, Co. Kerry, 7-3-1923.

BUCKLEY, Stephen: mine explosion when in PT custody, Countess Bridge, Killarney, Co. Kerry, 7-3-1923.

BUCKLEY, William: KIA, Riverstown, Co. Cork, 26-9-1922.

BURNS, Patrick: Cork, 21-8-1922.

BUTLER, E.: KIA, Glenbower, Co. Tipperary, 3-12-1922.

BYRNE, James: KIA, Aungier St, Dublin, 18-8-1922.

CAMPBELL, Joseph: from WIA, 44 Parnell Square, Dublin, 2-5-1922.

CAREY, Harry: after period of imprisonment in the *Argenta* prison vessel, 1922.

CAROLAN, Michael: GSW, Grafton St, Dublin, 28-7-1922.

CASEY, Jeremiah: GSW, Beaufort, Co. Kerry, 20-3-1923.

CASEY, Jerry: KIA, Co. Cork, 5-12-1922.

CLARKE, William: GSW, Parnell St, Dublin, 28-6-1922.

CLIFFORD, Dan: KIA, Killorglin, Co. Kerry, 5-3-1923.

COLE, Sean: Yellow Lane, Whitehall, Drumcondra, Dublin, 26-8-1922.

COLLEY, Alfred: Yellow Lane, Whitehall, Drumcondra, Dublin, 26-8-1922.

CONDON, Michael: GSW, Kilkenny Jail (some sources say Clonmel Town Hall), 19-8-1922.

CONNOLLY, James (Capt): KIA, Finner Camp, Co. Donegal, 29-6-1922.

CONNOLLY, Patrick: KIA, Monk St, Wexford, 7-7-1922.

CONSIDINE, Joe: Jervis St Hospital, Dublin (from WIA at Four Courts), 28-6-1922.

COONEY, Patrick (Capt): KIA, Bantry, Co. Cork, 30-8-1922.

CORCORAN, Nicholas: Tuam, Co. Galway, 24-3-1923.

COSTELLO: KIA, Waterford, 23-7-1922.

COURTNEY, Michael: GSW and mine explosion, Bahaghs, Cahirciveen, Co. Kerry, 12-3-1923.

COX, Liam: KIA, Ladysbridge, Cork, 25-10-1922.

CRAWLEY, Thomas: KIA, Bessbrook, Co. Armagh, 14-6-1922.

CREGAN, Edward: KIA, 1922.

CREGGAN, Patrick: KIA, Bessbrook, Co. Armagh.

CROWLEY, Mick (Lt): KIA, Bantry, Co. Cork, 30-8-1922.

CULL, Michael: KIA, Ballyconnell, Co. Cavan, 1922.

CUMMINS, John: Ballyvoile, Co. Waterford, 6-6-1922.

CUNNINGHAM, Larry (Capt): Lyre, Co. Cork, 15-2-1923.

CURTIS, Bernard: premature mine explosion, Inchicore, Dublin, 26-9-1922.

CUSACK, Sean: KIA, Four Courts, Dublin, 30-6-1922.

DALTON, Paddy: KIA, Mollsheen Cross, Co. Tipperary, 26-10-1922.

DALY, Bernard: Dublin, 25-8-192.

DALY, Daniel: GSW, Tralee, Co. Kerry, 23-1-1923.

DALY, John: mine explosion when in PT custody, Ballyseedy Cross, Co. Kerry, 7-3-1923.

DEASE, George (Vol): KIA, Kealkil, Co. Cork, 8-12-1922.

DEVINS, Seamus (Brig): KIA, Ballintrillick-Glencar, Co. Sligo, 20-9-1922.

DONOGHUE, Daniel: mine explosion when in PT custody, Countess Bridge, Killarney, Co. Kerry, 7-3-1923.

DONOGHUE, Jeremiah: mine explosion when in PT custody, Countess Bridge, Killarney, Co. Kerry, 7-3-1923.

DONOVAN, Dan (Vol): KIA, Timoleague, Co. Cork, 4-10-1922.

DOYLE, John: Waterford, July 1922.

DOYLE, William: from WIA, Ormond Quay, Dublin, 5-7-1922.

DUGGAN, Patrick (Vol): KIA, Glengarriff, Co. Cork, 17-11-1922.

DUNNE, Thomas: GSW, Castledermot, Co. Kildare, 16-6-1922.

DURKAN, John: KIA, Ballymote, Co. Sligo, 13-9-1922.

DWYER, Denis: KIA, Tonduff, Co. Laois, 28-7-1922.

DWYER, Eugene: GSW and mine explosion, Bahaghs, Cahirciveen, Co. Kerry, 12-3-1923.

DWYER, John (Vol): KIA, Kealkil, Co. Cork, 8-12-1922.

EGAN, Paddy: premature mine explosion, Inchicore, Dublin, 26-9-1922.

ENGLISH, Paddy: KIA, Longfordpass, Co. Tipperary, 8-7-1922.

ENGLISH, Theo: KIA, Castle Blake, Cashel, Co. Tipperary, 16-4-1923.

FANNIN, Patrick: died while imprisoned in Mountjoy Jail, Dublin.

FITZGERALD, Eugene: Tralee, Co. Kerry, 16-1-1923.

FLEMING, John: Tralee, Co. Kerry, 28-3-1923.

FURLONG, Michael: KIA, Adamstown, 25-3-1923

GALLAGHER, Hugh: Cavan, 12-12-1922.

GALVIN, Jack: Ballyseedy, Co. Kerry, 30-9-1922.

GILLANDERS, Thomas: KIA, Monaghan, 18-8-1922.

GLEESON, William: GSW, in custody, Cloughjordan Barracks, Co. Tipperary, 2-3-1923.

GLEESON: Curragh Camp, Co. Kildare, 26-1-1923.

GORE, John: shot by British forces, Cushendall, Co. Antrim, 23-6-1922.

GRADY, Frank: Glenbeigh, Co. Kerry, 11-3-1923.

GRAHAM, William: GSW, Leeson St, Dublin, 25-11-1922.

GUILMARTIN, Denis: GSW from British forces, Derry.

HALPENNY, Sean: KIA, Ravensdale, Co. Louth, 8-10-1922.

HANLY, Con: KIA, Ballinard, Co. Tipperary, 18-9-1922.

HANNELLY, Thomas: from WIA, Ballaghadereen, 21-1-1923.

HARKIN, Dan: KIA, Rockhill House, Letterkenny, Co. Donegal, 22-7-1922.

HARRINGTON, William: KIA, Limerick, 8-12-1922.

HARTNETT, Patrick: mine explosion while in PT custody, Ballyseedy Cross, Co. Kerry, 7-3-1923.

HAYES, Jim: KIA, Moyglass, Co. Tipperary, 18-11-1922.

HAYES, Michael (Vol): killed in custody, Upton, Co. Cork, 4-10-1922.

HEFFERNAN, Mick: KIA, Drangan, Co. Tipperary, 8-9-1922.

HEGARTY, Edward: KIA, Newport, Co. Mayo, 27-7-1922.

HENNESSY, Sean: 1922.

HICKEY, Patrick J.: GSW, Portlaoise Prison, Co. Laois, 30-8-1922.

HILL, John: shot by British forces, Cushendall, Co. Antrim, 23-6-1922.

HOGAN, Martin: Grace Park Rd, Drumcondra, Dublin, 21-4-1923.

HOULIHAN, Brendan: Clondalkin, Co. Dublin, 7-10-1922.

HOURICAN, Gerry: KIA, Rochestown, Co. Cork, 9-8-1922.

HOWELL, John (Vol): KIA, Enniskeane, Co. Cork, 4-11-1922.

HUDSON, Joe: KIA, Glasthule, Dun Laoghaire, Co. Dublin, 17-8-1922.

HUGHES, Eamonn: Clondalkin, Co. Dublin, 7-10-1922.

JACKSON, Frank: KIA, Crown Alley, Dublin, 29-6-1922.

KANE, Daniel: KIA, Sally Gap, Co. Wicklow, 22-8-1922.

KEATING, Jeremiah: KIA, Killorglin, Co. Kerry, 2-10-1922.

KEATING, Thomas: KIA, Coolnasmear, Co. Waterford, 19-4-1923.

KEENAN, Owen: KIA, 1922.

KELLY, Denis (Lt): GSW, Kealkil, Co. Cork, 17-4-1923.

KENNEDY, Thomas: KIA, Golden, Co. Tipperary, 28-7-1922.

KENNEFICK, Timothy: KIA, Coachford, Co. Cork, 8-9-1922.

KENNEFICK, Timothy (Capt): 11-12-1922, Coachford, Co. Cork.

KEVINS, John: Gap Cross, Killarney, Co. Kerry, 15-3-1923.

KIELY, Gerard: KIA, Lisvarnan, Glen of Aherlow, Co. Tipperary, February 1923.

KIELY, Jerry: KIA, Glen of Aherlow, Co. Tipperary, 1-4-1923.

KILROY, Edward: KIA, Charlestown, Co. Mayo, 23-12-1922.

KING, George: KIA, Rathmines, Dublin, 1922.

LACEY, Denis (Comdt Gen): KIA, Ballydavid, Glen of Aherlow, Co. Tipperary, 18-2-1923.

LACEY, Denis: KIA, Crory, Ballyboggan, Co. Wexford, 23-3-1923.

LACEY, John: KIA, Crory, Ballyboggan, Co. Wexford, 23-3-1923.

LANGAN, Tom (Vol): KIA, Ballintrillick-Glencar, Co. Sligo, 20-9-1922.

LAWLOR, John: Ballyheigue, Co Kerry, 30-10-1922.

LAWLOR, Francis: Orwell Bridge, Dublin, 28-12-1922.

LEAVY, Joseph: KIA, Mullingar, Co. Westmeath, 27-4-1922.

LINNANE, John: Trineragh, Co. Kerry, 13-4-1923.

LOHAN, John: KIA, Killeen, Co. Galway, 22-9-1922.

LONG, Jeremiah: Cork, 24-9-1922.

LOONEY, Con: KIA, Killorglin, Co. Kerry, 27-9-1922.

LYNCH, Liam: St Joseph's Hospital, Clonmel (from WIA at Newcastle, Co. Tipperary), 10-4-1923.

LYNCH, Patrick: Moyrisk, Co. Kerry, 30-11-1922.

LYONS, Jerry: GSW, Clonmel Military Barracks, Co. Tipperary, 3-4-1923.

LYONS, Timothy ('Aeroplane'): from injuries received while being apprehended, Clashmealcon Cave, Co. Kerry, 18-4-1923.

MACKEY, Tom: GSW, Jervis St Hospital, Dublin, 2-7-1922.

MAGILL, Owen: shot by 'B Specials', Castlecaulfield, Co. Tyrone, 8-5-1922.

MAGUIRE, Thomas: premature mine explosion, Naas Road, Inchicore, Dublin, 26-9-1922.

MALLEY, Charles: KIA, O'Connell St, Dublin, 30-6-1922.

MALONEY, James: KIA, Rochestown, Co. Cork, 9-8-1922.

MALONEY, Murt: 9-4-1923.

MANGAN, Joseph: from WIA, Nenagh General Hospital, Co. Tipperary, 9-3-1923.

MANGAN, Patrick: GSW, Cork Jail, 25-9-1922.

MANNING, M.: GSW, Cork Jail, 24-9-1922.

MANNION, Patrick: Mount St, Dublin, 17-9-1922.

MANNION, Toby: GSW received escaping capture, 1922.

McALINDON: shot by British forces, Co. Down, 20-6-1922.

McALLISTER, Charles: shot by British forces, Glenariff Rock, 24-5-1922.

McALLISTER, Seamus: shot by British forces, Cushendall, 24-5-1922.

McCARTHY, Con (Lt): KIA, Spencerstown, Co. Wexford, 10-1-1923.

McCARTHY, Daniel (Lt): Cork, 20-8-1922.

McCARTHY, Donal (Lt): KIA, Bantry, Co. Cork, 30-8-1922.

McCARTHY, Patrick (Sec Cdr): KIA, Skibbereen, Co. Cork, 10-8-1922.

McCARTHY, Robert: Co. Kerry, 25-3-1923.

McCONVILLE, Anthony: shot by British forces, 6-5-1922.

McDONAGH, Joseph: Mater Hospital, Dublin, after removal from Mountjoy Jail, 25-12-1922.

McDONAGH, Paddy: from GSW, Tipperary Hospital, 19-2-1923.

McEVOY, Sean: Bishop St, Dublin, 12-9-1922.

McGOWAN, John: GSW, St Vincent's Hospital, Dublin, 2-7-1922.

McGRATH, Tom: drowned during capture, Clashmealcon Cave, Co. Kerry, 16-4-1923.

McGUINN, James: KIA, Co. Sligo, 4-2-1923.

McGUINN, Martin: KIA, Curry, Co. Sligo, 13-3-1923.

McKENNA, Patrick (Brig): KIA, Dundalk Barracks, Co. Louth, 14-8-1922.

McKENZIE, Kennedy: KIA, Rochestown, Co. Cork, 9-8-1922.

McKEON, Christy: KIA, Moate, Co. Westmeath, 3-12-1922.

McNALLY, Charlie: shot by 'B Specials', Crannagh, Co. Tyrone, June 1922.

McNEILL, Brian (Comdt): KIA, Ballintrillick-Glencar, Co. Sligo, 20-9-1922.

McNULTY, Patrick: 1922.

McVEIGH, Patrick: shot by British forces, Glenariff Rock, 24-5-1922.

MONKS, John: Clondalkin, Co. Dublin, 29-6-1922.

MONKS, R.: died while imprisoned in Curragh Camp, Co. Kildare, 30-8-1922.

MORIARTY, John: Ballonagh, Co. Kerry, 27-8-1922.

MULCHRONE, Patrick: 1-11-1922.

MULRENNAY, Seamus: GSW while attempting to escape, Derrynacartha, 6-10-1922.

MURPHY, Charles: Stillorgan, Dublin, 2-9-1922.

MURPHY, Patrick: Leemount, Co. Cork, 12-9-1922.

MURPHY, Bertie: Killarney, Co. Kerry, 19-9-1922.

MURPHY, Patrick: KIA, Killorglin, Co. Kerry, 27-9-1922.

MURPHY, Timothy: mine explosion when in PT custody, Countess Bridge, Killarney, Co. Kerry, 7-3-1923.

MURPHY, Dan: Knocknagashel, Co. Kerry, 24-4-1923.

MURRAY, Leo: Stillorgan, Dublin, 2-9-1922.

MURRAY, Peter: KIA, Armagh, 19-6-1922.

NAGLE, George: KIA, Derrynafeena, Co. Kerry, 6-4-1923.

NAUGHTON, Paddy: KIA, Broadford, Co. Limerick, 8-8-1922.

NEARY, Tommy: Castlerea, Co. Roscommon, 2-12-1922.

NEVILLE, Michael: Killester, Dublin, 22-9-1922.

NOLAN, Martin: KIA, Crory, Ballyboggan, Co. Wexford, 23-3-1923.

NOONAN, Richard: 11-10-1922.

O'HALLORAY, Sean: KIA, 1922.

O'BRIEN, William: KIA, Broadford Barracks, Co. Clare, April 1922.

O'BRIEN, Patrick, Comdt: from WIA, Enniscorthy, Co. Wexford, 11-7-1922.

O'BRIEN, John: Cork, 14-9-1922.

O'BRIEN, Albert: GSW, Co. Clare, 10-2-1923.

O'BRIEN, Pat: KIA, Talbot St, Dublin, 23-4-1923.

O'CALLAGHAN, Dan: KIA, Killavullen, Co. Cork, 6-10-1922.

O'CARROLL, Patrick, Lt: KIA, Ballintrillick-Glencar, Co. Sligo, 20-9-1922.

O'CARROLL, Myles: KIA, Myshall, Co. Carlow, 5-12-1922.

O'CONNELL, Michael: mine explosion while in PT custody, Ballyseedy Cross, Co. Kerry, 7-3-1923.

O'CONNOR, Henry: KIA, Ferns, Co. Wexford, 26-4-1922.

O'CONNOR, John: mine explosion while in PT custody, 7-3-1923.

O'CONNOR, John: KIA, Crory, Ballyboggan, Co. Wexford, 23-3-1923.

O'CONNOR, Conway: KIA, Derrynafeena, Co. Kerry, 6-4-1923.

O'DEA, Padraic: KIA, Kilrush, Co. Clare, 15-7-1922.

O'DONNELL, Hugh: KIA, Kilfinnane, 7-12-1922.

O'DONOGHUE, Sean: Dublin Hill, Cork, 28-9-1922.

O'GORMAN, John: KIA, Killadysert, Co. Clare, 11-8-1922.

O'LEARY, Tadhg (Sec Cdr): KIA, Ballineen, Co. Cork, 4-11-1922.

O'LEARY, Thomas: Rathmines Road, Dublin, 23-3-1923.

OLDEN, Christy: from WIA, Rochestown, Co. Cork, 12-8-1922.

O'LOUGHLIN, Peter: 1-8-1922.

O'MAHONEY, John: KIA, Moore St, Dublin, 29-6-1922.

O'MAHONEY, Patrick: KIA, Limerick, 17-7-1922.

O'MEARA, James: KIA, Tipperary, 29-7-1922.

O'NEILL, Michael (A/Comdt): Bandon, Co. Cork, 25-4-1922.

O'RIORDAN, Sean: KIA, Ballingarry, Co. Tipperary, 12-12-1922.

O'SHEA, George: mine explosion while in PT custody, Ballyseedy Cross, Co. Kerry, 7-3-1923.

O'SHEA, Patrick: drowned during capture, Clashmealcon Cave, Co. Kerry, 16-4-1923.

O'SULLIVAN, William: KIA, Cork, 18-7-1922.

O'SULLIVAN, Daniel (Vol): killed in custody, Upton, Co. Cork, 4-10-1922.

O'SULLIVAN, Michael: KIA, Headford, Co. Kerry, 2-11-1922.

O'SULLIVAN, Thomas: Ballineanig, Co. Kerry, 18-2-1923.

O'SULLIVAN, John: KIA, Gleesk, Co. Kerry, 6-3-1923.

O'TOOLE, Seamus: KIA, Myshall, Co. Carlow, 5-12-1922.

PEARSE, Patrick (Vol): killed in custody, Upton, Co. Cork, 4-10-1922.

PHELAN, Patrick: KIA, Tonduff, Co. Laois, 28-7-1922.

PHELAN, Thomas: premature mine explosion, Inchicore, Dublin, 26-9-1922.

POWER, Francis: KIA, Portobello, Dublin, 10-10-1922.

POWER, Francis: KIA, Rathmines Rd, Dublin, 2-11-1922.

POWER, Andrew: died in custody, Kilkenny Prison Hospital, 28-1-1923.

PRENDERGAST: KIA, Dublin, 1922.

QUIRKE, James: KIA, Golden, Co. Tipperary, 28-7-1922.

RADFORD, Bernie: from WIA, Spencerstown, Co Wexford, 10-1-1923.

RIORDAN, Willie: GSW and mine explosion, Bahaghs, Cahirciveen, Co. Kerry, 12-3-1923.

ROCHE, Thomas: 27-9-1922.

ROGERS, Joseph: Clondalkin, Co. Dublin, 7-10-1922.

ROSS, Gibbs (Brig): KIA, Bantry, Co. Cork, 30-8-1922.

RYAN, Joseph: Drumshanbo, Co. Leitrim, 14-11-1922.

RYAN, Matt: KIA, Curreeney, Co. Tipperary, 29-3-1923.

SADLIER, Michael: Cashel Hospital (from WIA at Marlhill), Co. Tipperary, 4-11-1922.

SHEA, Dan: GSW and mine explosion, Bahaghs, Cahirciveen, Co. Kerry, 12-3-1923.

SHEEDY, John: KIA, Curreeney, Co. Tipperary, 29-3-1923.

SHEEHAN, Thomas: from WIA, Sligo, 9-7-1922.

SHEPPARD, Sylvester: KIA, Castledermot, Co. Kildare, 5-7-1922.

SHINNICK, Daniel: KIA, Glencurrane, Co. Cork, 4-9-1922.

SINNOTT, Michael: Currahane, Tralee, Co. Kerry, 13-2-1923.

SOMERS, Eamonn: KIA, Castle Blake, Cashel, Co. Tipperary, 16-4-1923.

SOMERS, William: KIA, Capel St, Dublin, 4-9-1922.

SPAIN, James: Donore Ave, Dublin, 8-11-1922.

SPILLANE, Maurice: KIA, Broadford, Co Limerick, June 1922.

SPILLANE, Maurice: KIA, Enniscorthy, Co. Wexford, 11-7-1922.

SPILLANE, William: KIA, Cork, 30-6-1922.

ST JOHN, James: KIA, Ballingarry, Co. Tipperary, 16-2-1923.

STENSON, Patrick: KIA, Curry, Co. Sligo, 13-3-1923.

STEPHENS, John J.: 2-9-1922.

SUGRUE, John: GSW and mine explosion, Bahaghs, Cahirciveen, Co. Kerry, 12-3-1923.

SULLIVAN, John: KIA, Sammy's Rock, Spa, Co. Kerry, 2-8-1922.

SWEENEY, Laurence: KIA, Castledermot, Co. Kildare, 5-7-1922.

SWEENEY, Michael: KIA, Grafton St, Dublin, 21-4-1922.

SWEENEY, Michael: KIA, Shrone, Co. Kerry, 4-2-1923.

TAYLOR, Seamus: Ballyseedy Wood, Co. Kerry, 14-3-1923.

TIERNEY, James: KIA, Dorset St, Dublin, 17-4-1923.

TOMKINS, Matt: KIA, Parnell St, Dublin, 29-6-1922.

TUMULTY, Patrick: shot by British forces, Co. Down, 20-6-1922.

TWOMEY, Timothy: mine explosion when in PT custody, Ballyseedy Cross, Co. Kerry, 7-3-1923.

WALL, Tom: from WIA, Four Courts, Dublin, 1-7-1922.

WALSH, James: mine explosion while in PT custody, Ballyseedy Cross, Co. Kerry, 7-3-1923.

WALSH, John: from ill-health resulting from imprisonment in Kilkenny, 14-3-1923.

WALSH, W.J.: from WIA, Whitehall, Dublin, 23-3-1923.

WALSH, James: Cordal, Co. Kerry, 27-3-1923.

WARD, Frank: from WIA, Dunamore, Co. Tyrone, 15-4-1922.

WHELAN, Patrick: KIA, Clonaslee, Co. Laois, 1922.

POST-CEASEFIRE

AHERNE, Jack: 1923.

BARRY, Denis: hunger-strike, Newbridge Camp, Co. Kildare, 20-1-1923.

BERGIN, Joseph: Milltown Bridge, Co. Kildare, 15-12-1923.

BOYLE, Niall Plunkett (Comdt): Vallymount, Co. Wicklow, 15-5-1923.

BOYLE, Owen: died in custody, Newbridge Camp, Co. Kildare, 13-11-1923.

BURKE, George: Cork, 22-12-1923.

DOWNEY, Daniel: ill-health due to imprisonment and hunger-strike, Curragh Camp, Co. Kildare, 10-6-1923.

GREEHY, Thomas: mine explosion, 5-5-1923.

HANLON, Charles: Bruree, Co. Limerick.

HEALY, Joseph: GSW, 5-6-1923.

HUMES, Dick: died in custody, Curragh Camp, Co. Kildare, 9-11-1923.

LACEY, Joseph: died as result of hunger-strike, Curragh Camp, Co. Kildare, 24-12-1923.

LANDERS, Edward: died in custody, Ballykinlar Camp, Co. Down, 1923.

LEMASS, Noel: body found on Glencree Mountain, Co. Dublin, 12-10-1923.

MACKEY, Thomas: Fountain, Co. Waterford, 10-5-1923.

McENTEE, Henry: Finglas, Co. Dublin, 1-8-1923.

McGRATH, Michael: GSW in custody, 1923.

MOONEY, James: Mater Hospital, Dublin, (from ill-health due to imprisonment and a fall in Mountjoy), August 1923.

MORAN, James: Glenhest, Co. Mayo, 1923.

MULRENNAN, Pat: Athlone Barracks, 1923.

MURPHY, Patrick: GSW, Granard, Co. Longford, 1923.

MYLES, William: GSW, Curraheen, Co. Kerry, 11-10-1923.

NEARY, Michael: from WIA, St Michael's Hospital, Dun Laoghaire, 24-5-1923.

O'DONOHUE, Frank: GSW, Athlone, 1923.

O'KEEFE, Frank: died in custody, Curragh Camp, Co. Kildare, 1923.

QUINN, Sean F.: 22-5-1923.

RADFORD, Mick (Comdt): GSW, Tomhaggard, Co. Wexford, 21-6-1923.

RYAN, Denis: 4-6-1923 (from WIA 10-1-1923).

SULLIVAN, Andy: died on hunger-strike, Mountjoy, Dublin, 22-11-1923.

TOBIN, Michael: Ballineen, Co. Cork, November 1923.

WHITTY, Joseph: died on hunger-strike, Curragh Camp, Co. Kildare, 2-9-1923.

CIVIL WAR EXECUTIONS

Order of details, when given: name, address, method of trial, place of execution and date.

BAGNALL, Patrick (Fairgreen, Kildare): Committee, Dublin, 19-12-1922.

BARRETT, Richard (Ballineen, Co. Cork): Untried, Mountjoy, Dublin, 8-12-1922.

BOURKE, Martin (Caherlistrane, Co. Galway): Committee, Athlone, 20-1-1923.

BRADY, Terence: GCM, Kilmainham, Dublin, 8-1-1923.

BROSNAN, Michael (Ballyfadora, Tralee, Co. Kerry): Military court, Tralee, 20-1-1923.

BURKE, Frederick (Borrisoleigh, Co. Tipperary): Committee, Roscrea, Co. Tipperary, 15-1-1923.

BURKE, Luke [alias Henry Keenan] (Keady, Co. Armagh): Committee, Mullingar, Co. Westmeath, 14-3-1923.

BYRNE, Joseph (Cruit Croghan, Co. Offaly): Committee, Portlaoise, Co. Laois, 27-1-1923.

CASSIDY, Peter (7 Usher St, Dublin): Military court, Kilmainham, Dublin, 17-11-1922.

CHILDERS, Erskine. Military court, Dublin, 24-11-1922.

CLIFFORD, John (Cahirciveen, Co. Kerry): Military court, Tralee, Co. Kerry, 20-11-1923.

COLLINS, Herbert (Kilkeane, Headford, Co. Galway): Committee, Athlone, 20-11-1923.

CONROY, William: Military court, Birr, Co. Offaly, 26-1-1923.

CREANE, John (Taughmon, Co. Wexford): Committee, Wexford, 13-3-1923.

CUNNANE, Francis (Headford, Co. Galway): Committee, Tuam, Co. Galway, 11-4-1923.

CUNNINGHAM, Patrick (Tullamore, Co. Offaly): Military court, Birr, Co. Offaly, 26-1-1923.

DALY, Charles (Knockane, Co. Kerry): Military court, Drumboe, Co. Donegal, 14-3-1923.

DALY, James (Killarney): Military court, Tralee, Co. Kerry, 20-1-1923.

DOWLING, Leo: GCM, Dublin, 8-1-1923.

ENRIGHT, Daniel (Listowel, Co. Kerry): Military court, Drumboe, Co. Donegal, 14-3-1923.

FARRELLY, Patrick (67 Chancery Lane, Dublin): Military court, Dublin, 30-11-1922.

FERGUSON, Joseph (Greenore, Co. Louth): Committee, Dundalk, Co. Louth, 22-1-1923.

FISHER, James (Eckland St, Dublin): Military court, Kilmainham, Dublin, 17-11-1922.

FITZGERALD, Michael (Youghal, Co. Cork): Committee, Waterford, 25-1-1923.

GAFFNEY, John (3 Usher St, Dublin): Military court, Kilmainham, Dublin, 17-11-1922.

GERAGHTY, Patrick (Rochfortbridge, Mullingar, Co. Westmeath): Committee, Portlaoise, Co. Laois, 27-1-1923.

GIBSON, Thomas: GCM, Portlaoise, Co. Laois, 27-2-1923.

GREANEY, Edward (Ardfert, Co. Kerry): Committee, Tralee, Co. Kerry, 25-4-1923.

GREERY, Michael (Athenry, Co. Galway): Committee, Mullingar, Co. Westmeath, 14-3-1923.

HANLON (or Hannon), James (Ardfert, Co. Kerry): Military court, Tralee, Co. Kerry, 20-1-1923.

HATHAWAY, Reginald (Ardfert, Co. Kerry): Committee, Tralee, Co. Kerry, 25-4-1923.

HEALY, William (Donaghmore, Co. Cork): Unspecified, Cork, 13-3-1923.

HEANEY, Sylvester: GCM, Keogh Barracks, Dublin, 8-1-1923.

HENNESSY, Patrick (Clooney, Ennis, Co. Clare): Committee, Limerick, 20-1-1923.

HOGAN, Patrick (William's St, Wexford): Committee, Wexford, 13-3-1923.

HUGHES, Thomas (Athlone): Committee, Athlone, 20-1-1923.

JOHNSTON, Joseph (Station Rd, Kildare): Committee, Dublin, 19-11-1922.

JOYCE, Stephen (Derrymore, Caherlistrane, Co. Galway): Committee, Athlone, 20-1-1923.

KELLY, Colm (Tullamore, Co. Offaly): Military court, Birr, Co. Offaly, 26-1-1923.

LARKIN, John (Magherafelt, Co. Derry): Military court, Drumboe, Co. Donegal, 14-3-1923.

LENNON, Thomas (Dundalk, Co. Louth): Committee, Dundalk, 22-1-1923.

LILLIS, James (Bagenalstown, Co. Carlow): Military court, Carlow, 15-1-1923.

McINERNY, James (Slieveadra, Ardfert, Co. Kerry): Committee, Tralee, Co. Kerry, 25-4-1923.

McKELVEY, Joseph (Stewartstown, Co. Tyrone): Untried, Mountjoy, Dublin, 8-12-1922.

McKEON, Thomas (Piedmount, Co. Louth): Military court, Dundalk, Co. Louth, 13-1-1923.

McMAHON, Cornelius (Ennis, Co. Clare): Committee, Limerick, 20-1-1923.

McNAMARA, Patrick (Nenagh, Co. Tipperary): Military court, Roscrea, Co. Tipperary, 15-1-1923.

McNULTY, John [alias Murphy, Belleek, Co. Fermanagh] (Currymannon, Co. Louth): Committee, Dundalk, Co. Louth, 13-1-1923.

MAGUIRE, John (Galway): Committee, Tuam, Co. Galway, 11-4-1924.

MANGAN, Patrick (Fairgreen, Kildare): Committee, Dublin, 19-11-1922.

MELIA, James (Dundalk, Co. Louth): Committee, Dundalk, Co. Louth, 22-1-1923.

MELLOWS, Liam (Castletown, Co. Wexford): Untried, Mountjoy, Dublin, 8-12-1922.

MONAGHAN, Michael (Clonmehan, Headford, Co. Galway): Committee, Tuam, Co. Galway 11-4-1923.

MOORE, Brian (Rathbride, Kildare): Committee, Dublin, 19-12-1922.

MOYLAN [or Nolan], Martin (Farmistown, Annadown, Co. Galway): Committee, Tuam, Co. Galway, 11-4-1923.

MURPHY, John (56 Bellview Buildings, Dublin): Military court, Dublin, 20-11-1922.

MURPHY, John (Bishopslough, Co. Kilkenny): Committee, Kilkenny, 29-12-1923.

MURRAY, Charles [or Thomas] (White's Cross, Co. Armagh): Military court, Dundalk, 13-1-1923.

NEWELL, James [or John] (Galway): Committee, Tuam, Co. Galway, 11-4-1924.

NOLAN, Patrick (Rathbride, Co. Kildare): Committee, Dublin, 19-12-1922.

O'CONNOR, James [or Joseph] (Bansha, Co. Tipperary): Committee, Dublin, 19-12-1922.

O'CONNOR, Rory (Monkstown, Co. Dublin): Untried, 8-12-1922.

O'MAHONEY, Patrick (Market St, Ennis, Co. Clare): Committee, Ennis, 26-4-1923.

O'MALLEY, James (Oughterard, Co. Galway): Committee, Tuam, Co. Galway, 11-4-1924.

O'REILLY, Anthony: GCM, Dublin, 8-1-1923.

O'REILLY, Patrick (Youghal, Co. Cork): Military court, Waterford, 25-1-1923.

O'ROURKE, James (1 Upper Gloucester St, Dublin): Committee, Dublin, 13-3-1923.

O'ROURKE, Joseph (Ardrahan, Co. Galway): Tuam, Co. Galway, 13-5-1923.

O'SHEA, Martin (Carrinagreena, Borrisoleigh, Co. Tipperary): Committee, Roscrea, Co. Tipperary, 15-1-1923.

O'SULLIVAN, Timothy (William's St, Listowel, Co. Kerry): Military court, 18-1-1923, Drumboe, Co. Donegal, 14-3-1923.

PARLE, James (Clover Valley, Taughmon, Co. Wexford): Committee, Wexford, 13-3-1923.

PHELAN, John: Committee, Kilkenny, 29-12-1923.

QUINN, Christopher (Turnpike, Ennis, Co. Clare): Military tribunal, Ennis, 2-5-1923.

RUSSELL, Patrick (Summerhill, Borrisoleigh, Co. Tipperary): Committee, Roscrea, Co. Tipperary, 15-1-1923.

SHAUGHNESSY, William (Ennis, Co. Clare): Committee, Ennis, 2-5-1923.

SHEEHY, Laurence: GCM, Dublin, 8-1-1923.

SPOONER, Joseph (36-37 McCaffery's Estate, Dublin): Military court, Dublin, 30-11-1922.

TWOHIG, Richard (1 O'Connor Buildings, Dublin): Military court, Kilmainham, Dublin, 17-11-1922.

WALSH, Michael (Derrymore, Caherlistrane, Co. Galway): Committee, Athlone, 20-1-1923.

WHITE, Stephen (Abbey St, Kildare): Committee, Dublin, 19-11-1922.

WINSLEY, Bernard: Cork County Prison, September 1922.

226

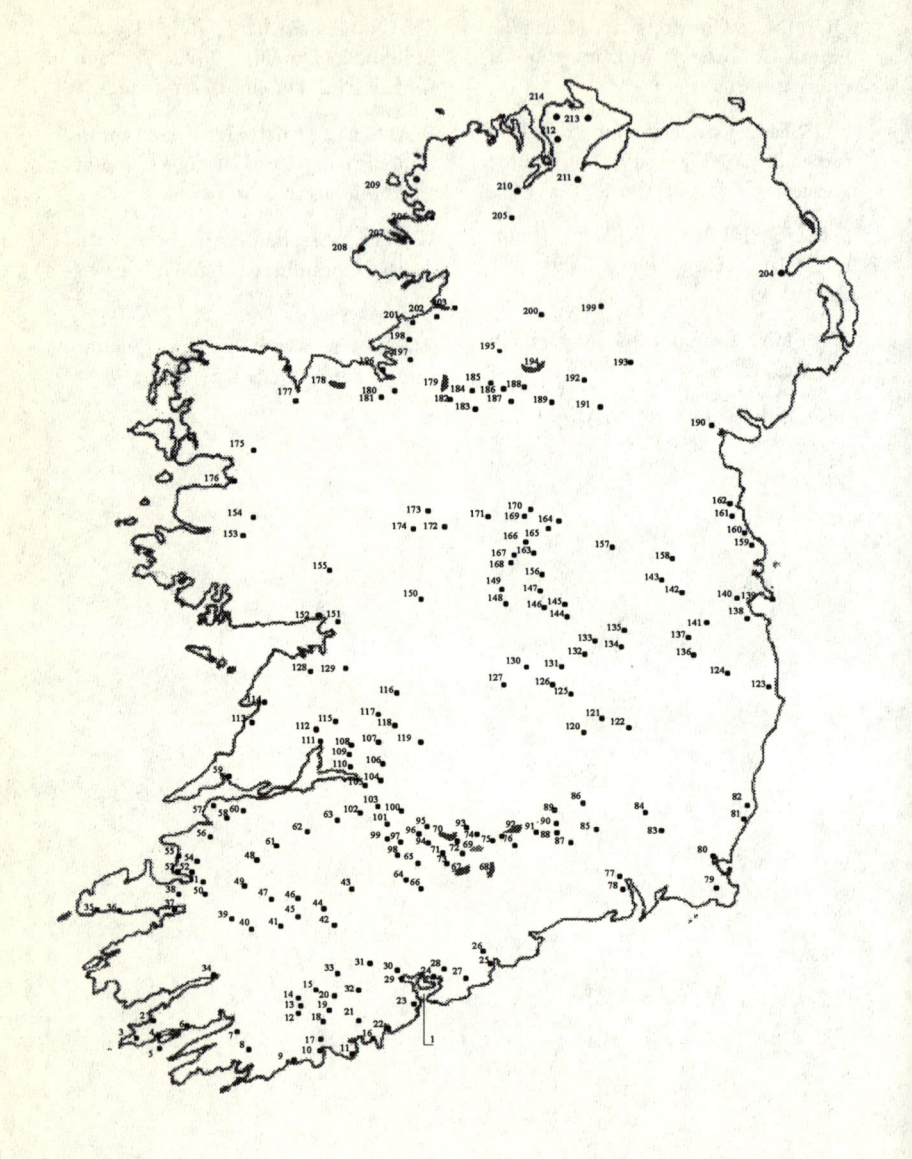

SITES OF ENGAGEMENTS AND RELATED EVENTS

Abbeydorney 54
Abbeyleix 125
Adare 63
Adrigoole 6
Allihies 3
Annacarthy 100
Ardara 207
Ardfinnan 73
Ardrahan 129
Ashbourne 158
Ashtown 140
Athlone 148
Balbriggan 160
Baldonnel 141
Ballina 177
Ballinalee 167
Ballinamuck 170
Ballinasloe 150
Ballinlough 174
Ballinphellic 20
Ballintrillick/Glencar 198
Ballykissane 38
Ballylanders 66
Ballylongford 58
Ballymoe 172
Ballymote 181
Ballyseedy 50
Ballyshannon 203
Ballytrain 192
Bandon 17
Banna Strand 55
Bantry 7
Béal na mBláth 12
Belfast 204
Bere Island 5
Berehaven 4
Birr 130
Blarney 30
Blessington 137
Borrisokane 127
Boyle 182
Broadford 108
Buncrana 212
Burtonport 209
Cahir 68
Callan 89
Carlow 121
Carndonagh 213
Carrick-on-Shannon 183
Carrick-on-Suir 176
Carrigaphooca 33
Carrigtwohill 28
Cashel 96
Castlebar 175

Castleisland 49
Cavan 189
Clara 146
Clonakilty 11
Clonalis 173
Clonbanin 46
Clonfin 166
Clonmany 214
Clonmel 74
Clonmult 26
Coachford 32
Cobh 24
Collooney 180
Comeragh Mountains 71
Cootehall 184
Cork 29
Crookedwood 163
Crookstown 13
Crossbarry 19
Cuilcagh Mountains 194
Curlew Mountains 179
Curragh 134
Derry 211
Dingle 35
Drangan 93
Drimoleague 8
Dripsey 31
Drogheda 162
Dromkeen 102
Drumboe 205
Drumlish 169
Dublin 138
Dundalk 190
Ennis 111
Enniscorthy 83
Eyeries 2
Fenagh 187
Fenit 53
Fermoy 42
Fethard 94
Finner Camp 202
Galway 152
Garadice 188
Glen of Aherlow 67
Glendalough 124
Glenties 206
Glenwood 109
Gorey 81
Gormanston 161
Granard 165
Headford 40
Howth 139
Inistiogue 85
Innishannon 21

'Katmandu' 90
Keadue 185
Kenmare 34
Kesh 186
Kilbeggan 145
Kilbrittain 16
Kilcock 143
Kildare 133
Kildorrery 43
Kilkenny 86
Killaloe 107
Killane 84
Killarney 39
Killorglin 37
Killurin 79
Kilmaganny 87
Kilmallock 64
Kilmichael 14
Kilrush 59
Kiltyclogher 200
Kinsale 22
Kinvara 128
Knockanure 57
Knocklong 65
Knockmealdown Mts 70
Knocknagashel 48
Lahinch 114
Letterkenny 210
Limerick 105
Lispole 36
Listowel 56
Longford 168
Macroom 15
Mallow 44
Manorhamilton 195
Maynooth 142
Meelick 75
Midleton 27
Millstreet 41
Moate 147
Mollsheen's Cross 69
Monaghan 199
Monreal 112
Mounterown 153
Mountshannon 117
Mullinahone 91
Mullingar 156
Myshall 122
Nenagh 118
Newbridge 135
Newcastle West 61
Newport 104
Newtownhamilton 193
Nire Valley 72

O'Brien's Bridge 106
Oldcastle 164
Oola 101
Oranmore 151
Ox Mountains 178
Pallis 82
Passage West 23
Portarlington 132
Portlaoise 131
Poulnacapal 90
Quaker Island 149
Rathcoole 45
Rathkeale 62
Rear Cross 103
Redmondstown 75
Rineen 113
Rosscarbery 10
Roscrea 126
Rosgreen 95
Rossan Point 208
Ruan 115
Scramogue 171
Shercock 191
Sinnotts Cross 77
Sixmilebridge 110
Skerries 159
Slievenamon 92
Sligo 196
Solohedbeg 99
Spa 52
Spike Island 1
Strandhill 197
Tarbert 60
Templemore 119
Thomastown 97
Tipperary 98
Tourmakeady 154
Tralee 51
Trim 157
Tuam 155
Tullaghan 201
Tullamore 144
Tureengarriffe 47
Union Hall 9
Upton 18
Uskerty Wood 120
Valleymount 136
Waterford 78
Westport 176
Wexford 80
Wicklow 123
Windgap 88
Youghal 25

227

SOURCES

PRIMARY SOURCES

National Library of Ireland, Dublin
Collins papers
Gallagher papers
RIC records
Report of Royal Commission on the Rebellion in Ireland

University College Dublin Archives
Connolly papers
Mulcahy papers
O'Malley papers

Franciscan House of Celtic Studies, Dún Mhuire, Killiney
MacEoin papers

Army Archives, Cathal Brugha Barracks, Dublin
National Army Census Returns, 1922
Military and Chaplain's records of Civil War Casualties
Operation and Intelligence Reports, 1922/1923
Collins papers
MacBride diary
MacBride papers
Mulcahy papers
O'Malley papers

State Paper Office of Ireland, Dublin
Cabinet and Ministry Records of Dáil Éireann
RIC investigations reports on incidents, 1922
Documents relating to RIC activity in Northern Ireland

The King's Inns Law Library
Law reports

SOURCES

Oireachtas Library
Lists of Dáil Deputies and constituencies

BBC Written Archives
Transcript of interview with Ernie O'Malley

Whitehall Library
Designation of British Army units

Irish Bureau of Military History, Dublin
Chronology of events, 1918-21

Unpublished memoirs of Kathleen Napoli McKenna

Interviews
Sean MacBride, Sean MacEoin, Seamus MacEoin, Kathleen Trappe, Todd Andrews, Peadar O'Donnell, Col Dan Bryan, Lt Gen Michael J. Costello, Lt Gen Michael Brennan, Col D. Neligan, Sighle Bean Uí Dhonnchadha (Humphreys), Máire Comerford, Sean Dowling, John L. O'Sullivan, Aodhgán O'Rahilly, Tom Brady, Jack Hughes, Mick Gormley, Niall Harrington, Bill McKenna, close relatives of Ernie O'Malley, Dr Breandán Mac Giolla Choille (former Keeper of State Papers)

Letters and documents
Contributed by participants or relatives, many of whom requested anonymity.

NEWSPAPERS AND JOURNALS

British: *The Evening Standard, Daily Mirror, The Sunday Express, People, The Times*
Irish daily: *Cork Examiner, Irish Independent, Irish Press, Irish Times*
Irish weekly: *Anglo-Celt, Clare Champion, Connaught Tribune, The Echo* (Wexford), *Free Press, The Kerryman, Leinster Leader, Limerick Leader, Longford Leader, Longford News, Midland Tribune, Sligo Champion, Tipperary Nationalist, Westmeath Examiner, Westmeath Guardian, Wicklow People*
Other journals: *The Irish Bulletin, An Cosantoir, Journal of the Irish Railway Record Society, An tOglach, The Irish Sword, The Past, Old Limerick Journal, Teathbha, The Other Clare, The Leitrim Guardian* (annual), *Tipperary Historical Journal, Études Irlandaises, Capuchin Annual, Journals of British Army Units.*

BOOKS
Ambrose, Joseph G., *The Dan Breen Story* (Cork 1981).
Andrews, C.S., *Dublin Made Me* (Dublin & Cork 1979).
Barry, Tom, *Guerilla Days in Ireland* (Cork 1955).
Beaslaí, Piaras, *Michael Collins and the Making of a New Ireland* (2 vols, Dublin 1926).

SOURCES

Bell, J. Bowyer, *The Secret Army: History of the IRA 1916-1970* (London 1970).
Boylan, Henry, *A Dictionary of Irish Biography* (Dublin 1988).
Breen, Dan, *My Fight for Irish Freedom* (Tralee 1964).
Brennan, Michael, *The War in Clare* (Dublin 1980).
Browne, Vincent, (ed.), *The Magill Book of Irish Politics* (Dublin 1981).
Campbell, Col., *Emergency Law in Ireland 1918-1925* (Oxford 1994).
Caulfield, Max, *The Easter Rebellion* (London 1964).
Collier, Basil, *Brasshat: A Biography of Field Marshal Sir Henry Wilson 1864-1922* (London 1961).
Collins, Michael, *The Path to Freedom* (Dublin & London 1922).
Colum, Padraic, *Arthur Griffith* (Dublin 1959).
Comerford, Judge, *My Kilkenny IRA Days 1916-1922.* (Kilkenny 1978).
Coogan, Tim Pat, *Ireland Since The Rising* (London 1966).
——*Michael Collins: A Biography* (London 1990).
Cowell, John, *Where They Lived in Dublin* (Dublin 1980).
——*Sligo* (Dublin 1989).
Crowley, Flor, *In West Cork Long Ago* (Dublin & Cork 1979).
Crozier, Brigadier-General F.P., *Ireland For Ever* (London 1932).
Dalton, Charles, *With the Dublin Brigade 1917-1921* (London 1929).
Deasy, Liam, *Brother against Brother* (Dublin & Cork 1982).
——*Towards Ireland Free* (Dublin & Cork 1973).
Doherty, J.E., and D.J. Hickey, *A Chronology of Irish History since 1500* (Dublin 1989).
——*A Dictionary of Irish History 1800-1980* (Dublin 1987).
Dudley Edwards, Ruth, *James Connolly* (Dublin 1981).
Duggan, John P., *A History of the Irish Army* (Dublin 1991).
English, Richard and O'Malley, Cormac (eds) *Prisoners – The Civil War Letters of Ernie O'Malley* (Dublin 1991).
Feehan, Sean, *The Shooting of Michael Collins* (Cork 1981).
Figgis, Darrell, *Recollections of the Irish War* (London 1927).
Fisk, Robert, *In Time of War* (London 1983).
Forester, Margery, *Michael Collins – The Lost Leader* (1972).
Gleeson, James, *Bloody Sunday* (London 1962).
Hammond, Bill, *Soldier of the Rearguard* (Fermoy 1977).
Harrington, Niall C., *Kerry Landing, August 1922* (Dublin 1992).
Herlihy, Jim, *Peter Golden, The Voice of Ireland* (Cork 1994).
Hogan, David, *The Four Glorious Years* (1954).
Hopkinson, Michael, *Green against Green* (Dublin 1988).
Irish Times, The, *Who's Who What's What and Where in Ireland* (London 1973).
Irwin, Wilmot, *Betrayal in Ireland* (Belfast n.d.).
Kee, Robert, *Ireland – A History* (London 1980).
Kelly, Freida, *A History of Kilmainham Gaol* (Dublin & Cork 1988).
Kerryman, The, *Dublin's Fighting Story* (Tralee 1947).
——*Limerick's Fighting Story* (Tralee 1947).
——*Rebel Cork's Fighting Story* (Tralee 1947).

―――With the IRA in the Fight for Freedom (Tralee n.d.).
Kilgannon, Tadhg, *Sligo and its Surroundings* (Sligo 1926).
Kilroy, Patricia, *The Story of Connemara* (Dublin 1989).
Litton, Helen, *The Irish Civil War – An Illustrated History* (Dublin 1995).
Lloyd George, David, *War Memoirs* (1933-6).
Loch Mowat, Charles, *Britain between the Wars* (London 1955).
Lyons, F.S.L., *Ireland Since the Famine* (London 1979).
Macardle, Dorothy, *The Irish Republic* (Dublin 1951).
Mac Eoin, Uinseann, *Survivors* (Dublin 1980).
MacLysaght, Edward, *Changing Times* (Gerrard's Cross 1978).
Macready, General Sir Nevil, *Annals of an Active Life* (2 vols, London 1924).
Mac Suain, Seamus, *County Wexford's Civil War* (Wexford 1995)
―――*Republican Wexford Remembers 1922-1923* (Wexford 1993).
McGinley, J.P., *Dr McGinley and His Times.* (Letterkenny 1985).
Mitchel, Arthur, and Padraig Ó Snodaigh, *Irish Political Documents 1916-1949* (Dublin 1985).
Moody, T.W., & Martin, F.X., *The Course of Irish History* (Cork 1984).
Morrison, George *The Irish Civil War – An Illustrated History* (Dublin 1981).
National Graves Association, *The Last Post* (Dublin 1976).
Neeson, Eoin, *The Civil War in Ireland* (Cork 1969).
Neligan, David, *The Spy in the Castle* (1968).
O'Brien, Barry, *Munster at War* (Dublin & Cork 1971).
Ó Broin, Leon, *Michael Collins* (Dublin 1980).
O'Callaghan, Michael, *For Ireland and Freedom* (Boyle 1964).
O'Connor, Batt, *With Michael Collins in the Fight for Irish Independence* (London 1929).
O'Connor, Frank, *The Big Fellow* (Dublin 1979).
O'Connor, Ulick, *Oliver St John Gogarty* (London 1964).
―――*A Terrible Beauty is Born* (London 1981).
O'Donnell, Peadar, *The Gates Flew Open* (Dublin & Cork 1965).
O'Donoghue, Florence, *No Other Law* (Dublin 1954).
O'Dwyer, Liam, *Beara in Irish History* (New York 1977).
O'Farrell, Padraic, *The Blacksmith of Ballinalee* (Mullingar 1993).
―――*The Ernie O'Malley Story* (Dublin & Cork 1983).
―――*The Sean MacEoin Story* (Cork 1981).
―――*Who's Who in the Irish War of Independence 1916-1921* (Dublin & Cork 1980).
O'Malley, Edward, *Memories of a Mayoman* (Dublin 1981).
O'Malley, Ernie, *On Another Man's Wound* (Dublin 1979).
―――*Raids and Rallies* (Dublin 1982).
―――*The Singing Flame* (Dublin 1978).
Ó Suilleabháin, Micheál, *Where Mountainy Men Have Sown* (Tralee 1965).
Pakenham, Frank, *Peace by Ordeal* (London 1972).
Robbins, Frank, *Under the Starry Plough* (Dublin 1977).
Ryan, Desmond, *Michael Collins & the Invisible Army* (Dublin 1977).

SOURCES

——*Sean Treacy and the Third Tipperary Brigade IRA* (Tralee 1945).
Ryan, Meda, *The Day Michael Collins Was Shot* (Dublin 1989).
——*The Real Chief: The Story of Liam Lynch* (Cork & Dublin 1986).
——*The Tom Barry Story* (Cork 1982).
Ryle Dwyer, T., *Eamonn de Valera* (Dublin 1980).
——*Michael Collins and the Treaty: His Differences with De Valera* (Cork 1981).
——*Michael Collins, 'The Man Who Won the War'* (Cork 1990).
Taylor, Rex, *Michael Collins* (London 1958).
Ward, Margaret, *Maud Gonne: Ireland's Joan of Arc* (London 1990).
——*Unmanageable Revolutionaries* (Kerry 1983).
Weekly Irish Times, The, *The Sinn Féin Rebellion Handbook* (Dublin 1916).
Valiulis, Dr Maryann Gialanella, *Portrait of a Revolutionary: General Richard Mulcahy and the founding of the IFS* (Dublin 1992).
Vane, Sir Francis, *Agin the Governments* (London 1931).
Younger, Carlton, *Ireland's Civil War* (London 1968).